BERKELEY

The Arguments of
the Philosophers

EDITOR: TED HONDERICH
Reader in Philosophy, University College London

The group of books of which this is one will include an
essentially analytic and critical account of each of the
considerable number of the great and the influential
philosophers. Each book will provide an ordered
exposition and an examination of the contentions and
doctrines of the philosopher in question. The group of
books taken together will comprise a contemporary
assessment and history of the entire course of
philosophical thought.

Already published in the series

Plato J. C. B. Gosling

Meinong Reinhardt Grossman

Santayana Timothy L. S. Sprigge

Wittgenstein R. J. Fogelin

Hume B. Stroud

BERKELEY

George Pitcher
Professor of Philosophy
Princeton University

Routledge & Kegan Paul
London, Henley and Boston

First published in 1977
by Routledge & Kegan Paul Ltd
39 Store Street,
London WC1E 7DD
Broadway House,
Newtown Road,
Henley-on-Thames,
Oxon RG9 1EN and
9 Park Street,
Boston, Mass. 02108, USA
Set in 11 on 12 Garamond
by Kelly and Wright, Bradford-on-Avon, Wiltshire
and printed in Great Britain by
Morrison & Gibb Ltd
Copyright George Pitcher 1977

British Library Cataloguing in Publication Data

Pitcher, George

Berkeley.—(The arguments of the philosophers).
1. Berkeley, George
I. Series
192   B1348   77-30062

ISBN 0-7100-8685-7

For E.T.C., in friendship

Contents

	Preface	ix
	Three Dialogues between Hylas and Philonous	xi
I	Biographical Sketch	1
II	The Visual Perception of Distance	4
III	Visible Objects; the Visual Perception of Magnitude	25
IV	Retinal Images; the Heterogeneity of Tangible and Visible Objects	42
V	Abstract Ideas	62
VI	The Objects of Immediate Perception: Ideas of Sense	91
VII	The Attack against Lockean Matter	110
VIII	Berkeley's World View I: Ideas of Sense	125
IX	Berkeley's World View II: Berkeley and Common Sense	140
X	Berkeley's World View III: the Existence of Unperceived Objects	163
XI	Berkeley's View of the Mind	180
XII	Passive Obedience	228
	Notes	255
	Works (other than Berkeley's) Referred to in the Text	268
	Additional Selected Bibliography	271
	Index	275

Preface

Quotations from Berkeley's writings are taken from *The Works of George Berkeley, Bishop of Cloyne*, edited by A. A. Luce and T. E. Jessop. In referring to passages from Berkeley's works, I use the following abbreviations:

Alciphron x y	*Alciphron, or the Minute Philosopher*, Dialogue x, section y
De Motu x	*De Motu*, section x
NTV x	*An Essay towards a New Theory of Vision*, section x
PC x	*Philosophical Commentaries*, entry x
PHK Intro. x	Introduction to *A Treatise concerning the Principles of Human Knowledge*, section x
PHK I X	Part I of *A Treatise concerning the Principles of Human Knowledge*, section x
PO x	*Passive Obedience*, section x
Siris x	*Siris: A Chain of Philosophical Reflexions and Enquiries*, section x
TVV x	*The Theory of Vision or Visual Language shewing the immediate Presence and Providence of a Deity Vindicated and Explained*, section x
W x y	*The Works of George Berkeley, Bishop of Cloyne*, vol. x, page y
3D x	*Three Dialogues between Hylas and Philonous*, Dialogue x

Note: The three dialogues are each fairly long, and Berkeley does not divide them into smaller numbered or lettered sections; so it is difficult for the reader to find in his own text passages quoted from the work. To help solve this problem, I give page references to three different volumes, using the following abbreviations:

(1) *W* II x   *The Works of George Berkeley, Bishop of Cloyne*, Vol. II, page x

(2) A x   *Berkeley's Philosophical Works*, edited by D. M. Armstrong, page x

(3) T x   *George Berkeley: Principles, Dialogues, and Philosophical Correspondence*, edited by C. M. Turbayne, page x

For readers who use G. J. Warnock's edition of Berkeley in the Fontana Library I provide a schedule that shows how page numbers from his edition correspond to those from vol. II of the Luce and Jessop edition.

When I refer to works that are not Berkeley's, I usually do so by giving just the author's name (sometimes followed by a number in parentheses). The titles and other bibliographical data are to be found at the end of the book in the section called 'Works (other than Berkeley's) Referred to in the Text.'

In writing this book, I received generous help of various kinds from my friends Willis Doney, Gilbert Harman, Richard Rorty, James Ward Smith, Morton White, and Margaret Wilson. I profited, too, from correspondence with Gary Thrane. I am happy to record my debt to all of them. To Princeton University I am grateful for a year's leave of absence and for other released time from teaching. Thanks are due to the Princeton University Press for permission to reprint a short passage from my book *A Theory of Perception*, and to the editor of the *American Philosophical Quarterly* for permission to reprint my article 'Minds and Ideas in Berkeley.' (The latter appears here as part of Chapter XI, pp. 189–203.) Finally, I want to express my gratitude to Mrs Helen Wright, once again, for her flawless typing of the manuscript.

G.P.

Three Dialogues between
Hylas and Philonous

	Works II	Warnock
Dialogue I	171–5	149–54
	176–80	154–61
	181–5	161–7
	186–90	167–73
	191–5	173–8
	196–200	178–84
	201–7	184–92
Dialogue II	208–12	193–8
	213–17	198–204
	218–22	204–11
	223–6	211–15
Dialogue III	227–31	216–21
	232–6	221–7
	237–41	227–33
	242–6	233–9
	247–51	239–45
	252–6	245–51
	257–63	251–9

I

Biographical Sketch

George Berkeley, an Irishman of English descent, was born on March 12, 1685 near Kilkenny, Ireland.[1] At the age of ten, he entered Kilkenny College, and at fifteen, Trinity College, Dublin. He received his B.A. there at nineteen, and then stayed on to prepare for a fellowship examination. In 1707 he was made a fellow of the college, and, as the appointment required, took Holy Orders. At about that time, he began the notebooks that we know today as the *Philosophical Commentaries*; they were finished a little over a year later. *An Essay towards a New Theory of Vision* appeared in 1709, *A Treatise concerning the Principles of Human Knowledge* in 1710, and the *Three Dialogues between Hylas and Philonous* in 1713. By the age of twenty-eight, then, Berkeley had completed the great works that give him a secure place in the history of philosophy.

He left Ireland for London early in 1713, intending to be gone for only a few months, but in fact he stayed away for eight years. In London, he quickly met and became friends with many of the country's intellectual élite; Addison, Steele, Pope, and Swift, among others.[2] After ten months in London, there was a trip, of roughly the same duration, to the Continent. The story goes that in Paris Berkeley met Malebranche, who was ill, and that the excitement of their philosophical conversation brought on an attack that resulted in the death of the Occasionalist a few days later. The two men certainly met in November 1713, but there can be no truth in the other part of the story since Malebranche did not die until nearly two years later. Berkeley returned to England in the late summer of 1714, and after two years, spent mostly in England, returned to the Continent for an extended tour of four years as the tutor and companion of young George Ashe, son of the Bishop of Clogher.

After his extended leave of absence, Berkeley returned to Trinity

College, Dublin, as a senior fellow, and proceeded to take an active part in the life of the college. In 1724, he resigned his fellowship to become Dean of Derry. All of Berkeley's energies, now, were focused on his famous Bermuda project: to build a college or seminary in Bermuda to educate the sons of English settlers in America and the native Indians from the mainland, so that they could return as missionaries to their own people. In the autumn of 1728, Berkeley and his new wife set out for Newport, Rhode Island, thinking that the funds for the college were forthcoming. Why Newport, rather than Bermuda? Because he was beginning to have doubts that Bermuda was the ideal place for his seminary, and Newport appeared to be a better site. And even if the college were built in Bermuda after all, it would need a base on the mainland for the supply of provisions, and again Newport would be suitable for that purpose. Berkeley bought a small estate of about 100 acres in Middletown, just north of Newport, and lived there for more than two and a half years, waiting for the British government to provide the promised funds.[3] By March 1731, at least, he realized that the money would never be paid, and returned to London in the autumn.

Berkeley had the manuscript of *Alciphron*, anyway, to show for his stay in America, and it was published early in 1732. While in London, awaiting preferment, he wrote *The Analyst* (published in 1734), which contains, in the words of two recent writers, a 'brilliant and devastating critique of the infinitesimal method.'[4] He showed, in brief, that mathematicians inconsistently treated infinitesimals both as finite quantities and as equal to zero. The work caused a stir in mathematical circles: there were attacks on Berkeley and his own counterattacks. If he achieved nothing else, Berkeley forced the mathematicians to re-examine the foundations of their work to ensure that there were no contradictions lurking there.

In 1734, Berkeley returned to Ireland upon being appointed Bishop of Cloyne. His days of travel and adventure were now over, and in the remaining years of his life, he ministered quietly and faithfully to the needs of his people. He was concerned not simply with their spiritual health, but also with the improvement of their economic and physical condition. He published *The Querist* (in three parts, from 1735 to 1737), which contained a great deal of sensible economic and political advice to the Irish. He urged them, for example, to enact legislation that would restrict foreign imports, especially the import of luxuries such as wine and silk. The general thrust of his advice, in fact, was that Ireland should be more nearly self-sufficient economically. Above all, he exhorted his compatriots to *get busy*. The work also contains theoretical reflections about money and credit that were years ahead of his time. *The Querist* is notable for its literary form, too, for it consists of nothing but questions! It is a tribute to Berkeley's art as a writer that one reads the tract with genuine pleasure.

It was during this period that he sought, with the greatest vigor and high seriousness, to educate the general public about the medicinal virtues of tar-water. *Siris*, which begins as a tract on tar-water, and then passes on through chemistry and cosmology to religion, was published in 1744. Though there was strong, predictable, opposition to tar-water from certain medical men, Berkeley actually met with some success here; for a few years, people in Ireland, especially, but also in England and on the Continent, from all classes, drank it to cure a large variety of complaints. There were numerous reports of cures: enough to encourage Berkeley to think that tar-water might well be a panacea.[5]

Three of Berkeley's seven children died in infancy; but the death in 1751 of his fourteen-year-old son William, whom he adored, must have caused him the greatest sorrow. A few days after the boy's death, Berkeley wrote to Bishop Benson:

> I was a man retired from the amusement of politics, visits, and what the world calls pleasure. I had a little friend, educated always under mine own eye, whose painting delighted me, whose music ravished me, and whose lively, gay spirit was a continual feast. It has pleased God to take him hence. God, I say, in mercy hath deprived me of this pretty, gay plaything. His parts and person, his innocence and piety, his particularly uncommon affection for me, had gained too much upon me. Not content to be fond of him, I was vain of him. I had set my heart too much upon him—more perhaps than I ought to have done upon anything in this world.
> (*W* VIII 304)

Berkeley moved to Oxford in the summer of 1752, apparently to oversee the education of his second son, George, at the university. He died peacefully there on January 14, 1753.

II

The Visual Perception
of Distance

Berkeley's metaphysics rises in the garden of British thought like some fantastic plant—beautiful and extravagant. Nevertheless, when one digs among its roots, one finds there a sober, well-informed account of that most familiar of processes—sense perception. How these ordinary roots yield such wondrous foliage is the story of Berkeley's philosophy.

Berkeley read and thought about perception throughout his career. The *Philosophical Commentaries* are full of his musings on the subject, and his first published work was *An Essay towards a New Theory of Vision*. The first of the *Three Dialogues between Hylas and Philonous* deals almost exclusively with the nature of the objects of perception, and twenty-four years after the first appearance of the *New Theory of Vision*, Berkeley vigorously defended it in *The Theory of Vision Vindicated and Explained*. One cannot fully understand or properly evaluate Berkeley's metaphysical views without having a clear picture of what goes on in his theory of perception.

The *New Theory of Vision* deals essentially with only one general kind of perception, although it is a kind that, for Berkeley's system, is of the greatest importance—namely, our visual perception of certain spatial characteristics of objects, that is, of those characteristics that every object, in so far as it exists in space, must have. Any spatial object must have a location in space; this means that it must be at some particular distance from a given perceiver in some direction or other. Berkeley does not concern himself with a person's visual perception of a thing's direction, but he does deal with the problem of how one knows, by sight, its distance. Berkeley realized that it was necessary for him to examine this kind of perception; for he had to reconcile his metaphysical view of so-called physical objects, according to which they consist of nothing but ideas, with the

4

disturbing fact, borne in on us whenever we use our eyes, that things just do look to be disposed around us in space, and so to be located at various different distances from us. It was precisely this problem of reconciliation, Berkeley tells us, that gave rise to the *New Theory of Vision*:

> that we should in truth see external space, and bodies actually existing in it, some nearer, others farther off, seems to carry with it some opposition to what hath been said, of their existing no where without the mind. The consideration of this difficulty it was, that gave birth to my *Essay towards a new Theory of Vision*, which was published not long since. (*PHK* I 43)

Berkeley deals with the visual perception of distance in sections 2–51 of the *New Theory of Vision*.

Another spatial characteristic of objects is their size; Berkeley discusses our visual perception of this in sections 52–87 of the *Essay*. Objects on or near the earth must have some spatial orientation with respect to the earth and to each other; for example, a man doing a handstand is upside down, since his feet, which are normally closer to the earth than other parts of his body, are now farther away. Berkeley refers to this feature of spatial objects as their *situation*, and he deals with our visual perception of it in sections 88–120. The fourth and final section of the work (sections 121–59) seeks to establish the heterogeneity of the objects of sight and touch, including *all* their properties. In this chapter, I shall investigate Berkeley's views about the visual perception of distance—what is nowadays called visual depth perception.

Berkeley begins with this bold deliverance:

It is, I think, agreed by all that
(A) distance, of itself and immediately, cannot be seen.
(B) For distance being a line directed end-wise to the eye, it projects only one point in the fund of the eye, which point remains invariably the same, whether the distance be longer or shorter.[1] (*NTV* 2)

William Molyneux, in his *Dioptrica Nova* (1692) had urged that '*distance* of it self, is not to be perceived; for 'tis a line (or a length) presented to the eye with its end toward us, which must therefore be only a *point*, and that is *invisible*' (p. 113). Berkeley obviously adopts (A) and (B) directly from Molyneux. He seems to regard (A) as almost self-evident, for he gives it a mere one-sentence gesture of a defense, namely, proposition (B). But one ought not to grant (A), and its meager defense (B), until one knows precisely what they mean—and this is far from clear.

What *does* (A) mean, then? It can't mean that:

(1) objects that are in fact located at a distance, of themselves and immediately, cannot be seen

because (B), which is supposed to imply (A), does not, on any interpretation, imply (1). Moreover, Berkeley, as we shall discover (see below, pp. 25–7), carefully distinguishes (1) from (A),[2] and seeks to establish it by considerations that have nothing to do with (B).

We obviously cannot read (A) to be saying that:

(2) although visual perceivers do see objects that are located at some distance from them, still they cannot normally see the intervening distance itself, since that is usually just a space of clear air which is invisible

for (B), which is supposed to support (A), does not even appear to provide any justification for (2). In addition, (2) suffers from the fact that it confuses two quite different things—namely, the distance between a perceiver and what he sees, on the one hand, and, on the other, the mass of air whose extent, in the direction running between the perceiver and what he sees, is the same as the distance separating the two.

By (A), Berkeley does not mean to be asserting, either, that:

(3) a perceiver cannot tell, by looking at an object, how far away it is from him

because he later lists some ways that a person *can* tell, by looking at a thing, how far away it is. But with (3), we are surely getting warm.

The clue to understanding the meaning of (A) lies in its tricky word 'immediately': (A) says that distance cannot be *immediately* seen.[3] What Berkeley means by 'immediately' in this context is made somewhat clearer by his discussion a bit later in the *Essay* of how distance *is* perceived visually. It is perceived, he says, by our first becoming aware of something else. Consider, for example, the following passage:

It is certain by experience that when we look at a near object with both eyes, according as it approaches or recedes from us, we alter the disposition of our eyes, by lessening or widening the interval between the pupils. This disposition or turn of the eyes is attended with a sensation, which seems to me to be that which in this case brings the idea of greater or lesser distance into the mind. (*NTV* 16)

Berkeley maintains here that whenever we see an object that is

6

relatively near to us, we feel a certain kind of sensation in our eyes. Each sensation of this kind has been associated, in our past experience, with the object's being a certain specific distance away (cf. *NTV* 17). So we first feel one of these peculiar ocular sensations, and then, by the association of ideas, the idea of the object's being at such-and-such a distance from us is produced in our mind. This is one of the ways we have, so Berkeley claims, of perceiving distance visually.

Notice that although Berkeley allows himself to speak of our visual perception of distance (e.g., *NTV* 11), on his view we really do not see distance at all: 'the ideas of space, outness . . . are not, strictly speaking, the object of sight' (*NTV* 46; see also *NTV* 45). On Berkeley's view, one's visual perception of distance is like his visual perception of the back of something he is looking at. Suppose, for example, that someone is looking at a sofa from the front. Experience has taught him that things which look like *that* generally have backs; his view of the front may therefore cause him to have the idea that this sofa has a back—but that does not imply that he actually *sees* the back of the sofa. In fact, he does not. Similarly, according to Berkeley, he does not see the distance that separates him from the sofa.

In one respect, however, the sofa example is a bad one; because the backs of sofas are visible, after all, whereas Berkeley holds that distance is not. Since we do have an idea of distance, it must be perceived by some sense or other; in fact, according to Berkeley, it is really perceived only by touch (although, as we shall see, he uses the term 'touch' in an extended sense). A better example, then, would be this: a person, when he views a red, glowing poker that has just been taken from a roaring furnace, may gather from what he sees that the poker is extremely hot. He sees *that* the poker is very hot, but he does not really see the heat itself; heat can be felt, but not seen. Again, a person may see a ringing bell or a vibrating tuning fork, but he does not see the sound; he sees *that* the bell is ringing and *that* the tuning fork is sounding, but he does not, and cannot, see the sound—for sounds can only be heard. Just so, Berkeley tells us, a person can see *that* something is located at such-and-such a distance from him; but he cannot see the distance, for distance can be perceived, in the strict sense, only by 'touch.'

Let us try to understand better exactly what Berkeley's claim that we do not, in the strict sense (or literally), see distance amounts to. The examples just cited will again prove helpful. To say that we do not literally see the heat of the poker or the sound of the bell is to say that the visual manifold of which we are aware when we see a hot poker or a ringing bell does not contain any heat or sound in it.

7

Similarly, to say that we do not literally see the distance of objects is to say that the visual manifold of which we are aware when we see them does not contain distance—that is, does not contain a third dimension running between us (i.e., the perceivers) and the things perceived. To put it another way: the 'visual appearances' of things are two, not three, dimensional.

The lack of a third dimension in visual appearances entails that:

(i)   visual appearances are altogether flat.

This means that no seen object looks, in what I shall call the full-blooded sense, to be any nearer to, or farther away from, the visual perceiver than any other—although in what I shall call the anemic sense, objects do normally look to be closer, or farther away, than others. Here's what I mean by the *full-blooded* and the *anemic* senses of 'look.' When you see a fire engine under standard conditions it looks, in the full-blooded sense, red to you; redness is magnificently there before your visual consciousness. When, however, you see, at a safe distance, a glowing red poker being removed from a fire, although the poker looks red to you in the full-blooded sense, it looks hot to you only in the anemic sense; heat is not there before your visual consciousness. You merely infer that it is hot from, among other things, the fact that it looks (in the full-blooded sense) red.

The lack of a third, or distance, dimension in visual appearances also entails that:

(ii)   nothing ever looks, in the full-blooded sense, to be at any distance at all from the visual perceiver, although of course things do normally look, in the anemic sense, to be at various different distances from him. (Cf. *NTV* 50)

To say that things do not look, in the full-blooded sense, to be any distance from the perceiver, is not at all the same thing as to say that they look to be quite close to the perceiver—pressed, as it were, against his eyes—or even that they look to occupy the very same place that the perceiver does. It is rather to say that it simply doesn't make sense to speak of an object's looking, in the full-blooded sense, to be at any distance from the perceiver. It follows from this that it doesn't even make sense to speak of an object's looking, in the full-blooded sense, as though it were at a distance of zero feet (inches, or whatever) from the perceiver—for that presupposes that distance concepts can intelligibly be applied to the 'visual appearances' and that the distance always happens to be zero; whereas what Berkeley specifically means to hold is that distance concepts cannot intelligibly be applied to the 'visual appearances' at all. According to him, distance concepts are in exactly the same boat with heat concepts on this score. It makes no sense to say that a glowing red poker looks, in the *full-blooded sense*, hot or cold. It cannot look hot in the way it looks red. So (ii), above, has the following analogue: nothing ever looks, in the full-blooded sense, to be anywhere on the spectrum from extremely hot to extremely cold (although of course things do often look, in the anemic sense, to be somewhere on that spectrum—e.g., to look hot, or to look cold). To say that objects look, in the full-blooded sense, to be at some distance from the perceiver would, on Berkeley's view, be just as nonsensical as saying that a thought appeared to be at some distance from the thinker or that anger appeared to be at some distance from the angry person: distance concepts apply to visual appearances as little as they apply to thoughts or emotions.

(ii), of course, entails (i), but not vice versa: for it is conceivable that visual appearances should present themselves to a perceiver in a flat (i.e., two dimensional) plane that seems to be at some, perhaps indeterminate, distance from him—like a cinema screen, for instance. In that case, (i) would be true, but not (ii). So (ii) is much stronger than (i); and Berkeley wisely pays more attention to (ii) than he does to (i).

We now have some intuitive idea of what Berkeley means by his proposition (A) (p. 5). According to him, distance is no part of the manifold directly presented to a person in visual perception, no part of the immediate 'look' of things. To be sure, one can normally tell, just by looking, how far away a thing is; but he can do it only in the way that he can tell, by looking, that an object is hot or cold or slimy—that is, by first detecting something else and then from this, as the result of some sort of mental process, arriving at the idea (or belief) that the object is such-and-such a distance away.

Let us have a look, now, at Berkeley's distinction between immediate (or direct) perception and mediate (or indirect) perception. The first thing to notice is that there are actually two distinctions here, not just one. The first distinction hinges on whether or not some 'intellectual' process is involved in the perception; the second distinction hinges on whether or not an intermediary is involved in the perception. Let us consider these distinctions in order.

Immediate perception of something in the first distinction is a sensuous awareness of it that is devoid of any 'intellectual' element, such as an interpretation of the object or a belief about it. Immediate seeing of this sort is, I believe, what Fred Dretske has called non-epistemic seeing.[4] Mediate perception of the first sort, by contrast, essentially involves both an 'intellectual' process and a resultant belief. It requires that the person immediately perceives something and then acquires, by some kind of mental process (e.g., by inference or by what Berkeley will call 'suggestion') a relevant belief. I shall designate this first kind of immediate (or direct) perception *immediate (or direct) perception*$_{without\ inference}$ or, for short, *immediate (or direct) perception*$_{w/o.\ inf.}$. I shall label the first kind of mediate (or indirect) perception as *mediate (or indirect) perception*$_{with\ inference}$ or, for short, *mediate (or indirect) perception*$_{w.\ inf.}$. For example: when I see the glowing poker removed from the furnace, I directly see$_{w/o.\ inf.}$ the redness of it, and indirectly see$_{w.\ inf.}$ its heat.

Let us turn, now, to the second distinction. Here I shall consider mediate or *in*direct perception first. In the second distinction, mediate perception of something is the perception of it by first perceiving a distinct intermediary. For example: if the lookout spies a bubbling oil slick and infers, correctly, that there is a damaged submarine below the surface, we may say that he mediately sees, in this second sense, the submarine. He sees it by first perceiving an intermediary—something wholly distinct from it—namely, the bubbling oil slick.[5] In the second distinction, immediate perception of something is the perception of it without the perception of any such intermediary: in our naval example, a direct realist would hold that the lookout sees the oil slick immediately, for there is no third thing between him and the oil slick that he must first perceive in order to perceive the oil slick. I shall designate this second kind of immediate (or direct) perception *immediate (or direct) perception*$_{without\ intermediary}$ or, for short, *immediate (or direct) perception*$_{w/o.\ inter.}$, and the second kind of mediate (or indirect) perception *mediate (or indirect) perception*$_{with\ intermediary}$ or, for short, *mediate (or indirect) perception*$_{w.\ inter.}$.[6]

These two distinctions are quite distinct. It is no doubt true that there cannot be a case of immediate perception $_{w/o.\ inf.}$ that is not also a case of immediate perception $_{w/o.\ inter.}$, and it is also true that many cases of mediate perception$_{w.\ inf.}$ are also cases of mediate perception $_{w.\ inter.}$ (as in the glowing poker example). But mediate perception $_{w.\ inter.}$ is nevertheless different from mediate perception $_{w.\ inf.}$, because (to consider the case of vision) while mediate seeing $_{w.\ inter.}$ of x can normally occur neither with immediate seeing $_{w/o.\ inter.}$ of x nor with immediate seeing $_{w/o.\ inf.}$ of x, mediate seeing $_{w.\ inf.}$ of x, on the contrary, often occurs with both kinds of immediate seeing of x. This may be seen from the following examples. Suppose you have been told by a friend that she has lost her black Persian cat, Gremlin, and that she is worried about the animal because he has injured his right front paw and limps

10

badly. The next day, seeing a black Persian cat, obviously lost, limping badly on its right front paw, you sagely infer that the cat is none other than Gremlin. Since you made a (correct) inference from what you saw and arrived at a belief about it, clearly you mediately saw $_{w.\ inf.}$ Gremlin. But it is not the case that you saw it only by first perceiving some intermediary—some third thing, distinct from Gremlin. You, therefore, immediately saw$_{w/o.\ inter.}$ Gremlin (assuming, for the present, a direct realist view of perception). So mediate perception$_{w.\ inf.}$ of x is compatible with immediate perception$_{w/o.\ inter.}$ of x. It is even compatible, perhaps surprisingly, with immediate perception $_{w/o.\ inf.}$ of x. Gremlin will do again for an example. You mediately saw $_{w.\ inf.}$ this lost cat, but you doubtless immediately saw $_{w/o.\ inf.}$ his black color, his shape, his walk, etc., and so you could not avoid immediately seeing $_{w/o.\ inf.}$ *him*. Of course, it sounds odd to say that you mediately saw $_{w.\ inf.}$ and, at the same time, immediately saw $_{w/o.\ inf.}$ a single object; but the oddity disappears when we recall that in this kind of case mediately seeing $_{w.\ inf.}$ an object O is merely seeing that the object before you is indeed object O, or of the kind O, or whatever (depending on what sort of term 'O' is)—i.e., is merely a matter of *recognizing O*—for there is no oddity in the claim that a person both immediately sees $_{w/o.\ inf.}$ an object and at the same time recognizes it. Indeed, mediately seeing $_{w.\ inf.}$ an object O, in the Gremlin sort of case, must positively *include* immediately seeing $_{w/o.\ inf.}$ O.[7]

We shall find Berkeley in this later works invoking both of the distinctions we have been discussing. In the first of the *Three Dialogues*, for example, we find these two passages within the scope of a single page:

Are those things only perceived by the senses which are perceived immediately? Or may those things properly be said to be *sensible*, which are perceived mediately, or not without the intervention of others? (3D I (*W* II 174; A 138; T 111))

in truth the senses perceive nothing which they do not perceive immediately: for they make no inferences. (3D I (*W* II 174f; A 138; T 112))

In the first passage, Berkeley is clearly talking about mediate perception $_{w.\ inter.}$, and in the second, immediate perception $_{w/o.\ inf.}$. More about this later: it suffices for now to say that according to Berkeley, our visual perception of distance is never immediate in either of our two ways; on the contrary, it is always mediate in both of our two ways. That is, we can see distance only in a way that is both mediate seeing $_{w.\ inf.}$ and mediate seeing $_{w.\ inter.}$; and we can never immediately see $_{w/o.\ inf.}$ distance nor immediately see $_{w/o.\ inter.}$

it. So Berkeley's proposition (A) is to be understood as denying the existence of both kinds of immediate seeing of distance.

It is part of Berkeley's view, not at all surprisingly, that any kind of mediate perception presupposes (an act of) immediate perception (cf. *NTV* 11); in order to mediately perceive w. inf. or w. inter. something, O, one must immediately perceive w/o. inf. and w/o. inter. something—either O itself or something wholly distinct from, but regularly connected with, O. So in accepting (A), Berkeley is committed to the consequence that our visual perception of distance can be accomplished only by noting something *in our consciousness*, something *of which we are aware* (*NTV* 9–11). This consequence allows him to reject accounts that were then current, according to which we judge the distance of a seen object by means of such things as the size of the angle that our two optic axes make when they meet at the object (*NTV* 4) and the amount of divergency in the light rays from the object as they impinge on the eye (*NTV* 6). These accounts are false, says Berkeley, because we are not in the least conscious of 'those lines and angles,' and so they cannot possibly help us to determine what the distance is to a seen object (*NTV* 12f).

Let us call those things the detecting of which allows a person to tell, by looking, how far away an object is, *distance clues*. We have already mentioned one of Berkeley's distance clues—namely, the sensation caused by the act of turning the eyes so that they are both aimed directly at the object (see p. 6). Another is the degree of 'confusion' (i.e., blurriness or out-of-focus-ness) that characterizes the look of things when they are very close to one's eyes (*NTV* 21). A third is the sensation of ocular strain that accompanies the effort to prevent an object from looking blurred, or out-of-focus, as it approaches closer and closer to the eyes (*NTV* 27). Berkeley also mentions some other distance clues—e.g., 'the particular number, size, kind, etc., of the things seen' (*NTV* 28; see also *NTV* 3). (In the *Philosophical Commentaries*, he remarks that objects that are higher in our visual field are judged to be farther away than those that are lower (*PC* 302a); and he makes the same point, in a modified form, in *NTV* 77.)

On Berkeley's view, when a perceiver sees an object, he is at the same time normally aware of one or more distance clues; his mind then passes to the idea that the object is at such-and-such a distance. What sort of process is it by which the mind of a visual perceiver passes from the awareness of an object and the accompanying distance clues to the idea of its distance? Berkeley insists that it is no process of deductive, or necessary, inference; for there is, he says, no necessary connection between any of the distance clues and the idea of a particular distance (*NTV* 17, 23, 28). The connections between them cannot be reasoned out in advance; they simply have to be learned by experience. This does not mean, however, that in an actual case of perception, the mind's passage from an awareness of distance clues to the idea of the object's distance constitutes an *inductive* inference. Perceivers are not aware of making any such inferences (except perhaps in a few rare cases), and this is enough to convince Berkeley that no such process of inference occurs in the normal case; he would consider it nonsense to speak of something going on in a person's mind if the person is not aware of it (*NTV* 19). The truth is that in the course of his experience the perceiver learns that, say, a certain ocular sensation, S, goes with a certain distance, d—that is, he finds S and d constantly conjoined in his experience. As a result, when he now feels S, the idea of d spontaneously comes into his mind. His earlier experience has conditioned him to think of d whenever he feels S (see *NTV* 17, 20). Thus do we find in Berkeley the principle of the association of ideas being put to an important philosophical (and, of course, psychological) use.

The passage from the sight of an object accompanied by the awareness of one or more distance clues to the idea of the object's distance, then, is normally not at all a process of conscious inference, either deductive or inductive; it is simply a conditioned, or as Berkeley might rather put it, 'an habitual or customary,' response. He uses the term 'suggestion' in a quasi-technical sense to designate the process—as the result of prior experience, the distance clues *suggest* the idea of this or that distance—and suggestion is not to be confused with inference:

> To perceive is one thing; to judge is another. So likewise, to be suggested is one thing, and to be inferred another. Things are suggested and perceived by sense. We make judgments and inferences by the understanding. (*TVV* 42)

In visual perception, the transition from the distance clues to the 'suggested' idea of a certain distance is extremely rapid. There is an analogous fast transition, says Berkeley, in reading or conversation: the words immediately suggest their meanings to the reader or hearer (*NTV* 17). (Locke draws precisely the same analogy: see *An Essay Concerning Human Understanding*, Bk II, ch. 9, § 9.)

Distance, then, for Berkeley, is not actually seen; what one sees merely suggests the idea of distance. But what *is* this idea of distance? Berkeley would obviously not dream of holding that it is an innate idea; he must, and does, hold, rather, that it is derived from some form of sense perception. Distance, Berkeley tells us, is genuinely perceivable only by touch—although under the heading of 'touch' he includes in addition to the tactual sense, the awareness one has of one's own bodily movements (kinesthesis). Suppose a person is some distance away from a tree; if he walks from where he is standing (call it place x) towards the tree, being aware all the time of the kind and rate of his motion, until he actually touches the tree, he will be perceiving by 'touch,' the distance between x and the tree. (None but the very shortest distances, therefore, can be perceived in a flash; the perception of most distances will require a certain amount of time.) To say that visual distance clues suggest to the perceiver the idea of a certain distance is to say, then, that they suggest to him the possibility of a certain kind and amount of bodily motion:

> Having of a long time experienced certain ideas, perceivable by touch, as distance, tangible figure, and solidity, to have been connected with certain ideas of sight, I do upon perceiving these ideas of sight forthwith conclude what tangible ideas are, by the wonted ordinary course of Nature like to follow. Looking at an object I perceive a certain visible figure and colour, with some degree of faintness and other circumstances, which from what I have formerly observed, determine me to think that if I advance forward so many paces or miles, I shall be affected with such and such ideas of touch. (*NTV* 45)

So far we have examined how Berkeley's crucial principle (A) (p. 5) is to be understood and what some of its consequences are; let us see how Berkeley attempts to justify it. It is true, as I remarked earlier, that he seems almost to regard (A) as wearing its truth on its face; but he does at least offer, with proposition (B), the bare suggestion of a defense. Here is (B) again:

> (B) Distance being a line directed end-wise to the eye, it projects only one point in the fund of the eye, which point remains invariably the same, whether the distance be longer or shorter. (*NTV* 2)

This is a curious remark: what does it mean to speak of distance as 'a line directed end-wise to the eye'? Distance can presumably be *represented* in a drawing by a line; but surely it *is* not a line. Since vision and the eye are the topics under discussion, it seems reasonable to suppose that Berkeley is really talking about light rays, or a light ray, and not distance at all. In fact, as a plausible reading of (B) I suggest the following: when one of the rays from a point of light, P, stimulates a point on the retina of a perceiver, he cannot tell, just from the visual awareness thus caused, how far away P is, since the very same retinal stimulation and hence the very same visual presentation would have been caused by that light ray no matter what the distance of P from the perceiver happened to be. This claim of

14

Berkeley's need not be confined to a single point of light and a corresponding single point of retinal stimulation: it can, and for convenience should, be generalized, as follows. When rays of light from an object, F, cause a pattern of retinal stimulation in a perceiver, he cannot tell, just from the visual awareness that this stimulation in turn produces, how far away F is, since the very same pattern of retinal stimulation and hence the very same visual presentation could have been caused by light rays from objects at indefinitely many different distances from the perceiver. Berkeley's point can be illustrated—see Figures 1 and 2.

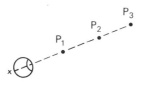

Figure 1

In Figure 1, P_1, P_2, and P_3 represent points of light. Notice that the retina of the perceiver is stimulated just at point x no matter where along the line running from x towards P_3 the light source happens to be located; so the stimulation will not give the perceiver enough information to be able to tell how far away the light source actually is. Similarly, in Figure 2, light from any of the figures indicated, and of course from any of an indefinitely large number of others, would produce the same pattern of retinal stimulation, so that the perceiver is not able to tell how far away the actual figure before him is.

If this is the way (B) is to be understood, then what it says, essentially, when generalized, is this:

(B′) The pattern of retinal stimulation that is produced by light rays from an object contains no information whatever about the distance separating the visual perceiver and the object.

But (B′) is false. Notice, first, that the retinal stimulation with which (B′) deals is of a restricted kind, in the following two respects: (i) it is restricted to the stimulation of a single retina, taking no account of the differences between the patterns of stimulation on the two retinas, and (ii) it is restricted to an unchanging pattern of stimulation, taking no account of the changes that occur in retinal stimulation as the perceiver or the seen object move in various ways. (B′) deals, in short, only with a stationary monocular retinal image.

But even within this restricted range, (B′) is false; for stationary monocular images *do* contain information about distances, both absolute and relative. For example, if, with only one eye open, you extend your arm straight in front of you, open your hand, and look at it, you can tell that it is roughly 2½ or 3 feet away from your eye. Moreover, your hand will no doubt blot out some surrounding objects, or parts of them, from your vision, while those objects will not blot out any part of your hand: from this, you can tell that your hand is closer to your eye than those surrounding objects. But such examples would not disturb Berkeley in the least. The heart of his position is that a person cannot immediately see[8] distance; and he would argue, plausibly, that neither example upsets that claim. When you look at your open hand, he would say, you merely infer, from the facts that it is your hand and that your arm is extended, that it is roughly 2½ or 3 feet away from your eye; so you only mediately see that distance. Similarly, you merely infer, from the fact that your hand's outline is complete while that of the surrounding objects is interrupted by the appearance of your hand, that your hand is closer to your eye than the others; again, you only mediately see the relative distance involved.

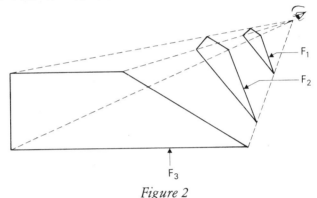

Figure 2

Nevertheless, the examples show that (B′) needs to be reworded, since it is false as it stands. I shall use the term '*effective information*' to designate any information that *would* cause a visual perceiver to immediately see the distance of an object—i.e., that would make it look, in the full-blooded sense, to him as though the object is at the distance from him that it actually is.[9] (B′), then, must give way to:

(B″) The pattern of retinal stimulation that is produced by light rays from an object contains no effective information about the distance separating the visual perceiver and the object.

So if we restrict ourselves, as Berkeley does, to stationary monocular retinal images, (B), understood as in (B″), seems reasonably safe. But one cannot legitimately so confine oneself, for there is binocular disparity, among other things,[10] to consider: except for objects at a great distance, the things one sees normally cause slightly different

16

images on his two retinas—and this difference is, in general, a function of the object's distance from him. Furthermore, the way the images change, as the object or the perceiver moves, will vary with the distance of the object. Berkeley must have known about binocular disparity, but its role in the perception of distance was not known until the nineteenth century.[11] But suppose he were told about this role: would he then have abandoned (B″)? The answer is clearly 'No.' He would reply that visual perceivers are simply not aware of the fact that the images on their two retinas are different. Since that is so, Berkeley would treat binocular disparity just as he treats, say, 'the greater or lesser divergency of the [light] rays' as they fall on the pupils of the eye (cf. *NTV* 6)—that is, he would dismiss it as irrelevant to our perception of distance. His reason for doing so, in both cases, would be that he takes it to be 'evident' that 'no idea which is not it self perceived can be the means of perceiving any other idea' (*NTV* 10). Since binocular disparity is 'not it self perceived,' it cannot 'be the means of perceiving' the different idea of distance. Berkeley would thus deny that binocular disparity is a distance cue at all; it does not contain, in other words, *any kind* of distance information, and so *a fortiori*, it does not contain *effective* distance information. It, therefore, poses no threat to (B″).

From this defense of (B″) that Berkeley would assuredly make, and from the way he handles his three distance clues, we can detect an important assumption that he is making, no doubt without realizing that he is doing so. It is an assumption about psycho-physical correlations in visual distance perception; or, more accurately, an assumption about the workings of the brain, the workings of the mind, and the correlation between the two in the visual perception of distance. The assumption is that each event[12] in the brain that is an integral part of the normal physical mechanism of visual distance perception (in that it is one of the events that normally cause the mind to become aware of the distance between the person and the various objects he is seeing) directly causes its own individual mental event. There is a direct one-to-one correspondence between those brain events and certain states of consciousness; then the mind, using those mental items, produces in itself the awareness of (i.e., the idea of) distance. So the picture of our visual perception of distance that Berkeley has is that shown in Figure 3.

r.s. is the brain event caused by the patterns of retinal stimulation, and v.p. is the visual presentation that they produce in the mind of the perceiver.[13] $c_1, c_2, c_3, \ldots$ are the other brain events that are also parts of the normal physical mechanism of visual distance perception; they correspond to the various different distance clues—thus, c_1

might be the brain event caused by the turning of the two eyes so that they are both aimed directly at the object. Each of these brain events (r.s., c_1, c_2, . . .) produces its own special mental event (v.p., x_1, x_2, . . .). Then the mind, on the basis of these separate mental items, produces in itself, by suggestion or (sometimes) inference, the idea of a certain distance—the distance that separates the person from the object he is looking at.

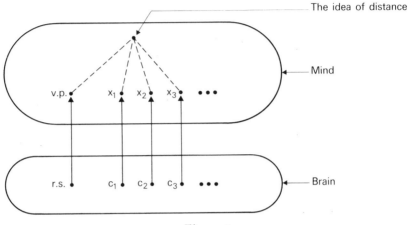

Figure 3

Anyone who, like Berkeley, has this picture of psycho-physical correlation in the visual perception of distance is bound to think that (B) implies (A); for given that brain event r.s. contains no distance information (which is a direct consequence of (B)), the visual presentation (v.p.) that it directly causes, in accordance with this picture of psycho-physical correlations, cannot contain any representation of distance, which means that (A) is true.

The various different distance clues, on this picture, cannot possibly cause the perceiver to immediately see distance. Consider, for example, Berkeley's first distance clue. He explicitly states that the turning of the two eyes so that they are both aimed directly at the object 'is attended with a sensation, which seems . . . to be that which in this case brings the idea of greater or lesser distance into the mind' (*NTV* 16). So the turning of the eyes causes a brain event (c_1 in Figure 3, say) that produces its own special mental event (x_1 in Figure 3)—namely, the sensation of the two eyes turning in a particular way. Sensation x_1 is obviously *not* the same thing as an awareness of distance. Guided (or rather, constrained) by his picture of psycho-physical correlations, Berkeley supposes that c_1 can be connected with the perceiver's awareness of distance only by first causing a sensation x_1 which then suggests to the perceiver's mind the idea of a certain distance. This means that as far as this source of distance information goes, our visual perception of distance is not immediate, but mediate. And the same kind of story would apply to all the distance clues known to Berkeley.

It seems pretty clear that Berkeley's general position on distance cues (or clues) and on our visual perception of distance is not satisfactory. Thus, it is false to deny that binocular disparity is a distance cue; so there must be something wrong with Berkeley's principles, for they surely entail that it is not a distance cue. And Berkeley's view of how convergence works in our visual perception of distance cannot be right; for we know that it is effective *whenever* we are looking at objects that are relatively close to us—but we seldom feel the convergence sensation that Berkeley appeals to. In saying this, I mean only to point out that Berkeley's system fails to fit certain facts. Of course, in one sense it would be grossly unfair to criticize Berkeley for not realizing these inadequacies—for the truth about the way binocular disparity, accommodation, convergence, and the rest, actually work in our visual perception of depth was unknown in his day[14]—indeed, there is much about it that is still unknown. But I do think it is fair to remark that Berkeley's view about the character of psycho-physical correlations in visual distance perception is almost certainly false and would prevent him from ever achieving a satisfactory theory of visual depth (or distance) perception.

The role of distance cues can, I believe, be properly understood and appreciated only on some more nearly adequate view of the kind of psycho-physical correlations that obtain in visual distance perception. One plausible possibility may be depicted as in Figure 4.

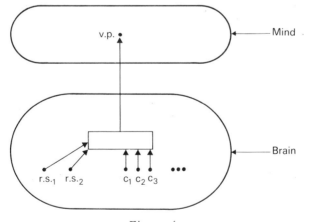

Figure 4

In this diagram, $r.s._1$ and $r.s._2$ are the brain events caused by the retinal stimulation of the two eyes. $c_1, c_2, c_3, \ldots$ are the brain events answering to the various other distance cues, such as accommodation, convergence, etc. All of these events serve as inputs to a brain mechanism that has, as output, a complex brain event which in turn causes a visual presentation (v.p.) of the object in the perceiver's mind. He is not, or anyway not necessarily, aware of the separate inputs $r.s._1, r.s._2, c_1, c_2 \ldots$ etc. On the view represented in Figure 4, it is the brain, not the mind, that 'operates' with the visual distance cues; this makes it perfectly intelligible that an input can be a distance cue and yet not, *by itself*, enter the consciousness of the perceiver. (This view, by the way, ought to be acceptable to Berkeley, for it need not be construed as including unconscious inferences or unconscious processes of any sort.)[15] Notice that the mental event v.p. might very well be—and I should think is—an act of immediately seeing both an object and the distance separating the perceiver from it!

We must conclude that Berkeley's case for (A) is weak. Is (A) nevertheless true? Let us first ask how Berkeley can even *think* that it is true. (A) implies that nothing ever looks, in the full-blooded sense, to be at any distance at all from the visual perceiver, where this means not that things look to be at no distance from him (i.e., to be inside his head), but rather that distance concepts are not even applicable to visible objects. But how can that be true? Is there anything more certain than that the things we see at least *look*—and look in the full-blooded sense—to be disposed about us at varying distances? And yet this evident truth is one that Berkeley without doubt denies. Visible objects, he says, 'neither are, nor appear to be, without the mind, or at any distance off' (*NTV* 50). And again: 'In truth and strictness of speech I neither see distance it self, nor anything I take to be at a distance' (*NTV* 45). Berkeley must hold, therefore, that we are all perpetually the victims of an illusion when we think that the things we see look to be various distances away from us. Let us call it *the distance illusion*. The distance illusion is the effect of long conditioning. We have found certain features of visible objects, and certain sensations accompanying visual experience, to be associated with the appropriate tangible objects' being various distances away from us; we are now so conditioned, therefore, that when we detect one of those features, or feel one of those sensations, the idea of such-and-such a distance immediately suggests itself to us. This alone, of course, would not account for the alleged illusion; so Berkeley takes the further step of claiming that the suggested idea of distance, being so closely wedded in our minds with the features of our visual experience, is mistakenly taken by us to be itself a feature of our visual experience—that is, we (erroneously) suppose that the 'visual appearances' contain a third, or distance, dimension:

> We cannot open our eyes but the ideas of distance, bodies, and tangible figures are suggested by them. So swift and sudden and unperceived is the transition from visible to tangible ideas that we can scarce forbear thinking them equally the immediate objects of vision.
>
> The prejudice which is grounded on these, and whatever other causes may be assigned thereof, sticks so fast that it is impossible without obstinate striving and labour of the mind to get intirely clear of it. (*NTV* 145–6)

This is an ingenious attempt to reconcile a central tenet of Berkeley's theory (namely, proposition (A)) with a phenomenological fact that seems bluntly to contradict it. The account does, however, raise doubts and questions. According to Berkeley, the ideas of distance that are, after long conditioning, immediately suggested to the mind of the visual perceiver, are tangible ones—an idea, for example, of his walking so many steps forward, reaching out with his hand, and feeling a certain kind of surface (cf. *NTV* 45). It might seem implausible to say that an idea from one sense modality can be confused with, and mistaken for, an idea from a different sense modality; but in point of fact, this seems to happen quite frequently, and especially where vision is involved. A glowing coal in the fireplace looks hot; the association between that kind of glowing visual appearance and the feeling of heat is so close, that we imagine that we are positively *seeing* the heat. Similarly, we suppose that we can see the slickness of an icy pavement or the softness of velvet, thus showing how readily we project, as it were, a tangible property onto a visual appearance, in cases where the correlation between the two is very high. So Berkeley would seem to be within his credibility rights in claiming that this common human propensity towards perceptual projection is at work when we think, mistakenly, that we actually *see* distance.

Nevertheless, doubts remain. Berkeley's explanation of the distance illusion characterizes it as just another instance of a kind of illusion that is familiar to everyone; and let us grant that it is of that kind. Still, Berkeley's general view of the mind creates difficulties for his account of the distance illusion, and, in addition, makes it very difficult indeed to understand that account. By 'Berkeley's general view of the mind,' I mean, here, his view of the mind as a sort of transparent medium, so to speak: there are no dark or hidden regions in it—everything that goes on in it is fully and clearly known to the person whose mind it is. There is no such thing as an unconscious mental act, state, event, process, or whatever: everything that exists, or takes place, in the mind is completely conscious. This conception of the mind and its close associate—namely, the view of psycho-physical correlations depicted in Figure 3—determine the kind of explanation that Berkeley can, and in fact does, give of the distance illusion.

According to that explanation, when a normally sighted person in broad daylight stands facing a tree that is, say 20 feet in front of him, when he has his eyes open and aimed in the direction of the tree, when there are no obstructions between him and the tree, and so on—that is, when he *sees* the tree, as we would ordinarily put it—he literally sees only a certain flat expanse of light and colors; but as the result of long conditioning, tangible ideas of an appropriate kind are immediately suggested to him. These ideas must of course, for Berkeley, be fully conscious ones.

But, first, it seems to be just false that we are aware, whenever we see something, of any such tangible ideas; so Berkeley's explanation rests on at least one falsehood. Second, in his explanation, he appeals, as we have seen, to a transition in the mind (the transition, namely, from visible ideas to the (tangible) ideas of distance) that is so swift and sudden as to be 'unperceived.' We must all agree that this transition, if it does indeed take place, is 'unperceived'; for we are certainly not aware of it. But unfortunately Berkeley's conception of the mind as a transparent medium does not permit him to posit any such event, for according to that conception, it makes no sense to speak of something's being, or occurring, in a person's mind if he is not aware of it. Berkeley chides his opponents for seeking to explain our visual judgments of distance by appealing to things of which we are not in fact aware; thus he claims that to make judgments or draw conclusions 'without knowing that I do so, seems altogether incomprehensible' (*NTV* 19; see also *NTV* 12). But then he cannot, without inconsistency, allow himself the luxury of unperceived transitions in the mind.

Third, and finally, even if we were to grant that tangible ideas of distance do always occur to visual perceivers and that the kind of transition just described does always take place in their minds, it would still be far from clear how Berkeley's story of what happens in the minds of visual perceivers can provide a genuine explanation of the distance illusion. It is extremely difficult to see precisely how the occurrence of: (i) the awareness of a flat expanse of light and colors, quickly followed by (ii) tangible ideas of distance (e.g., the idea of walking straight ahead so many paces, of reaching out with one's hand, and of feeling such-and-such a tactual sensation) is supposed to yield, or could conceivably yield, the illusion of three-dimensionality in the flat expanse of light and colors. In order to understand

Berkeley's explanation of the illusion, we need to be told why, and how, the conjunction of (i) and (ii) is anything more than simply that—a bare conjunction of two radically different mental items. Berkeley, to be sure, does try to tell us, in a passage already quoted. He says, remember: 'So swift and sudden and unperceived is the transition from visible to tangible ideas that we can scarce forbear thinking them equally the immediate object of vision' (*NTV* 145). But this doesn't help, for it is literally incredible that ideas such as those given in (ii), above, should ever be taken for 'immediate objects of vision.' So there is an essential link missing in Berkeley's account of the (alleged) distance illusion—and I cannot myself think how to provide it.

There can now be little doubt that in the visual perception of distance, a process of conditioning, or learning, involving numerous kinds of bodily movement—e.g., walking toward objects, reaching out to touch or grab them, etc.—plays an essential part. Berkeley deserves full credit for anticipating this truth; but, as I have argued, it cannot really be accommodated within the system determined by his other doctrines. Ironically enough, it is the behaviorists—whom Berkeley would regard as his arch-enemies—who have stressed the importance of bodily movements in learning to perceive distance (and other spatial properties—e.g., shape, verticality, etc.) visually.[16]

Is (A) true? We have not answered that question, and I propose to leave it unanswered. But it is highly implausible, and Berkeley has certainly given us no good reason for accepting it. I believe that all of Berkeley's troubles in this area could be resolved at once, and painlessly, if he simply abandoned thesis (A) and thus admitted— what seems obviously true—that visual appearances are three dimensional, that things just do normally look, in the full-blooded sense, to be at various different distances from the visual perceiver. I say 'painlessly' because I think that the rejection of (A) would still allow Berkeley to retain everything of importance in his system: in particular, it would by no means force him to give up (D), below, the proposition that the things we immediately see exist only in the mind (cf. p. 25). Berkeley himself later realizes this, for he writes in the *Principles of Human Knowledge*:

> It will be objected that we see things actually without or at a distance from us, and which consequently do not exist in the mind, it being absurd that those things which are seen at the distance of several miles, should be as near to us as our own thoughts. In answer to this, I desire it may be considered, that in dream we do oft perceive things as existing at a great distance off, and yet for all that, those things are acknowledged to have their

existence only in the mind. (*PHK* I 42; see also *3D* I (*W* II 201; A 164; T 141f)

But the rejecting of (A) is a possibility that never occurred to Berkeley—and perhaps it could not have occurred to him, given that the working out of the plausible empiricistic alternatives to (A) would require a knowledge of eye- and brain-physiology that was not available to him.

III

Visible Objects; the Visual Perception of Magnitude

Visible objects

It is important to distinguish Berkeley's proposition (A):

(A) Distance, of itself and immediately, cannot be seen

from the quite different proposition (C):

(C) Objects that are in fact located at a distance, of themselves and immediately, cannot be seen.

Notice, in particular, that (A) in no way entails (C); for it might be true both that a perceiver does see things that are located at some distance from him and that nevertheless he does not see the distance that separates them from him. This state of affairs would obtain where the distant objects cause, in the standard way, the perceiver's 'visual presentations' of them (so that it is really they that he sees) but where the perceiver has no way of telling how far away any of the objects are or even whether they are any distance away at all. Berkeley considers it a matter of the greatest importance to prove (C), but he is too shrewd to imagine that (A) entails it; he is fully aware that he needs new arguments to establish it.

At the time of writing the *Essay*, Berkeley is in fact convinced that:

(D) The things we see 'of themselves and immediately' exist only in the mind.

Thus, he writes:

what we immediately and properly see are only lights and colours in sundry situations and shades and degrees of faintness and clearness, confusion and distinctness. All which visible objects are only in the mind. (*NTV* 77)

25

If proposition (D) were available to Berkeley at this point, it seems that he might well use it to prove (C). Of course, we cannot be sure, yet, that we know what it is 'to exist in the mind'; but if to exist in the mind is to be something like an idea, or an image, or a thought, then if what we immediately see exists only in the mind (as (D) avers), then we do not immediately see things that are located at some distance from us (as (C) asserts). But (D) is not thus available to Berkeley, for at the stage of his argument where he sets out to prove (C), he has not demonstrated the truth of (D).

To be sure, he does attempt a kind of conditional proof of (D), as follows. He seeks to show that anyone who is willing to grant proposition (E) must also admit the truth of (D):

(E) Colours, which are the proper and immediate object of sight, are not without the mind. (*NTV* 43)

He argues that the extension of an object we see is 'in the very same place' that its color is; and where its extension is, there too must be its figure (shape) and motion. Since, presumably, if all these properties of a visible object are in the mind, it would be impossible to place the object itself anywhere else, visible objects must all be located in the mind—which is just what (D) asserts. This argument is a total loss, but its badness is not now pertinent: the relevant point is that since, as he well knows, Berkeley has said nothing by way of justifying (E)—although he certainly believes it and thinks that 'all who have had any thoughts of that matter' do also—he realizes that he has not demonstrated the truth of (D). Therefore, his actual defense of (C) makes no use whatever of (D).

The proof of (C) is given in section 44. We commonly speak, Berkeley reminds us, of seeing something in the, or at a, distance; we think that what we (immediately) see is an object that is located at some distance from us. But this is a mistake. Imagine, for example, that I am looking at the moon. What I immediately see is just 'a round, luminous plain of about thirty visible points in diameter'; and I suppose it to be a great many miles away. But if I should travel to the moon, I shall not find there any 'round, luminous plain of about thirty visible points in diameter'; nothing answering to that description is to be found at the place where the moon is. So what I immediately saw, back on earth, was not the object that was then a great distance away from me.

The argument, then, is this: if what I immediately see (a visible object) were identical with an object that is really located at some distance from me, then it should not change as I move towards it—because the object that is supposedly located at some distance from me does not change simply because I move towards it. But what

I immediately see *does* always change when I so move. Therefore, what I immediately see is never identical with an object that is really located at some distance from me. And this is what (C) asserts. Later, in *Alciphron* IV 9, Berkeley argues that, quite generally, what one immediately sees has properties that are different from the (presumed) object that is located at some distance, and so cannot be identical with it. We shall have to examine this argument of Berkeley's very carefully later on; but for now we may let it pass, despite our uneasy feeling that it must not be possible to prove anything as earthshaking as (C) in the space of a medium-sized paragraph!

Our doubts are exacerbated by the astounding fact that Berkeley also seeks to prove, in the very same paragraph (i.e., section 44), a thesis that is stronger even than (C). Notice that (C) leaves open the possibility that what we immediately see is at least a representation, or idea, of the object that is located at a distance. Berkeley, for reasons that emerge only in his later works, will have none of this. He wants to foreclose that option, thus making still more tenuous the connection between what the perceiver immediately sees and the objects located at a distance from him. So he sets out to prove the extremely strong proposition:

(F) The immediate objects of sight are not so much as the ideas or resemblances of things placed at a distance. (*NTV* 44)

As we shall see, for Berkeley, in order for something, x, to be an idea of something else, y, x must resemble y. But what we immediately see, he contends, does not resemble the object that is located at a distance. Thus, consider the moon example again: when I get to the moon, not only do I not find the very thing I immediately saw when I was back on earth—namely, 'a round, luminous plain of about thirty visible points in diameter'—I do not even find anything that resembles it: 'by the time that I am advanced fifty or sixty semidiameters of the earth, I shall be so far from being near a small, round, luminous flat that I shall perceive nothing like it' (*NTV* 44). Again, if I see,[1] faintly, something I judge to be about a mile away, and then approach it, I shall not find anything like what I originally saw; for at every step 'the appearance alters, and from being obscure, small, and faint, grows clear, large, and vigorous' (*NTV* 44). As a proof of (F), these almost perfunctory observations leave a great deal to be desired. All that Berkeley has shown is that when I am close to an object 'what I see' (or 'that which I see'), as he here uses these phrases, is sometimes different, in certain respects, from 'what I see' when I am farther away from it. And there is obviously a huge gap between that meager truth and the truth of (F). One can only make conjectures as to why Berkeley offers this feeble defense of (F). My own guess is that since the metaphysical system of the *Essay* is but a half-way house to the full immaterialism of the works to follow, Berkeley feels (quite rightly, it seems to me) that the strenuous efforts required to prove (F) adequately would be wasted; for within the system of the *Essay*, (F) is naturally to be interpreted as presupposing that 'things placed at a distance' are not mind-dependent, that they exist 'without the mind'—a presupposition that Berkeley, even at the time of the *Essay*, in fact believes to be false. In the later works, he labors hard and long to demonstrate an immaterialistic analogue of (F); but meanwhile he must think there is little point in expending energy on (F) itself, with its false presupposition.

Assuming him to have proven (C), Berkeley is entitled to conclude that:

(G) We never see and feel one and the same object. (*NTV* 49)

What we feel are the tangible objects—i.e., the objects that are spread around us at various points in physical space. What we see are objects that exist only in the mind. The things we see and the things we feel thus constitute two wholly distinct classes of objects. They are not, however, totally unrelated: on the basis of my previous experience, I can tell, when I perceive a certain kind of visible object, that if I make certain bodily movements (e.g., if I walk in such-and-such a direction for such-and-such a distance, or if I reach out with my hand in such-and-such a way), I shall encounter a certain kind of tangible object (*NTV* 45). Although we cannot immediately see tangible objects, the existence of these connections is enough, Berkeley supposes, to warrant our saying that we *mediately* see them (cf. *NTV* 50).

Berkeley knows—how could he fail to?—that (G) constitutes an assault upon the beliefs of the so-called man in the street; that is to say, it contradicts something that we all take to be true. What could be more certain, we suppose, than this: that when you look at an apple that you are holding in your hand, what you see and what you touch are one and the same object? Berkeley dismisses this protest (*NTV* 49, 51) by remarking that one reason it is difficult for us to grasp the truth of (G) is that our language misleads us by containing the same word—e.g., 'apple'—for what we see and what we touch. He adds that 'the use and end of language' requires such common names, but their effect on philosophy is nevertheless disastrous. (Berkeley is certainly right when he suggests that our linguistic life would be enormously more complicated if we had different names for what we see and what we touch—not to mention the objects of our other senses.) We shall find that one of the themes that run through

28

all of Berkeley's philosophy—from the very start, in the *Philosophical Commentaries*, where it figures prominently—is that language is a powerful deceiver, making clear philosophical vision difficult. This important truth, which had been much stressed by Francis Bacon[2] and others, was mainly lost from view for over 200 years until, in our own day, Wittgenstein rediscovered it.

We have a reasonably clear, if not very detailed, idea of what, on Berkeley's view in the *Essay*, the nature of tangible objects is: they are the extended, solid, shaped things that exist around us in space. But if, as (G) asserts, the things we see—i.e., visible objects—are different from tangible objects, the question of what their nature is immediately arises. Berkeley makes it perfectly clear, as I said earlier (p. 25), that he thinks they are mental entities, that they exist 'in the mind.' I also said that by the time he gets around to proving (C), Berkeley has not argued for the truth of that proposition—i.e., for the truth of (D)—and that his proof of (C) makes no use of it: nor is there any attempt to defend (D) later in the *Essay*. And so it comes as a jolt to discover, in section 81, that Berkeley thinks he *has* demonstrated the truth of (D):

> To which I answer, the *minimum visible* having (in like manner as all other the proper and immediate objects of sight) been shewn not to have any existence without the mind of him who sees it, it follows there cannot be any part of it that is not actually perceived. (*NTV* 81)

(The same claim is made in section 117, and again in section 119.) The passage from section 77, already quoted (p. 25f), in which Berkeley calmly asserts (D), might have prepared us for the surprise; but still, it is one thing to assert a proposition you merely believe to be true, and it is another thing to claim that you have proved it.

After a bit of reflection, however, we can see that it is not really so surprising that Berkeley should think that he has shown (D) to be true. There is plenty of evidence in the *Essay* that he pictures a person's mind as a kind of place where objects can exist, and indeed where they must exist in case they don't exist at some distance from the person. A mind, in other words, is one—and a most important one—of the places where an object can be located: a thing either exists outside, or 'without,' all minds, or else it exists inside, or 'within,' some mind. There are no other places available in which an object might be located. (I shall dub this picture, according to which the mind is viewed as a kind of place where objects can exist, the *place-picture* of the mind.) On this place-picture, if the objects that we see are not located at a distance from the perceiver—and (C) says that they are not—then they must be located within our minds. So to someone who is under the influence of the picture, as Berkeley surely is, a proof of (C) would naturally be seen as tantamount to a proof of (D). The very fact that Berkeley fails to draw (D) explicitly as a consequence of (C) is evidence that something very like the place-picture is at work in his thinking; for such pictures, as Wittgenstein has taught us, lie deep and hidden in our thought, determining how we view things, in ways that we are not conscious of. To Berkeley, a captive[3] of the place-picture of the mind, the truth of (D) must seem too obvious to mention, once he has, as he supposes, proved (C).

Here is some textual evidence that the place-picture of the mind is, indeed, at work in Berkeley's thought: (a) In section 41 of the *Essay*, Berkeley says 'our judging objects perceived by sight to be at any distance, or without the mind, is (*vid.* sect. 28) intirely the effect of experience' (*NTV* 41). In this passage, judging objects to be 'at any distance' is assumed to be *equivalent* to judging them to be 'without the mind': this is precisely what anyone held captive by the place-picture of the mind would say.

(b) In his effort to persuade holders of (E) that they ought to accept (D) as well (an argument we discussed earlier, p. 26), Berkeley discusses the plausible but erroneous notion that visible extension, figure, and motion are 'at some distance from the mind' (*NTV* 43)—as though the mind were a place that other things could be some distance from. He goes on to claim that the (visible) extension of an object appears to be 'as near to' a person as its color; since colors are in the person's mind, Berkeley is clearly thinking of the mind as a place that is 'near' to the person—indeed, I rather imagine he would think that to be in a person's mind is to be as near as possible to that person. The whole of section 43 is stamped with the place-picture of the mind.

(c) In section 50 of the *Essay*, Berkeley speaks of a certain class of objects that 'neither are, nor appear to be, without the mind, or at any distance off.' Here again we see clearly the influence of the place-picture: it makes Berkeley suppose that being 'without the mind' is exactly the same as being 'at [some] distance off.' (See also the first sentence of section 55.)

In a moment, I shall suggest that the place-picture of the mind is an unhappy one. But notice, first, that there are two versions of the picture. According to one, the place that the mind is—the mind-place—is just one of the indefinitely many places in physical space. On this conception, the mind, and the things in it, would literally be so many inches (feet, miles, etc.) from the various objects in the surrounding physical space. According to the other, the mind-place is not in physical space at all, but constitutes, rather, a totally separate realm. On this version, the mind, and the things in it, cannot sensibly be spoken of as being literally so many inches (feet, miles, etc.) from the objects in physical space.

I take it that this second version of the place-picture is obviously preferable to the first. Berkeley *almost* always speaks in ways that are appropriate to the first picture, however—for instance, he does so in all three passages, (a)–(c), just cited. Here is another such passage: 'all visible things are equally in the mind, and take up no part of the external space: And consequently are equidistant from any tangible thing which exists without the mind' (*NTV* 111). In order for all the contents of the mind to be *equidistant* from any given object in physical space, the mind must be just one more place in a framework of locations that includes also the numerous points in physical space—and this accords with the first version of the place-picture of the mind. But Berkeley immediately corrects himself: 'Or rather, to speak truly, the proper objects of sight are at no distance, neither near nor far, from any tangible thing' (*NTV* 112). This accords with the second version of the place-picture. So when Berkeley is careful and consciously thinking about it, he rejects the first version of the place-picture of the mind. (Indeed, we shall find that when he comes to the problem of inverted retinal images and to the question of the heterogeneity of tangible and visible objects, he makes much of the point that visible objects stand in *no* spatial relations to tangible objects.)

The place-picture of the mind influences Berkeley's thought not only in the *Essay*, but in the later works as well. We shall find that it has baleful effects on his philosophy. Indeed, we have already noted one of its evil results—for it seduces Berkeley into thinking that he has proven the extremely important thesis (D) in the very act of proving (C), whereas that particular feat cannot, in fact, be accomplished. The picture is certainly a most unfortunate one, in any case. The first version has it that a person's mind is just one place in the system of spatial locations—one that is very much closer to the person than the others, so that his thoughts and emotions are the nearest possible things to him—and so the picture in this version leads the philosopher into nonsense.

But a more serious danger attaching to the picture, even in its better second version, is that it forces the philosopher, without his realizing it, into a certain way of viewing what it is to exist in the mind, and hence blinds him to certain possibilities that he ought to see and seriously consider. One plausible meaning for the phrase 'to be in the mind,' for example, is this: to be an object of awareness. Something, *x*, is in a person's mind just in case that person is aware of *x* in some fashion or other. Notice that on this view, there is no

31

necessary incompatibility between a thing's being *both* 'at some distance' from a person *and* in his mind; thus, for example, when a person sees a tree, the tree is both in his mind (since he is aware of it) and, of course, some distance away from him. An even more obvious example is this: a person can think of, or imagine, some real distant object, in which case it is in his mind and yet it actually exists some distance away. If a philosopher is held captive by the place-picture of the mind, he will not be able to see this alternative way of viewing existence in the mind, and hence the possibilities illustrated in the two examples just described will not receive their day in court—for the place-picture forces one to suppose that a thing *either* is located somewhere in space (i.e., at some distance from a given person)—in which case it is a spatial, or three dimensional, object—*or*, if it isn't, that it be 'located' in the mind—in which case it is some sort of mental, non-spatial, entity (state, process, or whatever). My purpose here is not to argue the virtues or faults of these two accounts of what 'to be in the mind' means: it is merely to point out that because his thought is (no doubt unconsciously) governed by the place-picture of the mind, Berkeley is prevented from seeing important possibilities that it would have been profitable for him to consider. This confining or channeling of thought, this shrinking of the conceptual field, is one of the most pernicious effects of such philosophically relevant pictures as the place-picture of the mind.

I said earlier that in the *Essay*, Berkeley does not, in fact, prove (D); and I have been arguing that it is the place-picture of the mind that seduces him into thinking he has proven it. But the full story has not yet been told. Two presuppositions underlying Berkeley's place-picture of the mind—and I attach no special importance to the image of *underlying*; we might as well say that they are part and parcel of his place-picture—are these:

(1) Everything is in, or occupies, some one place or other, and
(2) There are only two different kinds of places in the system of possible places.

These assumptions lie hidden very deep in Berkeley's thought, and so we cannot expect to find him explicitly stating them; nevertheless, it is possible to discern them in what he says. Anyone who falls prey to the place-picture is likely to make assumption (1); in Berkeley's case, however, the making of that assumption may well be one of the main causes that lead to his adoption of the place-picture. This may be seen as follows. According to the place-picture as it works in Berkeley's thought, if a thing is not located at some distance from a person, it must be located in his mind. But notice: this follows only if the assumption is made that everything must exist at, or in, some place or other—i.e., only if assumption (1) is made. If the possibility is left open that something may exist and yet be nowhere—i.e., in no place—then from the fact that it does not exist at some distance from a person, one cannot conclude that it exists in the person's mind. Perhaps it isn't at any place at all. And as far as 'objects of awareness' are concerned, this is a possibility that Berkeley never recognizes: he does not, cannot, see it.

Berkeley's version of the place-picture also clearly incorporates assumption (2). This is shown by the very way he argues. He reasons that if a thing does not exist at some distance from a person, it must therefore exist in his mind. By the phrase 'at some distance,' he means at some distance in tangible space, i.e., in what one ordinarily thinks of as physical space. The *only* alternative allowed by Berkeley to location in tangible space is location in the mind. Besides these two, there are no other kinds of places in which a thing might be. This confinement of possible places to just two kinds is not, of course, explicitly acknowledged by Berkeley: he simply talks everywhere as if there were just those two—for those two are the only ones he can see.

I said that Berkeley evidently assumes that a proof of (C) is tantamount to a proof of (D). This assumption is mistaken; for consider the following propositions:

(3) Visible things (i.e., the things we (immediately) see) are not located in any sort of place, but they are perfectly objective and accessible to different perceivers.

(4) There is an objective and publicly accessible visible space, different from tangible space, in which visible things are located.

Notice that both (3) and (4) are consistent with (C); for (C) says, in effect, only that visible objects are not identical with objects that are located in tangible space. But neither (3) nor (4) is consistent with (D) as (D) is interpreted by Berkeley; because on both (3) and (4) visible things are not mental entities (states, processes, or whatever), but are perfectly objective, and accessible to all. This shows that Berkeley is wrong in supposing that in proving (C) he has *ipso facto* proven (D); even if we grant him his proof of (C), he still owes us a further argument showing that (3) and (4) are false, and that (D) is true. Berkeley does not see the need for this additional step, because he unthinkingly accepts (1), which rules out (3), and (2), which rules out (4). But in the absence of any defense of assumptions (1) and (2) on Berkeley's part, our charge that he fails to prove (D) must stand. Once again: it is only because his thought is unconsciously influenced by a place-picture of the mind that embodies assumptions (1) and (2) that he can regard his proof of (C) as amounting to one of (D) as well.

It would, of course, be an extremely serious flaw in Berkeley's philosophy if (D) received from him no more of a justification than he provides for it in the *Essay*. But this is far from being the case: in the later works, he turns his attention directly to (D) and presents a powerful defense of it.

The visual perception of magnitude (NTV 52–87)

We need not labor nearly as hard over Berkeley's treatment of this topic as we did over his treatment of the visual perception of distance: in these sections, Berkeley simply applies to magnitude (size), principles that he formulated in the first part of the *Essay*. We know that according to Berkeley, there are (at least) these two distinct kinds of perceptual objects (cf. (C) and (G)): the things one sees (visible objects) and the things one feels (tangible objects). In speaking of the visual perception of size, then, we must take care to distinguish the size of visible objects from that of tangible objects.

Since Berkeley thinks that visible objects exist only in the mind, it might seem strange that he should speak of their size at all: they are nothing but ideas or sensations (*NTV* 41), and how can an idea or a sensation be thought of as having any size? But consider the difference between what you see when you are looking at Jones when he is half a mile away and what you see when he is only ten feet away. We are strongly tempted to say that although Jones is presumably the same size in both cases, still there is *something* that is larger in the second case. If we can divorce the phrase 'visual appearance of *x*' from any suggestion that it is an image or resemblance of *x* (so as to avoid conflict with (F)),[4] we may say that Jones's visual *appearance* when he is half a mile away is smaller than it is when he is ten feet away: his appearance bulks much larger in your visual field in the latter case. We might say that his visual phenomenal size is greater. It is to this visual phenomenal size that Berkeley refers when he speaks of the size of the visible object.

Naturally, this kind of size cannot be measured in terms of inches, feet, miles, or any other of our standard units of length; for it makes no sense to say that the visual appearance of a thing is so many inches or feet tall. To be sure, a man—e.g., Jones—may (visually) appear to be six feet tall, but this does not mean that his appearance is six feet tall: for Jones would doubtless appear to be six feet tall whether you were seeing him from half a mile away or from ten feet away—and we agreed that his appearance is larger when he is closer (cf. *NTV* 61). Instead, then, of using inches, feet, or any other unit that is ordinarily used in measuring the size of physical things, Berkeley elects to use minimum visibilia as his unit for specifying (it would be odd to say 'for measuring') the size of his visible objects. A minimum visible is the smallest amount of visible extension that can still be seen (*NTV* 54); it is any part of a visual appearance (or visual field) than which nothing smaller can be discerned. We might put it this way: it is the smallest possible phenomenal dot, in the visual mode. It is a phenomenal, or appearance, dot, not a physical one, or, as Berkeley would have it in the *Essay*, not a tangible one. To see the difference between the two kinds of dot: consider a small physical dot—an ink mark made by a fine-pointed pen on a piece of white paper, for instance. To a person looking at it, it may present the smallest possible (visual) appearance—that is, it may appear to him as a single minimum visibile; but to a tiny insect, it will doubtless appear as a great many minimum visibilia (cf. *NTV*, appendix to the second edition (W I 238f)). In order to avoid confusing the two kinds of dots, we should probably *not* say that a minimum visibile is something of such a size that if it were any smaller, it could ńot be seen; for this seems to suggest that if you were to take something away from a minimum visibile, it would still exist, although it would be too small to see. That way of talking is appropriate only to physical, or tangible, dots; first, there can be no such thing as really 'taking something away from' a minimum visibile, and second, if you take something away from it *in thought*, or imagine it to be smaller, it is not 'still there' although invisible—on the contrary, it necessarily does not exist.

Berkeley points out that there is no such thing as *the* (one and only) size of a visible object, because the visible object keeps 'changing as you approach to, or recede from, the tangible object' (*NTV* 55); 'it hath no fixed and determinate greatness' (*ibid.*). (Notice that this way of describing the situation seems to presuppose that there is a single, enduring visible object—e.g., the visible Jones, in our earlier example—that exists while you 'approach to, or recede from, the tangible object,' and that has the peculiar property of constantly changing in size. We shall have to ask later whether this presupposition is warranted, or whether Berkeley ought to hold instead that there is no single enduring visible object, but rather only a series of different ones.) We do often speak of *the* size of such-and-such an object—a tree, for example—and indeed we assume that most things have a (single) size that remains more or less constant through time. When we speak and think in this way, we must, in view of the changeable character of the visible object (e.g., the visible tree), mean the tangible object—i.e., the object that exists 'without the mind,' at some distance (*NTV* 55).

Clearly, the question of how we perceive, visually, the size of an object is really the question of how we perceive, visually, the size of a *tangible* object. It is easy to predict, from the principles already laid down, what Berkeley must say about this. We know, from (C), that we do not (immediately) see the tangible object. Our visual perception of its size, then, must be like our visual perception of its distance (*NTV* 65). First, we learn, through experience, that certain features of what we do see (or perhaps also that certain items of consciousness that accompany the act of vision) are associated, or conjoined, with a certain given size of the relevant tangible object. (Let's call them *visual size clues*—or, for short, simply *size clues*.) Then, whenever we detect one of these clues, our mind is carried, by a process of suggestion—or perhaps inference—to the idea of the associated size. So we see the size of a (tangible) object only in the weak sense in which we can see heat or a sound—we see it, that is, only mediately.

Berkeley lists the following size clues (*NTV* 56). First, the size of the relevant visible object, 'which being immediately perceived by sight, is connected with that other which is tangible and placed at a distance.' Actually, as Berkeley realizes, the connection between the magnitude of the visible object (in terms of minimum visibilia) and that of the tangible object is more complex than this. There is no direct association in anyone's experience between a given size of a visible object and a given size of a tangible one; a visible object of 32 minimum visibilia arranged roughly vertically, for example, could be the visual appearance[5] of a pin six inches away, of a man ten feet away, of a tree one hundred yards away, and so on. The experienced correlations, then, are between the size of a visible object *when that object is the appearance of a tangible object located at such-and-such a distance from the perceiver* and the size of the tangible object; if a person is viewing a tangible object from a certain distance away, then, all else being equal, the larger the visible object, the larger the tangible object, normally. No doubt Berkeley had all this in mind when he included the words '*caeteris paribus*' in the following sentence: '*Caeteris paribus*, by how much the greater or lesser the visible object is, by so much the greater or lesser do I conclude the tangible object to be' (*NTV* 56).

Berkeley's second size clue is 'the confusion or distinctness' of the visible object, and the third, 'the vigorousness or faintness of the . . . visible appearance' (*NTV* 56). Notice that both are also distance clues;[6] indeed, the natural presumption would be that they have their status as size clues only *because* they are also distance clues. Thus, it is most plausible to suppose that the second size clue, for example, works this way: the 'confusion' of a visible object shows that the associated tangible object is close to the perceiver's eyes, and therefore he knows that even a quite large visible size betokens only a small tangible size. In the next paragraph of the *Essay* (i.e., 57), Berkeley mentions some additional size clues—notably, 'the figure, number, and situation' of the visible object. From these features, the perceiver can tell what kind of object it is—e.g., whether it is a tower or a man. Berkeley suggests that this knowledge leads directly to an estimate of tangible size, since the perceiver knows what the heights of men and towers generally tend to be. But towers vary enormously in size, and to a lesser degree, so do men. When presented with a visible object of such-and-such a size, then, a perceiver can make an accurate judgment of tangible size from his knowledge of the object's kind only when he also knows, at least roughly, how far away the object is.

It seems to be perfectly clear that a visual perceiver's judgments of (tangible) size and distance are very closely interconnected. In one passage, Berkeley seems to deny this patent truth, for he says of those ideas that suggest both distance and magnitude, that they 'suggest magnitude as independently of distance as they do distance independently of magnitude' (*NTV* 53). But this is just a case of unfortunate wording. What he clearly means to be saying here is that *making* the judgment of size is independent of *making* the judgment of distance, in that one does not cause the other. In fact the two judgments, he says, occur simultaneously:

> I say, [the ideas which suggest both distance and magnitude] do not first suggest distance, and then leave it to the judgment to use that as a medium whereby to collect the magnitude; but they have as close and immediate a connexion with the magnitude as with the distance. (*NTV* 53)

This is quite compatible with holding, what is true, that the two judged quantities—namely, distance and size—are not independent of each other. So I think we can, and ought to, interpret Berkeley as maintaining that we learn correlations between, on the one hand, certain visual clues and, on the other, a complex 'tangible state of affairs' consisting of the object's being a certain distance away *and* its being a certain size.

In an extended passage (i.e., sections 67–78), Berkeley uses his principles (of our visual perception of size) in an effort to explain a 'celebrated [visual] phenomenon,' the moon illusion. The moon looks much larger when it hangs low over the horizon than it looks when it is high in the sky, at or near its zenith, despite the fact that the number of degrees it subtends in our visual field is the same in both cases—or, as Berkeley might have put it (though he didn't), despite the fact that the size of the *visible* moon (i.e., the visible object corresponding to the tangible object that exists many miles away, the *tangible* moon) is the same in both cases. The illusion has degrees, moreover: sometimes the horizon moon looks larger than it does at other times (*NTV* 67).

Berkeley offers a two-part explanation of the moon illusion. (A) More rays of light from the horizon moon are intercepted than are intercepted from the zenith moon, because in the former case, the rays have to travel through more of the dense earth's atmosphere to reach us. The result is that the (visible) horizon moon is fainter, and according to Berkeley's third size clue, fainter visible objects are associated in our experience with larger tangible ones; hence, we judge the (tangible) moon to be larger when it is over the horizon (*NTV* 68).

Is Berkeley right that faintness is a (partial) explanation of the moon illusion? Nowadays this sort of problem would be regarded as one that experimental scientists should cope with, not philosophers. This was not true in Berkeley's time; and certainly experimentation in psychology is a relatively new phenomenon. Berkeley conducted no tests as far as I know:[7] with only some skimpy facts at his disposal, he simply thought about the problem and devised a clever solution that fits in well with his general theory of the visual perception of size. Unfortunately, experiments have now shown fairly conclusively that this first side of Berkeley's account plays no part in the true explanation of the moon illusion. Using an optical device that allows an observer to see an artificial moon against the (real) sky, Kaufman and Rock easily proved that the faintness of the horizontal moon has nothing to do with the moon illusion: 'Neither decreasing the relative brightness of the artificial horizon moon nor increasing the contrast of the zenith moon against its background had any measurable effect on this illusion'[8] (Kaufman and Rock, p. 128).

(B) Berkeley thinks that something else, besides the faintness of the horizon moon, contributes to the moon illusion; he tells us what it is in section 73.[9] Anything that serves as a visual size clue (or as a distance clue either, for that matter) does so only in a certain surrounding of circumstances, Berkeley tells us. To explain what he means, he appeals, as we find him doing again and again, to the analogy with language: a size clue suggests its associated tangible size to us 'in the same way that words suggest the notions to which they are annexed.' But the meaning of a word is not the same in all contexts; the words that provide its setting can sometimes alter its meaning. So is it, too, in the case of size clues. Any size clue suggests a certain tangible size to us only in those circumstances in which we have found it to be associated with that size; if the clue occurs in some different context, it will not—except perhaps by chance—suggest that same size to us at all. In the case of all size clues, however, one of the surrounding circumstances in which we have found them to be associated with their corresponding tangible sizes is this—that our head and eyes have usually been directed (roughly) forward and (roughly) on a level, that is, neither up nor down. As Berkeley puts it:

> we are rarely accustomed to view objects at a great height; our concerns lie among things situated rather before than above us, and accordingly our eyes are not placed on the top of our heads, but in such a position as is most convenient for us to see distant objects standing in our way. (*NTV* 73)

This circumstance (namely, of head and eyes being directed roughly forward and level) is obviously missing when an observer gazes up at the zenith moon, which means that the size clues, occurring out of their normal context, will yield a different judgment of tangible size than they normally would.

Berkeley thinks that the resulting judgment will be that the moon is smaller than it would normally be thought to be, and that this fact also helps to explain the moon illusion. But why should the size clues, out of their normal surrounding circumstances, yield a judgment of *smaller* size in this case, rather than, say, larger?[10] Berkeley's answer is as follows. With very distant objects, if we had to judge their tangible size by relying just on their visible size alone, we would judge them to be much smaller than we actually do judge them to be. Berkeley does not actually explain why he thinks this should be so; but no doubt it is because he assumes, plausibly, that visible objects which are the size of the moon are highly correlated in our experience with tangible objects that are far smaller than those huge objects (such as the moon) that can be seen from enormous distances. So with very distant objects, the surrounding circumstances in which we normally view them[11] must be regarded as so many causes that result in a judgment of a *larger* tangible size than would result if the perceiver went just by the visible size alone. Therefore, when one or more of these causes is omitted, as in the case of the zenith moon, the object is judged to be smaller.

This is an ingenious (partial) explanation of the moon illusion—much more interesting, really, than the first half of his account. It warrants some discussion. Berkeley claims that the visual size clues suggest whatever (tangible) size they do only in those situations where they are accompanied by the old familiar circumstances—i.e., the circumstances in which the original correlations between the clue and the (tangible) size obtained. We can be sure that Berkeley's picture of psycho-physical correlations leads him to think that only those surrounding circumstances *of which we are conscious* are relevant. But there is a further restriction, too; for not all of the normal surrounding circumstances of which we are conscious, not even very many, can be in the least relevant to our judgments of size. Let us suppose, with Berkeley, that faintness is a size clue, betokening large size. Some of the circumstances in which the requisite correlation (i.e., between faintness and large (tangible) size) is to be found in an average person's experience, I imagine, are that he has hair of a certain color, that he hears something, that he feels some bodily sensation or other, and so on. None of these 'surrounding circumstances' presumably has the slightest relevance to a person's visual perception of size: if any one of them were to be different—e.g., if the person had hair of a different color—this would not make things look larger or smaller to him. So the surrounding circumstances that Berkeley means to be talking about in section 73 are just those that have some effect—i.e., some causal influence—on a person's visual perception of size. Berkeley's claim is that the usual position of one's head and eyes—that is, directed (roughly) forward and (roughly) on a level; that is, neither up nor down—is one such causally efficacious circumstance.

Evidence for the existence of such a causal connection, Berkeley suggests, is provided by the fact that an object on the top of a high steeple looks smaller to someone looking at it from the ground than it would look if it were the same distance away from him but at eye level (*NTV* 73). But observing 'external' evidence is not the favored way of discovering such causal connections. Berkeley describes the best method for discovering what the size clues are in the following passage:

> in order to discover by what means the magnitude of tangible objects is perceived by sight, I need only reflect on what passes in my own mind, and observe what those things be which introduce the ideas of greater or lesser into my thoughts, when I look on any object. (*NTV* 56; see also *NTV* 77)

As this very passage, with its use of the term 'introduce,' indicates, the size clues are causes: they are items in one's consciousness that cause him, or help cause him, to think of such-and-such tangible sizes. Berkeley presumably discovers in the same way—i.e., by introspection—that the forward-and-level attitude of the head and eyes is a causally efficacious circumstance in the visual perception of size.

But the method of introspection, which is a kind of inward looking-and-seeing, will not do. By merely looking-and-seeing, one can never be sure that he has found real causal connections even if he is lucky enough to discover genuine *de facto* correlations—and this is as true of correlations among purely conscious phenomena as it is of those among physical events or states of affairs. x may, as a matter of fact, be regularly followed by y; but this does not guarantee that x is the, or even a, cause of y. Some one or more (perhaps unnoticed) factors accompanying x might be the real cause of y. Berkeley is quite confident—more so than he has a right to be—that simply by 'reflect[ing] on what passes in [his] own mind' (i.e., by looking-and-seeing) he can easily pick out, from the features of visual perception, the causes of our various judgments of tangible size. This shows very clearly how radically transparent a medium he considers the mind to be: not only is everything that goes on in the mind fully conscious to the person, but it is also perfectly clear to the person, simply by inspection, what causal connections hold among various (conscious) items that occur in his mind.

As a matter of sad fact, however, recent experiments have shown that the forward-and-level attitude of the head and eyes, which Berkeley considers to be a causally efficacious circumstance with respect to judgments of tangible size, and moreover to be one that (partially) accounts for the moon illusion, is actually nothing of the sort, but a mere accompaniment of the true cause.[12] As Kaufman and Rock conclusively show, the explanation of the moon illusion is this: the horizon moon, in virtue of the fact that it is seen across a plane (i.e., the earth or the sea) that appears to extend for a great distance before the observer, looks to be farther away than the zenith moon, and therefore, because the two moons subtend the same angle in his visual field, the horizon moon looks much larger.

It would naturally be difficult, or impossible, for Berkeley to see the truth of this account, since, as we noted, he steadfastly refuses to acknowledge that our visual judgments of (tangible) size are causally influenced by our visual judgments of distance.[13] The reason Berkeley is so adamant in his refusal to allow that there is any causal connection between a visual perceiver's judgments of distance and his judgments of (tangible) size is simple: when he looks into his mind to notice what goes on there while he is visually perceiving some distant object, he just does not find that he goes through any such process of reasoning as the following: 'This object looks faint and faintness betokens great distance, so the object must be a fairly large one.' The judgments of distance and (tangible) size are 'sudden' or 'immediate,' and they occur simultaneously. It is, of course, his picture of psycho-physical correlations, discussed in Chapter II, that makes him view the matter in this manner—that makes him think, for example, that the only way to explain the moon illusion is to look into one's own mind to see what goes on there.

IV

Retinal Images; the Heterogeneity of Tangible and Visible Objects

The visual perception of situation (NTV *88–120*)

The purpose of this part of the *Essay* is to show how Berkeley's system provides, what other theories of perception do not, a solution to the problem of inverted retinal images. The problem is this: how is it to be explained that although the images of external objects are inverted on a perceiver's retina, he nevertheless sees those objects in their proper upright position (*NTV* 88)? One solution that was current in his day Berkeley quickly rejects. Suppose a perceiver is looking at a tree. According to this account, the person's mind, on perceiving a light ray striking the upper part of the retina, realizes that it has come from the base of the tree. Similarly, it realizes that a light ray striking the lower part of the retina has come from the top of the tree. So the mind traces the impinging light rays back to their proper source, and judges, correctly, that it is seeing an upright tree (*NTV* 89). True to his conception of psycho-physical correlations, Berkeley dismisses this explanation, on the ground that we are not in fact aware of light rays impinging on our retinas, nor of the direction from which they come, nor of any process of tracing them back to their external origin. Any such awareness, therefore, would have to be unconscious awareness, and this notion Berkeley professes not to understand: 'for the mind to judge of the situation of objects by those things without perceiving them, or to perceive them without knowing it, is equally beyond my comprehension' (*NTV* 90).

The secret of the true solution, Berkeley tells us, lies in the distinction he has drawn between the objects of sight (visible objects) and the objects of touch (tangible objects) (*NTV* 91). Indeed, most of the space in this part of the *Essay* (i.e., sections 92–112) is devoted to that distinction. No new theoretical ground is broken, but Berkeley draws some consequences of the distinction, defends his view that all connections between the two kinds of objects are purely contingent, and, in general, seeks to make the nature of the distinction clearer to the reader and rid him of the powerful, but false, idea that we see and touch the very same object. I do not propose to discuss this material at all fully, but there is one point that I must deal briefly with before discussing Berkeley's solution to the problem of inverted retinal images.

Tangible objects, in the system of the *Essay*, exist around us in real physical space. There is no difficulty in understanding what terms such as 'up,' 'down,' 'erect,' 'top,' 'bottom,' 'high,' 'low,' and so on, mean when applied to objects of that sort. But visible objects, as we know from (D) (p. 25), exist only in the mind; and so it is not clear that 'up,' 'down,' and the rest, can have any application at all to them. Yet we constantly do apply these terms to visible objects as well as to tangible ones. How can Berkeley explain this fact?

The answer contained in sections 96–9, as I understand what Berkeley says there, is as follows. We have all found in our experience that there is a highly complex, but extremely familiar, pattern of correlations between certain visible objects and certain tangible ones. When, for instance, we see a special kind of roundish, reddish visible object, we know that if we were to perform certain bodily movements—such as reaching out and grasping—we would encounter a tangible apple. There are a vast number of such connections known to everyone. Terms of spatial situation (such as 'above,' 'below,' and so on) apply primarily to tangible objects, but in virtue of the intimate correlations that exist between visible and tangible objects, their application can readily be, and is, extended to visible objects. Consider, for example, the spatial term 'above.' For the standard cases—i.e., cases of normal sense perception—we say that a visible object *x* seen by a perceiver is *above* a visible object *y* seen by him just in case the following conditions obtain:

(i) visible objects of type *x* are correlated in the familiar way with tangible objects of type *w*;

(ii) visible objects of type *y* are correlated in the familiar way with tangible objects of type *v*;

(iii) the *w* that is causing *x* is above the *v* that is causing *y*, so that (a) if the perceiver were to raise his (tangible) eyes, thus aiming them at the *w*, *x* would be nearer the center of his visual field, and (b) if the perceiver were to lower his (tangible) eyes, thus aiming them at the *v*, *y* would be nearer the center of his visual field.

(This is only a very rough statement of conditions, in need of many refinements, but it should serve us well enough.) For cases other than those of normal sense perception—e.g., after-images, visible objects brought about by the wearing of inverting spectacles, etc.—we may say (and here I go beyond Berkeley) that a visible object *x* is *above* a visible object *y* if, and only if, their arrangement looks, in the relevant respect, the same as the arrangement of two visible objects in a case of normal sense perception, where one is above the other.

Let us turn, now, to Berkeley's solution to the problem of inverted retinal images. The problem, remember, is supposed to be this: how does it happen that we see objects right side up despite the fact that our retinal images are upside down? This seems, on the face of it, to be a non-problem; we evidently do not see our own retinal images in normal cases of vision, so why should the fact that they are inverted be any cause for concern? A genuine problem exists only if one makes the assumption that:

(1) what one (immediately) sees is always nothing other than the retinal image itself.

But why should one assume any such thing? There are, after all, strong independent reasons for thinking (1) to be false: because we know what it is to see a retinal image—although oculists are about the only people who actually ever do it—and we know that nothing like that goes on in *every* case of seeing. (Would a defender of (1) dare to reply that what I have been talking about is seeing a retinal image from the *outside*, whereas his contention is rather that in every case of visual perception one sees a retinal image from the *inside*?)

Whatever the merits of (1) may be, it might seem as though Berkeley espouses it in the *Essay*, for he says: 'Let us suppose the pictures in the fund of the eye to be the immediate objects of sight' (*NTV* 114). Berkeley regards assumption (1) as the standard opinion of the writers on optics of his day; it was expressed, notably, by the esteemed Molyneux (cf. *Dioptrica Nova*, pp. 105–6). But the most plausible interpretation of the way he deals with (1) in the *Essay*, I suggest, is that he regards it neither as definitely true nor as definitely false, but as an hypothesis that he is willing to treat as if it were true. First, however, he subjects it to critical scrutiny. What, he wants to know, is the nature of these 'pictures in the fund of the eye' (i.e., retinal images)? Molyneux certainly thought that they are patterns of stimulation caused by light rays falling on the actual physical retina—that is, on what Berkeley would call the tangible retina. Berkeley admits, of course, that this image on the tangible retina is inverted, but insists that since it is 'by nature altogether of the tangible kind,' it cannot be (immediately) seen (*TVV* 50). So if (1) is to be acceptable, the retinal image it refers to cannot be that pattern of light stimulation on the tangible retina. On the contrary, it must be an image, or rather a picture (cf. *TVV* 51), on the *visible* retina.

But when (1) is thus properly understood, it creates no difficulties: the alleged problem of inverted retinal images simply disappears, Berkeley claims, because the picture on the visible retina is not inverted. For suppose Jones is looking at a man standing before him: in the picture on Jones's visible retina, the head of the man is farther from the (pictured) earth than his feet are, which means that the man looks upright to Jones, just as he should. There is no inversion, and hence no problem to solve (*NTV* 114).

This resolution of the problem of inverted retinal images will not do, however. It is based on a principle expressed in the following passage:

> But then we must well observe that the position of any object is determined with respect only to objects of the same sense. We say any object of touch is high or low, according as it is more or less distant from the tangible earth: And in like manner we denominate any object of sight high or low in proportion as it is more or less distant from the visible earth. (*NTV* 111)

The first half of the principle—concerning tangible objects—is all right, but the second—concerning visible objects—is false. Consider Jones again, looking at his man. The man's visible head is above his visible feet; and it is true that his visible head is farther from the visible earth than his visible feet are. But suppose that Jones puts on a pair of inverting spectacles and again looks at the man. Now the man will look upside down: his visible feet will be *above*, rather than below, his visible head. Berkeley's principle entails, however, that the man must look upright, that his visible feet are *below* his visible head—because his visible feet are still closer to the visible earth than his visible head is, just as before. So Berkeley's principle is false. He seems to have forgotten his earlier, different, account of the application of spatial terms such as 'above' and 'below' to visible objects (cf. p. 43f). That earlier account provides a perfectly good resolution of the (alleged) problem of inverted retinal images, because on that account, the man's visible head is above his visible feet, as it should be, when Jones is looking at him under normal conditions. (Note that the three conditions (i)–(iii) for visible object x being above visible object y are all satisfied when x is taken as the man's visible head and y as his visible feet.) Berkeley could add that when Jones puts on the inverting spectacles, the man's visible feet are then *above* his visible head because those visible objects are arranged just as they would be if the tangible man were really upside down and his 'visible appearance' were being caused under the normal conditions of sense perception.

So although Berkeley actually resolves the problem of inverted retinal images in a faulty way, he has at his disposal a much better way of doing it. In any case, he thinks he has shown that even if assumption (1) is true, there is no such problem, because the relevant retinal image—namely, the visible picture on the visible retina—is not inverted. Anyone who believes that the picture on Jones's visible retina is inverted must think it is inverted relative to the surrounding tangible objects, and thus must presuppose that visible objects stand in spatial relationships to tangible objects. But Berkeley has shown, he thinks, that visible objects exist only in the mind and, therefore, cannot stand in any spatial relationships with tangible objects (cf. *NTV* 111, 112, 115).

What tempts us to think that there is a real problem of inverted images is the fact that if someone (call him *the oculist*) were to look at another person's retina (say, Jones's retina) he would see something that could quite properly be called an inverted image of what Jones is looking at. But we should not succumb to the temptation, Berkeley tells us (*NTV* 116). For consider: the image that the oculist sees is a visible object, and like all visible objects, exists only 'in the mind'—in this case, in the oculist's mind, presumably. So Jones's retinal image is inverted only for the oculist, or in the oculist (as Berkeley himself would put it)—not for, or in, Jones. If this seems puzzling to anyone, perhaps that is because he persists in thinking that the oculist (immediately) sees the retinal image on Jones's *tangible* retina; for, of course, a tangible retinal image would have to be either upright or inverted—it would make no sense to say it was upright for (or in) Jones but inverted for (or in) the oculist. Indeed, it wouldn't be *in* the oculist at all, but only in Jones—for it is his retina that is in question. But, says Berkeley, no one can (immediately) see a tangible object. What the oculist sees exists in his own mind; and there is no difficulty about its being inverted for, or in, the oculist and right side up for, or in, Jones; that is to say, the visible object in the oculist's mind answering to the description 'Jones's retinal image' is inverted, but the one that matters—namely, the one in Jones's mind answering to that description—is not.

Proposition (1), then, when rightly understood, creates no problem of inverted retinal images; and a proper understanding of it requires that we keep firmly in mind the important distinction that Berkeley, in his system, makes—that is, the distinction between visible objects and tangible objects.

Before taking up a new topic, I want to discuss briefly the question of whether Berkeley does, in fact, accept proposition (1). In recent years, there has been something of a controversy over this issue.[1] Opinions range all the way from the view that he definitely does embrace it to the view that he definitely does not. In these discussions, it is often not clear that the writer realizes that there are (at least) two versions of (1); in the first, the retinal image it refers to is an image on the tangible retina, and in the second, it is a picture on the visible retina. Berkeley is explicit in his rejection of the first version of (1), as we have seen; so the only question can be whether he accepts the second version or not. The extreme positions—namely, that he definitely rejects it and that he definitely accepts it—both seem implausible; for if Berkeley thinks that (1) is true,[2] or if he thinks it is false, we should expect him to say so. But he does not say either of these things: he says 'Let us suppose the pictures in the fund of the eye to be the immediate objects of sight.'

I think we can be reasonably sure that Berkeley does not definitely reject (1) as false. If he were to think that (1) is false, he would dispose of the alleged problem of inverted images in much shorter order than he in fact does: he would say that we are no more aware of retinal images than we are aware of those lines and angles that his opponents talk of, and that therefore the so-called 'problem' of inverted retinal images is no problem at all. But he does not do that; he resolves the problem in a much more elaborate way—and in a way that presupposes the truth of (1).

It is true that in the *Philosophical Commentaries*, Berkeley explicitly rejects some version of (1):

Mem: To discuss copiously how & why we do not see the
Pictures. (*PC* 268)

From *PC* 274 and 275, it is clear that by 'the Pictures,' Berkeley means retinal images. But it is doubtless the view of the experts on optics that Berkeley means to be rejecting in these entries—namely, the first version of (1) (in which the retinal image is a pattern on the tangible retina); so the entries provide no evidence that Berkeley definitely rejects the second version of (1).

It might be thought that one good reason Berkeley has for rejecting (1) is this: if, as (1) asserts, we directly see just a picture on our (visible) retinas, then one cannot maintain, as Berkeley wants to do, that we directly see visible men, trees, rocks, and so on. Whatever the merits of this objection might be, Berkeley in any case does not acknowledge them. He sees no difficulty in a philosopher's accepting (1) and then holding that to immediately see a picture on one's retina *is* to immediately see a visible man, or whatever, on the grounds that the picture *is* the visible man, or whatever. Thus he says: 'I ask, what mean you by the picture of the man, or, which is the same thing, the visible man's being inverted? (*NTV* 115; see also *NTV* 117). So he sees no problem in assuming the truth of (1) and then treating the visible man and the picture of the man as the very same thing; both would be a particular (visible) idea of sense in the perceiver's mind.

My guess is that while Berkeley can think of no good reason for rejecting (1), neither can he think of any conclusive reason for accepting it; but that since (1) is the received opinion of the experts on optics, he is willing to be conciliatory, and to go along with what they say—i.e., with the form of words they use to express their opinion. But in the course of his discussion, he finds cause to spurn their version of (1)—that is, the first version—and is willing to assume only that its second version is true.

The heterogeneity of visible and tangible objects (NTV 121–59)

Berkeley has long ago established to his own satisfaction that visible and tangible objects are numerically distinct: this, indeed, is precisely what (G) (p. 28) asserts. (G) is but the first stage, however, of a campaign that Berkeley wages throughout the *Essay*—a campaign to make the metaphysical gulf between visible and tangible objects ever wider. To be sure, he provides a chasm-spanning bridge between the two; for visible objects are reliably connected, in our experience, with tangible ones, and are thus signs forewarning us of them. But this bridge connects objects whose intrinsic natures are, on Berkeley's view, totally disparate. With the advent of (F) (p. 27), we have already witnessed the second stage of the campaign; for (F) claims that 'the immediate objects of sight are not so much as . . . resemblances of things placed at a distance [i.e., tangible objects]' (*NTV* 44). Notice that (F), at least as defended so far by Berkeley, leaves open the possibility that visible objects and tangible objects share certain high-level or generic properties—sometimes called determinable properties—and that they simply fail to share lower-level, specific, or what are sometimes called determinate, properties. Consider the property of having a shape, for example: Berkeley's (F) would allow visible and tangible objects both to have some shape or other, provided only that the tangible object that is correlated with various different visible ones has a shape that is specifically different from theirs. The third, and final, stage of the campaign occurs in this last section of the *Essay*, where Berkeley attempts to foreclose even the meager possibility of resemblance that (F) keeps open.

Berkeley seems to assume, naturally enough, that visible and tangible objects cannot possibly share any such determinable properties as having a color, say, or having some degree of warmth or coldness: for colors can only be seen (not felt) and warmth or coldness can only be felt (not seen), and since, according to (G), visible and tangible objects are numerically distinct, colors must therefore belong exclusively to visible objects, and warmth or coldness must belong exclusively to tangible objects. Whatever the merits of this assumption may be, Berkeley in any case confines himself to the question of whether visible and tangible objects share certain of the characteristics that used to be called common sensibles—in particular, the spatial properties of extension, figure, and motion.

It might seem all too obvious that they do share them; for how can it be denied that both visible and tangible objects are extended, that both have shapes, and that both are capable of motion? Berkeley readily admits that words such as 'extended,' 'triangular,' 'wavy,' and so on, apply to visible and tangible objects alike; but he insists that this linguistic fact is by no means enough to justify the common assumption that the two kinds of objects really share the very same (determinable) properties—for perhaps the words do not have the same univocal sense in the two cases or, to put it in the way preferred by Berkeley, perhaps visible extension (shape, motion) are not of the same kind as tangible extension (shape, motion). We have seen, after all, he might say, that such spatial terms as 'above,' 'under,' and 'over' designate quite different relations when applied to tangible objects and when applied to visible ones; so is it not reasonable to think that the same thing is true of tangible and visible extension, shape, and motion?

One standard view of what it means to say that several individuals $x_1, x_2, \ldots, x_n$ share a common characteristic C, is this: there is an abstract idea of C-ness that rational beings can have, and $x_1, x_2, \ldots, x_n$ each exhibit the feature, or features, contained in that idea. Here, in sections 122–6 of the *Essay*, Berkeley lashes out, for the first time in his published work, against this conception of an abstract idea; he seeks to show that it is unintelligible, so that not only are there no abstract ideas, but there could not be any. I put off until later our discussion of this attack, which is extended and strengthened in the Introduction to the *Principles*. Here I want only to remark that the question of the existence or non-existence of abstract ideas is not terribly relevant to Berkeley's present inquiry. For consider: either there are abstract ideas, or there are not. Suppose first that there are none. There are, then, no abstract ideas of colors—no abstract idea, for instance, of greenness. But this would certainly not imply that the green of an apple, say, is not of the same kind as the green of a lime. Similarly, the non-existence of an abstract idea of extension or shape would not imply that visible extension and shape are not of the same kind as tangible extension and shape. Suppose, on the other hand, that there *are* abstract ideas. This would not imply that visible and tangible extension *are* 'of the same kind'; it would take some further arguments to show that they are, because the term 'extension' might be ambiguous, so that there are really two abstract ideas of extension—one for visible extension and one for tangible extension.

Berkeley realizes that his present problem is not resolved by his finding that there are no abstract ideas; for he begins section 127 by saying:

> It having been shewn that there are no abstract ideas of figure [or of extension] . . . . : The question now remaining is, whether the particular extensions, figures, and motions perceived by sight be of the same kind with the particular extensions, figures, and motions perceived by touch?

Why, then, does he even broach the question of abstract ideas before facing the real problem? I imagine that he does it merely to eliminate a seductive, but false, account of the issue. He is saying, as it were, 'Look here, if you should suppose—wrongly, as it happens—that the existence of an abstract idea of extension shows that visible and tangible extension are the *same*, let me point out that there are no abstract ideas.'

Having cleared the decks for action, Berkeley confronts the difficult question of whether visible extension (figure, and motion) are of the same kind with tangible extension (figure, and motion). This question is hard in a way that Berkeley does not seem to see, however; for he evidently supposes that there is a clear meaning attached to the phrase 'of the same kind' in this context, whereas in fact there is not. For instance: should the fact that visible and tangible extensions are both perceived by normal human beings entitle us to group them together as belonging to the same kind? Berkeley obviously does not think so; but then how would he justify his negative answer? There certainly are situations in which the purposes and standards of classification into kinds are clear and straightforward, so that there would be general agreement as to whether several individuals (or properties or whatever) do or do not belong to some same kind. But what precisely the point is of classifying visible and tangible extensions together, or of refusing to do so, where nothing is said about what is supposed to hinge on the decision, is anything but clear, and so Berkeley's question strikes us, as it were, dumb; we have no idea how to answer it, for we don't know what the relevant considerations are that would weigh on one side or the other. Berkeley tries to dispel the disturbing air of unreality that surrounds his question by telling us what determines him to classify things as he does; but the attempt must, on any account, be placed squarely in the kind known as 'dismal failures':

When upon perception of an idea I range it under this or that sort, it is because it is perceived after the same manner, or because it has a likeness or conformity with, or affects me in the same way as, the ideas of the sort I rank it under. In short, it must not be intirely new, but have something in it old and already perceived by me. It must, I say, have so much at least in common with the ideas I have before known and named as to make me give it the same name with them. (*NTV* 128)

In this passage of atypical wooliness, Berkeley hardly says anything more helpful than that he classifies a new thing under such and such an old heading if he feels right about doing so.

We need not, however, expend a lot of energy trying to find some precise meaning of our own to fit Berkeley's question. It is better simply to observe how he goes about answering it; his answer and its defense may be regarded as showing what sense he attaches. to the tricky phrase 'of the same kind,' and anyway it ought to tell us what thesis, exactly, it is that he holds concerning the relationship between visible extension (figure, motion) and tangible extension (figure, motion).

In reply to his question, Berkeley tells us—predictably—that visible extension, and the rest, are not of the same kind, or species, with tangible extension, and the rest:

(H) *The extensions, figures, and motions perceived by sight are specifically distinct from the ideas of touch called by the same names, nor is there any such thing as one idea or kind of idea common to both senses.* (*NTV* 127)

In the subsequent discussion of objections (*NTV* 139–48), we gain some insight into how this claim is to be understood. Although visible and tangible extension (figure, motion) are called by the same names, the reason for this, Berkeley tells us, is not that they have any 'natural resemblance' (*NTV* 144), for they don't, but simply and solely because they happen to be correlated with one another in sense experience. For example, when presented with a visible square, one can be reasonably sure that if he makes certain bodily movements, he will encounter a tangible square. A visible square does not resemble a tangible square,[3] and the term 'square' applies to both solely because they happen to be thus correlated in normal sense experience. Things might have been quite different: it is logically possible that the visible shapes represented in Figure 5 (a)–(c) should have been correlated in our sense experience with a tangible square.

(a)

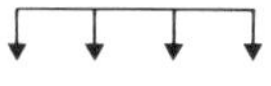

Figure 5

(b)

(c)

Figure 5b

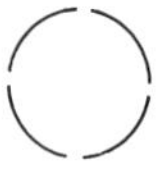

Figure 5c

In that case, those visible shapes would then be called (visible) squares. In this respect, Berkeley says, the relationship between a visible square and a tangible one is like that between the written sign 'adultery' and the spoken sounds 'adultery' (*NTV* 143). The written sign has as many parts (i.e., letters) as the spoken word has,[4] but the parts of each certainly bear no resemblance to one another: the written letters 'a,' 'd,' and so on, do not in the least resemble the spoken sounds 'a,' 'd,' and so on. There are no inherent characteristics in the written signs 'a,' 'd,' and so on, which demand that they, and no others, must in all possible worlds be used in representing the sounds 'a,' 'd,' and so on, in writing. We might easily have represented the sound 'a,' by the written sign 'f,' the sound 'd' by the written sign 'u,' and so on; the spoken sound 'adultery' might then have been written as follows: funsport. In that case, the written sign 'funsport,' not the written sign 'adultery,' would be the written expression of the spoken sounds 'adultery.' Similarly, says Berkeley, there are no inherent characteristics in a visible object that looks like that shown in Figure 5 (d), which

(d)

Figure 5 contd

demand that it, and no other visible object, must in all possible worlds be the 'visible expression' (i.e., the visible appearance, as we say) of a tangible square. On the contrary, a visible object such as that depicted in Figure 5 (a), (b), or (c) might, in some possible worlds, be the visible appearance of a tangible square; and if they were, then in those possible worlds, they would *be* (visible) squares, just as the written sign 'funsport,' in the possible world described earlier, would *be* the written version of the spoken word 'adultery.'

The crucial point, then, is this: just as the written letter 'a' and the spoken sound 'a' have no intrinsic characteristic in common, and are both called 'a's only because they happen (by human convention) to be correlated in a familiar way in our experience, so the visible shape depicted in Figure 5 (d) and tangible squares have no intrinsic characteristic in common, and are both called squares only because they happen (by decree of the Author of Nature, as it turns out) to be correlated in familiar ways in our experience. This is the essential message of (H), and it is a daring and provocative one.

Let us look at the three arguments that Berkeley offers in its support. Here is the first:

(1) The only things that we actually see—the only immediate objects of sight—are light and colors. Neither of these is identical with any tactual property, and so neither is identical, in particular, with any of the spatial characteristics, such as squareness, that are perceived by touch. So there cannot be any spatial characteristics common to both visible and tangible objects. (See *NTV* 129, 130)

Berkeley's proposition (H) explicitly concedes that visible objects do have some kind of extension and claims that it is of a different kind from tangible extension. But this first argument seems, on the face of it, to point to a much stronger (and stranger) thesis—namely, that visible objects are not extended at all, so that there are no visible lines, no visible shapes, and so on. It seems, in fact, to take this form: (i) we immediately see only light and color. (ii) So, we do not immediately see extension at all—i.e., visible objects are not extended. Therefore, (iii) visible and tangible objects do not have the property of extension (of being extended) in common (and so do not have the derivative properties of shape and motion in common, either). When we see how Berkeley seeks to defend (i), however, it is clear that he is not in fact offering any such argument as this: in particular, it becomes obvious that he does not want to assert (ii). Here is the key passage:

And as for figure and extension, I leave it to anyone that shall calmly attend to his own clear and distinct ideas to decide whether he has any idea intromitted immediately and properly by sight save only light and colours: Or whether it be possible for him to frame in his mind a distinct abstract idea of visible extension or figure exclusive of all colour: and on the other hand, whether he can conceive colour without visible extension? For my own part, I must confess I am not able to attain so great a nicety of abstraction: in a strict sense, I see nothing but light and colours, with their several shades and variations. (*NTV* 130)

It is obvious that in this passage Berkeley is assuming that we *do* immediately see (visible) extension—since he says that we cannot 'conceive colour without visible extension.' And elsewhere in the *Essay* he speaks in ways that presuppose that we do see (visible) extension (figure, motion).[5] In the *Three Dialogues*, moreover, Berkeley explicitly states that we do not 'immediately perceive by sight anything beside light, and colours, and figures'[6] (*3D* I (*W* II 175; A 139; T 112)).

I submit, then, that Berkeley's first argument is really the following: (i) Visible extension is identical with color. (ii) But color is a characteristic of visible objects only; tangible objects, in particular, do not have color. (iii) So, by (i), tangible objects do not have visible extension, either. Therefore, (iv) Visible extension and tangible extension are *different* properties.

Premiss (i) is the most important, and at the same time the weakest, element in this argument. Berkeley's defense of it occurs in the passage from *NTV* 130 quoted above. He argues there that an idea of color, abstracted from visible figure (and extension), cannot be formed; and that an idea of visible figure (or of extension), abstracted from color, cannot be formed. In other words, color cannot be conceived of without visible figure (and extension), and visible figure (and extension) cannot be conceived of without color. Berkeley infers from this that visible figure (and extension) are identical with color. Berkeley is fond of this form of argument. Thus, consider the following passage from the first of the *Three Dialogues*:

> Philonous. Or can you frame to yourself an idea of pain or pleasure in general, abstracted from every particular idea of heat, cold, tastes, smells, etc.?
> Hylas. I do not find that I can.
> Philonous. Doth it not therefore follow, that sensible pain is nothing distinct from those sensations or ideas, in an intense degree?
> Hylas. It is undeniable. (*W* II 177; A 140f; T 114f)

Even if we were to accept Berkeley's view of conceivability, and his claim that color is inconceivable apart from visible extension, and vice versa, his defense of premiss (i) would still need to be strengthened. Berkeley's defense clearly presupposes that:

> (a) If property x is inconceivable apart from property y, and vice versa, then x is identical with y.

Principle (a) seems plausible enough in some cases, not so plausible in others. For example: take x to be the property of being a brother, and y to be the property of being a sibling and being male. Here we are doubtless willing to conclude, in accordance with (a), that property x is identical with property y. But what if x is the property of being a closed plane figure having three angles (triangularity), and y is that of being a closed plane figure having three sides (trilaterality)?

If we grant that x in this case is inconceivable apart from y, and vice versa, ought we to conclude that x is identical with y? It is not at all obvious that we should: it even seems that we should not. The trouble here is that we have little more to go on than our intuitions. Most people's intuitive judgment about the properties of visible extension and color, I suspect, would surely contradict Berkeley's; it strikes us as highly implausible to hold that visible extension is the very same property as color.

I conclude that Berkeley's first argument for (H) is unconvincing, at least. Let us turn, now, to the second of the three arguments:

> (2) If a man born blind should one day achieve vision, he would not at first be able to classify the various spatial characteristics that he saw—he would not, for example, be able to tell which visible configurations were squares, which ones were circles, and so on. Consider the case of squares: if squareness were a property intrinsic to both tangible and visible squares, the newly-sighted man would certainly be able to recognize visible squares at once, since he would be familiar with that property of squareness from his experience of tangible squares. Since he cannot, in fact, do that, there is no intrinsic property of squareness shared by visible and tangible squares. (See *NTV* 128, 132, 133)

This is certainly a more plausible argument than the first. There is, today, a great deal of evidence confirming the view, shared by Locke, Molyneux, and Berkeley, that a man born blind is not able to recognize shapes visually at once when he gains the use of his eyes;[7] and if the squareness, say, thus presented to him visually were exactly the same property that he knew from his tactual experience, it seems reasonable to suppose that he should be able to recognize it easily. But let us examine the argument more closely.

Notice first of all that the argument presupposes that

> (β) when a man who has been blind from birth gains his sight, his visual presentations—i.e., the visual items of which he is aware —will, from the first moment, be at least fairly similar to the ones normally sighted people have; they will be at least fairly clear, sharp, determinate, coherent, and so on.

Let us take the particular example of squareness used in the argument: in order for the argument to get off the ground, we must imagine that among the items in the newly sighted man's visual consciousness is something which is of such a character that, if it were before our own visual consciousness, we would find it to be recognizably a square. If there were no such items, his inability to recognize squareness visually would not be surprising nor stand in any need of explanation.

There is reason to think that (β) is in fact false; for although people who have gained their sight after having been blind from birth quickly learn to recognize the colors of things, it invariably takes them a great deal of time, and costs them much effort, to become able to recognize shapes visually—indeed, some patients never do acquire that ability.[8] This fact would be inexplicable if (β) were true, and not difficult to explain if (β) is false.[9] Berkeley's argument fails, then, because it presupposes the truth of the highly dubious proposition (β).

Moreover, even if (β) were true, Berkeley's argument, though plausible, would still be defective. It looks plausible to us and to Berkeley, mainly, I think, because we tend to picture the mind as a kind of spiritual see-er, or viewer, that 'looks at,' and 'sees,' the objects of awareness that come before it. This is a dangerous picture, especially in the case that we are now considering, because it seduces us into thinking that tangible shape and visible shape are both really apprehended by a single sense—namely, by spiritual vision. So when the blind man gains his (physical) sight, he should be able to recognize visible squares at once, if visible squareness really were the same property as tangible squareness—because then visible squareness would simply be another example of a familiar property that he has been 'seeing,' with his spiritual eye, all along. If we put this seductive optical picture of the mind aside, however—as we surely ought to do, in the present case—we realize at once that even if visible and tangible squareness were the same property, there is no reason for thinking that the cured blind man ought immediately to recognize squareness visually just because he has been familiar with it tactually. The fact that he knows how squareness *feels* should establish no antecedent expectation that he ought instantly to know how it *looks*. To be sure, we, who have always had normal vision, can often recognize by sight a shape that we have previously only felt; but that is because we have had a long perceptual history during which we have learned to correlate the looks and feels of things—but the man born blind, who has had no such history, cannot be expected to have our hard-earned capability. I conclude that even if we grant (β) to Berkeley, the admitted fact that a man who is born blind and who then gains his vision cannot at first recognize squareness (and the other spatial characteristics) by sight does not show that there is no intrinsic property of squareness, and the rest, shared by visible and tangible objects.

What Berkeley would have to show, in order to make a reasonable case for (H), is that the newly sighted person could *never* figure out by himself, just by using his vision and his reasoning, which visible figures correspond to which tangible figures. He would have to show, that is, that the newly sighted person simply has to learn what the correlations are—by touching tangible objects and noticing what the corresponding visible objects look like, or perhaps by being told such things as 'Now you are looking at a [tangible] square.' (The best explanation of these facts, it could then be argued, is that visible shapes are intrinsically different properties from their tangible counterparts.)

How could such a thing be demonstrated? Well, Berkeley might argue that it is logically possible for any given tangible shape to correspond in our experience to any visible shape(s) whatever. I do not know how a general proof of such a thesis would go; but Berkeley might choose as an example, one given tangible shape—say, squareness—and try to demonstrate that it might possibly correspond to any of two or three different visible shapes—for instance, to any of the shapes depicted in Figure 5 (a)–(c) (p. 52). If successful, Berkeley would thus have shown that there are possible worlds in which tangible squares correspond to each of those visible shapes. If it could be shown that the relationship between visible and tangible shapes were of that character, then it might be reasonable to suppose that they are quite different properties. Berkeley, however, makes no effort to show that visible and tangible shapes are so related, and it is by no means clear that he could succeed if he were to try. Thus, a world in which tangible squares answered to what we, in our world, would call visible circles would be a world that is very radically different from our actual world, and its laws (e.g., its laws of physics and optics) would have to be so fantastically complicated, that it is uncertain whether any coherent description of it could possibly be formulated. It is, therefore, uncertain that it *is* a possible world.[10]

Let's turn now to Berkeley's third argument for (H):

(3) Visible lines and surfaces cannot conceivably be added to tangible ones so as to make single combined wholes. Visible and tangible objects, therefore, must not have quantifiable spatial characteristics (e.g., length) in common; for if they did, it would be possible to add, say, a visible line and a tangible line. (See *NTV* 131)

It is clear that the plausibility of this argument depends entirely on the acceptance of Berkeley's principle (D) (p. 25), which says that visible objects 'exist only in the mind.' If visible objects are mental entities, whose extension can be measured only in minimum visibilia, it would indeed seem to be inconceivable that a visible line could be added to a tangible one, whose length is measured in inches, feet, or whatever. In fact, if the truth of (D) were to be demonstrated, the plausibility of (H) would be increased. In the *Essay*, as we have seen, Berkeley does not in fact provide a proof of (D). But if we were to accept (D) anyway, would this mean that we should be forced to accept (H)? Not necessarily. An after-image 'exists only in the mind,' but it seems to have color and shape—e.g., to be red and circular, or green and square. Are these properties the *same* properties that tangible things have? I do not know how to set about answering this question. It is true, as Berkeley might point out, that the sides of a square after-image cannot be measured in feet or inches; but its sides are nevertheless unmistakably equal in length (measured in minimum visibilia, perhaps?) and its four angles are unmistakably right angles—so it would seem plausible to hold that the after-image is square, in the same sense of 'square' in which a tangible picture or a tangible card might be square. At any rate, we shall need more of an argument than Berkeley provides if we are to feel comfortable about denying this plausible claim.

We have now a fairly complete picture of the system Berkeley expounds in the *Essay*. The system comprises not only a theory of vision, but also a large fragment of a metaphysical scheme. Of the latter, some is simply assumed; but for other parts, Berkeley provides reasoned support. Perhaps the most important metaphysical assumption is that physical objects exist around us in three dimensional space; their existence is in no way dependent on our perception of them, nor on their being perceived by any other mind (e.g., God's) either. We perceive these objects via our sense of touch; so they are tangible objects. Moreover, Berkeley seems to assume a direct realist view of tactual perception. He attempts to demonstrate that the things that we (immediately) see—visible objects—are wholly distinct from the things we touch, that is, from tangible objects. They do not exist in the three dimensional space of tangible objects, and thus have no spatial relationships with them. Visible objects exist solely in the mind and hence are nothing more or less than ideas; but they in no way resemble tangible objects, and they do not represent them—i.e., they are not ideas *of* tangible objects. The sole connection between the two kinds of objects is this: visible objects are correlated in reliable and familiar ways with tangible objects. When, for example, I perceive a visible elephant, I can be sure that if I walk towards it and extend my hand, I shall encounter a tangible elephant. So visible objects are signs of impending tangible ones. Tangible objects are also presumably signs of visible ones; but since, as Berkeley points out (*NTV* 59), it is only tangible objects that can cause us pain and injury, they are of far greater importance to us, and hence we have more pressing reasons to regard visible objects as (mere) signs of tangible ones than to regard tangible objects as signs of visible ones. (Then too, a visible object can be perceived when we are at some distance from its corresponding tangible object, while a tangible object can be perceived only when we are near, or next to, it—and it is perhaps most natural to speak of x being a sign of y when we can perceive x when we are at a place that is some distance from where y is.)

Much in Berkeley's theory contradicts beliefs, some of them pretty basic, that we all cherish. For example, all of us are convinced that when we touch an elephant while at the same time looking at it, we feel and see the very same object. Berkeley flatly denies this in his principle (G): 'We never see and feel one and the same object' (*NTV* 49). As if that were not enough, he assaults us further with the claim that the things we see do not even resemble, and are not representations of, the things we feel (cf. (F), p. 27).

Berkeley often uses forms of words which suggest that what we ordinarily think of as a single object—e.g., a tree, the moon—is really two different objects. He speaks, for example, of the tangible earth and the visible earth, of the tangible man and the visible man (*NTV* 102). Again, right after announcing his principle (G), he says 'That which is seen is one thing, and that which is felt is another' (*NTV* 49). This assault on our commonsensical view of things is bad enough; but Berkeley's attack on it is yet more violent. First, he would presumably be committed to holding that there is a different object for each of our five external senses, not just the two for vision and touch. Perhaps Berkeley could avoid this by arguing that objects *make* sounds and *give off* smells, so that sounds and smells are distinct from the things that make them or give them off, rather than actually constituting two new dimensions of those objects themselves; but it is difficult to see how tastes could be handled in this way.

Second—and here we come to a more serious consideration—what Berkeley calls *the* (or *a*) visible object (e.g., the visible earth, a visible man), thus suggesting, at least, that it is in each case a single object, is in fact, on his view, numberless different objects. This follows from the doctrine that visible objects exist in the mind, that they are simply ideas. Thus, the visible tree over there is actually not just one thing, nor is it only as many things as there are creatures looking at it; for even within the mind of a single viewer of the tree, there are indefinitely many different objects (i.e., ideas of vision, or what might be called *visible ideas*) produced as he moves about the tree, approaches it, moves farther away from it, and so on. To be sure, it is far from clear what the principles are for individuating, and hence for counting, Berkeley's visible ideas, but on any reasonable account, there will have to be, within most viewers' minds, a great many visible ideas answering to what we would ordinarily assume to be a single visible object. This does violence to the conception we all have of the things we see. We naturally suppose, for example, if we turn a penny over in our hands, getting (as we say) lots of different views of it, that we are seeing the same enduring object the whole time; Berkeley tells us, however, that we are mistaken, and that we are actually seeing a series of different objects.

Again, when we approach an object from some distance, looking at it all the while, we take it for granted that the object we see when we are close to it is the same one we saw when we were farther away—indeed, the language we spontaneously use to describe the situation embodies that picture, making any rival to it seem almost unthinkable. Berkeley, ever aware of the pitfalls of language, rejects this picture altogether. To be sure, there are passages in which Berkeley's words strongly suggest, at least, that when we approach, say, a house or a tree, what we see—i.e., the visible object—does remain numerically the same, although it increases in size:

> The magnitude of the object which exists without the mind, and is at a distance, continues always invariably the same: But the visible object still changing as you approach to, or recede from, the tangible object, it hath no fixed and determinate greatness. (*NTV* 55)

(Actually, this conflicts with our usual picture in one important respect; for we do not normally suppose that what we see increases in size as we approach it, or that it decreases in size as we go away from it. But I shall reserve comment on this point until later.) When Berkeley speaks more carefully, however, he makes it clear that according to his scheme, we see a series of numerically different objects when we approach a (tangible) object. Thus, he points out that if I should approach the moon,

> by the time that I am advanced fifty or sixty semidiameters of the earth, I shall be so far from being near a small, round, luminous flat that I shall perceive nothing like it; *this object having long since disappeared*, and if I would recover it, it must be by going back to the earth from whence I set out. (*NTV* 44; my emphasis)

In Berkeley's system, it makes no sense to speak of *approaching*, or *going away from*, a visible object; only tangible objects can be approached or receded from. Thus, he says that visible objects 'may indeed grow greater or smaller, more confused, or more clear, or more faint, but they do not, cannot approach or recede from us' (*NTV* 50). By contrast to tangible objects which exist 'without the mind,' visible objects exist in the mind; and according to Berkeley's conception of what it is 'to exist in the mind,' one cannot reduce or increase the distance that separates one from something that exists in the mind. Berkeley cannot even grant that something analogous to approaching a visible object occurs—on the grounds, perhaps, that the visible object grows bigger as one approaches the corresponding tangible object—because the visible objects one sees at various distances from the tangible object are numerically different. For the same reason, Berkeley has to hold that it is nonsense to speak of getting a better (or closer) look at a visible object—through a microscope, for example. Any misguided attempt to gain a better look at a visible object can have only this result: that one no longer sees the original object and sees instead one or more different objects. So microscopes do not

> contribute to the improvement of sight; for when we look through a microscope we neither see more visible points, nor are the collateral points more distinct than when we look with the naked eye at objects placed in a due distance. A microscope brings us, as it were, into a new world: It presents us with a new scene of visible objects quite different from what we behold with the naked eye. (*NTV* 85)

All of this contradicts beliefs firmly held by virtually everyone. Later, we shall have to examine in some detail Berkeley's attitude toward such deep-seated commonsense beliefs.

V

Abstract Ideas

In the system of the *Essay*, the things one immediately sees—i.e., visible objects—exist only in the mind (cf. (D), p. 25). Although they are not ideas *of* the tangible objects spread around us in various directions and at various distances (cf. (F), p. 27), they are, nevertheless, ideas. This means, according to Berkeley, that they exist when, and only when, they are perceived by some mind; their existence, indeed, is nothing other than their being so perceived. (Let us assume, for the moment, that we perfectly understand all of this; later we shall have to examine it with a more critical eye.) There is no suggestion in the *Essay* that being perceived by a mind is at all required for the existence of tangible objects, however; they would exist even if there were no minds. This doctrine—namely, that tangible objects exist altogether independently of any mind—is one that Berkeley claims never, as a philosopher, to have believed. In the *Principles*, he labels it a 'vulgar error' (*PHK* I 44), and dismisses his apparent acceptance of it in the *Essay* with the words: 'It was beside my purpose to examine and refute it in a discourse concerning *vision*' (*PHK, ibid.*). The view that Berkeley really sets himself to defend, then, is that visible objects, tangible objects, and indeed everything that is perceived by any of the senses, exist only in the mind; so the existence not only of visible objects, but that of all sensible objects generally, consists in their being perceived by some mind. This is not, as Berkeley well knows, a popular view; on the contrary, 'it is . . . an opinion strangely prevailing amongst men, that houses, mountains, rivers, and in a word all sensible objects have an existence natural or real, distinct from their being perceived by the understanding' (*PHK* I 4). Berkeley finds the ultimate source of this widespread error in the doctrine of abstract ideas: 'For can there be a nicer strain of abstraction than to distinguish the existence of sensible objects from their being perceived, so as to conceive them existing unperceived?' (*PHK* I 5). Not surprisingly, therefore, Berkeley regards it as a matter of the first importance to reveal the doctrine of abstract ideas for the fraud and deception that he takes it to be: accordingly, he devotes the entire introduction to the *Principles* to this destructive labor. Later, we shall want to examine the connection that Berkeley alleges to exist between the doctrine of abstract ideas and the anti-Berkeleyan opinion that is so 'strangely prevailing amongst men' (cf. below, pp. 112–15); but first let us have a look at his attack on abstract ideas.

We may begin by asking: What is it, precisely, that Berkeley is attacking? What are abstract ideas supposed to be? They may be regarded, in the first place, as entities that play an essential role in a certain kind of fairly primitive, but strongly compelling, semantic theory—a theory designed to explain how a single word can refer to, denote, name, or be true of, a vast number of different individuals. It is a theory, therefore, about general terms, such as 'dog,' 'red,' 'animal,' 'square,' and so on. On the surface, at least, there does not seem to be any great mystery about the relation that holds between a proper name, such as 'Socrates' or 'Nassau Hall,' and the individual thing, person, or whatever, that it names; we think of the proper name as a kind of label that is attached just to that one thing and to nothing else. But general terms are different. They apply to a whole range of individuals dispersed, in many cases, through the long reaches of space and time. What determines that the word 'dog,' for example, applies to this, that, and the other object and does not apply to these other ones? What is it that connects 'dog' to just Lupa, Remus, Fido, Rover, Lassie, Rin-tin-tin, and the rest, and hence is missing between 'dog,' on the one hand, and, on the other, this pen I am using, that tree over there, Herbert Hoover, and lots of other things? It's no use answering that 'dog' applies to Lupa, Remus, Fido, Rover, . . . simply because they are *dogs*, and fails to apply to my pen, that tree, and Herbert Hoover simply because they are *not* dogs; for to say that those animals are dogs is just another, less stilted, way of saying that the term 'dog' correctly applies to them, and to say that those other things are not dogs is just another way of saying that the term 'dog' is not correctly applicable to them—so the proffered answer reduces to a tautology, and provides no real answer.

The doctrine of abstract ideas, on the contrary, is ready with a genuine answer—and it is a perfectly natural, plausible one. It says, first, that what connects a general term such as 'dog' with Lupa, Remus, Fido, and the others, is the idea that it stands for, or signifies, in the minds of the people who use it. The idea of a dog is the idea of a being that has characteristics $C_1, C_2, \ldots, C_n$, where $C_1, C_2, \ldots$ C_n are whatever characteristics we speakers of English take to be essential to a thing's being a dog.[1] Lupa, Remus, Fido, and the others, all have the listed characteristics; they satisfy the requirements contained in the idea of a dog, and hence may properly be called by that name. My pen, that tree, and Herbert Hoover, on the other hand, are none of them beings with all the characteristics C_1, C_2, . . . , C_n; they do not fit the idea of a dog and, therefore, the name is inapplicable to them. So what connects the general term 'dog' with just the *dogs* of this world is the idea it stands for, or signifies: 'dog' and dogs are connected via, or by means of, the idea of a dog.[2]

The idea that corresponds to a general term cannot be just any kind of idea. A philosopher who espouses the doctrine of abstract ideas—let us call him an abstract idea theorist—would, with reason, deny that the idea of a dog that is associated with the general term 'dog' could be a fully determinate mental image of a particular dog. Such an image, he would say, is too rich in detail. Thus, consider the image of Remus lying on his back with his paws up in the air: that image cannot be the idea of a dog that is associated with the general term 'dog,' because the animal it depicts has innumerable characteristics that are not shared by absolutely all dogs—e.g., it shows a handsome medium-sized male black and brown dog with semi-floppy ears, lying on his back, and only a few dogs answer to that description. The idea of a dog that is associated with the general term 'dog' must apply equally to all dogs, and so cannot require that a creature, in order to be properly called by the name 'dog,' be either small or large, be of this or that particular color, have curly or straight hair, and so on. It can require only that it be something having just those few characteristics C_1, C_2, . . . , C_n—whatever they may be—that we think all, and only, dogs share; otherwise it will not be the case that *all* dogs 'fit' the idea of a dog and hence can properly be called by the name 'dog.' The abstract idea theorist, therefore, claims that the idea associated with a general term must be, not a fully determinate mental image, but an abstract idea.

As the foregoing discussion indicates, an abstract idea of a kind of thing, x, picks out only certain features of x's—those, namely, shared by all x's. Take dogs, again. A particular dog, as we saw, has any number of characteristics that are simply irrelevant to its being properly called by the name 'dog'; if we mentally pare away all of these irrelevant features, we shall be left with the idea of an animal having just the essential canine features. Such an idea is an abstract idea of a dog or of doghood.

The doctrine of abstract ideas, then, is a theory, and a plausible one, that offers an account of how general terms apply to just the range of particular things they do apply to: thus, one might say that it explains how general words are connected with things in the world.

The words and the things, it says, are connected via the relevant abstract ideas in the minds of those who use the language to which the words belong. Thus Locke, an abstract idea theorist and Berkeley's very special target, speaks of abstract ideas as 'the bonds between particular things that exist and the names they are to be ranked under.' He also says that 'abstract *ideas* are the *medium* that unites [general names and particular beings].'[3]

Berkeley launches a vigorous attack on the entire doctrine of abstract ideas, seeking to destroy it utterly. He tries to establish not merely that there *are* no such things as abstract ideas, but that there could not possibly be. His thrusts here are of unequal force. We may begin by considering the weaker ones. In section 13 of the Introduction to the *Principles*, Berkeley quotes the following passage from Locke:

(1) For example, does it not require some pains and skill to form the general idea of a triangle (which is yet none of the most abstract comprehensive and difficult) for it must be neither oblique nor rectangle, neither equilateral, equicrural, nor scalenon, but *all and none* of these at once.

(2) In effect, it is something imperfect that cannot exist, an idea wherein some parts of several different and *inconsistent* ideas are put together. (Locke, Bk IV, ch. 7, § 9, Berkeley's emphasis; I have inserted the '(1)' and '(2)' for later reference.)

Berkeley regards this passage as making almost embarrassingly obvious the absurdity that he takes to be inherent in the very conception of an abstract idea:

What more easy than for anyone to look a little into his own thoughts, and there try whether he has, or can attain to have, an idea that shall correspond with the description that is here given of the general idea of a triangle, which is, *neither oblique, nor rectangle, equilateral, equicrural, nor scalenon, but all and none of these at once?* (PHK Intro. 13)

Indeed, we know from his early notebooks that Berkeley had thought from the very beginning that this single passage from Locke is enough to refute the doctrine of abstract ideas; for he wrote there: 'Mem: to bring the killing blow at the last v.g. in the matter of Abstraction to bring Lockes general triangle at the last' (PC 687).

It is, however, only the passage from Locke that deserves a 'killing blow,' not the entire doctrine of abstract ideas. In part (1) of the passage, Locke is seduced by the misleading 'surface grammar' of the expression 'general idea of a triangle'; the surface grammar easily suggests to the unwary that some real or imaginary *individual* triangle is meant—as if the expression 'general idea of a triangle' were in this respect just like the expressions 'diagram of a triangle' or 'picture of a triangle.' Locke falls into this disastrous construal of the expression, and the result is the nonsense that Berkeley derides. According to this construal, (1) says that the general idea of a triangle is the idea of a triangle—that is, of an individual triangle—that is neither oblique nor rectangle, neither equilateral, equicrural, nor scalenon, but all and none of these at once. This is an absurd assertion, of course. No wonder that Locke concludes, in part (2) of our passage, that there can be no such thing as an abstract idea of a triangle nor, by implication, any abstract ideas at all.

But on the assumption that Locke is a rational man, he cannot really believe that there can be no abstract ideas—for he continues to talk about them, and they continue to play a central role in his philosophy. Indeed, in the sentence that immediately follows (2), Locke says that the mind 'has need of such ideas.'

Can (1) and (2) be salvaged? I think they can. If we, unlike Locke and Berkeley, deliberately spurn the seductive surface grammar of the expression 'general idea of a triangle,' we can read (1) and (2) in a way that avoids absurdity. Here, then, is how I suggest that (1) and (2) should be understood:

(1′) It takes pains and skill to form the general idea of a triangle, for the general idea of a triangle cannot be the idea (just) of an oblique triangle, nor the idea (just) of a rectangle (i.e., right-angled) triangle, nor can it be the idea (just) of an equilateral, or of an equicrural (i.e., isosceles), or of a scalenon triangle. Rather, it has to be an idea that applies to *all* of these kinds of triangles; so, on the one hand, it is an idea of *all* of these kinds of triangles. Yet we have just seen that it cannot be the idea of any particular one of the specific kinds of triangles—so, on the other hand, it is an idea of *none* (i.e., no one) of these kinds of triangles.

(2′) Since the general idea of a triangle is abstract and so contains a representation of nothing more than the characteristics that are common to all triangles, anything that had *just* those common characteristics, and no others, would be imperfect and indeed could not exist. The general idea of a triangle is formed by combining certain parts—namely, the parts that they all have in common—from the ideas of an oblique and of a rectangle triangle, from the ideas of an equilateral, of an equicrural, and of a scalenon triangle. One may say, in other words, that it is formed by combining the common

parts from numerous different *inconsistent* ideas (for there
is a sense in which the ideas of an oblique triangle and of a
rectangle triangle, for example, may be said to be
inconsistent, in that no triangle could be both oblique and
rectangle).

These glosses show, I hope, that although (1) and (2) are
calamitously worded by Locke, they can nevertheless, when
sympathetically read, be seen to contain perfectly reasonable,
consistent points.[4]

Berkeley can hardly be expected to read (1) and (2) in any other
way than he actually does, since he assumes that all ideas are images.
In discussing (1) and (2), I have been talking as if Locke holds that
abstract ideas are *not* any kind of image, but are rather purely
intellectual, non-sensuous ideas. My gloss (2'), for example, makes
sense only on that non-imagist view of abstract ideas. If, however, as
Berkeley seems to assume, Locke thinks that abstract ideas are
(sketchy) images, then I admit that there is no saving those passages.
My excuses for defending Locke along *non*-imagist lines are these.
First, it is far from certain that Locke does, in fact, think that abstract
ideas are images. Indeed, the miserable shambles to which (1) and (2)
are at once reduced if abstract ideas are taken to be images, is quite
good evidence that he does not hold any such view.[5] And second,
even if the actual Locke does think that abstract ideas are images, it
would still be instructive to show how a mythical, non-imagist Locke
might understand (1) and (2); because when we see that (1) and (2)
make good sense on a non-imagist view of abstract ideas, we realize
that Berkeley's attack, though it perhaps damages the imagist
conception of abstract ideas, has no force at all against the more usual
non-imagist conception of them.

This discussion, now concluded, of Locke's (1) and (2) might have
made it appear as though Berkeley was doing little more than taking
easy pot shots at a few unfortunate lines that Locke had written in a
moment of weakness. But implicit in Berkeley's remarks is a sober
philosophical argument against the possibility of abstract ideas—an
argument that is at least strongly hinted at in other passages in
Berkeley as well. Here it is (I shall use the abstract idea of motion as a
paradigm in stating the argument):

Premisses (a) There can be no idea of *x* if it is conceptually (or
logically) impossible that *x* should exist.

(b) It is logically impossible that (bare) motion should
exist—i.e., that there should be a motion that is
'neither swift nor slow, curvilinear nor rectilinear'
(*PHK* Intro. 10), that is not the motion of any object

or moving thing at all, and so on.

(c) The abstract idea of motion is the idea of (bare) motion.

(d) So, the abstract idea of motion is the idea of something that cannot—conceptually (or logically)—exist.

Conclusion Therefore, there can be no abstract idea of motion.

Berkeley's actual attack on (1) and (2), as we saw, has force only against a very special view of abstract ideas—i.e., the imagist one. The present argument, by contrast, does not *seem*, at first, to be so narrowly focused; if sound, it would seem to score a hit against any conception of abstract ideas whatever.

Berkeley states the first premiss more than once. In the first draft of the Introduction to the *Principles*, he writes: 'It is, I think, a receiv'd axiom that an impossibility cannot be conceiv'd' (*W* II 125).[6] Again, in the published Introduction to the *Principles* Berkeley says, 'But I deny that I can abstract one from another, or conceive separately, those qualities which it is impossible should exist so separated' (*PHK* Intro. 10). (In both these passages, Berkeley clearly means *logical* impossibility.) Finally, in section 5 of Part I of the *Principles*, he admits that he can conceive of the trunk of a human body without its limbs; such 'abstraction' is possible because it 'extends only to the conceiving separately such objects, as it is possible may really exist . . . asunder.' But, he warns, 'my conceiving . . . power does not extend beyond the possibility of real existence.'

The premiss has some plausibility, too. For example, there cannot be an idea of an animal that has exactly four legs and also has exactly five legs; we cannot conceive of such a thing, and the reason for this seems to be that there is a contradiction in the suggestion that an animal of that sort might exist. And wasn't Hume right when he said that to think of something and to think of it as existing, are one and the same thing?[7] If so, then Berkeley's first premiss must be true. For to say that (i) it is conceptually (or logically) impossible that x should exist, is just another way of saying that (ii) one cannot think of x as existing. But from (ii) it then follows, according to Hume's principle, that (iii) one cannot think of x—i.e., there can be no idea of x. So if Hume's principle is correct, if (i) then (iii). But Berkeley's first premiss just states: if (i) then (iii). I take it, therefore, that the first premiss of the argument is at least plausible to some degree. I shall leave it at that and not investigate its merits, or possible demerits, any further, since that inquiry would force huge issues into the open—the nature of conceptual (or logical) impossibility, and what it is to have an idea of something.

We may let premiss (b) pass. But what about the third premiss? Berkeley construes it as saying that the abstract idea of motion is the idea of motion that is not the motion of any moving thing, or motion that is neither slow nor fast, neither rectilinear nor curvilinear, and so on. But the abstract idea theorist would simply reject this reading of premiss (c). He would respond to Berkeley along the following lines: The sense in which the abstract idea of motion is the idea of (bare) motion is not at all what you take it to be. To say that the abstract idea of motion is the idea of (bare) motion is to say that it is the idea of motion in general, and hence not the idea of *swift* motion in particular, nor of *slow* motion in particular, not the idea of *curvilinear* motion in particular, nor of *rectilinear* motion in particular, and so on. It is the idea of what is common to all of these—i.e., the idea of (just) motion in general. Similarly, the abstract idea of motion is not the idea of this or that particular kind of thing moving (much less of this or that *individual* thing moving), but just the idea of something-or-other moving.

Berkeley has provided no reason for thinking that this reading of premiss (c) is unacceptable. But if it *is* all right, then premiss (d) is immediately rendered false—for there is no conceptual (or logical) difficulty, let alone impossibility, in the suggestion that *motion* should exist. Motion can and, of course, even *does* exist—that is, there are numerous individual motions. So the abstract idea of motion is *not* the idea of something that cannot—conceptually (or logically)—exist, contrary to what premiss (d) asserts. So if the abstract idea theorist's interpretation of premiss (c) is legitimate, Berkeley's argument collapses.

Berkeley's error here, as well as in his treatment of Locke's passages (1) and (2), may be put this way: he supposes that it follows, from the fact that the abstract idea of motion contains no representation of the motion's being slow and no representation of its being fast, that it is an idea of a motion that is neither slow nor fast. Again, he supposes that it follows, from the fact that the abstract idea of motion contains no representation of the motion's being the motion of this particular thing or being the motion of that particular thing, that it is an idea of a motion that is the motion of *no* thing. This is a mistake. It is like arguing that since my idea of a movie startlet contains no specification of what color hair she must have, it is therefore the idea of a girl with hair of no color. The idea of a girl with hair of no color is an idea that is *quite different* from my idea of a movie starlet; similarly, the idea of a motion that is neither fast nor slow, and so on, and that is not the motion of any moving thing, would be, if, indeed, it were a possible idea, a *quite different* one from the abstract idea of motion. Berkeley's mistake, then, is to suppose that

(α) if an idea of *x* lacks the representation of some feature,
   F, it must therefore be the idea of an *x* that lacks *F*.

The reason Berkeley can believe (α) , evidently, is that he takes all ideas to be *images*: it is easy enough to think that if an *image* of *x* (say, the image of a movie starlet) lacks the representation of some feature, *F* (say, the representation of any shoes), it must therefore be the image of an *x* (movie starlet) that lacks *F* (shoes). Despite the initial appearances, then, Berkeley's argument does, after all, rest on the assumption that all ideas are images.

But, in fact, (α) is not even universally true for images; thus the image of a fully-clothed movie starlet contains, we may assume, no representation of any particular number, or even of any vague number, of navels on her body; but it is surely not for that reason an image of a person who has no particular number, or even no vague number, of navels. If it were, an argument parallel to the very argument of Berkeley that we are now considering would show that there could not *be* an image of a fully-clothed movie starlet—because a person who has no particular number, or even no vague number, of navels on his or her body cannot conceivably exist.

What Berkeley's extremely unsympathetic treatment of abstract ideas in the foregoing argument, and his unkind words about Locke's (1) and (2), show more than anything else is that the point of view from which he regards abstract ideas is so alien to them that his logical vision is clouded. He looks at them from the standpoint, as we have seen, of a man who is convinced that all ideas[8] are images. Indeed, he does not think there is any real need for elaborate arguments to disprove the doctrine of abstract ideas; for if, as he thinks, all ideas are images, it follows at once that there cannot be any abstract ideas—or at least there can be only very few and perhaps none. There certainly cannot be any abstract idea of (bare) motion, for there cannot be an image of motion that is not the image of something moving, that is not the image of curvilinear or rectilinear motion, and so on. Nor can there be any abstract idea of a triangle, for an image of a triangle has to be the image of an equilateral or of an equicrural or of a scalenon triangle, of an oblique or of a rectangle triangle, and so on.

Berkeley sometimes speaks as though he thinks that all images must be perfectly determinate in all respects[9]—e.g., as though an image of a person must depict him as having hair of a certain color, as standing (or sitting, or whatever) in just a certain specific way, as smiling or frowning or having some other special facial expression, as wearing glasses or not, and so on and on. I do not think that images *can* be perfectly determinate in all respects. But there is no need to insist on that much here; it is enough to remark that images do not have to be perfectly determinate in all respects, and that there can be images in which certain details are simply missing or vague; there can be an image of a person, for example, of which it isn't true either that he is smiling or that he isn't, or of which it isn't true either that his hair totally covers his ears or that it doesn't. Nevertheless, there are limits—not precise ones, to be sure—as to how many or what kinds of details can be missing; if too many details are missing from a (purported) image of an x, or the wrong kinds of details, then there may be nothing that can properly be called an image of an x at all.[10] And these limits are assuredly not so liberal as to allow the possibility of an image of (bare) motion or the image of something that is just triangular and nothing more specific than that. The view that ideas are images, then, even if one grants, what Berkeley apparently does not, the existence of sketchy or non-detailed images, certainly rules out the possibility of great numbers of abstract ideas.

The force of Berkeley's attack so far on the existence of abstract ideas derives entirely from his doctrine that all ideas are images; his attack is exactly as strong—or as weak—as that doctrine is. Before we proceed, let me try to make a little more precise what the doctrine is that I attribute to Berkeley when I say that he holds that all ideas are images. I said that I am using 'idea of x' here to refer to what one has in his mind when he is (merely) thinking about x and not perceiving it. But the range of these x's, these objects of thought, must be restricted; for Berkeley does not hold that for *all* x's, whenever we (merely) think of x, our thinking of x consists in our having an image of x. He realizes that there are certain things—notably minds or spirits—that we can genuinely think about, of which images, nevertheless, cannot be formed. Of such things, he says, we have, not ideas (i.e., images) but notions. We shall examine notions thoroughly later; but for now I want merely to point out that for any object (property, process, or whatever) x that is capable of being seen, felt, heard, etc.—in short, of being perceived by one or more of our senses—Berkeley holds that when we (merely) think about x without actually perceiving it, what we have in our minds in every case is an *image of x*. In short, it is only for *perceivable* x's that Berkeley holds that all ideas of x's are images. This is a rough characterization, since it is not entirely clear what 'perceivable' is supposed precisely to mean; but it will do for our present purposes. In what follows, since I shall restrict the discussion to perceivable things, I shall, for convenience, speak as though Berkeley thinks that all ideas are images—but I ask the reader to bear in mind that actually he maintains this doctrine only for perceivable things.

There can be no doubt that Berkeley does think that ideas of perceivable (or 'sensible') things are all images (let us call this his imagist view); thus he writes:

> Besides, not to inquire into the nature of pure intellect and its spiritual objects, as *virtue*, *reason*, *God*, or the like; thus much seems manifest, that sensible things are only to be perceived by sense, or represented by the imagination. (*3D* I (*W* II 194; A 157; T 133))

But we shall need to know what grounds Berkeley has to support this view before we shall be able to tell whether or not he is justified in using it to disparage abstract ideas. Berkeley's principal target, to be sure, is Locke's theory of abstract ideas, and Locke is often, perhaps even usually, interpreted as holding that all ideas, including abstract ideas, of perceivable things are images.[11] Berkeley certainly reads Locke in this way. So he might take the line that there is no call for him to justify his imagist view, since it is one that his antagonist (i.e., Locke) shares with him. This, however, would be a tactically unwise course, because Berkeley's real target is, or anyway ought to be, the doctrine of abstract ideas in general, not just Locke's (alleged) special imagist version of it. If Locke does really think that abstract ideas of perceivable things are images, then his view is, indeed, a hopeless one and it falls easy victim to Berkeley's onslaught. But the usual non-Lockean, or anyway non-imagist, version of the doctrine of abstract ideas—i.e., the version that holds that abstract ideas are purely intellectual ideas formed in the mind not by the imagination at all, but by the intellect (reason, understanding, or whatever)—is untouched by the bare assertion that all ideas are images. It simply meets that assertion with the counterassertion that some ideas, and all abstract ones, are not images. To crush this more common, and far stronger, version of the doctrine of abstract ideas, Berkeley needs in some way to *show* that all ideas are images. Moreover, his imagist view is important for other parts of his philosophy as well; so on that score, too, he ought to have some justification for it.

The passage, quoted above, from the *Three Dialogues*, suggests that for Berkeley it is just self-evident that all our ideas of perceivable things are images. But that can seem self-evident only as long as the phrase 'an idea of a perceivable thing' is taken to mean an idea of an (actual or possible) *individual* thing, not when it is taken to mean an idea of a *type*, or *class*, or perceivable thing. In point of fact, however, Berkeley does not treat his imagist view as a self-evident truth; he offers support for it. One kind of support he offers might be called empirical evidence—or, more specifically, introspective evidence. Berkeley, as we know, regards the mind as a kind of transparent medium (cf. p. 21f); by introspection, he thinks, we can tell exactly what the mind contains—we can 'see' what goes on in it, what sorts of ideas it has, and so on. So it comes as no surprise to find Berkeley sometimes saying, in effect, 'If you look into your mind, you will find images there, but no abstract ideas.' For example:

> Philonous. But for your farther satisfaction, try if you can frame
> the idea of any figure, abstracted from all particularities of
> size, or even from other sensible qualities.
> Hylas. Let me think a little—I do not find that I can. (*3D* I (*W* II
> 194; A 157; T 133))

The opening sentence of Part I of the *Principles* carries the same message:

> It is evident to any one who takes a survey of the objects of human
> knowledge, that they are either ideas actually imprinted on the
> senses, or else such as are perceived by attending to the passions
> and operations of the mind, or lastly ideas formed by help of
> memory and imagination, either compounding, dividing, or
> barely representing those originally perceived in the aforesaid
> ways. (*PHK* I 1)

The relevant group of ideas for us at the moment is the last-mentioned one, for it includes what we have been calling ideas of perceivable things: it is perfectly clear from this passage that Berkeley thinks that they are all images—and he discovers this, like an explorer or a botanist, by taking 'a survey of the objects of human knowledge.' The great trouble with this kind of quasi-empirical support, however, is that it is extremely weak. One can take a first-hand survey of one's own mind, and then ask a few friends what sorts of ideas they find in theirs—but even if we obtained in this way a completely Berkeleyan result, this would provide no answer at all to the abstract idea theorist when he confronts us with the remark 'Ah, but you see I *do* find abstract ideas in my mind.' So more substantial backing is needed.

The strongest support Berkeley may be said to provide for his imagist view comes, I believe, from the following line of argument—a line that constitutes at the same time his most forceful attack on the doctrine of abstract ideas. First, he urges that abstract ideas are not, in fact, needed for any of the purposes for which abstract idea theorists think they are needed. Some of these purposes turn out to be bogus; in such cases, a false theory about language has generated the (mere) illusion that there is a need for an entity, a need which abstract ideas are then posited to satisfy. Actually, there is no such need, so no need for an entity of any kind to satisfy it. Others of these purposes are perfectly legitimate—but then determinate images (as opposed* to sketchy ones) can adequately serve those purposes. Next, Berkeley points out that images are non-controversial entities, in so far as everyone concedes their existence. Abstract ideas, on the other hand, are at least highly controversial; many competent people deny that they have any such ideas, and some deny that they can even understand what sort of thing they are supposed to be. Everyone will grant, presumably, that ideas of *individual* perceivable things are images; and since images can serve all the purposes for which abstract ideas, viewed as ideas of *kinds* of perceivable things, were posited, there is good reason to reject abstract ideas and to accept the view that *all* ideas of perceivable things are (determinate) images.

I have presented Berkeley's line of reasoning in the guise of an argument that seeks to show that his imagist view is, all things considered, a better theory than the theory of abstract ideas. This is not at all the way Berkeley himself sees it. He thinks he has shown 'the impossibility of *abstract ideas*' (*PHK* Intro. 21); so he would hardly regard the theory of abstract ideas as a viable alternative to his own imagist doctrine, to be judged, side by side with his own doctrine, according to how well the two theories cope with certain problems. Berkeley would suppose that he has ruled out the doctrine of abstract ideas long before any such stage of impartial weighing is reached. But if I am right, he has done no such thing. The most he could be thought to have shown so far is that if his imagist doctrine is true, there can be no abstract ideas—that is to say, his imagist view is incompatible with that of the abstract idea theorist. So what I have tried to do, in presenting this last stage of Berkeley's attack, is to reconstruct, or interpret, it in a way that takes account of the weakness of his actual results to date, while still maintaining the essential thrust of his remarks—for he does argue that even if, contrary to fact, there could be such things as abstract ideas, they would be of 'no use for those ends, to which they are thought necessary' (*PHK* Intro. 21).

Let us see how strong a case we can find in Berkeley for the claim that determinate images can perform all the legitimate functions that abstract ideas are supposed to perform. He discusses three alleged functions of abstract ideas: (i) They are thought to play an essential role in interpersonal verbal communication. (ii) They are said to be needed for 'the enlargement of knowledge' (*PHK* Intro. 15). (iii) It is claimed that they are the necessary links between general terms and the particular things they apply to. The third (alleged) function is the most fundamental, and so Berkeley's treatment of it will be our primary concern in what follows. But, first, let us see what he has to say about the other two.

I begin with the second alleged function of abstract ideas. It is Locke, of course, who makes the claim that abstract ideas are needed for the enlargement of our knowledge; he makes it in the long passage containing (1) and (2), above, that Berkeley quotes in section 13 of his Introduction to the *Principles*. By 'knowledge,' here, Locke apparently means all kinds of knowledge, but in his rebuttal of Locke's claim, Berkeley chooses geometrical knowledge as his particular target. The aim of a geometrical proof, according to Locke, is to allow us to perceive a connection of 'agreement or disagreement' among certain of our ideas. From beginning to end, it deals exclusively with our own ideas. (See Locke, Bk IV, ch. 1, §§ 1, 2; and Bk IV, ch. 2.) And since the truth that is demonstrated is always general, applying to all things of a certain kind (e.g., all triangles), the ideas employed must be abstract ideas; for 'what is known of such general *ideas* will be true of every particular thing in whom that essence, i.e. that abstract *idea*, is to be found' (Locke, Bk IV, ch. 3, § 31).

Berkeley concedes, of course, that a geometrical proof—e.g., of the proposition that the sum of the interior angles of a triangle is equal to two right angles—demonstrates a general truth about all triangles; but this does not mean that the proof demonstrates something about the abstract idea of a triangle, nor even that in going through the proof, one must have an abstract idea of a triangle in one's mind. The proof requires only a diagram of a particular kind of triangle (or a corresponding determinate image of a triangle); the proof holds good of all triangles, to be sure, not just of the triangle depicted in the diagram—but the generality is adequately accounted for by the fact that the individual triangle depicted in the diagram is used to stand for all triangles (*PKH* Intro. 15):

> Though the idea I have in view whilst I make the demonstration
> be, for instance, that of an isosceles rectangular triangle, whose
> sides are of a determinate length, I may nevertheless be certain it
> extends to all other rectilinear triangles, of what sort or bigness
> soever. And that, because neither the right angle, nor the equality,
> nor determinate length of the sides, are at all concerned in the
> demonstration. It is true, the diagram I have in view includes all
> these particulars, but then there is not the least mention made of
> them in the proof of the proposition. (*PHK* Intro. 16)

Berkeley's view, then, is that a demonstration in geometry—e.g., of the theorem that the sum of the interior angles of a triangle equals two right angles—really consists of two stages. First, the theorem is proved of just the determinate kind of triangle depicted in the diagram used in the proof, and then, second, the conclusion is drawn, with certainty, that the theorem is true of all kinds of triangles. The justification for this second step of 'universal generalization' is that no mention is made, in the first stage proof, of the relative sizes of the angles and sides of the triangle depicted in the diagram. Berkeley's thought is that since no mention is made of these things, they could have been anything—the relative sizes of the three angles and sides could have been anything, and the proof would have gone through just as well. He, therefore, supposes that the relative sizes of the three angles and sides of the diagrammed triangle is as irrelevant to the proof as, say, its color. No mention is made of the color of the triangle: it could have been anything, and the proof would not have been affected.

But against Berkeley, I would urge that although we can be absolutely sure that the proof would apply to triangles of any color whatever, we have no right to conclude, from the lone fact that no mention is made of the relative sizes of the three angles and sides, that the proof would apply to triangles of any determinate shape whatever. For all we know, the determinate shape of the diagrammed triangle, unlike its color, may make a relevant difference to the various constructions carried out, and inferences made, in the course of the proof; so if the relative sizes of the angles and sides had been different, perhaps the proof would not have gone through. The fact, cited by Berkeley, that no mention is made of these things in the proof, counts for nothing. True, no mention is made of them in the actual words of the demonstration, but since a perfectly determinate kind of triangle is depicted in the actual diagram used in the proof, the relative sizes of its angles and sides *are*, as it were, mentioned. They are 'mentioned' in the diagram. So Berkeley does not, I think, satisfactorily account for the generality of geometrical demonstrations. No doubt abstract ideas do not account for it either, but Berkeley has not *shown* that they are not needed for this purpose.

Let us turn, now, to the first of the three alleged functions of abstract ideas. Berkeley offers two not-so-serious arguments against the claim that abstract ideas are required for interpersonal verbal communication. One of them (in *PHK* Intro. 14) goes like this. Locke himself admits that it requires a lot of skill and effort to form abstract ideas. Berkeley thinks that the truth of this admission is perfectly obvious from what he has said (in *PHK* Intro. 13) about the notorious passage from Locke that contains (1) and (2), above (p. 65f). Grown men, Locke urges in the same passage, may not regard abstract ideas as difficult to form, but that is only because they are familiar with them from prolonged use. But then, says Berkeley, these ideas must have been formed in childhood—and that is absurd because no child could possibly construct such monstrosities as Locke describes in the

(1)-and-(2)-passage, and yet they certainly can, and do, 'prate together of their sugarplumbs and rattles and the rest of their little trinkets.' There is a second, similar, argument implicit in what Berkeley says at the end of section 10 of the Introduction to the *Principles*:

> The generality of men which are simple and illiterate never
> pretend to *abstract notions*. It's said they are difficult and not to
> be attained without pains and study. We may therefore reasonably
> conclude that, if such there be, they are confined only to the
> learned. (*PHK* Intro. 10)

But if only the learned have abstract ideas, and abstract ideas were necessary for verbal communication, it would follow that only the learned could talk intelligibly, and then only to one another. This, too, reduces the notion that abstract ideas are necessary for verbal communication to absurdity.

There is a strong flavor of irony in these arguments, for Berkeley, in heaping scorn on Locke's (1)-and-(2)-passage, and in his earlier critique of abstract ideas (in *PHK* Intro. 10), thinks he has shown not that it takes great skill and effort to form abstract ideas (which is a premiss of the arguments) but that it is utterly inconceivable that any such ideas should ever be formed by anyone. But treating them anyway as serious arguments, we find that they are weak indeed. We saw that Berkeley's assault on the (1)-and-(2)-passages leaves the most common (i.e., the non-imagist) view of abstract ideas unscathed; he does not show even that it takes extraordinary human skills to form abstract ideas. (Locke's own concessions on this head do not help Berkeley, for he only said that 'abstract ideas are not so obvious or easy to children or the yet unexercised mind as particular ones' and that it requires 'some pains and skill' to form any abstract idea.) Moreover, the earlier critique of abstract ideas (in *PHK* Intro. 10) fails because it assumes, mistakenly, that abstract ideas, if they exist, would have to be a species of *images*. So in the second of his two arguments, Berkeley has no right to the lemma that only the learned can have abstract ideas; and that does not, in fact, seem to be a proposition that an abstract idea theorist has to accept. And against the first argument, an abstract idea theorist might plausibly urge that if a child uses a general term (e.g., 'sugarplum') perfectly, this shows that he *does* have the correct abstract idea answering to that term, but if, on the other hand, he uses it imperfectly, this shows that he has only a half-formed, incorrect, confused, or in some other way inadequate idea answering to that term. Berkeley simply hasn't given us any good reasons for thinking that children cannot have adequate abstract ideas, and yet surely the doctrine of abstract ideas makes it understandable, too, that children, especially very young ones, should often have inadequate or imperfect ideas of things. To sum up: the not-so-serious arguments pose no threat to the abstract idea theorist.

A bit later, Berkeley raises some more serious, and far more interesting points that bear on the idea-communicating function of language. He begins by remarking that it is a 'received opinion' that

(i) language has no other end but the communicating our ideas (*PHK* Intro. 19)

and that

(ii) every significant name stands for an [i.e., one single] idea (*ibid.*).

(By 'name,' here, Berkeley means: general term.) The abstract idea theorist then claims that these ideas must, in every case, be *abstract* ideas. When we come to the third alleged function of abstract ideas, we shall find Berkeley attacking proposition (ii); but here he concentrates on proposition (i). Berkeley begins his assault on proposition (i) not by making a direct attack on (i) itself, but by removing its strongest support. This prop is the belief that:

(β) when a word stands for an idea, it must be the case that every time the word is significantly used, its associated idea occurs in the mind of the speaker (or writer) and is subsequently raised in the mind of the hearer (or reader).

What I mean by a word's being *significantly* used on a given occasion is just that on that occasion both the speaker and hearer[12] understand it in that particular context. To many philosophers of Berkeley's day, (β) would have been a highly plausible belief; for they assumed that to understand a word on a given occasion is just to have in one's mind the idea for which it stands. Most of Berkeley's contemporaries would also have accepted proposition (ii) which Berkeley is not, for the moment, calling into question. But once propositions (ii) and (β) are embraced, proposition (i) immediately becomes tempting, for then it is easy to suppose that the speaker's purpose—or his *immediate* purpose, anyway—in making an utterance must always be just to raise in the minds of his hearers the very same ideas he has in his own mind and that he puts into words when he makes the utterance. The sole function of language, in short, is to serve as a public medium for transferring ideas from the mind of the speaker to the minds of his audience—and this is precisely what proposition (i) says.

Berkeley, as I said, starts by impugning (β). He points out, in an extremely important observation, that most of the time when we speak or write, we deal just with the words alone, never stopping to think of the associated ideas:

> And a little attention will discover, that it is not necessary (even in the strictest reasonings) significant names which stand for ideas should, every time they are used, excite in the understanding the ideas they are made to stand for: in reading and discoursing, names being for the most part used as letters are in *algebra*, in which though a particular quantity be marked by each letter, yet to proceed right it is not requisite that in every step each letter suggest to your thoughts, that particular quantity it was appointed to stand for. (*PHK* Intro. 19)

This seems obviously true, and yet it is important that the point be made, for the following reason. Proposition (β) was then, and perhaps to a degree still is, a most compelling thought. Gripped, as one well might be, by this thought, one is apt to overlook mere matters of obvious fact. So it is important to be forced to see them, to be reminded of what one should all along have known, to be brought back from theory to reality.

Berkeley has, I think, effectively sabotaged belief (β), and thus, to the extent that (β) serves to support proposition (i), undermined (i) as well. In section 20, he turns to a direct assault on (i) itself. Here is what he says:

> Besides, the communicating of ideas marked by words is not the chief and only end of language, as is commonly supposed. There are other ends, as the raising of some passion, the exciting to, or deterring from an action, the putting the mind in some particular disposition; to which the former is in many cases barely subservient, and sometimes entirely omitted, when these can be obtained without it, as I think doth not infrequently happen in the familiar use of language. (*PHK* Intro. 20)

This passage—or rather the whole of sections 19 and 20 of the Introduction—marks the birth of a view of language (which might be called the instrumentalist view) that was first to be taken up again in a serious way only much later; it was destined to receive its most influential formulation and richest development in the later philosophy of Wittgenstein. We shall have occasion later to discuss Berkeley's instrumentalist view of language; but for now, it suffices to say that in section 20 he resoundingly refutes proposition (i).

As Berkeley well knows, this refutation of proposition (i) does not constitute an argument against the claim that abstract ideas are required for interpersonal verbal communication—for it leaves entirely open the possibility that *one* of the important ends of language is the communicating of our ideas and that certain of these communicated ideas (those, namely, associated with general terms) must be abstract ideas. What the refutation does, rather, is chip away at a certain picture of language that an abstract idea theorist is likely to have—a picture that includes the 'received opinions' expressed in propositions (β), (i), and (ii). The abstract idea theorist can easily afford to lose propositions (β) and (i); he can make retrenchments to accommodate the loss without serious jeopardy to his essential position.

But what about his version of proposition (ii)? Well, he could retrench a bit here, too. He might be forced to concede that not *every* general term stands for an abstract idea, but then he must hold fast to the view that *most* or *very many* general terms stand for abstract ideas. Notice, however, that nothing Berkeley says in sections 19 and 20 requires the abstract idea theorist to make this retrenching move; for in those sections Berkeley does not show that there is even a single general term that does not stand for an idea. Elsewhere in the Introduction, however, he launches an attack on proposition (ii) in which he seeks to show that (ii) ought not to be merely weakened, but that it ought to be altogether abandoned. In this attack, he allows that general terms all stand for ideas of some sort,[13] but denies that they ever stand for a single abstract idea and claims rather that they each stand for any one of a large range of 'particular ideas.' And this brings us to Berkeley's critique of the third alleged function of abstract ideas—namely, that they are the necessary links between general terms and the particular things they apply to.

The main text is section 18 of the Introduction. Berkeley begins by attributing to the abstract idea theorist the following beliefs, which he takes to be mistaken:

> 'Tis thought that every name hath, or ought to have, one only precise and settled signification, which inclines men to think there are certain *abstract, determinate ideas*, which constitute the true and only immediate signification of each general name. And that it is by the mediation of these abstract ideas, that a general name comes to signify any particular thing. (*PHK* Intro. 18)

There is a temptation for us, today, to read passages like this as if they expressed the semantical views of, say, Mill. According to Mill, general terms *denote* a number of individuals, but they also *connote* certain attributes of those individuals. This connotation, moreover, is what we are actually talking about when we speak of the meaning of a general term.[14] But we must not read Locke and Berkeley through Mill's eyes if we are to understand them properly: they employ but a single semantic category—the relation of signifying, standing for, or denoting. (Berkeley uses all three terms interchangeably.)

Keeping as close as we can to Berkeley's own concepts, then, we see that in the passage just quoted from *PHK* Intro. 18, he is attributing to the abstract idea theorist (i.e., Locke) the following cluster of propositions:

(a) Each term signifies (denotes), or anyway ought to signify (denote), just one thing.

(b) Each general term signifies (denotes), primarily and immediately, just one specific abstract idea.

(c) By means of directly signifying (denoting) an abstract idea, each general term also signifies (denotes), in a secondary and indirect way, a range of particular things.

Berkeley then proceeds to state his own contrary view: 'Whereas, in truth, there is no such thing as one precise and definite signification annexed to any general name, they all signifying indifferently 'a great number of particular ideas' (*PHK* Intro. 18). In the first clause, Berkeley opposes (a): as far as general terms are concerned, he says, they do not signify just one thing. In the second clause, he opposes (b): according to him, each general term signifies any one of a great number of 'particular ideas.'

Notice that there is nothing resembling an *argument* here: Berkeley simply affirms his own view. We can, however, along the lines I suggested earlier (cf. p. 73f), construe him as implicitly arguing that there is no need to posit those exotic and highly problematical entities, i.e., abstract ideas, as the links between general terms and the particular things in the world that they apply to. But then a question about Berkeley's own view arises. Does he think there is no need to posit abstract ideas as word-world links on the grounds that there is no need for any such links, or rather on the grounds that although there is a genuine need for word-world links, determinate images (which are familiar and non-problematical entities) can play that role equally well? In other words, which of the following propositions would Berkeley accept?

(3) There is no need for ideas of any sort to mediate between general terms and the particulars they apply to (their referents),

or:

(4) There is a genuine need for such mediating ideas, but determinate images will do the job as well as abstract ideas.

(Note that if (3) is Berkeley's view, the 'particular ideas' mentioned in the passage from *PHK* Intro. 18, just quoted, will be individual

81

things in the world, whereas if (4) is his view, they will be determinate images that mediate between general terms and individual things.)

G. J. Warnock thinks that (3) is Berkeley's true view:

> Locke holds . . . that language has reference to the world, not directly, but in some way through the ideas in human minds. . . . Berkeley is in fact eager to deny this. He . . . objects to the 'interposition' of ideas between the words and the world of which we speak. . . . The main burden of his case is that the language in which we speak of the physical world refers directly to what we see and feel, taste, hear, and smell. Indeed he regards this, rightly, as one of his most important principles.[15]

There can be no doubt whatever that Berkeley did hold precisely this view in the unpublished first draft of the Introduction, as the following passages from that work show:

> Sure I am, as to what concerns myself, when I say the word Socrates is a proper or particular name, and the word Man an appellative or general name, I mean no more than this viz that the one is peculiar & appropriated to one particular person, the other common to a great many particular persons, each whereof has an equall right to be called by the name Man. This, I say, is the whole truth of the matter. (*W* II 127)

> Suppose I have the idea of some one particular dog to which I give the name Melampus and then frame this proposition Melampus is an animal, where 'tis evident the name Melampus denotes one particular idea. . . . [But the word 'animal' does not] indeed in that proposition stand for any idea at all. All that I intend to signify thereby being only this, that the particular thing I call Melampus has a right to be called by the name animal. (*W* II 136)

> Now I would fain know, why a word may not be made to comprehend a great number of particular things in its signification, without the interposition of a general idea. (*W* II 127)

There seems, however, to be evidence supporting the view that Berkeley abandons (3) after writing the first draft of the Introduction and adopts (4) in the published version. For consider: what would someone have to think about determinate images if he were to accept (4)? He would have to think that they can be (or serve as) *general* ideas; he would have to think that a determinate image (of a triangle, for example) can be used to represent all things of a relevant kind (e.g., all triangles), just as the abstract idea theorist holds that the abstract idea of a triangle represents all triangles. We should expect anyone who accepts (4), then, to make a case for the thesis that determinate images can, after all, be general. If, therefore, Berkeley moves to (4) in the published version of the Introduction, we should expect him to say there that determinate images can be general, and we should expect not to find any such claim in the first draft, where (3) is firmly defended.

Both of these expectations are in fact fulfilled. Indeed, the latter expectation is more than fulfilled: for in the first draft, Berkeley explicitly denies that determinate images can be general:

> An idea [i.e., a determinate image] is not capable of representing indifferently any thing or number of things it being limited by the likeness it beares to some particular existence, to represent it rather than any other. The word Man may actually be put to signify any particular man I can think of. But I cannot frame an idea of man, which shall equally represent & correspond to each particular of that sort of creatures that may possibly exist. (*W* II 129)

(Berkeley's unfortunate habit of calling determinate images 'particular ideas' reinforced this position, for it would naturally seem self-contradictory to think that a particular idea might be a general idea.) So in the first draft, Berkeley everywhere firmly identifies abstract ideas and general ideas; there is simply no room at all in his scheme for determinate images that are general. Since he thought that there are, and can be, no abstract ideas, Berkeley's identification of general ideas and abstract ideas meant that general ideas, too, were relegated to non-existence. In the published version of the Introduction, however, the existence of general ideas is starkly affirmed:

(5) By observing how ideas become general, we may the better judge how words are made so. And here it is to be noted that I do not deny absolutely there are general ideas, but only that there are any *abstract general ideas*. (*PHK* Intro. 12)

Does this mean that Berkeley really abandons (3) and accepts (4) in the published version of the Introduction? The affirmative answer seems guaranteed, at first glance, by two passages. The first is that just quoted: for to say that we may better judge how words are made general by observing how ideas become so, suggests that the generality of words derives from that of ideas, as (4) avers. The second occurs in the preceding section of the Introduction:

(6) But it seems that a word becomes general by being made the

sign, not of an abstract general idea, but of several particular ideas, any one of which it indifferently suggests to the mind. (*PHK* Intro. 11)

This seems almost to be a paraphrase of (4). So it certainly looks as though Berkeley has abandoned the (3) of the first draft and embraced (4).

On closer inspection of the two cited passages and what immediately follows them, however, we in fact find no trace of (4), and in one of the two cases, a virtual reassertion of (3). Thus, consider the second of the two passages—i.e., (6). Berkeley goes on at once to give an example to illustrate what he means in that passage. He says that if we have a general proposition about, say, motion, then of course the proposition says something about motion in general; but this does not imply that the abstract idea of motion is raised in our minds—it implies rather only that whatever (particular) motion we happen to think of, the proposition claims to hold good for it. But then the passage is revealed as having nothing whatever to do with (4), for in the example the fact that the (particular) motions are ones that we happen *to think of* is obviously irrelevant to the generality of the proposition and thus to the generality of the term 'motion.' So Berkeley might as well have said that the generality of the proposition implies that the proposition claims to hold good for any and all (particular) motions *that there are*. He is, in other words, simply asserting that the general proposition is *general*, and he is not saying anything at all about how this generality is achieved—he evidently sees no need to explain that. He is, thus, so far from affirming (4) in this passage, that he seems rather to be implying the truth of (3).

Let us turn now to the first of the two passages quoted above—i.e., (5): it turns out, from what Berkeley goes on to say, that he does not mean to be asserting in (5) that the generality of words derives from that of ideas, but only that the way ideas (i.e., determinate images) are made general is a good model for understanding how words are made general. A determinate image, he says, can be a general idea by being used, by the person who has it, to represent all the particulars of its kind:

An idea, which considered in it self is particular, becomes general, by being made to represent or stand for all other particular ideas of the same sort. To make this plain by an example, suppose a geometrician is demonstrating the method, of cutting a line in two equal parts. He draws, for instance, a black line of an inch in length, this which in it self is a particular line is nevertheless with regard to its signification general, since as it is there used, it represents all particular lines whatsoever; for that what is demonstrated of it, is demonstrated of all lines or, in other words, of a line in general. (*PHK* Intro. 12)

The diagram that is used in a geometrical proof is Berkeley's primary exemplar of a particular that is used to represent an entire class of things: it is appealed to again in sections 15 and 16 of the Introduction. Later, we shall want to examine this view that a determinate image can be a general idea, but for now let us uncritically accept it. Notice that although Berkeley began by saying that we may better judge how words are made general by observing how *ideas* become general, his actual exemplar is not an *idea* becoming general, but a (physical) thing—that is, a black line. This should already indicate that Berkeley is not in the process of defending (4) at all; for anyone who says that a black line, by being used in a certain way, can become general and who says so without appealing to any *ideas* to explain the fact, might also be expected to say that a word (i.e., 'motion') can become general, without his supposing that any ideas are necessary to account for its generality. And this expectation is realized in the very next lines:

And as that particular line becomes general, by being made a sign, so the name *line* which taken absolutely is particular, by being a sign is made general. And as the former owes its generality, not to its being the sign of an abstract or general line, but of all particular right lines that may possibly exist, so the latter must be thought to derive its generality from the same cause, namely, the various particular lines which it indifferently denotes. (*PHK* Intro. 12)

This passage may not commit Berkeley to (3) in the ineluctable way that the explicit (3)-passages cited earlier and suppressed in the published version of the Introduction did, but it can leave no doubt in the reader's mind that Berkeley still does, in fact, accept (3) and therefore rejects (4).

There is a puzzling element in all this: if Berkeley, after rejecting the existence of general ideas in the first draft of the Introduction, comes to acknowledge their existence in the published version, and yet makes no use of them as links connecting each general term with its referents, what does he think their role is? As we saw earlier, Berkeley says that general terms all 'signify . . . indifferently a great number of particular ideas' (*PHK* Intro. 18); but it isn't clear why Berkeley says this, since he doesn't say it as a first step towards asserting a linkage, via ideas, between general terms and their referents.

The solution to this problem is easy, however: Berkeley needs general ideas to account for the fact that people have non-verbal general thoughts, and indeed, to account for the fact that they have non-verbal thoughts even about individuals. Consider Berkeley's position in the first draft of the Introduction, where he denies the existence of general ideas. On this view, general terms refer directly to their referents, without the interposition of any ideas, and there simply are no non-verbal ideas corresponding to any general term. This comes out with exquisite clarity at the end of the notorious Melampus passage:

> And I do intreat any one to make this easy tryal. Let him but cast out of his thoughts the words of the proposition and then see whether two clear and determinate ideas remain in his understanding whereof he finds one to be conformable to the other. I perceive it evidently in my self that upon laying aside all thought of the words 'Melampus is an animal' I have remaining in my mind one only naked and bare idea viz that particular one to which I give the name Melampus. Tho' some there be that pretend they have also a general idea signified by the word animal, which idea is made up of inconsistencys and contradictions as has been already shewn. Whether this or that be the truth of the matter I desire every particular person to consider and conclude for him self. (*W* II 136; see also *PC* 600)

It follows from this that all purely general truths can only be verbal—and, indeed, almost all truths about individuals (e.g., 'Melampus is an animal') will have at least one unavoidable verbal element in them. The point is not that one cannot think such thoughts at all, but rather that all, or part, of the thoughts will have to be *in words*. For example, the thought corresponding to the sentence 'Melampus is an animal' cannot, as we have just seen, consist of an idea of Melampus combined with a (non-verbal) idea of animal-in-general, since the latter idea does not exist. So it must consist of a single (non-verbal) idea of Melampus plus the thought, *expressed in words*, '[This] is an animal' or perhaps '[This] has a right to be called by the name "animal." '

Berkeley came to think that this dependence of all thought, or of very nearly all thought, on language is intolerable; for it is one of his deepest convictions that language, although useful for various practical purposes, cannot fail to mislead us intellectually. In the last five sections of the Introduction, he urges us to shun words in our philosophical and other kinds of reflections, and to keep only our ideas, 'bare and naked' (i.e., divested of words), firmly before our minds.[16] In this way, we shall avoid error, since we cannot, Berkeley thinks, be mistaken about our own ideas: 'So long as I confine my thoughts to my own ideas divested of words, I do not see how I can easily be mistaken' (*PHK* Intro. 22). When Berkeley thus urges us to shun words in favor of our own ideas, he must mean totally *non-verbal* ideas—for, of course, there would be no deliverance from the 'embarras and delusion of words' (*PHK* Intro. 25) if we simply moved from words themselves to ideas that are either wholly or partially verbal. And yet this is all we can do, apparently, when the existence of general ideas is denied. In order, therefore, to be free from the wheel of words, to be able to move from words to non-verbal ideas, there must be (non-verbal) ideas that are general. This, then, is the role of the general ideas whose existence Berkeley affirms for the first time in the published version of the Introduction—not, as we had previously suspected, to provide links between general terms and their referents, but rather to serve as those (non-verbal) constituents of our thoughts that correspond to general terms. So Berkeley's view in the published version of the Introduction is that words may be general—i.e., may denote a great many particulars—and ideas may be general—i.e., may stand for, or represent, a great many particulars—but that the generality of these two different sorts of things are totally independent of one another; in particular, the generality of ideas in no way accounts for the generality of general terms.

Evidently, then, Berkeley still accepts (3) in the published version of the Introduction to the *Principles*. (3) might very well be a true proposition, for perhaps there is no need for *ideas* to mediate between general terms and their referents—or, for that matter, to mediate between proper names (and other singular terms) and their referents. But then some other account must be provided of the connection between words and things in the world. It cannot be maintained that *nothing at all* is needed to constitute the word-world links, for, as Berkeley acknowledges, all men have 'an equall right to be called by the name Man' and his dog Melampus 'has a right to be called by the name animal'; and surely such rights cannot be brute facts, but must be based on something. There must, for example, be something that links the general term 'man' with Socrates, Plato, Herbert Hoover, the next man you see, and the rest of us, and that fails to link 'man' with that tree out there, snow, this pen, and all the other non-men—and thus something that gives Socrates, Plato, Herbert Hoover, and so on, but not the tree, snow, this pen, and so on, 'an equall right to be called by the name Man.' If there were no such right-giving link, the claim that Socrates, Plato, etc., have a right to be called by the general term 'man' would be left floating in air, without any support.

Does Berkeley, in embracing (3), simply fail to see the need for word-world links, or does he see the need, but have an account of them that does not appeal to ideas? I think he simply fails to see the need. There are, to be sure, in Berkeley's thought the makings of an interesting alternative explanation of how words might be connected with their referents. These beginnings lie in his instrumentalist view of language. Throughout his career, Berkeley never wavers from his conception of language as a device used by human beings for various practical purposes. One of its important uses is to communicate ideas from one mind to another; but there are others—e.g., to cause emotions, and to alter people's conduct (*PHK* Intro. 20).

How could this instrumentalist view of language be used to provide an account of the needed word-world links? Well, it is clear that the connection between words and the world must involve the people who actually use the language of which the words are part—and it seems plausible to suppose that, in particular, it must involve their understanding of what the words mean. Berkeley's instrumentalist view of language, moreover, gives him a way of forging a conception of what it is to understand the meaning of a word that would not appeal just to ideas; to understand the meaning of a word, on this view of language, would be, roughly, *to know how to use the word.* Berkeley even comes close to expressing such a conception in a passage cited earlier:

> that there are many names in use amongst speculative men, which
> do not always suggest to others determinate particular ideas, is
> what no body will deny. And a little attention will discover, that it
> is not necessary (even in the strictest reasonings) significant names
> which stand for ideas should, every time they are used, excite in
> the understanding the ideas they are made to stand for: in reading
> and discoursing, names being for the most part used as letters are
> in *algebra*, in which though a particular quantity be marked by
> each letter, yet to proceed right it is not requisite that in every step
> each letter suggest to your thoughts, that particular quantity it was
> appointed to stand for. (*PHK* Intro. 19)

In this passage, Berkeley comes close to saying that understanding the meaning of a word just *is* knowing how to use it. If he were to pursue this line, he might develop a dispositional account of 'understanding the meaning of a word' that would allow him to explain the connections between words and their referents.

In the Introduction to the *Principles*, however, Berkeley does not in fact pursue any such line. The point of the passage just quoted is simply that we can sometimes use language without actually entertaining any relevant ideas; but Berkeley clearly enough thinks that there must be some relevant ideas in the offing. That is, he thinks that in order to know what the meaning of a word is, one must be *able*, if occasion should demand, to conjure up some appropriate ideas (i.e., determinate images).

Berkeley, I say, apparently sees no need to explain the word-world links; at any rate, he offers no account of how words are connected to their referents. It is, I suppose, just possible that he sees the need for such connections, and that he thinks his determinate images provide them. But, then, it is exceedingly strange that he does not say so.

In any event, determinate images could not, by themselves, provide the needed word-world links. An account of these links that appealed just to determinate images, for the case of general terms, would go like this: a general term directly signifies (denotes) any one of a range of determinate images, and the determinate image stands for (or represents) all the relevant particular things. So a general term denotes its referents indirectly, by directly signifying (denoting) any one of a range of determinate images. The account, then, would include the claim that a determinate image can be general—a claim that Berkeley in fact makes, as we have seen.

But there are difficulties here. An image is not general in itself, so to speak: it represents a range of particular things only for someone on a particular occasion. Consider, for example, an image of a right triangle, outlined in black against a white background, with the lengths of its sides in the ratio 3:4:5, with the right angle at the apex and the hypotenuse horizontal. (Call this image, I_r.) Berkeley says that I_r may be a general idea of a triangle—i.e., it may represent all triangles. I agree that it can. But for whom? Someone who is languishing in total ignorance of what triangles are might have I_r: he might, for instance, have seen some architectural detail that exactly resembles I_r and now visualizes it. But I_r does not, and cannot, *for him* represent all triangles: if it represents *anything* for him, it no doubt represents only the previously seen architectural detail. Again, suppose that Jones is pondering the question of whether white outlined in black is or is not a more pleasing color combination than white outlined in red, and that as an example of the former he happens to conjure up I_r. Jones may know a lot about triangles, but on this occasion, I_r represents for him not all triangles, or any triangle, but rather a certain pattern of colors.

For whom then *can* I_r represent all triangles? Only, it would seem, someone who satisfies two conditions. First, he knows what the relevant characteristics of I_r are—relevant, that is, to its being an image of, precisely, a *triangle*: he knows, for instance, that its three-sidedness is relevant, but not the fact that it has one right angle, not its color, and so on. Second, unlike Jones, he intends, on the occasion in question, that I_r should represent just all *triangles*, not a pattern of colors, not an architectural detail, and, in sum, not any of the countless other things that I_r could be used to represent.

I conclude, then, that no account of word-world links that appeals *only* to determinate images can work. In the case of general terms (the only ones we have considered here), a determinate image can connect a word to its referents only if it is backed up by an act of intending and a state of knowing what the relevant characteristics of the determinate image are.

I do not really think, however, that Berkeley wants to defend this, or any other, account of word-world links, for I believe he sees no need for any account of those connections. He sees no need for anything, idea or non-idea, to serve as a connecting link between general terms and their referents: general terms, according to him, simply denote their referents directly. I lament the fact that Berkeley takes this line, because, as I tried to show, some account, some analysis, of the relation that binds a general term to just the particulars it denotes (i.e., its referents) is called for. On this point, at least, it seems to me that the view of abstract idea theorists such as Locke is superior to that of Berkeley; for whatever the inadequacies of their doctrine may be,[17] they at least see the problem and offer a solution to it, whereas Berkeley, apparently, does not even see it.[18]

VI

The Objects of
Immediate Perception:
Ideas of Sense

Berkeley's views on general ideas are largely negative: they are, above all, anti-Lockean. We must see them as being formulated and defended in conscious opposition to Locke's views about abstract ideas. The same may be said of Berkeley's doctrines on the nature of reality and our knowledge of it. True, he offers here many more arguments in defense of his own positions than he does in the case of general ideas, but still his doctrines cannot be fully understood without viewing them against the background of Locke. Locke is the Philosopher for Berkeley, but again he treats his predecessor not as the infallible authority but rather as the Enemy. Let us try to see why.

Locke was a metaphysical dualist: he held that there are two radically different kinds of substances—extended material substances and unextended mental substances (minds). The physical world consists of material substances disposed in space. Human beings are complexes of a mental substance (or mind) united, via causal connections running in both directions, with a material substance (a human body). God is an infinite mental substance. Material objects in our vicinity affect our bodies—in particular, our sense organs—in various ways, causing changes in our brains which then cause ideas of these objects to occur in our minds. We are therefore not, in sense perception, directly confronted with the material things that surround us; we are directly aware only of the ideas they cause in our minds. We can, however, infer that the objects exist, since they cause our (perceptual) ideas of them; and we can know certain of their properties, since some, though not all, features of our ideas resemble features of the objects that cause them.

Berkeley has a long list of complaints against this picture of the world, but its major faults in his eyes are that it leads to skepticism and that it leads to atheism. Locke, of course, was not an atheist; he even had a proof of God's existence that he regarded as absolutely certain. But Berkeley rightly senses the danger of atheism lurking in Locke's system. Once the existence of interacting mental and material substances is acknowledged, it is but a short step to the view that they have always existed—and then what need is there of God? At the very least, God will be needed only to create the mental and material substances in the first place and to set the material ones in motion: after that, the laws of motion—discovered in Locke's own day by Newton—will see to it that the world keeps running without God's help. So at best Locke's scheme removes God far from man's world of everyday concerns.

The charge of skepticism against Locke is most powerfully and eloquently urged by Berkeley: indeed, it is without doubt one of his lasting achievements that he perceives so clearly the epistemological rocks and shoals lying beneath the calm surface of Locke's philosophy. Berkeley's vision of these hidden horrors will be revealed in Chapter VII.

Berkeley seeks to rectify the faults he finds in Locke's system by the simple, but extraordinarily dramatic, expedient of eliminating all material substances. All that exists are minds and their ideas. Many of a finite mind's ideas are caused by its own acts of volition, but those that arise in sense perception (ideas of sense) are obviously caused by some other power. This power, in Berkeley's system, is none other than God. Atheism and skepticism are thus swept away. What we call objects in the physical world—trees, chairs, human bodies, and the like—are no longer lurking behind a veil of appearance: they simply *are* congeries of ideas of sense. There is no longer any excuse for atheism, because each of us can be assured of God's existence at any moment just by—literally—opening our eyes. Our ideas of sense constitute utterances in a divine language of nature in which God constantly assures all of us, or anyway those of us who are willing to receive the message, that He exists and cares for us.

This remarkable system, whatever merits it may have on the score of avoiding Locke's difficulties, cannot fail to strike any reader with a robust sense of reality as fantastic and altogether incredible. But Berkeley cannot be so brusquely dismissed; certainly not, anyway, on the basis merely of the crude sketch of his system that I have just given. Berkeley defends his views with sober, rational, and highly persuasive arguments; no assessment of his system can fairly be made before one evaluates the cogency of these arguments—and this latter task will occupy the greatest part of our energies in what follows.

As my sketch of his system indicates, the fundamental metaphysical categories for Berkeley are that of a *mind* and that of an *idea*. A mind, at least in his great published works, the *Principles* and

Three Dialogues, is a mental substance—i.e., an unextended spiritual entity that exercises volition, and is conscious of various sorts of ideas and perhaps also of itself. There are several grave problems connected with Berkeley's conception of a mind that we shall have to face; but I propose to save them for later treatment and to concentrate now on the other basic category, that of *ideas*.

We have already discussed one kind of Berkeleyan idea—i.e., general ideas. I turn now to another—i.e., ideas of sense. Berkeley, following Locke, maintains that in sense perception, what we have before our minds in every case is nothing more nor less than an idea—what I have called, and shall continue to call, an *idea of sense*, to distinguish it from general ideas, ideas of memory, ideas of the imagination, and so on.[1] I regard this as the single most important principle in all of Berkeley, since virtually everything that is distinctive and exciting in his thought ultimately stems from it. We shall be wanting to refer to this principle; so let us give it a designation and restate it as follows:

> (a) In sense perception, what the perceiver has before his mind in every case is just one or more ideas of sense.

Berkeley makes it perfectly clear in the very first section of Part I of the *Principles* that he espouses (a). In the opening sentence, where he speaks of taking 'a survey of the objects of human knowledge,' he gives primacy of place to the 'ideas actually imprinted on the senses.' He goes on to say that 'by sight I have the ideas of light and colours with their several degrees and variations' (*PHK* I 1). In the final sentence of the section, he refers to congeries of perceived properties—e.g., the perceived properties of an apple—as 'collections of ideas.' So right from the start, Berkeley boldly announces his acceptance of principle (a).

Ideas of sense, like all other ideas, are, for Berkeley, necessarily mind-dependent. It is a conceptual truth that there can be no such thing as a free-floating idea—i.e., an idea that is had by, and exists in, no mind whatever, but simply exists by itself or combined with other ideas. An idea necessarily exists only in the mind that has it, or, to put it in another way that Berkeley is fond of, exists only in the mind that perceives it. (He tells us that an idea's existing in a mind is 'the same thing' as its being perceived by that mind (*PHK* I 2).) Since Berkeley, as we know, does not acknowledge even the possibility of *unconscious* ideas, when he says that an idea must be perceived by a mind, he means it must be *consciously* perceived by it. An idea, then, exists when, and only when, it is (consciously) perceived by a mind: an idea that is not (consciously) perceived[2] by some mind is a logical impossibility. Berkeley summarizes all of this by saying that the existence of ideas 'consists in being perceived' (*PHK* I 2), their '*esse* is *percipi*' (*PHK* I 3).

Given this conception of an idea of sense, what principle (*a*) says is that in every case of sense perception, the perceiver has before his mind—i.e., is aware of—something that is mind-dependent, something that exists only in his own mind. This is very far from being a self-evidently true proposition. On the contrary, one's first impulse is to suppose that it must be false; for we naturally think that in sense perception a perceiver is aware, typically, of such things as tables, trees, houses, and automobiles—and none of these is normally considered to be something mind-dependent, or to exist only in some mind. It is a matter of the first importance to determine why Berkeley accepts principle (*a*), because most of his metaphysical doctrines are ultimately supported, in large part, by it—e.g., the doctrine that so-called material things (such as automobiles) are collections of ideas, and the doctrine that nothing exists apart from minds and their ideas.

As soon as one searches, in Berkeley, for considerations to support principle (*a*), the first thing one discovers, disconcertingly, is that he seems to take its truth for granted, as if it stood in need of no defense. This is plain from the very opening words of Part I of the *Principles*:

> It is evident to any one who takes a survey of the objects of human knowledge, that they are either ideas actually imprinted on the senses, or else such as are perceived by attending to the passions and operations of the mind, or lastly ideas formed by help of memory and imagination, either compounding, dividing, or barely representing those originally perceived in the aforesaid ways. (*PHK* I 1)

The specific wording of this sentence is significant: Berkeley speaks of the objects of human *knowledge*—i.e., of what we can be *certain* about—and he speaks of ideas '*actually imprinted* on the senses.' These phrases suggest that there might be other kinds of ideas involved in sense perception that are *not* actually imprinted on the senses and that are *not* objects of human knowledge. As it turns out, we can tell from things Berkeley says elsewhere that he does, in fact, think there are such other ideas involved in sense perception. Indeed, we know this already from our study of the *New Theory of Vision*. Recall, for example, that Berkeley says there that when we are looking at a distant object, the ideas of sight we have suggest to our minds the idea of a certain distance and also other 'tangible ideas' we would be likely to have if we were to perform certain bodily movements. In such cases, the ideas of sight are 'actually imprinted on the senses,' but the others are not. Again, in the *Three Dialogues*, Berkeley points out that the only things perceived by the senses are the things that are perceived *immediately*, where the term 'immediately' is meant to rule out ideas that occur in the mind as the result of inference or suggestion. (See *3D* I (*W* II 174f and 204; A 138 and 167f; T 111f and 145).) In a typical case of sense perception, then, the perceiver will have a certain number of ideas that are 'actually imprinted on the senses' and, in addition, certain other ideas that these suggest to him or that he infers from them. It is only the first kind of idea—the imprinted ones—that deserve the title 'ideas of sense.'

From all of this, it becomes clear that (a) is misleadingly worded. (a) states that in sense perception, the perceiver is aware of *only* ideas of sense. In one way, this does actually express Berkeley's view, as we shall see, since he holds that the processes of inference and suggestion are not parts of sense perception, strictly speaking: thus, when we infer something from an idea of sense, it is our *reason* that is at work, not our senses (*3D* I (*W* II 174f; A 138; T 111f)), and when further ideas are suggested to our minds by ideas of sense, this is the work of our *imagination*, again not of our senses (*3D* I (*W* II 204; A 167f; T 145)). Nevertheless, (a) might be thought to imply, wrongly, that *when*, or *while*, we perceive something, it is only ideas of sense that we are aware of (or, as Berkeley would put it, that we perceive). To remove this erroneous suggestion, let us make (a) more precise, as follows:

(I) In sense perception, what the perceiver in every case is directly (or immediately) aware of—or, to use Berkeley's preferred terms, what the perceiver directly (or immediately) perceives— is just one or more ideas of sense.

(It is obvious that by 'direct perception,' here, we must understand *both* direct perception_{without} inference *and* direct perception without intermediary (cf. p. 9f).

Now that we have abandoned (a) in favor of (I) as a statement of Berkeley's crucial principle, let us start afresh, and try to determine why Berkeley accepts (I). It has to be said, again, that Berkeley treats (I) as if it were obviously true. We learn this from the opening sentence of Part I of the *Principles*, already quoted above. And we learn it, too, from remarks such as: 'That we are affected with ideas from without [in sense perception] is evident' (*3D* III (*W* II 239; A 201; T 184)),[3] and from the rhetorical character of the question: 'And what do we perceive besides our own ideas or sensations?' (*PHK* I 4). In Berkeley's day, it was certainly the received opinion that in sense perception what we are (directly) aware of is nothing but ideas: Locke, for example, held such a view. Berkeley himself makes the point: 'That the objects immediately perceived are ideas, is on all hands agreed' (*3D* III (*W* II 237; A 199; T 183)), and '[Philosophers are of the opinion that] *the things immediately perceived, are ideas which exist only in the mind*' (*3D* III (*W* II 262; A 224f; T 211)). The fact that all, or most, philosophers accept a certain proposition may provide one with some reason for accepting it; but in the case of a principle as momentous as (I), we shall naturally hope that Berkeley has better grounds than that.

I think that when he wrote the *Principles*, Berkeley regarded (I) as self-evidently true, and therefore as standing in no need of any proof, just as Locke before him had done. But later, he evidently came to realize that (I) is in fact a controversial proposition that needs some support, for in the *Three Dialogues* he makes a strenuous effort to provide it.[4]

Berkeley's defense of (I) consists, broadly speaking, of two stages. In the first, he seeks to establish that:

(II) In sense perception, the perceiver directly perceives nothing but a certain restricted range of perceptual properties.

Then, by considering each of these properties in turn, he tries to show that:

(III) All perceptual properties are ideas (of sense).[5]

The conjunction of (II) and (III) yields (I). Let us take up each of the arguments in turn.

Here is Berkeley's clearest statement of (II):

Philonous. You will farther inform me, whether we immediately perceive by sight any thing beside light, and colours, and figures: or by hearing, any thing but sounds: by the palate, any thing beside tastes: by the smell, beside odours: or by the touch, more than tangible qualities.
Hylas. We do not. (*3D* I (*W* II 175; A 139; T 112))

Let us concentrate on the case of vision. According to Berkeley,

(IIa) We immediately see only light, colors, and figures (i.e., shapes).

(Let us call these three properties the *basic visual properties*.) Berkeley nowhere tries to *demonstrate* that we immediately see nothing but these basic visual properties. His view seems to be that no proof is either required or possible, and that all one has to do in order to see its truth is to carefully examine one's own ideas (cf. *NTV* 130). But surely it simply is not obvious that we immediately see nothing but three basic visual properties, and so some argument for that proposition is required. If he were to be confronted with this challenge, Berkeley might try to argue that all visual objects and properties can be reduced to the three basic visual properties, just as he argued in the *New Theory of Vision* that visual figure and extension reduce to light and color. However, in Chapter IV we discussed this latter argument (cf. pp. 54f) and found it wanting; if we were right, then Berkeley would do well to avoid using that argument to demonstrate the truth of (IIa).

There is a different, and perhaps more promising, defense of (IIa) that can be constructed from Berkeleyan principles. It would go something like this:

(IV) Whatever a person immediately (or directly) sees he has incorrigible knowledge of.

(V) Of all the things a person learns about through vision, he has incorrigible knowledge only of the basic visual properties.

From these two premises, (IIa) follows as a conclusion.

Berkeley is firm in his espousal of (IV): thus, he says of a person who is deceived by an optical illusion:

His mistake lies not in what he perceives immediately and at present (it being a manifest contradiction to suppose he should err in respect of that) but in the wrong judgment he makes concerning the ideas he apprehends to be connected with those immediately perceived: or concerning the ideas that, from what he perceives at present, he imagines would be perceived in other circumstances. (3D III (W II 238; A 200; T 184))

It is clear from this passage that Berkeley considers (IV) to be a self-evident truth. No doubt he does so mainly because he thinks that what we immediately see is, in every case, nothing but an *idea*—and he takes it to be perfectly obvious that we have incorrigible knowledge about our own ideas (cf. e.g., *PHK* I 25). But since (IV) is here being used in an attempt to prove that what we immediately see is, in every case, nothing but an idea (i.e., in an attempt to prove (I)), we cannot allow Berkeley to support (IV) in that question-begging way.

I think Berkeley would insist that whether or not the things one immediately sees are ideas, (IV) is anyway self-evidently true. Many philosophers through the ages have certainly accepted something like it as axiomatic. This unquestioning faith in the truth of something like (IV) is understandable: after all, if you directly see something, it is right there before your consciousness, and what could keep you from infallibly knowing those features of it that you are thus (directly) aware of? To be sure, what you directly see may be blurred, have an indefinite shape, and be of an indeterminate color; but that it is blurred in just *that* way, has just *that* indefinite shape, and is of just *that* indeterminate color, are things that you cannot, so it might seem, be mistaken about. In recent times, the doctrine that there can be, and are, incorrigible empirical statements (in the form of reports of immediate experience), has come under heavy fire.[6] It would take us much too far afield to discuss the difficult and important issues that are raised in this debate; let us merely note that Berkeley does explicitly accept (IV), that it does not occur to him to question it (virtually all of his contemporaries would be at one with him on this score), and, finally, that the proposition has at least an air of plausibility about it.

Berkeley does not explicitly assert (V), but it, like (IV), seems plausible and he might well assume it to be true. I see no way of proving (V)m but anyone who accepts (IV) might easily be persuaded to accept (V) as well by trying, with the help of examples, to think of anything other than the basic visual properties that a person might, by using his eyes, acquire incorrigible knowledge of. Thus suppose someone, Smith, is looking, in broad daylight, at an object, ten feet away, that he takes to be a black cat. This cat, we may imagine, has typically soft fur, and Smith, let us further suppose, acquires the (true) belief that the cat does, in fact, have soft fur. This belief does not, however, constitute infallible knowledge. Smith has merely inferred, from the fact that what he sees is a *cat*, that it has soft fur; or else the idea of its soft fur has merely been *suggested* (in Berkeley's sense) to Smith as a result of his previous dealings with cats—and such inferences and suggestions can always be wrong. This cat, it might turn out, has a tough bristly coat. What about Smith's belief that what he sees is an animal and, in particular, a cat? This does not qualify as incorrigible knowledge either, for something with just that visual appearance might actually be a stuffed toy, a cardboard cut-out, a puppy dressed up in a cat suit, or any number of other things. Smith does not even incorrigibly know that he is seeing some sort of physical thing—for if he were having an hallucination, he might be presented with precisely the same visual appearances that he is aware of now. By considering such examples, one can be driven to the conclusion that the only 'objects' of whatever incorrigible knowledge a visual perceiver, as such, can have are the basic visual properties—that is, according to Berkeley's best-considered list, light, colors, and shapes. (We know from the *New Theory of Vision* why distance is not included on Berkeley's list; but we might wonder why relative direction from the perceiver, motion, and certain relations (e.g., the relation of being above, being bigger than, and so on) are not on it. Berkeley would doubtless answer that all of these either are, or essentially involve, relations, and on his view all relations includ[e] an act of the mind' (*PHK* I 142) and hence are not directly perceived. Let us not pursue this issue here.)

Notice that if we continue to espouse the principles we did just now in dealing with the example of Smith seeing the black cat, then we cannot hold that a visual perceiver has incorrigible knowledge of the colors and shapes that the objects he sees actually have; for, of course, a thing can look purple when it is really red, and look square when it is really trapezoidal. Color and shape are no better off, on this score, than cathood, animality, or objecthood. But there is, apparently, a difference between the basic visual properties and those others. When a person sees a piece of meat that is actually red but that looks purple to him (due, perhaps, to unfortunate lighting conditions), then purpleness seems to be undeniably there before his consciousness. He sees purple, or the color purple, even if it is not true to say that he sees something that is (objectively) purple. We may say that he surely sees *something*—call it a (visual) appearance[7]—that is purple, and—so it might plausibly be maintained—he cannot be mistaken about that color. Similarly, if a person sees something that looks square to him, he may be said to see a (visual) appearance that contains squareness, and—so it might again plausibly be maintained—he cannot be mistaken about that shape. All that our man Smith, qua visual perceiver, knows with absolute certainty, on this plausible view, is that he is seeing a (visual) appearance that contains an expanse of black that has a certain shape, namely, a feline shape. Indeed, if we grant Berkeley's contention in the *New Theory of Vision* that the visual appearances of things are always two, not three, dimensional, it would seem that we must acknowledge that the visual appearances of things contain only the properties of color and shape, and, in addition, the features of light and shade. And since it seems entirely reasonable to suppose that it is only about the visual appearances of things that a visual perceiver cannot be mistaken, we seem warranted in holding that a visual perceiver, as such, has incorrigible knowledge only of its characteristics—that is, color, shape, light-and-shade, or, in other words, Berkeley's three basic visual properties. (We agreed, at the end of the last paragraph, not to ask whether such things as motion, direction, the relation of being to the right of, and so on, don't also belong on Berkeley's list.) But this is just what (V) asserts.

Considerations of the foregoing kind can make propositions (IV) and (V)—and hence proposition (IIa)—seem unavoidable. It is certain that Berkeley espouses (IV), and it is not unreasonable to think that he accepts (V) as well; so perhaps he partially bases his firm conviction in the truth of (IIa) on those two propositions, or something quite like them. Analogous arguments for the senses other than vision would yield the generalization of (IIa)—namely, proposition (II) itself.

Even if we were not convinced of the truth of (II), this should not necessarily make us think that Berkeley's further efforts on behalf of (I) are abortive; for if he can prove that (III) is true—i.e., that all perceptual properties are ideas (of sense)—then this would be a giant step towards proving (I). We should still want to see, of course, some extra support for (I), but a proof of (III) would by itself give us good reason to think that (I) might well be true.

Let us turn, then, to Berkeley's proof of (III). His defense of (III) is presented most fully in the first of the *Three Dialogues*. There are three arguments:

1 the pleasure/pain argument,
2 the argument from the relativity of perception, and
3 the argument from the causation of perception.

1 *The pleasure/pain argument*

Berkeley employs this argument in the cases of heat and cold (*W* II 175–8; A 139–42; T 112–16), taste (*W* II 179f; A 143f; T 118f), and odor (*W* II 180f; A 144f; T 119), but I want to concentrate just on the first, since here the argument receives its best and most detailed treatment. Let us further restrict ourselves to heat alone, for the two branches of the argument that deal with heat and cold, respectively, are exactly parallel. Here is how Berkeley reasons:

(a) An intense degree of heat is a very great pain.
(b) Any pain is a sensation—i.e., an idea of sense.
(c) Therefore, an intense degree of heat is an idea of sense.

(Berkeley goes on to identify a moderate degree of heat with pleasure and hence with an idea of sense, for he thinks that pleasure, like pain, is a sensation. I shall ignore this part of the argument; it is anyway less plausible than the argument from (a) and (b) to (c), mainly because, as recent work has shown, it seems wrong to rank pleasure among the sensations.)

Let us focus our critical attention on (a). Notice, first, how odd (a) sounds to the ear: it seems ungrammatical, at least. Our impulse is to read it as if it said (a'): 'An intense degree of heat is very painful.' But (a') won't do as a reading of Berkeley's (a), for what it suggests is that if something (a furnace, or a fire, for example) is very hot, and someone touches it or anyway comes too close to it, he will feel pain as a result. This won't do, because it has the intense heat *causing* the pain, which means that the heat is presumably distinct from the pain;

and such a premiss, when combined with (b), would not yield the desired conclusion, (c). On the contrary, it would yield only the barren conclusion that an intense degree of heat *causes* an idea of sense. In order, then, to get (c), which is an identity statement, (a), too, must be an identity statement; it has to say that what we are (directly) aware of when we feel an intense heat is nothing other than a great pain.

Is (a), so understood, true? Well, there do seem to be some situations, anyway, in which (a) is highly implausible. Thus, consider the very example employed by Berkeley, in which I put my hand near a blazing fire. I certainly feel the heat of the fire, and what (a) says, according to Berkeley, as far as I can tell, is that *this* heat—i.e., the heat of the fire—is nothing other than a great pain. But this is surely wrong. There are two objects whose heat I feel: the heat of the fire and the heat of that part of my hand that is nearest the fire. The former heat causes the latter, but there is no credibility at all in the idea that the former—the heat of the fire—might actually *be* a pain; because, for one thing, I feel the heat of the fire for some time before I begin to feel the pain—and since the heat of the fire, which is presumably unchanging, cannot be the pain *before* the pain begins, it is wildly implausible to suggest that it might be the pain *after* the pain begins. Moreover, as Donald Henze points out (p. 177), if Berkeley says that the heat of the fire is identical with your pain, then he must also say that your pain, like the heat, is in the fire! So in this example, at least, (a) has a chance of being true only if the intense degree of heat it refers to is understood to be the heat of my hand (or of the skin of my hand). There are other kinds of cases where it is less obvious that one must distinguish the intense heat of the external object (or whatever) from the heat of the relevant part of the perceiver's body—for example, where one happens to touch a pot of boiling water: but our earlier example (of putting one's hand near a fire) no doubt makes us suspect, at least, that in *all* cases, it is in fact only the heat of a part of a perceiver's body that can possibly be identified with his pain. If this suspicion should be correct, then nothing that Berkeley says in support of premiss (a) would show it to have the unrestricted degree of generality that he needs it to have and that he thinks it does have; he would at most have shown that an extremely limited class of intense heat is a great pain—that is, the intense heat of bodily parts that are exposed to extremely hot external objects (or whatever). Then, in order to achieve the desired, and necessary, extra degree of generality for premiss (a), so that it would apply to *all* kinds of intense heat, Berkeley would need some new arguments; but he in fact supplies none, and I strongly doubt that any sound ones exist.

But it is premature to speculate about additional arguments that Berkeley might or might not be able to give, before examining the ones he does offer. Therefore, resigning ourselves, as I think we must, to the view that the support Berkeley actually offers for premiss (a) can at most show it to be true for the radically restricted type of intense heat indicated above, let us see whether his reasoning establishes even that much. To have a concrete example before us, imagine that you accidentally put your hand too close to a roaring fire. You feel the heat of the fire, you feel the resulting heat of that part of your hand that is nearest the fire, and you feel a pain. As we noted earlier, Berkeley seems to hold that the first heat—the heat of the fire—is none other than the pain, but we are supposing that this suggestion lacks credibility. Let us interpret him as saying, then, that it is the second heat—the heat of your hand—which is none other than the pain you feel. One's first reaction is to think that this cannot be right; for, after all, you feel the heat and you feel the pain—so aren't you feeling *two* things? But Berkeley is ready for this reaction: he claims that what you feel in your hand is 'one simple or uncompounded' sensation (*W* II 176; A 140; T 114), and so the heat that you feel must *be* the pain that you feel. We thus find that Berkeley's whole case here rests on his contention that what you feel is 'simple or uncompounded,' for this proposition constitutes his entire support for premiss (a).

Berkeley takes it for granted that one need only 'look and see'—i.e., introspect—in order to tell whether a sensation is simple or complex, as if simplicity and complexity were two incompatible properties, one or the other of which every sensation intrinsically has. Locke and Hume, along with everyone else at that time, make the same, by no means unreasonable, assumption. But in our hand-too-close-to-the-fire example, introspection yields no clear decision; we really have no idea whether we ought to agree with Hylas and Philonous that what you feel is to be called simple or whether we ought rather to say that it is complex. The whole question has an air of unreality about it. This is a sure sign that the question is being raised in a vacuum—that is, outside of any living context in which it can breathe. It now seems obvious that one and the same thing can be classified as simple *or* as complex, depending on what our particular interests happen to be with respect to that issue and on what scheme of classification we adopt. (cf. Wittgenstein, I, §§ 47–8.) So in order for any sense to attach to the claim that something is simple, or that it is complex, there must be some reason, provided by the background of one's interests, for so classifying it. For example, if I ask you, out of the blue, whether a pane of glass, or a patch of yellow, or a one-inch line, is simple or complex, a proper response is that, so far, there is no answer to the question; only if I tell you what I am up to, what issues are at stake—in short, what *reasons* there might be for classifying the thing one way or the other—will you be able even to consider what the answer to my question might be.

If this Wittgensteinian way of looking at simplicity and complexity is right, as I think it is, then Berkeley and all his contemporaries are wrong in assuming that one can tell just by inspection whether a thing is simple or complex. Still, there may *be* good reasons, in our hand-too-close-to-the-fire example, for classifying what you feel as simple, so that Berkeley's premiss (a) may yet be saved.

What sorts of reasons are there either for saying that your sensation is 'simple or uncompounded' or for saying that it is complex or compounded? Here is one possibility: a philosopher could be interested in formulating a general theory about the nature of pain, and for this purpose it will make a difference whether he says that your sensation is simple or says instead that it is complex. Can Berkeley's contention that the sensation is 'simple or uncompounded' be justified on the grounds that it leads to a satisfactory theory of the nature of pain? Let us see.

If your sensation is simple, then the *pain* that you feel must be the very same thing as the intense *heat* that you feel. It is obviously false, however, that *all* pains are intense heats; so in order to achieve a satisfactory general theory about the nature of pain, Berkeley will have to find some other characterization of the felt heat. The only plausible option open to him, it would seem, is to characterize the heat as 'an excessively high degree of a sensible property' or as 'a sensible property that has reached, or passed, a certain level of intensity,' or something of the sort. His general theory of pain would then be that pain is any sensible property when it reaches a high enough degree of intensity. And this is precisely the theory of pain that Berkeley *does*, in fact, espouse: 'Doth it not therefore follow, that sensible pain is nothing distinct from those sensations or ideas [i.e., of heat, cold, tastes, smells, etc.], in an intense degree?' (*W* II 177; A 140f; T 114). But unfortunately for this theory, there are a tremendous number of pains that it does not cover—e.g., stomach aches, tooth aches, the pain of a knife wound, the pain of a heart attack, and so on. It looks, then, as though Berkeley's calling your sensation simple will not, after all, allow him to devise a satisfactory general theory of what pain is.

I conclude that Berkeley most likely does not have a good reason *of the sort we have been considering* for classifying your sensation as simple, rather than as complex. Unless there are good reasons of some different kind for classifying it as simple—and I do not know what they might be—he has no such reasons, and his claim that the sensation is 'simple or uncompounded' is thus not justified. Since he needs the claim, as we saw, if his pleasure / pain argument, even in its radically restricted form, is to succeed, we must conclude that the argument fails.

2   The argument from the relativity of perception

This argument, which has sometimes also been called the argument from illusion, is employed over and over again by Berkeley in the first of the *Three Dialogues*. He uses it in an attempt to show that each of the following sensible properties is nothing but an idea (of sense): heat and cold (*W* II 178f; A 142f; T 116f), taste (*W* II 180; A 144; T 119), odor (*W* II 181; A 145; T 119), color (*W* II 184–6; A 148–50; T 123–5), size (*W* II 188f; A 152f; T 127f), shape (*W* II 189; A 153; T 129), motion (*W* II 190; A 154; T 129f), and solidity (*W* II 191; A 154f; T 130). I shall concentrate on one version of the argument that deals with color.

The argument goes as follows. The colors of distant objects, such as clouds that look red or purple, or hills that look bluish-purple, are merely apparent, because when one approaches the objects, those colors disappear. But the colors of nearby objects must also be only apparent, for if one inspects them with a microscope, the colors one saw with the naked eye are no longer seen. Berkeley puts his conclusion in the form of a rhetorical question: 'From all which, should it not seem to follow, that all colours are equally apparent, and that none of those which we perceive are really inherent in any outward object?' (*3D* I (*W* II 185; A 149f; T 124)). When we recall that for Berkeley, if a property is not 'really inherent in any outward object,' then it must exist 'in the mind' (cf. p. 32f), it becomes clear that for 'are apparent' in this passage, we may read 'exist in the mind'; so the conclusion of the argument is supposed to be that all colors exist only in the mind, i.e., are ideas of sense.

The argument, so far, is a rickety affair that needs shoring up. Why should it be thought to follow, from the fact that things look different in color under different circumstances, that colors cannot be really inherent in outward objects? Berkeley replies to this worry as follows:

The point will be past all doubt, if you consider, that in case colours were real properties or affections inherent in external bodies, they could admit of no alteration, without some change wrought in the very bodies themselves: but is it not evident from what hath been said, that upon the use of microscopes, upon a change happening in the humours of the eye, or a variation of distance, without any manner of real alteration in the thing itself, the colours of any object are either changed, or totally disappear? (*3D* I (*W* II 185f; A 149; T 124f))

The trouble with the principle that Berkeley here appeals to is that it is an arid tautology, and so cannot possibly provide the support his argument needs. *Of course*, if color is a real property of an object, it cannot change without there being some change in the object; for on that assumption, a change in its color obviously *is* a change in the object. No one could dispute that point. What can be disputed, and certainly would be disputed by Berkeley's adversary in this debate, is the assumption Berkeley makes in the passage just quoted—the assumption, namely, that what a perceiver sees in each of the different mentioned circumstances is properly termed 'the color of the object.' It is only by making this dubious assumption that Berkeley can think his argument receives strong support from the above-mentioned tautology. Thus, for example, *if* what you see when you look at some distant hills can properly be called 'the color of the hills'—let's say the color is purple—and *if* what you see when you look at them close up can also properly be called 'the color of the hills'—let's say the color is green now—then the thesis that color is 'really inherent' in those hills is in serious trouble. It is in trouble because then what is called 'the color of the hills' would have changed without any change having taken place in the hills themselves, which means that the color of the hills cannot be a property that is 'really inherent' in the hills.

But Berkeley's opponent can plausibly dispute the assumption on which this conclusion depends; he can argue that when a person is looking at the distant hills, it is not correct to say of him that he sees the color of the hills and that the color is purple. One should describe the situation, rather, by saying that the hills (merely) *look* purple to him. This description carries no implication that the color of the hills really *is* purple, and hence no implication that the color of the hills must have changed when, on closer approach, they no longer look purple; it thus effectively blocks Berkeley's argument against the thesis that color is 'really inherent' in 'outward objects.' Berkeley, his opponent would urge, simply stacks the cards in his favor when he describes the example of the distant hills in the way he does.

If Berkeley's opponent makes the move just indicated, he will, it is true, then find himself in some at least apparent trouble; but the trouble will be of an epistemological kind, rather than of a straightforwardly metaphysical sort. If, as he claims, the hills (merely) *look* purple when viewed from a great distance, because, under different conditions of observation they no longer look so, then no matter what the conditions of observation may be, it seems that we shall perpetually be confined to the color they *look* to be and shall never be able to tell what color they *are*, because however you specify the conditions of observation, the hills will look to have a different color under some different conditions of observation. In other words, there seems to be no non-arbitrary way of specifying those conditions of observation in which an object may be seen to have the color it really does have. Berkeley expresses this worry in the following passage:

> I would fain know . . . from you, what certain distance and position of the object, what peculiar texture and formation of the eye, what degree or kind of light is necessary for ascertaining that true colour, and distinguishing it from apparent ones.
> (*3D* I (*W* II 186; A 150; T 125))

Berkeley evidently thinks there is no satisfactory answer to this challenge; others have, of course, attempted to provide one—but for our purposes, it is not necessary to enter upon that debate. What is important for us is that if Berkeley's opponent on the big issue is right, then Berkeley's argument from the relativity of perception shows *at most* that we can never know what the true color (taste, smell, etc.) of anything is, and it fails to show that color, and the rest, are not 'really inherent' in 'outward objects,' and hence that they are only ideas of sense. It fails, in other words, to provide any support for principle (III). Although Berkeley does not say so in the *Three Dialogues*, he nevertheless agrees with this estimate of his argument, for he says of it in the *Principles*: 'It must be confessed this method of arguing doth not so much prove that there is no extension or colour in an outward object, as that we do not know by sense which is the true extension or colour of the object' (*PHK* I 15). Since it seems to be acknowledged on all sides that Berkeley's version of the argument from the relativity of perception does not support (III), we need consider it no further.[8] To be sure, his argument can be fixed up, and added to, so as to make it constitute a defense of principle (III), though I think it can never be made into a *cogent* defense of that principle;[9] but since we are concerned here primarily with Berkeley's own actual arguments, we are justified in pursuing the matter no further.

3   The argument from the causation of perception

Berkeley employs this argument in the cases of heat and cold (*W* II 179; A 143; T 117), sound (*W* II 181f; A 145f; T 119f), and color (*W* II 186f; A 150f; T 125f). It goes like this. Let us suppose for the moment that there really are, surrounding us, physical objects that exist independently of any mind, and that have colors, emit sounds, and so on. The question then arises: how can anyone perceive the supposed properties of these supposed distant objects? The answer must be that the properties start, or anyway contribute to, a causal chain of events that includes the stimulation of the perceiver's relevant sense organs and, later, of his brain. The brain stimulation, finally, produces in the perceiver's soul sensations of red, C-sharp, or whatever—i.e., ideas of sense. The properties that a person directly perceives, then—i.e., what we have called perceptual properties— are, in every case, nothing but ideas of sense. And this is precisely what proposition (III) asserts.

Berkeley's argument, while psychologically persuasive, is never- theless not valid. Let us examine it as it applies to vision. The crucial consideration in the argument is that the ultimate brain stimulation in the visual perceiver occurs at some distance from the object that he sees and that figures in an early stage of the causal chain leading to that brain stimulation. It is this consideration alone that is supposed to force us to admit that the perceiver must be directly aware of an idea of sense, and to deny that he can be directly aware of the light-emitting, or light-reflecting object itself. But clearly there is a link missing in the argument; for we need to know what the connection is between (a) the fact that event x (the brain stimulation in the observer) occurs at some distance from event y (the object's emitting or reflecting light rays toward the observer), and (b) the (alleged) facts that event x cannot immediately give rise to a direct awareness of the object, and that event x must immediately give rise to a direct awareness of nothing but an idea of sense. Why should (a) be thought to imply (b)?

I think that anyone who, like Berkeley, believes that (a) implies (b) must reason along something like the following lines. He starts with the natural assumption that if one event immediately causes another, the latter must occur at a place contiguous to the former. Applying this principle to the event x (the observer's brain stimulation), he imagines that since x immediately causes the occurrence of some object of awareness O, O must occupy a spatial position contiguous to x. But only an idea of sense is close enough to x to be able to fulfill the requirement placed on O: the object that figures in event y (the emitting or reflecting of light rays toward the observer) is too far away.

But this picture is obviously full of confusion. Imagining that x immediately causes *the occurrence of some object of awareness O*, makes it look as though x directly causes some *thing*, some *object*, which then must be (at least) quite close to x. Well, even if one were to grant the legitimacy of this way of putting things, it would still be false, or senseless rather, to say that an idea of sense satisfies the requirements placed on O—because an idea of sense occupies no place in (real physical) space and hence is not at, or quite close to, or yet any distance from, the spatial position occupied by x. But, in fact, we cannot allow this way of putting things: for x is not the direct cause of *the occurrence of some object of awareness O*, but is rather the direct cause of *the observer's state (or act) of awareness of something, O*. And as soon as we put the matter in this correct way, we see that there is no evident reason to think that O *cannot* be (identical with) the physical object from which light rays are being emitted or reflected. It is no whit easier to understand how x might cause the (direct) awareness of an idea of sense than it is to understand how it might cause the (direct) awareness of a physical object. So a direct realist need have no qualms about admitting all the physiological, and other physical, facts involved in the causation of sense perception. He can perfectly well insist that what happens as a result of the light rays, neural impulses, and brain stimulation is that the (physical) things before the perceiver's eyes are (directly) revealed to him, just as they are in themselves. There is no reason to think that just because the brain stimulation occurs at some distance from the objects perceived, it must therefore give rise to the (direct) awareness of a mere idea of sense. It is perfectly possible to look upon the light rays, neural impulses, and brain stimulation as being the physical preconditions of the perceiver's ability to apprehend, directly, certain objects in his environment.[10]

Berkeley's attempts to establish (III)—the proposition that all perceptual properties are ideas (of sense)—which is supposed, in turn, to support (I)—the proposition that in sense perception, what the perceiver directly (or immediately) perceives in every case is just one or more ideas of sense—are failures. We must, therefore, judge that his efforts to prove (I) are not successful. This need not, however, be regarded as a catastrophe for Berkeley's philosophy, causing any intelligent person to lose interest in it at once. Far from it. Proposition (I) expresses a basic tenet that Locke accepts, along with most other philosophers of that day and many of this. It certainly lies at the very heart of Locke's philosophy; it is central, in fact, to much of the Western philosophy that derives from Descartes. What Locke tries to do is to incorporate (I) into a view of the world that satisfies most of our fundamental intuitions about it—i.e., into a philosophy that gives a place to our ordinary, commonsensical beliefs about the world. Berkeley's twofold achievement, as I see it, and the source of the lasting interest that rightly attaches to his philosophy, is, first, that he shows, with devastating clarity, that Locke's way of making (I) respectable, as it were, is fraught with hidden dangers, and, second, that he goes on to defend, with extraordinary vigor and ingenuity, another world-view—a positively intoxicating one—that, according to Berkeley, is far superior to Locke's. In Chapter VII, we shall discuss the attack on Locke, which focuses on his notion of matter. In Chapters VIII–X, we shall examine Berkeley's quite different world view.

VII

The Attack against
Lockean Matter

Berkeley raises, and insists on an answer to, the following question: if, as Locke and Berkeley both believe, proposition (I) is true—so that one is directly aware, in sense perception, of nothing but ideas of sense—then what reasons have we to believe that there are any Lockean material objects? By a 'Lockean material object,' I mean an extended non-mental entity that exists whether or not any mind is aware of it—that is, an entity whose existence is totally independent of mind or, as Berkeley misleadingly puts it, an entity that exists 'without the mind.'

Berkeley's answer to his question is: we have no reason whatever to believe in the existence of such objects. His complaint is not that their existence is an intelligible hypothesis for which there happens to be painfully little, or no, evidence; he charges, rather, that it is an unintelligible hypothesis (if something that is unintelligible can be called an hypothesis). It is unintelligible because we have, and can have, no conception whatever of a Lockean material object. Let us see how Berkeley seeks to justify this very serious charge against Locke's metaphysical scheme.

The most natural way of expressing a conception of a certain kind of entity is, of course, to specify its intrinsic properties, preferably its essential properties. But what properties are we to say that Lockean material objects have? They must either be properties that we can directly perceive (i.e., perceptual properties) or some other, non-perceptual, properties. Berkeley claims that there are insuperable difficulties either way.

He quickly disposes of the suggestion that Lockean material objects might have perceptual properties. Perceptual properties—e.g., the color and shape that we are familiar with—are directly perceived, and Berkeley has already shown, he thinks, that they are all ideas of sense (cf. (III), p. 96). Whatever a Lockean material object may be, it is certainly not a mind, not a thinking thing: therefore, it would be a contradiction to say that it has perceptual properties, because this would be to say that a non-thinking thing has ideas—i.e., that a non-thinking thing thinks (*PHK* I 7, 9; *3D* III (*W* II 233, 237; A 195, 199; T 178; 182f)).

This argument is full of confusions; but let us not pause to examine it further, because Locke himself accepts its conclusion—namely, that the properties of Lockean material objects are not directly perceivable. Let us turn, rather, to the suggestion that Lockean material objects have properties other than perceptual ones. Berkeley considers the two leading claims here—namely, that Lockean material objects have the characteristic of existing unperceived and unthought of by any mind, and that they have properties that resemble certain perceptual properties—i.e., that they resemble certain features of our ideas of sense. Let us take up Berkeley's attack on each of these two claims, in order.

Berkeley argues that we can have no conception of an object that exists 'without the mind'—i.e., that exists whether or not it is being perceived or thought of by a mind. He boldly claims that we can conceive of no such thing. He admits that we can think of something—a desert island, for example—that is not being perceived by anyone, but he adds that when we realize what is involved in doing so, we will see that his bold claim is after all substantiated:

> But say you, surely there is nothing easier than to imagine trees, for instance, in a park, or books existing in a closet, and no body by to perceive them. I answer, you may so, there is no difficulty in it: but what is all this, I beseech you, more than framing in your mind certain ideas which you call *books* and *trees*, and at the same time omitting to frame the idea of any one that may perceive them? But do not you your self perceive or think of them all the while? This therefore is nothing to the purpose: it only shows you have the power of imagining or forming ideas in your mind; but it doth not shew that you can conceive it possible, the objects of your thought may exist without the mind: to make out this, it is necessary that you conceive them existing unconceived or unthought of, which is a manifest repugnancy. When we do our utmost to conceive the existence of external bodies, we are all the while only contemplating our own ideas. But the mind taking no notice of itself, is deluded to think it can and doth conceive bodies existing unthought of or without the mind; though at the same time they are apprehended by or exist in it self. A little attention will discover to any one the truth and evidence of what is here said,

and make it unnecessary to insist on any other proofs against the existence of material substance. (*PHK* I 23)

Berkeley's argument, as I understand it, is this: Of course you can conceive of an object, *x*, that is not being perceived by anyone.[1] In order to do that, however, you must yourself think of, or conceive of, *x*. But then *x* is just an idea in your mind, and so you have failed, as you must always do, to conceive of an object that exists 'without the mind.'

That this is, indeed, Berkeley's argument is perhaps more clearly seen from another statement of it that he offers in the *Three Dialogues*:

> Philonous. I am content to put the whole upon this issue. If you can conceive it possible for any mixture or combination of qualities, or any sensible object whatever, to exist without the mind, then I will grant it actually to be so.
>
> Hylas. If it comes to that, the point will soon be decided. What more easy than to conceive a tree or house existing by itself, independent of, and unperceived by any mind whatsoever? I do at this present time conceive them existing after that manner.
>
> Philonous. How say you, Hylas, can you see a thing which is at the same time unseen?
>
> Hylas. No, that were a contradiction.
>
> Philonous. Is it not as great a contradiction to talk of *conceiving* a thing which is *unconceived*?
>
> Hylas. It is.
>
> Philonous. The tree or house therefore which you think of, is conceived by you.
>
> Hylas. How should it be otherwise?
>
> Philonous. And what is conceived, is surely in the mind.
>
> Hylas. Without question, that which is conceived is in the mind.
>
> Philonous. How then came you to say, you conceived a house or tree existing independent and out of all minds whatsoever?
>
> (*3D* I (*W* II 200; A 163f; T 140f))

If this argument were acceptable, it would show that we cannot possibly conceive of a Lockean material object; the range of the conceivable would be limited to the contents of minds—i.e., to ideas.

But the argument is not acceptable. It is far too strong. As several commentators have remarked, Berkeley's argument, if valid, would also prove that one cannot conceive of anything that does not exist in one's *own* mind—i.e., that is not an idea of one's own.[2] Indeed, it would prove the even stronger proposition that one cannot conceive of anything that does not exist in one's own mind *now*. These consequences would be as unacceptable to Berkeley as they are to the rest of us. So something is wrong with the argument.

The fault lies in the fact that Berkeley overlooks a crucial distinction. (I shall concentrate on the *Three Dialogues* version of the argument.) The false step is taken when Philonous asserts, and Hylas agrees, that 'what is conceived . . . . [exists] in the mind.' There is an ambiguity in the expression 'what is conceived' that Berkeley misses. 'What is conceived' can refer to what is conceived *of*, or it can refer to what one conceives *with*, if I may put it so. The distinction, couched in terms of ideas, is between what an idea is an idea *of*, and the idea itself; couched in terms of representation, it is the distinction between what is represent*ed* and what represents. An idea, say an idea of x, that a person, P, has is indeed something that exists in his mind; that is, it would not exist if P were not having it. But what the idea is an idea of—that is, x—will not as a rule, and certainly not necessarily, be something that exists in his mind. Suppose, for example, he has an idea of Nassau Hall; the existence of Nassau Hall does not depend on P's thinking of it, and so does not in that sense exist in his mind. Nassau Hall exists whether P thinks of it or not. Suppose he has an idea of a winged horse; again, its existence does not depend on P's thinking of it, and so again does not in that sense exist in his mind. A winged horse has no existence, whether P thinks of it or not.[3]

Berkeley, in thus confusing an idea and what an idea is of,[4] makes the same sort of mistake in his argument that a man (call him Jones) would make if he claimed that there necessarily could not be a public performance of a play about a man (call him Robinson Crusoe) who is alone on a desert island, on the ground that hundreds of people in the audience would be with him. Jones might even say: It is a manifest repugnancy to speak of a man being alone when he is surrounded by hundreds of people. Jones's claim, of course, is obviously absurd, for it confuses the actor who portrays Robinson Crusoe with the character, Robinson Crusoe. The actor cannot, of necessity, be alone when there are hundreds of people in the audience, but the character he portrays, Robinson Crusoe, can be alone on his desert island. The hundreds of people in the audience are irrelevant to Robinson Crusoe's lonely condition, because Robinson Crusoe is not in the theater at all. Robinson Crusoe is not, for example, six feet from a big piece of canvas painted to look like palm trees, though the actor who portrays him is; nor is Robinson Crusoe looking into the face of Suzy Smith, who is sitting in the third row of the theater, even though the eyes of the actor portraying him are focused squarely on her face.[5]

The nature of Jones's mistake may be put like this: given a statement that contains a claim about a character in a play, Jones tries to rebut the statement by citing a reason that has application to the actor who portrays the character, but has no application to the character himself. The statement Jones seeks to rebut is this: a play about a man alone on a desert island (e.g., Robinson Crusoe) can be performed before an audience of many people. Jones tries to disprove this statement by pointing out that the man in the play, if it were performed in public, would be standing and walking about before many other people, and therefore he could not possibly be described as being *alone*, contrary to what the statement says. Jones's alleged refutation is spurious, of course, because he cites a fact about the actor who portrays Robinson Crusoe; this fact (namely, that the actor would not be alone) has no force against the original statement, and is indeed irrelevant to it—for that statement makes a claim only about the character in the play (namely, that he is alone), and does not say, or imply, that the actor who portrays the character would be alone. On the contrary.

Similarly, Berkeley attacks a statement that contains a claim about what an idea is of, by citing a fact not about what the idea is of, but about the idea itself. So this fact has no bearing at all on the statement it is supposed to destroy. The statement is this: I can have an idea (can conceive) of a tree or a house that is thought of by no one. The relevant claim contained in this statement is that what the idea is of, i.e., the tree or the house, is thought of by no one. Berkeley replies that the statement cannot be true because my conception exists in my own mind and hence is thought of by myself. But 'my conception' here can only refer to my *idea*, not to what my idea is *of*, since it is only my idea that exists in my mind.

Let me make the point in a different way. Suppose that Hylas were actually resting against a certain tree and at the same time having an image of that very tree with no one near it. Would the fact that he is actually next to the tree refute his claim that he has an idea of the tree with no one near it? Obviously not. Suppose, now, that Hylas were actually looking at the tree: would this make it logically impossible for him to imagine the tree and to imagine that no one is looking at it? Again, obviously not. It is also true, if not equally obvious, finally, that there is no logical incoherence in the suggestion that Hylas might imagine the tree and imagine that no one is thinking of it, contrary to what Berkeley contends. One might be tempted to suppose that this last case of thinking about the tree is essentially different from the earlier cases of being near the tree and seeing the tree: isn't Hylas' claim that he is imagining that no one is thinking about the tree as incoherent as the claim someone makes when he says

'I am not speaking'? Not at all. The remark 'I am not speaking' is indeed self-refuting;[6] it asserts something about the speaker, and his very act of making the remark renders it false. But Hylas' situation is quite different. When he says he is imagining the tree and imagining that no one is thinking about it, he makes no claim about who is doing what to the tree in the real world. He is, rather, imagining a non-factual, but possible, world in which no one is thinking about the tree. The fact that someone else inhabiting Hylas' actual world—Philonous, say—might happen to be thinking about the tree could not possibly be regarded as showing that Hylas cannot be imagining what he says he is imagining. Why, then, should the fact that Hylas himself is thinking about the tree be thought to show it? The answer is that it shouldn't.

We must conclude that Berkeley's attempt to show that we cannot conceive of an object existing 'without the mind' is a failure. It is time, now, to take up the Lockean doctrine that his material objects have properties that, although not directly perceived, nevertheless resemble certain perceptual properties. Assuming the truth of (I), the doctrine is, then, that Lockean material objects resemble our ideas of sense in certain respects.

Berkeley bluntly contends, against Locke, that our ideas of sense cannot possibly resemble Lockean material objects in any respect, because 'an idea can be like nothing but an idea' (*PHK* I 8; see also *PC* 378, *PC* 861, and *3D* I (*W* II 206; A 169; T 147)). If Berkeley can make good this contention, he will have gone a long way, at least, toward proving his belief that we can have no conception of a Lockean material object. Let us try to see, then, what reasons there might be for accepting Berkeley's dictum that 'an idea can be like nothing but an idea.'

One plausible way to defend the dictum would be to argue as follows: Whether or not the dictum is true *generally*, one must grant at least that an idea of sense cannot resemble a Lockean material object with respect to the *primary* qualities. For suppose it could. This would mean that ideas could be square, or three feet long. But it makes no sense to speak of square ideas, or of ideas that are three feet long.

There is considerable force in this restricted defense of the dictum; but Berkeley does not argue for it in this way, and in fact he could not so argue. For him, both primary and secondary qualities 'exist in the mind,' and they exist there, as he puts it, 'only by way of *idea*' (*PHK* I 49); this must mean that ideas of sense—either individual ones or classes of them—are in some way characterizable in terms of primary and secondary qualities. So the suggested defense of his dictum goes directly against Berkeley's own principles and is thus not available to him. (He would dismiss as unimportant the odd sound of such expressions as 'square ideas' just as he dismisses, later, the complaint of his opponents that 'it sounds very harsh to say we eat and drink ideas, and are clothed with ideas' (*PHK* I 38).)

We must find some other support for Berkeley's dictum that 'an idea can be like nothing but an idea.' Our willingness, or unwillingness, to accept it is, of course, going to depend in large part on what we take it to mean—and there is some doubt as to how it is to be properly understood. We surely cannot construe the dictum to be saying that nothing can be *exactly* like an idea, *even in its essential nature*, except another idea, because that is trivially true. But if we interpret 'like' in a more liberal way, then it appears, on the face of it, as though Berkeley's dictum is just false; for why can't a mental image of a piano, say, be 'like'—i.e., resemble—a piano, in the perfectly straightforward way in which a painted picture of a piano is like a piano? Looked at in this way, Berkeley's dictum that an idea can be like nothing but an idea seems to be as false as the claim that a picture can be like nothing but a picture.

Berkeley would object strenuously to this rude treatment of his dictum. He would respond along the following lines: Look here, I am supposing that my principle (II) (p. 96) has been established. According to it, in sense perception we directly perceive nothing but a certain restricted range of basic perceptual properties—and all of these properties, by my principle (III) (p. 96), are ideas (of sense). My dictum (namely, that an idea can be like nothing but an idea) should be understood in terms of these basic perceptual properties. What it says is that these properties can resemble only themselves. A color or a figure, for example, can be like only a color of a figure (cf. *PHK* I 8; *PC* 861). And if we follow out the implications of this, we will see that the properties of a Lockean material object, in particular, cannot resemble any of these basic perceptual properties—i.e., Lockean material objects cannot resemble any of our ideas of sense.

Berkeley is surely right that a color, as such, or a shape, as such, can exactly resemble only a color or a shape. (I use '*exactly* resemble' to rule out the kind of resemblance that holds, as the blind man is reputed to have claimed, between scarlet and the sound of a trumpet. That loose kind of resemblance is not what either Locke or Berkeley has in mind.) Thus, the redness (squareness) we are directly aware of—i.e., the redness (squareness) that characterizes an idea of sense—surely cannot exactly resemble something that isn't a color (a shape) at all. But—and this is the really important question here—how does that speak against the Lockean hypothesis? It speaks against it if, and only if, Lockean material objects do not have colors, and do not have shapes. Locke himself concedes that his material objects do not have colors, but he insists that they do have shapes—and it is only with respect to shape and the other so-called primary qualities that he claims a resemblance between characteristics of our ideas of sense, on the one hand, and characteristics of material objects, on the other. But then Berkeley's dictum, as we are now construing it, has no force whatever against the Lockean hypothesis; Locke could simply agree with it—e.g., could agree that a figure can be like nothing but another figure—and then add: But of course Lockean material objects do have figures (i.e., shapes), and so, as I have always maintained, our ideas of sense do resemble material objects with respect to figure and the other primary qualities.

Berkeley might respond to this objection as follows: Colors and shapes, and the rest, are characteristics that we are directly aware of (that we directly perceive), and so if Lockean material objects had these qualities, it would have to be possible for us to be directly aware of them—and Locke himself, as well as all other Lockeans, concede that we cannot be directly aware of the characteristics of Lockean material objects. Therefore, Lockeans cannot claim that their material objects have any of the sensible characteristics (e.g., color and shape) that pertain to our ideas of sense.

But the answer to this countercharge is that Berkeley has by no means shown that what we directly perceive (i.e., ideas of sense) are the *only* kinds of things that can have colors and shapes. We do, let us grant, directly perceive the colors, shapes, and so on, that characterize ideas of sense; but it does not follow from this, nor from anything else that Berkeley has so far established, that there cannot be colors and shapes that (a) characterize other kinds of entities—e.g., Lockean material objects—and that (b) we do not, and cannot, directly perceive. And there is no reason, either, why such colors and shapes should not be exactly like the colors and shapes that characterize our ideas of sense.[7]

Berkeley has yet another way of formulating his dictum; let's see if this new way can show the dictum to have some force against the Lockean hypothesis:

How can that which is sensible be like that which is insensible?
Can a real thing in itself *invisible* be like a *colour*; or a real thing which is not *audible*, be like a *sound*? In a word, can any thing be like a sensation or idea, but another sensation or idea?
(*3D* I(*W* II 206; A 169; T 147); see also *PHK* I 8, and *PC* 862)

The whole force of Berkeley's rhetorical questions derives from the fact that it sounds odd to speak of invisible colors and inaudible sounds; our immediate reaction is to think that if the Lockean hypothesis commits one to such nonsense, then we shall have nothing further to do with it. But let us examine the matter a bit more carefully. *Why* does it sound funny to speak of, for example, invisible colors or invisible shapes? The answer, I think, is that without fully or consciously realizing what we are doing, we try to imagine some object of direct awareness that is colored (or shaped), and yet invisible. And we find, of course, that the very attempt is ridiculous; we cannot possibly perceive a color (or a shape) that is at the same time invisible. But the futility of such an experiment provides no warrant for rejecting the Lockean hypothesis; for when viewed within the framework of the Lockean hypothesis, rather than within the framework we unconsciously adopted when conducting our futile thought experiment, expressions such as 'invisible color,' 'invisible shape,' and 'inaudible sound' are seen to be not nonsensical but perfectly intelligible—or anyway *apparently* intelligible. On the Lockean hypothesis, material objects and their properties are invisible, inaudible, etc.—at least, we cannot *directly* perceive them. But no reason has so far been given for thinking that it makes no sense to suppose that these objects nevertheless might have, for example, colors and shapes; and if they did have them, those colors and shapes would be *invisible* colors and shapes. There seems to be no logical or conceptual oddity involved in this suggestion, and so Berkeley's dictum once again fails.

But we have not yet penetrated to the heart of Berkeley's dictum. In order to do that, we must consider the following interesting passage from the *Philosophical Commentaries*: 'A man cannot compare 2 things together without perceiving them each, ergo he cannot say any thing which is not an idea is like or unlike an idea' (*PC* 51; see also *PC* 378 (16)–(19)). The phrase 'he cannot say' in this passage could mean simply 'he cannot know whether'; on this reading, which is perhaps the most natural one, it would make sense to say that Lockean material objects are like, or unlike, ideas, but, alas, no one can ever know whether they are or not. This point is weaker than Berkeley's dictum itself, for the dictum says flatly that a Lockean material object cannot be like an idea, while the present point is just that no one can ever tell whether such an object is, or is not, like an idea. The point is also more plausible than the dictum and, though weaker than it, would still be, if true, terribly damaging to the Lockean hypothesis—for that hypothesis would then be revealed as being little more than an idle shot in the dark, forever beyond the reach of human knowledge.

But *is* the point asserted in *PC* 51, construed in this way, true? I do not think its truth should be conceded without more of an argument in its defense than Berkeley offers. What he offers is only the bold claim that in order to know whether two things, x and y, are alike or unlike in some way, one must perceive both x and y. But why should we accept this unadorned claim?[8] To be sure, in the case of two observable objects, perhaps the best way to tell whether, and how, they are alike or unlike is to perceive them both—but it isn't the only way, even for observable objects. Someone can tell you about one of two objects (or both), or you could read a description of one (or both), and this might enable you to tell that the two objects are alike in certain respects. But this, though true, is a trivial consideration that Berkeley could easily have handled. More important is the case where one of the objects, w, is one that can in principle be perceived, while the other, u, is not. If Berkeley's defense of the point maintained in PC 51 were true, no one would ever be able to tell whether w and u were alike or unlike in any respect. But it does not seem to be true. It seems to be quite possible that a philosopher might invent an argument that successfully shows that · all unobservable material objects have certain characteristics that render them similar to observable objects, or anyway that a philosopher might devise an argument showing that we have good reasons for thinking that unobservable material objects have such characteristics. An argument of either kind would render PC 51 false. Moreover, plausible arguments of the second kind are actually at hand. One such argument can, I think, be constructed from Jonathan Bennett's well-known discussion of the distinction between primary and secondary qualities.[9] Another is offered by E. M. Curley.[10] Curley takes Locke to be maintaining that in a scientific explanation of our perception of both primary and secondary qualities, it will be necessary to posit that the material objects have primary qualities, but not necessary to posit that they have any secondary qualities. He sums up his case by saying: 'Locke's characterization of the primary qualities as "original" qualities of objects rightly suggests what we would now put by saying that they are qualities designated by the primitive terms in the scientific theory of perception' (p. 454). If the reasoning that Curley attributes to Locke is sound, then despite the fact that we cannot compare material objects and ideas of sense by perceiving both, we nevertheless have good reason for thinking that unobservable material objects resemble our ideas of sense in certain respects, and the point Berkeley makes in PC 51 is thus false. I shall not attempt to evaluate Curley's argument; I want simply to point out that although Berkeley makes an interesting claim in PC 51, it needs more of a defense than Berkeley provides, since there are plausible arguments against it.

I have been supposing when, in PC 51, Berkeley says that a person 'cannot say any thing which is not an idea is like or unlike an idea,' that for 'cannot say' we may substitute 'cannot know whether.' What

PC 51 says, on this reading, is that although it makes sense to say that a non-idea is like, or unlike, an idea, no one can ever know whether any such statement is true or false. I have tried to show that even on this weaker reading of *PC* 51, Berkeley's claim is problematical. Actually, however, he means to be making an even stronger claim; for 'he cannot say,' we should read not 'he cannot know whether,' but rather 'it makes no sense to say.' Thus, in *PC* 51, Berkeley really means to maintain that since we cannot perceive any non-ideas and hence cannot compare any non-ideas with ideas, it makes no sense to say that a non-idea is either like, or unlike, an idea.[11] This reading of the passage conforms more closely to the spirit of Berkeley's remarks in his published works—e.g., when he says:

> If we look but ever so little into our thoughts, we shall find it impossible for us to conceive a likeness except only between our ideas. (*PHK* I 8)

> Upon inquiry, I find it impossible for me to conceive or understand how any thing but an idea can be like an idea.
> (*3D* I (*W* II 206; A 170; T 148))

I tried to show earlier that even if we read *PC* 51 as expressing a weaker claim than this, Berkeley provides no good grounds for accepting *PC* 51; therefore, *a fortiori*, he provides no good grounds for accepting *PC* 51 when we read it as expressing this *stronger* claim that Berkeley evidently intends.

Berkeley thinks he has shown, now, that we can have no conception of a Lockean material object, *if having such a conception requires that we be able to specify what its intrinsic properties are.* But on Berkeley's view, this does not yet rule out the possibility that we might have another sort of legitimate conception (or notion) of a Lockean material object—what he calls a *relative* notion. We have a relative notion of an entity, x, just in case there are good grounds for supposing that x exists as the thing that bears a certain relation R to something else, y, where y is directly perceived by us. In short: we have a relative notion of x just in case we have reason to believe that $(\exists x)\,(xRy)$, where y is directly perceived. And x may be such that it is not directly perceivable:

> That from a cause, effect, operation, sign, or other circumstance, there may reasonably be inferred the existence of a thing not immediately perceived, and that it were absurd for any man to argue against the existence of that thing, from his having no direct and positive notion of it, I freely own. But where there is nothing of all this; where neither reason nor revelation induce us to believe the existence of a thing; *where we have not even a relative notion*

of it; where an abstraction is made from perceiving and being perceived, from spirit and idea: lastly, where there is not so much as the most inadequate or faint idea pretended to: I will not indeed thence conclude against the reality of any notion or existence of any thing: but my inference shall be, that you mean nothing at all: that you employ words to no manner of purpose, without any design or signification whatsoever. (*3D* II (*W* II 223; A 186; T 166); my emphasis)

So Berkeley does not reject Lockean material objects *solely* because we have, as he thinks he has shown, no 'direct and positive notion' of them; no, he would concede that they probably, or perhaps even necessarily, exist if we had a *relative* notion of them. But we don't. Let us see why.

If we had a relative notion of a Lockean material object, Berkeley seems to think, it would be the notion of that which has, or supports, perceptual properties. But this is nonsense. Perceptual properties, as he has already demonstrated, are ideas (of sense), and only a mind can have, or 'support,' ideas of sense.

Moreover, even if perceptual properties were *not* ideas, the situation would still be quite as desperate. In that case, the notion of a (complete) Lockean material object would not be a relative notion: it would be the notion of a complex entity consisting of two kinds of components—namely, perceptual properties and a material substratum that supports them. But then the required notion of a material substratum would be a relative notion: it would be the notion of that which supports certain properties. Such a notion, however, would be totally incomprehensible. We do not understand what we are talking about when we speak of material substratum *supporting*, or *standing under*, properties. The terms 'supporting' and 'standing under' obviously cannot have their usual sense—'as when we say that pillars support a building' (*PHK* I 16); but what *un*usual, non-literal sense those words may have is entirely unknown. So the notion of material substratum is unacceptable, because unintelligible (*PHK* I 16, 17; *3D* I (*W* II 197–9; A 161–2; T 137–9)).

Berkeley's criticism shows, I think, that the notion of material substratum, embraced by Locke,[12] must be rejected. Strangely enough, Locke himself clearly sees its conceptual inadequacy (see Locke, Bk I, ch. 3, § 19; Bk II, ch. 13, § 17–19; Bk II, ch. 23, § 1, 2). Yet, he is unable to give it up. 'I conclude there is substance,' he says, 'because we cannot conceive how qualities should subsist by themselves' (*Third Letter* to Stillingfleet).

Berkeley concludes that there can be no conception—neither a 'direct and positive' nor a relative conception—of a Lockean material object. As if not content with this fundamental attack, he has two further shots to fire at Locke. In both cases, Berkeley concedes, what he takes to be demonstrably false, that we *do* have a conception of a Lockean material object; and he argues that even if we do, the Lockean system is woefully deficient.

The first of these attacks occurs in the *Three Dialogues*. It is part of the Lockean hypothesis that in vision (or hearing), physical objects cause our visual (or auditory) ideas of sense by means of light rays (or sound waves). Philonous gets Hylas, who espouses the Lockean hypothesis, to assert that although 'light and colours, as immediately perceived by us . . . cannot exist without the mind,' nevertheless 'in themselves they are only the motions and configurations of certain insensible particles of matter' (3D I (*W* II 187; A 151; T 126)). Similarly, he claims that the sound we immediately perceive 'is a particular kind of sensation,' but the sound 'which exists without us' is 'merely a vibrative or undulatory motion in the air' (3D I (*W* II 182; A 145; T 120)). On the Lockean hypothesis, in other words, light and color, in themselves, are light rays, and sounds, in themselves, are sound waves.

Berkeley, as Philonous, now swoops in for the kill. If light and color, in themselves—i.e., real light and real color—are light rays, then it follows that no one ever has, or ever can, see real light and color. And this is absurd; it is absurd to say that light and color are invisible. Again, if sounds in themselves—i.e., real sounds—are sound waves, then 'real sounds may possibly be *seen* or *felt*, but [can] never [be] *heard*' (3D I (*W* II 182; A 146; T 121)). And this, too, is obvious nonsense. In this way, Berkeley thinks he has shown that one part of the Lockean hypothesis is nonsensical.

However, a clever Lockean, unlike Hylas, would have little difficulty answering this objection. He would never fall into the trap that Philonous sets for Hylas; that is, he would not concede that real light and colors are (invisible) light rays, nor that real sound is (inaudible) sound waves. He acknowledges the 'subjectivity' of secondary qualities, and ranks light and colors, as well as sounds, among them; so he holds that they exist only as (directly) perceived by us—that is to say, only as ideas of sense. Light rays and sound waves therefore, on his view, are simply parts of the postulated *cause* of light, color, and sound; they are not themselves light, color, and sound. The absurdity that Berkeley thinks he finds in this part of the Lockean hypothesis, then, is just not there.

The second of Berkeley's two parting shots against Locke is aimed at his contention that Lockean material objects cause our ideas of sense. Berkeley's objection is that such objects cannot possibly explain how our ideas of sense come about, since it is agreed on all sides that no one understands how any material object can produce an effect in a mind or spirit (*PHK* I 19).

It might seem, at first glance, as though Berkeley is asking too much of a good hypothesis; for after all there are lots of good hypotheses that are incomplete. One can, for example, imagine that the best hypothesis we have to explain how migrating birds find their way between their nesting and wintering areas each year, is that they navigate by the stars or the sun, or, alternatively, by the earth's magnetic field. These could be perfectly good hypotheses even though we do not know how the stars, or the earth's magnetic field, actually guide the birds in their extraordinary migrations. But there is, Berkeley could say, a crucial difference between such scientific hypotheses and the Lockean one. When we admit that we don't know how the stars, say, guide the birds' flight, we mean that we 'don't know how *in fact* it is done; we can conceive of all sorts of possible mechanisms that might do the job, but we simply don't know which of these, or whether perhaps some other, is the actual one. In this case, then, the difficulty is just that certain facts—important ones, to be sure—are missing. But the difficulty with the Lockean hypothesis is of a more serious kind, at least if one assumes, with Locke and Berkeley, that the mind is an unextended, immaterial substance.[13] Here, it isn't just that some facts are missing; rather, it looks as though it is inconceivable that there should be the kind of causal connections required by the hypothesis—i.e., causal connections between Lockean material objects and unextended spiritual substances—for how can something extended in any way influence something unextended, or vice versa?

How cogent is this complaint of Berkeley's against the Lockean hypothesis? Well, given the then-prevailing mechanistic conception of matter, according to which any bit of matter can influence something else solely in virtue of its motion, hence by pushing against the other thing or pulling on it, Berkeley's complaint can look powerful indeed, for it seems unintelligible to suggest that an unextended immaterial thing might be pushed or pulled. To be pushed or pulled, one naturally supposes, a thing must at least have extension.[14] To someone with a less mechanistic conception of matter than was available to Berkeley or Locke, Berkeley's complaint would not look so devastating to the Lockean hypothesis; for if pushing and pulling are not essential to causal efficacy, then there is no *a priori* obstacle in the way of supposing that an extended thing might causally interact with an unextended thing.

Hume, too, sees no virtue in Berkeley's objection to the Lockean hypothesis. He sees no virtue in it even on a mechanistic view of matter. According to Hume's constant conjunction view of causality: 'any thing may produce any thing, and . . . we shall never discover a reason, why any object may or may not be the cause of any other, however great, or however little the resemblance may be betwixt them' (Hume, Bk I, Pt IV, § 5, p. 247 of the Selby-Bigge edition). So for Hume, no *a priori* considerations prevent us from supposing that an extended thing can produce effects (e.g., ideas) in an unextended thing. The mistaken notion that this is an unintelligible supposition arises as follows. First, one thinks he understands perfectly the causal efficacy involved in one material object's pushing or pulling another, and he therefore treats pulling and pushing as the prototype for all intelligible causal efficacy on the part of material objects. Then, when he realizes that it is nonsense to speak of an unextended substance being pulled or pushed, he concludes at once that it is nonsense to speak of an extended thing exerting a causal influence on an unextended one, since his favored prototype fails for such cases. But according to Hume, we do not in the least understand the connection between two physical objects when one of them pulls or pushes the other, and we would therefore be wrong to treat that kind of causality as the model for any possible causal efficacy on the part of physical objects, on the ground that it alone is intelligible. We are, in fact, perfectly free to admit the possibility that physical objects can produce causal effects (e.g., ideas) in spiritual substances; that kind of causal connection is as intelligible as—i.e., no less unintelligible than—any other. (Berkeley would think there is no merit in Hume's position, for he, unlike, Hume, thinks that *activity* is an essential element in causality, and that only minds are genuinely active. We shall discuss Berkeley's views on causality later.)

In this chapter, we have examined the various aspects of Berkeley's attack on Lockean material objects. Convinced, with Locke, that one is directly aware, in sense perception, of nothing but ideas of sense (cf. proposition (I), p. 95), Berkeley seeks to show that not only do we have no reason to think that such material objects exist, but the very suggestion that they might is unintelligible. I have argued that Berkeley's anti-Lockean arguments are not so damaging as he thinks they are. Nevertheless, it is one of Berkeley's great contributions to philosophy that he sees with such clarity that once proposition (I) is accepted, the very notion of a material object, as envisaged by Locke, immediately becomes problematical. Given that he is trapped, as it were, with Locke, in proposition (I), Berkeley challenges Locke on precisely the right points. A Lockean may, as I have suggested, be able to answer these challenges, but answer them he must—and to do it adequately, even if it can indeed be done, is certain to be a long and difficult project.

VIII

Berkeley's World View I: Ideas of Sense

In Chapter VI we found, discouragingly, that Berkeley fails in his attempts to demonstrate the truth of his fundamental principles—in particular, that he fails to prove the crucial principle (I) that he shares with Locke, namely that in sense perception, what the perceiver directly (or immediately) perceives in every case is just one or more ideas of sense. He fails, too, as we saw in Chapter VII, to prove that Locke's representational realism is false or unintelligible. But these failures should not of themselves cause us to abandon Berkeley and his immaterialism. They should, rather, make us realize that Berkeley's aims here are too ambitious, that such aims cannot be achieved by any philosopher, or anyway not by the methods that Berkeley has at his disposal. Instead of trying to *demonstrate*—i.e., prove with certainty—that his fundamental metaphysical and epistemological principles are *the* correct ones, Berkeley might better treat them as hypotheses that cannot be established with absolute certainty, but are judged better or worse depending on how well or how badly they fit into a general philosophical system (which is itself a more comprehensive hypothesis) that is satisfactory, by whatever criteria of satisfactoriness philosophers have. (Berkeley himself mentions this interpretation of his philosophy: see *PHK* I 133.)

I suggest that the most sensible way to read Berkeley is to regard him as a philosopher who simply *assumes* principle (I), along with Locke and most other thinkers of the time, and who tries to build a metaphysical system that includes (I) and is better than any of its competitors—and the most visible competitor is, of course, Locke's system. Although Berkeley seeks to *demonstrate* the truth of (I), the principle plays the same logical role in his system that it would play if it were, for him, a (mere) hypothesis, and we may therefore so view it, without doing violence to his arguments. In this way we can, as it were, set aside Berkeley's unsuccessful attempts to demonstrate such propositions as principle (I), and thereby see the rest of his philosophy for what it is—a masterpiece of metaphysical system building. (Note that to the extent that Berkeley's system turns out to be adequate, the principles on which it is built will to that degree receive support; not the absolutely firm support that Berkeley thinks he provides for them, but the only kind of support, perhaps, that they are capable of having.)

It is time now to examine the system that Berkeley builds on his fundamental principles. (For expository purposes, I shall, in the discussion to follow—most of the time, anyway—join Berkeley and Locke in assuming the truth of principle (I).) We know that Berkeley rejects Lockean material substances, thinking that no sense can be attached to the hypothesis that such things exist. But if Lockean material objects are swept away, we seem then to be deprived of the entire physical world in which, as we naturally think, we live, breathe, and have our being. Without them, aren't we left in nothing but an unreal dream world, alone with our own ideas? Indeed, if the existence of Lockean material objects is denied, what can then be understood by 'sense perception,' 'ideas of sense,' and related notions? For anyone who accepts principle (I), it would seem, sense perception can only be thought of as a process in which real physical objects (processes, events, or whatever)—i.e. Lockean objects (or processes, events, and so on, in which they figure)—cause various ideas of sense to arise in the minds of the perceivers of those objects (processes, etc.); so if there *are* no Lockean material objects, we cannot understand what sense perception, ideas of sense, and the rest, can possibly be. Certainly on that conception of sense perception and ideas of sense (and what other conception of these is there?), there can be, in Berkeley's system, no such thing as sense perception, and no ideas of sense. As far as objectivity goes, then, this means that all of our ideas are on a par, and there is no distinction to be made between, on the one hand, our awareness of real things—for the real things have been eliminated!—and, on the other hand, what we would normally call figments of our imagination, day dreams, ordinary dreams, after-images, and the like.

This is a complex objection to Berkeley, with several interwoven strands that have to be distinguished and treated separately. The general line of defense that Berkeley pursues is as follows. First of all, he points out that the distinction between ideas of sense and such things as dreams, figments of the imagination, etc. (let us, for convenience, lump all these latter ideas together, and call them *ideas of imagination*) is, after all, a distinction between different kinds of *ideas*. Moreover, it is a distinction that we make, and *can* only make, on the basis of certain *detectable* features of our ideas; it would be absurd to suggest that we can determine which of our ideas are ideas of sense by noting which ones are caused by Lockean material objects. But then Berkeley has at his disposal, in his system, the very same means of distinguishing between ideas of sense and ideas of imagination that Locke has in his. There are, says Berkeley, the following three detectable differences between ideas of sense and ideas of imagination:

(a) 'The ideas of sense are more strong, lively, and distinct than those of the imagination.' (*PHK* I 30; see also *3D* III (*W* II 235; A 197; T 180))

(b) Ideas of imagination have 'an entire dependence on the will' of the person who has them, whereas ideas of sense 'have not a like dependence on our will.' (*3D* III(*W* II 235; A 197; T 180); see also *PHK* I 28, 29)

(c) Ideas of sense have 'a steadiness, order, and coherence, and are not excited at random, as those which are the effects of human wills often are, but in a regular train or series.' (*PHK* I 30) Unlike ideas of imagination, ideas of sense are 'connected, and of a pice with the preceding and subsequent transactions of our lives.' (*3D* III (*W* II 235; A 197; T 180))

These three tests, or criteria, for distinguishing between ideas of sense and ideas of imagination do not hold good universally. Thus, in the case of (a), some ideas of imagination—e.g., some hallucinations —are stronger and more lively than some ideas of sense, though, for the most part, (a) is true enough. (b) is true only for one or two limited kinds of ideas of imagination, but not true at all for dreams, hallucinations, and after-images, none of which has 'an entire dependence on the will.' The third criterion, (c), is of far greater importance than the other two. Our perceptual experiences of what we take to be the real world are marked, above all, by their orderliness and coherence, in sharp contrast to our dreams, hallucinations, and the rest. A real bunch of keys left on a real table is likely to be there when you look for it again, or anyway is to be found somewhere; but dream keys left on a dream table are not reliable at all. If, in a dream, you should return to the table and not find the keys, it doesn't even follow, as it does in the real world, that they must be somewhere else. Again, the perceptual experiences we have in walking around a real tree—looking at it, touching it, and so on—are orderly and predictable in a way that the experiences we have of an hallucinatory tree (where, as we might put it, anything can happen) are not. We may summarize this difference by saying that in the perception of real things, what we are aware of—that is, in

127

Berkeley's terminology, ideas of sense—are, we think, subject to (natural) laws, or at any rate to lots of generalizations, whereas our ideas of imagination are not. To be sure, ideas of imagination do figure in certain kinds of laws or generalizations; for example, it is doubtless true that if a certain amount of alcohol is swallowed at such-and-such a rate by a person with such-and-such a kind of brain, then he will have a certain specific type of idea of imagination— hallucinatory dancing pink elephants, perhaps. Ideas of imagination (e.g., hallucinations) are real things that people really have, and are therefore subject to (natural) laws and generalizations, just as other real things are. But there is still an enormous difference between the laws and generalizations about, for example, hallucinatory elephants, and those that concern real elephants. If there were any laws or generalizations that could tell us what to expect of hallucinatory elephants, they would deal almost exclusively with our central nervous system and would be known only to a few experts. There would, presumably, be no such simple laws or generalizations as that hallucinatory elephants are pugnacious, have rough skin, or drink through their trunks, nor even that they are heavy, are three dimensional, and have a far, or back, surface (i.e., a surface that is not 'visible' to the person having the hallucination). In this sense, there can hardly be reasonably simple, easily learned, laws or generalizations about hallucinatory elephants, hallucinatory trees, and so on, and hence none about hallucinatory *objects* in general. But we all know hundreds of thousands of such laws and generalizations—even if we can state only a few of them—about real physical objects, many of which have direct implications for our perceptual experiences (i.e., ideas of sense) of such objects. And so Berkeley is right when he claims, in (c), that our ideas of sense have 'a steadiness, order, and coherence' that is lacking in our ideas of imagination.

Berkeley's criterion (c) introduces the important point that our perceptual experiences of real objects (i.e., in Berkeley's terminology, our ideas of sense) are distinguished from all our other sensuous experience (e.g., images, dreams, and so on—i.e., our ideas of imagination) mainly by the fact that they are orderly and coherent—i.e., are 'lawful'—in a way that our ideas of imagination are not. This is a theme that is later developed by Hume and, still later, made one of the foundation stones for the whole Kantian philosophy.

When principle (I) is accepted, as it is by Locke and Berkeley alike, then, as Berkeley rightly points out, criteria (a)–(c)—or anyway some improved and perhaps expanded version of those criteria—are required in order to distinguish genuine ideas of sense from mere ideas of imagination. A Lockean, in other words, is in the same boat with Berkeley on this score; both must appeal to exactly the same criteria for making the crucial distinction. (cf. *3D* III (*W* II 235; A 197; T 180)).

What Berkeley has done, so far, is to prove that the complex objection raised earlier against his system is wrong at least in this respect: it contained the claim that he could not distinguish ideas of sense from ideas of imagination—and he has now shown that, and how, he can. But it is by no means clear how far this reply goes toward quelling the doubts and worries expressed in the objection. Berkeley has given us tests for distinguishing, in his system, between ideas of sense and ideas of imagination. But does he mean to assert, further, that:

(i) the satisfying of his criteria (a)–(c) is what *constitutes* an idea's being an idea of sense (or a set of ideas' being a set of ideas of sense)

or does he rather want to say that:

(ii) his criteria (a)–(c) merely enable us to *identify*, or *pick out*, ideas of sense, but what makes them ideas of sense is their possession of some further property, *P*, or their standing in some relation, *R*, to something (or some things)?

Locke clearly chooses (ii): he should, and probably would, agree with Berkeley that we need something like criteria (a)–(c) in order to pick out the genuine ideas of sense from all the others, but their being ideas of sense is not a matter simply of their satisfying those criteria—it is a matter of their being caused, in certain ways, by something else, namely, by Lockean material objects (or by events, processes, and so on, in which such objects figure). Locke would say, further, that their being caused in this way explains why ideas of sense do, in fact, satisfy criteria (a)–(c). Thus, consider (b): the reason ideas of sense have very little 'dependence on our will' is just that they are caused in us by the action of Lockean objects on our sense organs. And the 'steadiness, order, and coherence' of ideas of sense, involved in criterion (c), is also explained by the same fact. (The full explanation requires additional assumptions about Lockean objects, to be sure—for example, that they endure, that they act in ways that do not radically change over the course of time, and so on.) A case could even be made out that criterion (a), too, is explained by the fact that ideas of sense, unlike ideas of imagination, are caused by the actual stimulation of our sense organs by real Lockean objects (or by signals from real Lockean objects).

But what, now, about Berkeley? Does he wish to assert (i), or does he wish instead to assert some non-Lockean version of (ii)? Here's one plausible answer to this question: Well, he really cannot assert (i). He cannot, that is, maintain that the mere satisfaction of criteria (a)–(c) by certain of our (sensuous) ideas is what makes them ideas of sense, for that would leave too many brute facts lying around—i.e., it would leave too much unexplained. Ideas of sense, by definition, are those we have when we are aware, perceptually, of real objects in the world. But it is part of our conception of a real object that two or more perceivers may be aware of the very same object at the same time. This means that there will be a considerable amount of interpersonal agreement about the properties and behavior of real objects; two or more observers of a single object will normally have very similar ideas of sense of it. But if (i) were true, this very important feature of our ideas of sense would be wholly unexplained; for why should ideas that happen to satisfy criteria (a)–(c) also enjoy this kind of intersubjective harmony? Locke, who espouses a version of (ii), has, of course, no difficulty in answering this question, unlike a defender of (i). Again, a defender of (i) has nothing to offer by way of explaining why ideas of sense have a 'steadiness, order, and coherence' (criterion (c), and why they have little 'dependence on our will' (criterion (b)). If they are not generated by ourselves, then we shall naturally want to know what does cause them to occur.

Whether or not this reply, above, is sound, Berkeley apparently agrees with it, for he espouses a version of (ii). If we recall the tangible objects of his *New Theory of Vision*, we might expect him to say that it is they that cause our ideas of sense; but clearly his attack on the Lockean hypothesis leaves him in no position, now, to assert the existence of tangible objects as they were conceived of in the *New Theory*. Berkeley tells us in the *Principles* that when he wrote the *New Theory*, he did not really believe that tangible objects 'exist without the mind,' and that he simply wrote as if this 'vulgar error' were true, since it was 'beside [his] purpose to examine and refute it in a discourse concerning *vision*' (*PHK* I 44). His real view is that our sense of touch does not put us in direct contact with any such tangible objects as were assumed to exist in the *New Theory*, but that it provides us, rather, with a special kind of ideas of sense (tangible ideas of sense), and that these are on a par with all other ideas of sense; so it is no more intelligible to suppose that tangible ideas of sense represent (Lockean) objects existing 'without the mind' than it is to suppose that, say, visible ideas of sense represent them. All such objects, Berkeley thinks, have been swept away by his critique of the Lockean hypothesis.

The cause of our ideas of sense, on Berkeley's view, is none other than God. A philosopher who thinks that God created the world—where 'the world' includes a realm of Lockean material objects—and that He constantly maintains it in existence, could also say that God is the cause of our ideas of sense; for such a philosopher could say that God is the cause of the Lockean material objects and that these, in turn, cause our ideas of sense. So God would cause our ideas of sense *indirectly*, *via* Lockean material objects. But this, of course, is not at all what Berkeley wishes to say. For him, God causes all of our ideas of sense *directly*, with no intermediary whatsoever.

What reasoning lies behind this remarkable proposal? Well, first of all, Berkeley takes it for granted, as anyone must, that our ideas of sense have some cause or other. Next, he never doubts that our ideas of sense must be caused by something other than ourselves. This does not quite follow at once from criterion (b), but it almost does. According to (b), recall, our ideas of sense are not dependent on our own wills in the way that ideas of imagination are supposed to be. (b) leaves open the outré possibility that although our wills have no control over them, ideas of sense are nevertheless generated out of our own unconscious minds, just as dreams presumably are; but this Leibnizian view never occurs to Berkeley and if it were to occur to him, he would reject it at once, since it presupposes the notion of the unconscious mind. (Remember that for Berkeley the mind is a transparent medium.) After his attack on Locke, Berkeley cannot say that material objects, in Locke's sense, cause our ideas of sense. In fact, he has narrowed his options down to just two. He must say either (1) that our ideas of sense are caused by some other *ideas*, or else, (2) that they are caused by some other *mind* or *minds*. Let us consider these options.

Given certain of Berkeley's assumptions, there is, at first blush, some plausibility in the first option, but it quickly fades. One might naturally suppose that our ideas of sense are caused by those very things that we are aware of in sense perception—and, since these are nothing but ideas, on Berkeley's view, why shouldn't he say that our ideas of sense are caused by ideas? But the suggestion is full of difficulties. Suppose you are looking at a tree, so that you have an idea of sense, I_1—the visual appearance of a tree. According to the suggestion just made, I_1 must be caused by that *very same idea*, I_1, since that is what you are now aware of. But surely it is absurd to think that an idea might be caused by itself. As if that were not enough, I_1 is an idea in your own mind, and Berkeley is looking for a cause of it that is *other than* yourself, and hence other than your own mind or any of its ideas.

Even if we could solve problems of this sort—that is, even if we could find some idea (or set of ideas) other than I_1 existing in some mind other than yours that might appear to be a plausible candidate for the cause of I_1—still Berkeley would refuse to allow that it could possibly be the real cause of I_1 (or, indeed, of anything else). His reason is this:

> All our ideas, sensations, or the things which we perceive, by whatsoever names they may be distinguished, are visibly inactive, there is nothing of power or agency included in them. So that one idea or object of thought cannot produce, or make any alteration in another. . . . [T]he very being of an idea implies passiveness and inertness in it, insomuch that it is impossible for an idea to do any thing, or, strictly speaking, to be the cause of any thing. (*PHK* I 25)

Berkeley thus assumes that if something is to be the *cause* of anything, it must have power, activity, or agency in it, and he claims that since ideas include nothing of the sort, they cannot cause anything—not even other ideas.

The assumption that a cause must include some power or activity in it is a perfectly natural one for Berkeley to make; after all, it was only Hume who first had the genius to subject the assumption to critical scrutiny.[1] And if one does make the assumption, then Berkeley's rejection of ideas as causes can look plausible, at least. Thus suppose, for example, that you are sitting near a fire, and that you have certain visual ideas of sense—perhaps of reddish and yellow areas constantly changing their shapes—and certain 'tangible' ideas of sense—of heat, let us say. Berkeley says of ideas that 'there is nothing in them but what is perceived' (*PHK* I 25); but you perceive nothing in your ideas of the fire but redness, yellowness, flickeringness, and heat. In particular, you do not perceive something else, in addition to these perceptual properties, that could reasonably be called 'agency,' 'power,' or 'activity.'[2] Those ideas of sense of the fire, then, are passive and inert (to use Berkeley's terms), and so cannot cause anything.

It is clear that Berkeley, the empiricist, wants to find something answering to the words 'power,' 'activity,' and 'agency' somewhere in his experience. Failing to find it among his ideas, he looks elsewhere in his mind, and finds it in his acts of volition or willing:

> I find I can excite ideas in my mind at pleasure, and vary and shift the scene as oft as I think fit. It is no more than willing, and straightway this or that idea arises in my fancy: and by the same power it is obliterated, and makes way for another. This making and unmaking of ideas doth very properly denominate the mind active. (*PHK* I 28)

For Berkeley, a volition is not an idea; it is an action. (As we shall see, one cannot even have an idea of a volition, since an idea, being passive, cannot represent something active.) In the published work, Berkeley simply assumes that volitions are actions and that these actions are totally different in kind from any ideas (or combinations of ideas). It might, therefore, seem as though he were somewhat naïve and uncritical on the point. But in his notebooks (*The Philosophical Commentaries*), he gives a great deal of thought to the question of how volitions are to be understood, what their connections with perception (i.e., the having of ideas) is, and so on. We shall discuss all of this in a later chapter.

For Berkeley, mind is the sole principle of activity; and so minds are the only true causes of anything. It is regrettable that he does not work out and defend this position, so central to his whole philosophy, more fully in his published works; perhaps he did so in Part II of the *Principles*, the incomplete manuscript of which was tragically lost.[3] But his view is an immensely appealing one, even without an elaborate defense. There is something altogether special about the causality of our own actions; we can just feel ourselves making them happen. Thus, if I decide to raise my left arm now, and do it, there is no temptation for me to think that I have merely learned from experience that such acts of volition are generally followed by my left arm going up. One is irresistibly drawn to the idea that here, with volitions, and only here, we experience real causality, real agency. Berkeley doubtless thinks that a truth as obvious as this needs no extended defense.

To return, now, to the question of what it is that causes our ideas of sense: we have seen that Berkeley must reject proposal (1)—namely, that they are caused by some other ideas—and must espouse (2)—namely, that they are caused by some other mind or minds. Berkeley quickly infers that the cause can be none other than God Himself. At one point, he claims that this proof of God's existence does not need to take into account 'the contrivance, order, and adjustment of things' in the universe, but rather hinges entirely on 'the bare existence of the sensible world' (*3D* II (*W* II 212; A 175; T 154)). In this, he errs badly. If we consider only the bare existence of the sensible world, then, assuming that we accept Berkeley's argument up to this point, we have as much right to infer that there are two minds that cause our ideas of sense, or that there are sixteen, or even that there is one for each different sensible object (a spirit for each living and non-living thing), as we have to infer that there is one infinite mind, namely God's, causing our ideas of sense. Whatever plausibility there is in making God the cause of all our ideas of sense stems from the fact that the sensible world is so tremendously vast, complex, and orderly: only a single mind possessing infinite powers, so the reasoning must go, can be responsible for such a world. Berkeley, except when he wrote the passage just cited, realizes this full well:

the far greater part of the ideas or sensations perceived by us, are not produced by, or dependent on the wills of men. There is therefore some other spirit that causes them, since it is repugnant that they should subsist by themselves. See *Sect.* 29. But, if we attentively consider the constant regularity, order, and concatenation of natural things, the surprising magnificence, beauty, and perfection of the larger, and the exquisite contrivance of the smaller parts of the creation, together with the exact harmony and correspondence of the whole, but above all, the never enough admired laws of pain and pleasure, and the instincts or natural inclinations, appetites, and passions of animals; I say if we consider all these things, and at the same time attend to the meaning and import of the attributes, one, eternal, infinitely wise, good, and perfect, we shall clearly perceive that they belong to the aforesaid spirit, *who works all in all*, and *by whom all things consist.* (*PHK* I 146)

The positing of God as the cause of our ideas of sense cannot look, now, to be as reasonable a move as it does to Berkeley, living in the early eighteenth century, when God was a standard feature of world views. But in any case, Berkeley certainly considers his hypothesis to be superior in every way to Locke's. In the first place, Locke's system has need of God, too—to create our souls and all material objects, and, at the time of creation, to set matter in motion. Berkeley sees this as demeaning God, however, because it implies that God has to create matter to serve as an instrument to produce ideas of sense in our minds—as if He lacked the power to do so directly (*3D* II (*W* II 217–19; A 180–2; T 160–2); *PHK* I 60f). We can put Berkeley's point in a different way: Berkeley's system is simpler than Locke's, in that he has need only of God where Locke needs both God and a whole extra realm of being—i.e., the material world of Lockean objects.

Second, the entities that Locke posits as the cause of our ideas of sense—i.e., material objects—are never experienced by us and are, according to Berkeley, wholly incomprehensible; whereas in employing God for the same purpose, Berkeley is positing a kind of thing—i.e., a mind—that we do know, with certainty, to exist, since each of us knows that he is himself a mind. Third, Locke's system has what Berkeley considers to be the egregious flaw of requiring that matter causally influence our minds (by producing ideas of sense in it); it is a flaw, remember, because no one is supposed to understand

134

how extended matter can have any effect on an unextended, spiritual substance. Berkeley sees himself as escaping this kind of criticism by having a *mind*—namely, God's—causing our ideas of sense. We have a great deal of first-hand knowledge that minds can cause ideas, since each of us can produce ideas in his own mind at will (*PHK* I 28).

Of this last—third—alleged advantage over Locke, however, I would say that I think Berkeley ought not to be quite so self-assured. The only kind of experience we have of a mind *directly* causing ideas, as Berkeley himself seems to concede, is of our own mind causing ideas *in itself*.[4] We presume, to be sure, that one mind can produce ideas in another, but not without the mediation of physical objects (processes, events, or whatever), as, for example, when one person speaks to another. But Berkeley has God producing ideas of sense in our minds *directly*, and we have, I should judge, no more understanding of how that is supposed to be accomplished than we do of how a Lockean physical object can produce ideas in our minds. So although he does not realize it, Berkeley is no better off on this score than Locke.

Perhaps the most striking advantage that Berkeley sees in his view that it is God who causes all our ideas of sense is that it moves God into the very center of our lives. It has God producing fantastically complex, conscious effects in each of our minds during every moment of our waking life. The intimate concern that God thus demonstrates for our individual welfares can only make us love and trust Him. Atheism is thereby crushed. We have but to open our eyes to have a living proof of God's existence—assuming, of course, that we accept Berkeley's argument that God must be the cause of our ideas of sense. Once we accept that argument, we have more assurance of the existence of God (and of His concern for us) than we do even of the existence of other people (*PHK* I 147f):

> It is therefore plain, that nothing can be more evident to any one that is capable of the least reflexion, than the existence of God, or a spirit who is intimately present to our minds, producing in them all that variety of ideas or sensations, which continually affect us, on whom we have an absolute and entire dependence, in short, *in whom we live, and move, and have our being*. (*PHK* I 149; see also *Alciphron* IV 14, 15)

Berkeley, as we see, has great confidence in the virtues of his thesis that God causes our ideas of sense. However I must once again play the villain and introduce a disturbing note. Our conception of seeing something, of hearing something, and so on for the other senses, includes the idea that the thing we see, hear, etc., must cause our sensory awareness of it—in Berkeley's terms, must cause our ideas of sense of it. This is clearly shown in a well-known example of Grice's.[5] Imagine someone sitting in a room facing a wall that has a shelf with a clock on it. (Call this the *original* clock.) Unknown to the person, there is a large clear mirror between him and the wall; in the mirror, he can see the reflection of an exactly similar clock on an exactly similar shelf. (Call this the *second* clock.) The person thinks he sees a certain kind of clock that is in front of him; in fact, there is such a clock there—and we can even imagine that if the mirror were to be removed, the man's visual ideas of sense would be no different from what they are now. Nevertheless, we would all agree that with the mirror standing between him and the original clock, the man does not see that clock. He sees the second clock; he sees it, as we say, in the mirror. The reason for this, evidently, is that we require a certain kind of causal connection to exist between our ideas of sense and the object that we perceive; such a connection does exist between the man's ideas of sense and the second clock, and is lacking between his ideas of sense and the original clock.

But if, now, we apply this principle to Berkeley's system, we encounter difficulties. Let us confine ourselves to the sense of sight. According to our principle, what we see is what causes our visual ideas of sense. Therefore, it seems that Berkeley will have to hold either that everything we directly see is some part or aspect of God (we might call this the direct realism option), or else that everything we directly see *represents* some part or aspect of God (we might call this the representational realism, or Lockean, option). Neither of these options can be attractive to Berkeley. The first—the direct realism option—goes against received theological doctrine, in that it is pantheistic, since it makes all of nature either identical with, or anyway part of, God. The second—the representational realism option—destroys at once all the epistemological advantages that Berkeley has been striving so hard to achieve; it is as bad as the skepticism that he finds in Locke's system, is indeed a transposed version of it. Berkeley, alert to the danger, rejects both options:

Not that I imagine we see God (as some[6] will have it) by a direct and immediate view, or see corporeal things, not by themselves, but by seeing that which represents them in the essence of God, which doctrine is I must confess to me incomprehensible. (*PHK* I 148)

Mark it well; I do not say, I see things by perceiving that which represents them in the intelligible substance of God. This I do not understand; but I say, the things by me perceived are known by the understanding, and produced by the will, of an infinite spirit. (*3D* II (*W* II 215; A 178; T 157))

But the question remains: how does Berkeley seek to justify this blunt rejection of the two options? The answer is that he does it by rejecting our principle—namely, the principle that there is a real causal link between what we perceive and our perceiving of it. But how can a principle that strikes us as so obviously true be rejected? At this point, just when Berkeley seems poised on the brink of one disaster or another, he executes a masterstroke that allows him, as he thinks, to triumph on all fronts. I refer to his brilliant move of simply identifying what we call real physical objects (events, processes, or whatever) with ideas of sense. Fire, water, thumbs, hammers, trees, and every other thing (event, etc.) that we commonly consider to be *physical* or *material* in nature, are nothing but sets, families, or collections of ideas of sense. (See *PHK* I 1 and *3D* III (*W* II 245, 249; A 207, 211; T 191, 195f).) This allows Berkeley to escape from the troubles I have just been trying to burden him with. Let us see how.

Recall that Berkeley takes himself to have shown that all ideas are inactive and that real causality requires activity, agency, or power. But then if physical things are just so many ideas of sense, they cannot really cause anything at all. This shows that most of our ordinary, commonsensical judgments of causality are fundamentally mistaken—I mean such judgments as that fire can cause water to boil, that hitting your thumb with a hammer causes pain, and so on. The principle of ours that is supposed to be so troublesome for Berkeley, therefore, must also be rejected, since it employs the same ordinary, commonsensical notion of causality that has just been shown to be defective. With this principle safely out of the way, Berkeley can now triumphantly hold both that God is the real cause of our ideas of sense and that nevertheless what we perceive (i.e., what we see, hear, feel, and so on) is not God but real physical things such as trees, fire, and water—or anyway, that we perceive real *parts* of such things. (We shall later consider the question of whether, in Berkeley's system, it is legitimate to say that we perceive so-called physical objects, or whether one has to say, instead, that we perceive merely individual ideas of sense that are parts, or members, of such objects.)

Let us consider for a moment Berkeley's rejection of our ordinary, commonsensical judgments of causality. They are, I said, on his view, fundamentally mistaken. This rejection, we saw, enables him to avoid disaster. But perhaps this should be regarded as too high a price to pay. Any theory that requires one to deny that fire can cause water to boil, or that hitting one's thumb with a hammer causes pain, thereby loses much of whatever attractiveness it might otherwise have. But Berkeley is easily able to repair this apparent damage. When I said he rejects as fundamentally mistaken such statements as 'Fire can cause water to boil' or 'Hitting one's thumb with a hammer causes pain,' I meant that he considers them to be false *if they are construed in what Berkeley takes to be the literal way*—namely, as asserting that fire (or a hammer blow) contains real activity and so really causes water to boil (or pain). So construed, they are indeed false, according to Berkeley. But if they are understood in a different way, then they can all be accepted as true and can, thus, regain their accustomed place in our body of cherished beliefs. What is true in the judgment, for example, that 'Fire can cause water to boil,' and what we therefore ought to understand it to be asserting, is just that under appropriate conditions, fire is always followed by boiling water. When, for example, cold water in a kettle is placed over a fire, if the conditions are right the water will boil in the fullness of time. The world is characterized by this sort of sequence of events (or states of affairs); but note that they are merely *sequences*—the one state of affairs is generally *followed by* the other, it does not genuinely *cause* it. We may also say that the first state of affairs (water in a kettle over a fire) is a sign that the second (boiling water in the kettle) will ensue:

> [T]he connexion of ideas does not imply the relation of *cause* and *effect*, but only of a mark or *sign* with the thing *signified*. The fire which I see is not the cause of the pain I suffer upon my approaching it, but the mark that forewarns me of it. (*PHK* I 65)

Berkeley adds that as long as we remember how such sentences as 'Fire can cause water to boil' are properly to be understood, we can, and indeed ought to, continue to use them, despite the fact that they are actually false, when construed literally:

> [I]t will . . . be demanded whether it does not seem absurd to take away natural causes, and ascribe every thing to the immediate operation of spirits? We must no longer say upon these principles that fire heats, or water cools, but that a spirit heats, and so forth. Would not a man be deservedly laughed at, who should talk after this manner? I answer, he would so; in such things we ought to *think with the learned, and speak with the vulgar.* . . . In the ordinary affairs of life, any phrases may be retained, so long as they excite in us proper sentiments, or dispositions to act in such a manner as is necessary for our well-being, how false soever they may be, if taken in a strict and speculative sense. Nay this is unavoidable, since propriety being regulated by custom, language is suited to the received opinions, which are not always the truest. (*PHK* I 51, 52)

Although Berkeley strips things and events in nature of all activity, and hence denies that there are any real causal connections among states of affairs in the physical world, he nevertheless assures us that we can be confident that nature will behave in regular, dependable ways. There are, in fact, knowable laws of nature. Such laws summarize the ways in which God causes our ideas of sense to occur in our minds. Since we cannot conceive that God is subject to change, and in particular that He would change the laws of nature, the knowledge of which is so essential to our very existence, we can be sure that these laws will remain constant (but we can be only *morally* sure of this, apparently: see *PHK* I 107):

> Now the set rules or established methods, wherein the mind we depend on excites in us the ideas of sense, are called the *Laws of Nature*: and these we learn by experience, which teaches us that such and such ideas are attended with such and such other ideas, in the ordinary course of things. . . . [T]his consistent uniform working . . . evidently displays the goodness and wisdom of that governing spirit whose will constitutes the Laws of Nature. (*PHK* I 30, 32)

It is the job of the natural scientist, says Berkeley, to discover more and more laws of nature (*PHK* I 105); his work, thus, amounts to deciphering the system of signs[7] instituted by God. A scientist is simply mistaken if he regards himself as searching for, and finding, the real causes of anything (see *PHK* I 66, 108). Thus does Berkeley put science in its place—namely, below metaphysics, which genuinely does investigate, among other things, true causes.

IX

Berkeley's World View II:
Berkeley and Common Sense

There are many questions that need answering before we shall be able to judge how successful Berkeley's world view is—his metaphysical theory, I mean, of the so-called physical world. (We shall take up his theory of the mind in a later chapter.) In order to get at some of these questions, I want to indicate briefly what I take to be the standards by which such theories are to be judged.

There are, of course, some very general standards that any system of thought whatever ought to satisfy—for example, consistency, intelligibility, comprehensiveness, and simplicity; but I shall here pass these by. I want to concentrate, rather, on an important way—or perhaps I should say, pair of ways—in which a metaphysical system of physical reality, in particular, can be judged.

Note, first, that there are a number of extremely general propositions about the world that virtually everyone would subscribe to. It is not going too far to say that these propositions express our ordinary, or everyday—or, as I shall call it, our common sense—conception of the kind of world we inhabit. Let me characterize, very sketchily, this commonsense view of the world, and then describe the way (or pair of ways) of judging a metaphysical system such as Berkeley's that I want to focus on.

We exist, according to common sense, in a four dimensional world of three spatial dimensions and one temporal dimension. While on earth, at least, we are surrounded by, and move among, physical objects—that is, objects that also exist in our (single) space and time. These objects are individual things that exist, if I may put it so, in their totality at each instant; that is to say, they are precisely *not* classes or families whose existence at any given moment consists in the mere facts that (a) some members that belong to the class or family happen to exist, and (b) other, merely possible, members that belong to the class *could* exist if certain conditions were different. They endure more or less unchanged through short stretches of time, and some do so through quite long stretches of time as well; any changes they may undergo are the effects of regular causes, which may be either external or internal to the changing objects. We not only live and move among physical objects, we also perceive them with our various different senses; but their existence has nothing to do with our perception of them—indeed, they would exist whether or not there were any perceivers to perceive them. We can recognize quite a few individual objects; we can perceive that this object, here and now, is the same individual as that other one, there and then (or perhaps here and then). This means that we can, and do, make all sorts of identity judgments about physical objects through (or across) time. Many different people can perceive the same physical object at any given time (and at different times, too, of course). Each of us singly, and even two or more different people together, can see and touch the very same physical thing. This is only a crude and incomplete sketch of how almost all of us unthinkingly—even instinctively—view the world and ourselves in it—but it will do for our purposes.

Metaphysical systems of the world are considered by some to be good or bad according to how much or how little of this commonsense view of the world they are consistent with; or, on the contrary, the evaluator of such a system can count it of slight importance whether or not the system is consistent with the commonsense, or 'vulgar,' view of the world. Let us call these two opposing attitudes toward common sense on the part of evaluators of metaphysical systems the *conciliatory* attitude and the *non-conciliatory* attitude, respectively, and a critic who adopts these attitudes, a *conciliator* and a *non-conciliator*.[1] A radical conciliator regards all, or most, of the commonsense view of the world as true and as known to be true. He also holds these truths to be basic, in that other propositions—including those contained in a meta-physician's system—are judged by reference to them; anything that conflicts with them must be discarded. The radical non-conciliator, on the other hand, considers common sense to be little more than vulgar prejudice, and regards as foolish the suggestion that it should be set up as the yardstick for truth. He supposes that there are metaphysical principles which are either self-evidently true or demonstrably true, and that if a metaphysical system based on such principles should happen to conflict with the deliverances of common sense, then so much the worse for common sense. (Analogous positions are adopted by philosophers in virtually every branch of philosophy. In ethics, for instance, there are those who regard the dictates of an ordinary healthy moral conscience as inviolable, or nearly inviolable, data that a moral theory must deal with in various ways (conciliators), and others (non-conciliators) who consider a small number of general moral principles to be absolutely certain and who dismiss as mere prejudice our everyday moral convictions when they conflict with the fundamental moral principles.)

Berkeley, in constructing his system, judges it with a combination of a conciliatory and non-conciliatory attitude. On the one hand, he is a professed conciliator. It is a favorite theme of his that the philosophy of his day is beset with idle disputes and that he wants to return us to the truths of common sense:

> That the qualities we perceive, are not on the objects: that we must not believe our senses: that we know nothing of the real nature of things, and can never be assured even of their existence: that real colours and sounds are nothing but certain unknown figures and motions: . . . These are the novelties, these are the strange notions which shock the genuine uncorrupted judgment of all mankind; and being once admitted, embarrass the mind with endless doubts and difficulties. And it is against these and the like innovations, I endeavour to vindicate common sense. (3D III (W II 244; A 206; T 190))

On the other hand, we find in Berkeley's writings clear utterances of the non-conciliator. Recall, for example, his admonition 'to think with the learned, and speak with the vulgar' (PHK I 51). Here is another non-conciliatory passage:

> It is indeed an opinion strangely prevailing amongst men, that houses, mountains, rivers, and in a word all sensible objects have an existence natural or real, distinct from their being perceived by the understanding. (PHK I 4)

And in the preface to the *Principles*, there is this bold non-conciliatory pronouncement:

> *As for the characters of novelty and singularity, which some of the following notions may seem to bear, 'tis, I hope, needless to make any apology on that account. He must surely be either very weak, or very little acquainted with the sciences, who shall reject a truth, that is capable of demonstration, for no other reason but because it's newly known and contrary to the prejudices of mankind.*[2]

How can we explain this apparently conflicted attitude towards common sense? I offer the following hypothesis. Berkeley wants very much to defend common sense against what he takes to be its violation by the philosophers of his day—notably, Locke. However, as we know, he regards the subjectivist principle (I) as absolutely certain and, indeed, almost self-evidently true. He realizes, rightly, that ordinary, commonsense people would not recognize (I) as one of their own convictions: it is a purely philosophical principle (cf. *3D* III (*W* II 262; A 224f; T 211)). (I) seems to have consequences that directly conflict with certain aspects of the commonsense view of the world. Berkeley, then, finds himself in the awkward position of having to adopt both a conciliatory and a non-conciliatory attitude. Principle (I), for him, is more certain than any belief of common sense; so for its sake, he has to be non-conciliatory. But he is eager to defend any feature of the commonsense view of the world that can live happily with principle (I); to that extent, then, he is conciliatory.

Berkeley's world view, however, turns out to be quite decidedly non-conciliatory in a number of important ways. In his system, so-called physical objects (or *natural objects*, as I shall sometimes call them) are not at all what we ordinarily take them to be. Recall, to begin with, that according to Berkeley we never touch and see the same object (cf. (G), p. 28); this doctrine, first expounded in the *New Theory of Vision*, is not abandoned in the later works (cf. *3D* III (*W* II 245; A 207; T 191)). Our language hides this metaphysical complexity; for example, we refer simply to *a fig tree*, and not to a visual fig tree, a tangible fig tree—nor to the fig trees that correspond to our other senses. The truth, however, is that what we refer to, and ordinarily think of, as a single object is in reality a complex of several different objects.

But this is only the beginning of the complexity; for each of the several different objects—e.g., the visual fig tree—is itself, in turn, really a huge complex of many different objects, i.e., different ideas of sense. That this is Berkeley's view is clear from his discussion, in the *New Theory*, of our visual perception of magnitude: he points out that there is no such thing as *the* magnitude of what we commonly refer to as a single visible object, *O*, and the reason for this is that by sight we apprehend a host of different visible objects that comprise *O*, and these objects are of very many different sizes. (Cf. *NTV* 55; see also the discussion in *NTV* 44.) It is explicit, moreover, in these passages from the *Three Dialogues*:

> Sight therefore doth not suggest or any way inform you, that the visible object you immediately perceive, exists at a distance, or will be perceived when you advance farther onward, there being a continued series of visible objects succeeding each other, during the whole time of your approach. (*3D* I (*W* II 201; A 165; T 142))

> And when I look through a microscope, it is not that I may perceive more clearly what I perceived already with my bare eyes,

the object perceived by the glass being quite different from the former. (3D III (W II 245; A 207; T 191f))

So such terms as 'that visible fig tree' and 'this tangible fig tree' only seem to denote single objects, on Berkeley's view; in fact, they denote an indefinitely large series of different objects or ideas of sense. (Berkeley does not discuss the principles that determine how individual ideas of sense are assigned to the particular series to which they belong—i.e., to the particular visible (tangible, or whatever) objects that they comprise.)

All of this is non-conciliatory enough, but Berkeley draws from it two even more drastically non-conciliatory consequences:

(1) we never perceive so-called physical objects—e.g., never see such things as tulips and rocks; we perceive *only* things that exist in our own minds, that is, our own ideas.

Hence:

(2) different people must always perceive numerically distinct things.

Berkeley thinks that he is defending common sense when he asserts that we perceive real things (i.e., ideas of sense, on his view) and the properties they really have; but this is hardly enough to overcome the powerful non-conciliatory force of (1) and (2). Why, then, does Berkeley embrace (1) and (2)? Let us consider (1) first.

To understand Berkeley's reasons for accepting (1), we must see how he views sense perception. According to his picture of sense perception, some active entity other than the perceiver himself causes him to be aware of certain things—e.g., to be aware of redness, or of a high, shrill sound. Let us call such things *primal perceptual data.* So far—i.e., in the mere reception of the primal perceptual data—the perceiver is totally passive. In the course of his previous experience, the perceiver will have learned that certain combinations of primal perceptual data 'go with,' or are associated with, certain other such data; accordingly now, when he receives a few data from a larger set of associated data, some or all of the others in the set may be, and usually are, suggested to his mind. These further data will occur to him in the form of images, or ideas of the imagination. In other words, the receipt of primal perceptual data normally stimulates the perceiver's imagination to produce ideas (images) of associated data. It may also stimulate his reason, in which case he will make some inference from the primal perceptual data.

If one has this kind of picture of sense perception, then one may be led to suppose—and Berkeley does indeed suppose—that it is only what I called the primal perceptual data that are really perceived, in the strict and proper sense of that term. To prove this point, Berkeley uses the example of reading words:

> Philonous. In reading a book, what I immediately perceive are the letters, but mediately, or by means of these, are suggested to my mind the notions of God, virtue, truth, etc. Now, that the letters are truly sensible things, or perceived by sense, there is no doubt: but I would know whether you take the things suggested by them to be so too.
>
> Hylas. No certainly, it were absurd to think *God* or *Virtue* sensible things, though they may be signified and suggested to the mind by sensible marks, with which they have an arbitrary connexion. (*3D* I (*W* II 174; A 138; T 111); see also *NTV* 51)

This example is meant to show that the only things we really perceive (i.e., perceive by our senses) are the things we perceive as the result of the operation of just our perceptual systems alone (e.g., our visual system, auditory system, etc.); here, the operation of our perceptual systems is being contrasted with the activities of our *minds*—in particular, of our imagination and our reason. If we are aware of something, *x*, simply because it has been suggested to our imagination by some primal perceptual data, or simply because we have inferred its existence by reasoning from some primal perceptual data, then we do not really perceive *x*—we merely imagine it, or else we merely reason that it must, or probably does, exist. Accordingly, whatever is genuinely perceived is in every case *immediately* (or *directly*) perceived:

> Hylas. To prevent any more questions of this kind, I tell you once for all, that by *sensible things* I mean those only which are perceived by sense, and that in truth the senses perceive nothing which they do not perceive immediately: for they make no inferences. (*3D* I (*W* II 174f; A 138; T 112))

To be sure, we often speak of perceiving things that are merely suggested to our imagination by something we immediately perceive, or whose existence we merely infer from something we immediately perceive, but, says Berkeley, this is a loose, and in fact false, way of speaking:

> Though I grant we may in one acceptation be said to perceive sensible things mediately by sense: that is, when from a frequently perceived connexion, the immediate perception of ideas by one sense suggests to the mind others perhaps belonging to another sense, which are wont to be connected with them. For instance, when I hear a coach drive along the streets, immediately I perceive

only the sound; but from the experience I have had that such a sound is connected with a coach, I am said to hear the coach. It is nevertheless evident, that in truth and strictness, nothing can be *heard* but *sound*: and the coach is not then properly perceived by sense, but suggested from experience. So likewise when we are said to see a red-hot bar of iron; the solidity and heat of the iron are not the objects of sight, but suggested to the imagination by the colour and figure, which are properly perceived by that sense. In short, those things alone are actually and strictly perceived by any sense, which would have been perceived, in case that same sense had then been first conferred on us. As for other things, it is plain they are only suggested to the mind by experience grounded on former perceptions. (*3D* I (*W* II 204; A 167f; T 145))

So for Berkeley, to say that something is genuinely perceived (i.e., perceived by our senses), is to say that it is directly (or immediately, or non-epistemically (cf. p. 9)) perceived. And when something is genuinely perceived—i.e., immediately or non-epistemically—it is apprehended by the use of just our perceptual systems (e.g., our visual system) alone, with no help from the imagination or reason—i.e., with no accretion of ideas by suggestion or inference.

Does it follow from this view of perception that when an observer immediately perceives an idea of sense—e.g., a black rock-shaped visual idea of sense—he does not also perceive the appropriate natural object (e.g., a black rock)? Berkeley thinks it does follow. He says: 'I see, therefore, in strict philosophical truth, that rock only in the same sense that I may be said to hear it, when the word *rock* is pronounced' (*Alciphron* IV 11). In other words, I do *not* see that rock. Berkeley apparently reasons as follows: I immediately see a certain pattern of colors; I have to *infer* that the thing before my eyes is a rock—or the idea of a rock must come to me by *suggestion*. Therefore, I do not immediately perceive the rock—and hence I do not perceive it (see it) at all, since all genuine perception is *immediate* perception.

The non-conciliatory proposition (2)—namely, that different people must always perceive numerically distinct things—follows at once from (1); for if the only things one perceives are his own ideas, then different people can never perceive the numerically same thing. Hylas makes the point:

But the same idea which is in my mind, cannot be in yours, or any other mind. Doth it not therefore follow from your principles, that no two can see the same thing? And is not this highly absurd? (*3D* III (*W* II 247; A 209; T 193))

Berkeley thinks he can soften the harsh non-conciliatory effect of

(2). He notes that ordinary language allows us to speak of two people having different ideas, but it also permits us to say that two people have the *same* idea. For example, if you and I both have an idea of sense of a red triangle against a green background, where the colors and shapes are precisely the same, where the orientation of the triangle is the same, and so on, then we both have the *same* idea. This means, if we accept Berkeley's account of what ordinary language allows, that you and I have ideas that are numerically distinct (so that we have in this sense two *different* ideas) but that are qualitatively the same (so that we have in this second sense two ideas that are the *same*).[3] I take it that Berkeley is quite right in his claim that ordinary language permits us to say that several different people can all have the same idea.

I have been using the phrase 'having the same idea'; this corresponds to Berkeley's phrase 'perceiving the same idea.' Using Berkeley's terminology, now, we may express the claim I have just agreed to as follows: ordinary language permits us to say that several different people can all perceive the same idea. Berkeley takes it that because ordinary language permits one to say that different people can perceive the same idea, it is *ipso facto* open to him, in his system, to say that:

(3) different people can perceive the same thing. If the term *same* be taken in the vulgar acceptation, it is certain (and not at all repugnant to the principles I maintain) that different persons may perceive the same thing; or the same thing or idea exist in different minds. (*3D* III (*W* II 247; A 209; T 193f))

It is in this way that Berkeley seeks to bring his own metaphysical views closer to our common view of the world: according to both, in certain circumstances (call them circumstances *C*) it is permissible to say that different people are perceiving the same thing. (Circumstances *C* are those that obtain in such situations as the following: two friends are conversing and one says 'Look at that tree over there—the one with all the starlings in it,' and the other replies 'Oh yes, I see it.' That is, circumstances *C* are all those circumstances, whatever they are, in which, *as we might ordinarily put it*, different people are perceiving one and the same object.)

But this reconciliation is obviously only skin deep. Berkeley naturally construes the word 'same' in (3) to mean *qualitatively the same*: in circumstances *C*, different observers perceive things that are merely qualitatively the same. It is quite clear that he would deny that different people, even in circumstances *C*, can perceive the *numerically* same thing (or idea). He would hold, in other words, that:

147

(2) different people must always perceive numerically distinct things.

Since Berkeley would accept (2), there seems to be a deep conflict between Berkeley's system and our ordinary view of the world—for surely we all naturally assume that in circumstances C, several different people perceive the very same (i.e., numerically the same) thing. Berkeley makes what looks like a stab at resolving this apparent conflict by claiming that:

(4) In circumstances C, it so happens that our common linguistic practice is to say that different people perceive the *same* thing, but this is nothing more than an accident of linguistic usage; it could just as easily have been our practice to say that the different people perceive *different* things.

In asserting (4), Berkeley appears to be seeking to destroy the impression that there is a difference of opinion over a matter of substantial importance between his conviction that (2) is true and our ordinary common sense (according to which (2) is false). (4) is apparently meant to show that this difference of opinion is merely a verbal dispute, not a real one. It is not a real one, Berkeley seems to be claiming, because it is nothing more than an accidental convention that makes common sense insist that different observers, in circumstances C, perceive the same object. In other words, without changing any of its substantial beliefs at all, common sense could just as well maintain that, in those circumstances, different observers perceive different objects—which is precisely what Berkeley holds.

This attempt at reconciliation, if that is what it actually is, must be judged a failure, however. It is clear from the very way he defends (4) that Berkeley is simply assuming the truth of (2). Here is the relevant passage:

Let us suppose several men together, all endued with the same faculties, and consequently affected in like sort by their senses, and who had yet never known the use of language; they would without question agree in their perceptions. Though perhaps, when they came to the use of speech, some regarding the uniformness of what was perceived, might call it the *same* thing: others especially regarding the diversity of persons who perceived, might choose the denomination of different things. But who sees not that all the dispute is about a word? to wit, whether what is perceived by different persons, may yet have the term *same* applied to it? (3D III (*W* II 247f; A 210; T 194))

I think this passage must be read as presupposing that people in circumstances C are, *of course*, perceiving numerically different objects; because it suggests that the only, or anyway the main, reason men might have to apply the word 'different' to what they perceive in circumstances C is that there is a 'diversity of persons' who do the perceiving—and why should *that* be a reason for such a linguistic choice unless one takes for granted that different people must always perceive numerically distinct things (i.e., their own ideas)? So Berkeley is saying: Given that different people must always perceive numerically distinct objects, and that in circumstances C they can perceive objects that are closely (and perhaps even exactly) resembling, wouldn't it obviously be nothing but a verbal dispute if we should argue about whether one should say that in such circumstances they perceive different things or whether, instead, one should say that they perceive the same thing?

Well, *if* we could agree that 'different people must always perceive numerically distinct things,' we might accept what Berkeley says here. But that is precisely the point of the present dispute between Berkeley and common sense, as I see it. Therefore, since Berkeley everywhere assumes the truth of (2), what he says here, and in (4), obviously cannot count as any sort of reconciliation of his system and our ordinary view of the world—because the dispute is precisely over the truth of (2).

Berkeley goes on to cite the following example:

> Or suppose a house, whose walls or outward shell remaining unaltered, the chambers are pulled down, and new ones built in their place; and that you should call this the *same*, and I should say it was not the *same* house: would we not for all this perfectly agree in our thoughts of the house, considered in it self? and would not all the difference consist in a sound? (*3D* III (*W* II 248; A 210; T 194))

This is designed to show that 'men may dispute about identity and diversity, without any real difference in their thoughts and opinions, abstracted from names' (*3D* III (*W* II 248; A 210; T 195)). But it has been my contention that in the present dispute between Berkeley and common sense there certainly *is* a 'real difference in their thoughts and opinions.' It certainly does not follow, as Berkeley apparently thinks it does, from the fact that some disputes as to whether something is to be called the *same* or *different* are vacuous, that all such disputes are vacuous.

At the end of his treatment of Hylas' objection, Berkeley reveals a certain uneasiness about his own position, so it seems to me, by appealing to the archetype in God's mind of each object in the world. This does, indeed, provide some kind of unity for the objects that are perceived by several different observers who are in circumstances C; but what it provides is only a single cause[4] of those objects. It still does not provide a single object of perception for the different observers however, because, as Berkeley himself insists (cf. p. 136f), we do not perceive these archetypes in God's mind.

It is apparent, then, that although Berkeley holds that one can truly say 'Several different observers, in circumstances C, can perceive the same thing,' this represents only the most superficial kind of agreement with our common (or commonsensical) view of the world, for the meaning that Berkeley attaches to that sentence reveals a deep conflict between his beliefs and those of common sense.

I want to argue, now, that although Berkeley thinks he must accept both of the non-conciliatory propositions (1) and (2), he does not in fact have to do so. He could argue as follows: In circumstances C, it is true that each of two observers immediately perceives his own numerically distinct idea of sense—call them I_1 and I_2. But since I_1 and I_2 both belong to a collection of ideas that constitute a so-called physical object, O, each observer is also perceiving O, and hence both observers are perceiving the very same object, that is, O.

We have seen that Berkeley would reject this argument, on the grounds that since one immediately perceives only a certain pattern of colors and so must infer (or else it must be suggested to his mind) that this pattern belongs to a particular kind of so-called physical object (to a rock, say), one therefore does not immediately see the rock and hence does not see it at all.

But Berkeley would be wrong to reject the argument on such grounds. Even if his premises be granted, his reasoning shows at most only that one cannot immediately see*without inference* the rock: it does not show that one cannot, and does not, immediately see *without intermediary* the rock. Indeed, if the color and shape that one (immediately) sees are the color and shape that belong to that very rock, then I think it is obvious that one *does* (immediately) see the rock. (Recall our discussion of the Gremlin example, p. 10f.) In any case, it is certainly open to Berkeley to say that in (immediately) seeing an idea of sense, a perceiver is *also* (immediately) seeing*without intermediary* the appropriate natural object—and this is all he needs in order to reconcile his system with common sense on this issue. Berkeley *can*, then, accept the argument I suggested in the paragraph above and can thus eliminate the conflict with common sense. The reason Berkeley does not see this possibility is that he fails to make the distinction between immediate perception*without inference* and immediate perception*without intermediary*.

To this, the following objection might be raised: Because of his conception of what a natural object is, Berkeley's system cannot be reconciled with common sense on the issue we have been discussing. A natural object, for him, is a huge collection of ideas of sense, and although (to consider just the case of vision) one can see individual members of the collection, one cannot see the whole huge collection itself—and so one cannot see the natural object.

Bennett

There is little merit in this objection. The inference from the premiss that a person perceives only a few ideas of sense that belong to a much larger collection, to the conclusion that a person never perceives the collection itself (i.e., the so-called physical object), is like the inference that other philosophers make from the claim that:

(i) a person perceives only the front surfaces of physical objects

to the conclusion that:

(ii) a person never perceives physical objects,

or like the inference from the claim that:

(iii) a person perceives only the properties of physical objects,

to the same conclusion. These inferences are disturbing, because although in a sense they look valid enough, we can nevertheless see that they embody a gross mistake. Consider the inference from (i) to (ii). If, as (i) says, a person perceives only the front *surfaces* of physical objects, then it seems to follow, as (ii) says, that he can never perceive a physical object, since it is not the case that a surface of a physical object is identical with a physical object. And yet we sense that something is wrong. If a person perceives the surface of a physical object, then he *does* perceive a physical object, because to see the surface of a tree, in the standard cases, just *is* to see the tree. One could be tempted to deny this only if he had an impossibly exaggerated notion of what it is to see a tree: he would have to think that in order to see a tree, one would have to see not only the surface of the bark and leaves, but the insides of the tree as well. He would have to see the totality of the tree. But even if it made sense to speak of seeing the totality of a tree, so much is not required in order to see the tree.

I think the inference that Berkeley, according to the present objection, would have to make, is exactly analogous to the inference from (i) to (ii), and is just as invalid. So we have not yet seen any good reason why Berkeley could not, and should not, align himself with common sense to the extent of holding that to perceive one or more ideas of sense that belong to a certain kind of collection of them, *is* to perceive that collection (i.e., *is* to perceive a so-called physical object). Of course, the one or two ideas of sense that are actually perceived constitute only a small part of the entire collection; but the front surface of a physical object (as conceived of by common sense) is similarly only a small part of the entire physical object. For Berkeley to insist that in order to see the collection, one must see every single idea in the collection, would be as unreasonable as it would be for a realist to insist that in order to see a physical object one must see every single atom in the object.

If Berkeley does make the move I suggest, this will allow his system to be more harmonious with the commonsense view of the world; in particular, it will allow him to reject the non-conciliatory (1) and (2).

If Berkeley were to distinguish immediate perception without inference and immediate perception without intermediary and allow, as I have urged he should, that to perceive one or more members of a collection may be to perceive the collection itself, he would free himself from his much too restrictive interpretation of principle (I). (I), on this restrictive reading, says that a person, in sense perception, perceives *nothing but* one or more ideas of sense—in particular, he does not also perceive certain *collections* of such ideas. We may say that (I), on this narrow interpretation, asserts that individual ideas of sense are the *only* objects of perception. It is this overly restrictive reading of (I) that leads Berkeley into espousing the grotesque and non-conciliatory proposition that when (as we would ordinarily put it) a person—let's take Peter as an example—approaches an object, he is not continually perceiving the same object, but rather a series of different objects. Berkeley believes this because Peter is perceiving a series of different *ideas* and he supposes that this requires him to say that therefore Peter is perceiving a series of different *objects*. But once free of the notion that the only objects of perception are the one or two individual ideas of sense that a perceiver may happen to have at any given time, Berkeley can align himself with common sense by affirming that since the different ideas that Peter has are members of one and the same natural object (i.e., the same collection of ideas), Peter is continually perceiving the *same* object. By a precisely analogous argument, it can be shown that Berkeley does not need to embrace the non-conciliatory proposition that an object seen with the naked eye and an object seen through a microscope are always, necessarily, two *different* objects.

Just as Berkeley can, and should, abandon the proposition that when a person approaches an object, he is really perceiving a series of different objects, so he can, and should, abandon (G) (p. 28) —namely, the proposition that a person never sees and feels the (numerically) same object. There is some excuse for (G) in the system of the *New Theory of Vision*, where a visual object is a collection of (visual) ideas of sense and a tangible object is something of an altogether different character; but in the mature system of the *Principles* and *Three Dialogues*, where all natural objects are nothing but families of ideas, there is no reason to embrace it. To be sure, when a person simultaneously touches and sees a single object O (as common sense would have it), his visual idea of sense of O and his tactual idea of sense of O are two quite different ideas, and so he is perceiving two different 'objects' (i.e., ideas): but since Berkeley holds that both ideas belong to the single collection of ideas that constitutes O, he can, and should, maintain, with common sense, that in perceiving the two different ideas, the person is also perceiving, tactually and visually, one and the same object O.

So far, then, it would seem that Berkeley could be more of a conciliator than he allows himself to be. Now let us try to see how much further he can go along conciliatory lines. I shall consider this question as it pertains to two closely related issues:

(i) the distinction between the real properties of an object and its merely apparent ones, and
(ii) the question of whether, and to what extent, our senses reveal the real properties of objects.

Can Berkeley, in his system, capture the views of common sense in this area? It will be convenient, in discussing these issues, to assume that in Berkeley's system, it can be maintained that in standard cases, at least, of sense perception, we perceive (so-called) physical objects. I shall also assume that to perceive one of these natural objects, in Berkeley's system, is to perceive one or more of the ideas of sense in the family of ideas that constitute the object.

Consider, now, this fact: our senses present objects as having a bewildering variety of incompatible properties. Take color, for instance. Pure snow looks white under many conditions; but under red floodlights, it looks pink or red, to someone wearing green sunglasses it looks greenish, and so on. We naturally suppose that snow does not have all of these colors: we think it is *really* white, and that the pink, red, green, and the rest, are merely apparent colors of snow. But how is Berkeley to handle this distinction between the real properties of objects and their merely apparent ones; and how is he to avoid the possibility of skeptical doubts about what the real properties of objects actually are?

This question reminds us that Berkeley still owes us a lot more of the story about the nature of so-called physical objects after he has said merely that they are collections of ideas. The example of the colors of snow indicates that we need guidance to determine what ideas of sense are to be included in the collections that constitute these objects. Suppose, for example, that I am quietly contemplating a snowman. Suddenly, the red floodlights are turned on, and I begin to have reddish, snowman-shaped ideas of sense. These ideas meet all three of Berkeley's criteria for being genuine ideas of sense (cf. p. 127); they are definitely not ideas of imagination. Presumably, then, I am still perceiving some real object; indeed, one would naturally think it is still the original snowman that I am seeing. But if so, then those reddish, snowman-shaped ideas of sense must be included in the family of ideas that constitute this particular snowman. Berkeley might try to exclude them from the family—declare them to be illegitimate, as it were—by maintaining that when the red floodlights are turned on, I no longer perceive the original snowman at all, but some reddish imposter. This would be unacceptable, however; for the world would then be populated with a bewildering array of objects popping into, and out of, existence with every change of conditions of observation. Moreover, Berkeley would surely be unhappy about the new possibilities for skeptical doubts that such a complex ontology would introduce.

Berkeley must say, then—and it seems anyway to be true—that when the red floodlights are turned on, I continue, as before, to see the original snowman. So, as I have said, my reddish, snowman-shaped ideas of sense have to be included in the family of ideas that constitute the snowman. But consider, now, a snowman that, at various times in its career, is seen under red floodlights, green floodlights, and purple floodlights. This means that there are reddish, greenish, and purplish ideas of sense in the collection of ideas that constitute the snowman. What is Berkeley to say about these disquieting intruders? What relationship is supposed to hold between the snowman and all these diverse colors?

There are, so it would seem, two alternatives open to him (later, I shall suggest a third):

(a) He can adopt the principle that it makes no sense to attribute sensible properties to collections of ideas of sense (i.e., to objects as wholes); sensible properties are attributable only to individual ideas of sense. (Let us call this the principle of non-propertied collections—or principle non-P/C for short.)

The espousal of principle non-P/C would preserve Berkeley's system in a sound epistemological state—i.e., it would remain unblemished by any taint of skepticism concerning sensible properties. But non-P/C has a decidedly non-conciliatory bias, since it entails the anti-commonsensical proposition that our snowman cannot be said to be white, green, red, or any other color.

At this stage of the game, Berkeley might better pick the second of his two alternatives. Here, again, he would insist that sensible

154

properties are attributable to individual ideas of sense, but:

(b) he can adopt the principle that if, at a certain time t, an object O contains an idea of sense that is characterized by the sensible property Q, then O at t has the property Q. (Let us call this the principle of propertied collections—or principle PC for short.)

Adoption of PC would mean that Berkeley could maintain that the snowman, when the red floodlights are turned on, *is* reddish; that when the purple floodlights are turned on, it *is* purplish; and so on. By this account, then, our senses do not deceive us; they reveal to us real properties that the object, under different conditions, actually has. In this way, Berkeley could show that his system is free of skepticism. However, PC, too, marks a departure from the commonsense view of an object, for it attributes to the object a wide range of different real properties as the conditions of observation vary.

Consider, next, the familiar straight oar half immersed in water. We would ordinarily describe the situation as follows: the oar is really straight, but it looks bent. How can Berkeley's system cope with this example?

Notice, first, that the move I said Berkeley would probably prefer in the previous case of the snowman—that is, (b), with the adoption of principle PC—will not be enough here. If he does no more than that, he shall have to say that the oar when half immersed in water is straight and is also bent—but that would be a contradiction. The minimal additional step he would have to take, it seems, would be to distinguish, in what we, in our commonsensical way, call a single object, two different objects: the tangible oar and the visual (or visible) oar. The tangible oar, then, when half immersed in (tangible) water, would really be straight, while the visual oar, when half immersed in (visual) water, would really be bent. This would amount to a reassertion of the non-conciliatory proposition (G) (p. 28) from *The New Theory of Vision*.

If Berkeley were thus to adopt principle PC and make the minimal necessary move that I have suggested he make, he would once again have cleared his system from the suspicion that it harbors the possibility of a certain amount of skepticism. But, of course, at a price. He would have removed himself another big step away from the common view of the world; for what the latter view regards as a single object would have become, in Berkeley's system, two or more objects—the tangible object, the visual (or visible) object, and objects corresponding to our other external senses as well, presumably. The single object of common sense would have begun to crumble.

(Notice, too, that as the result of his earlier preferred move in the first example (involving the snowman), each of Berkeley's sense-specific objects—e.g., the visual oar, the tangible oar—would have a whole range of different sensible properties, varying with the conditions of observation.)

But what if Berkeley were to adopt not principle PC, but non-P/C instead, to deal with the case of the oar half immersed in water? Then he would not have to break up the oar into the different sense-specific objects. He could simply say, rather, that the oar is neither bent nor straight, but contains a tactual idea of sense that is straight[5] and a visual idea of sense that is bent. When Berkeley actually considers this example of the oar half immersed in water, although it is not *perfectly* clear that he opts for principle non-P/C rather than for PC, I nevertheless believe that he does. (See *3D* III (*W* II 238; A 200; T 183f).)

Berkeley's alternative (b), with its principle PC, started out with a slight advantage over alternative (a), with its principle non-P/C, in the case of the snowman. However, in the case of the oar half immersed in water, they appear to be about equally attractive (or unattractive, depending on one's philosophical tastes). But when we look at another kind of perceptual situation, we come to see that PC has almost no special appeal of its own, and is in fact virtually indistinguishable from non-P/C. Thus, consider a necktie that both Paul and Gil are examining: it looks red to Gil and muddy brown to Paul. If Berkeley were to choose PC to cope with this case, he would have to say that the (visible) tie is red and is muddy brown; it is muddy brown to (or for) Paul and red to (or for) Gil. PC thus leads a Berkeleyan to the view that a so-called physical object is really five different sense-specific objects, each one of which has different sensible properties under various different conditions of observation, and even sometimes has different sensible properties (e.g., different colors) at the same time to (or for) different observers. But when the sensible properties of an object are made as ephemeral as that, there seems to be no discernible non-verbal difference between such a view, based as it is on PC, and the view, based on non-P/C, that so-called physical objects cannot be said to have sensible properties and that *only* ideas of sense can have sensible properties attributed to them.

Let us summarize, now, what we have learned about Berkeley's conception of a natural object. It is in reality a huge collection of ideas of sense (leaving God's ideas still out of account). If Berkeley accepts the principle non-P/C, he will maintain that a natural object cannot be said to have any sensible properties whatever; individual ideas of sense are the only objects to which sensible properties can be ascribed. If, instead, he accepts the principle PC, he will maintain that a natural object consists of five different sense-specific objects, each of which has the bewildering array of different sensible properties cited earlier.

It may, as I believe, make no real difference whether Berkeley accepts PC or non-P/C, but we need not settle that point. Either way, Berkeley's system turns out to be radically non-conciliatory—for either way, natural objects turn out to be wildly different from what commonsense believes them to be.

There is, however, still a third principle available to Berkeley, in addition to non-P/C and PC—and it is one that would permit him to narrow somewhat the gulf between his system and the commonsense view of things. I mean a modified version of the PC principle. On this new principle, when an object O contains an idea of sense that is characterized by the sensible property Q, (a) if the conditions of observation are all normal, then O really has Q (Q is a real property of O), but (b) if the conditions of observation are not all normal, then O may not really have Q—O may merely appear to have Q.[6] (I shall dub this the *weaker PC principle*.) This principle would allow Berkeley to say the same thing about the examples we have been considering that the commonsense man would say about them: thus, it would allow him to say that the snowman illuminated by red floodlights is not really red, and that the straight oar half immersed in water is not really bent, but only looks so.

If Berkeley were to embrace this weaker PC principle, the reconciliation with common sense would still be far from complete, however; for he would have to construe the principle in an anti-commonsensical way, in at least one important respect. I mean that he would have to understand its distinction between the real and the merely apparent properties of a natural object in an anti-commonsensical way. If Berkeley, with his metaphysical system, were to embrace the principle, he could not regard its distinction between the real and the merely apparent properties of an object as being of a fundamental metaphysical sort. He could not understand the distinction as Locke, for example, does. In Locke's system, a real property of an object is one that actually inheres in it, that modifies its very being, while a merely apparent property of an object does not inhere in it at all. For Berkeley, however, the distinction cannot be so basically metaphysical: all the ideas of sense that go to make up a natural object, in his system, are on a par, metaphysically, and so are their properties. So Berkeley would have to understand the terms 'real property' and '(merely) apparent property' in the weaker PC principle as marking some other kind of distinction—a pragmatic one, most likely. He would have to understand the weaker PC principle in some such way as this: By the 'real properties' of a natural object O, I mean the properties it is most beneficial or useful, for a variety of reasons, for people to associate with O, and by the '(merely) apparent properties' of O, I mean the properties it is less beneficial or useful for people to associate with O. Since it is reasonable to suppose that people will benefit most from associating with an object, O, just those sensible properties $Q_1, \ldots, Q_n$ that ideas of sense in the O-family[7] have when the conditions of observation are normal, we can say that $Q_1, \ldots, Q_n$ are the real properties of O, and we can say that any other sensible properties that members of the O-family may have are (merely) apparent properties.

To make the distinction between the real and the merely apparent properties of a natural object in this pragmatic way is, I believe, to go against common sense; for I take it that common sense views the distinction as being an objective, metaphysical distinction, not as one that we make on grounds of convenience or usefulness. Still, it seems clear that the best line for Berkeley to take would be to adopt the weaker PC principle, and then charge that common sense has the wrong idea about the distinction—adding that perhaps the error is due to a confused or anyway mistaken notion of what the nature of so-called material objects is. This position would certainly put Berkeley closer to common sense than the adoption of either the non-P/C or the original, stronger PC principle would.

Whatever success we may have had so far in reconciling Berkeley and the commonsense view of the world, the stark fact remains that Berkeley's conception of a natural object as a collection of ideas of sense is radically different from the ordinary conception of those objects. Is there any way of narrowing this apparently vast gap between the two world views? Let us see.

Notice, first of all, that it is extremely unlikely that any satisfactory system can do without the ordinary commonsensical concept of a physical object. There are any number of important purposes that seem to require such a concept and that cannot, apparently, be achieved with Berkeley's concept of a physical object. I shall consider just the following one. We often want to identify some particular physical object for a person who doesn't know it, when we are not actually in the vicinity of the object, by using just language alone, and to do it in such a way that the hearer will be able to recognize it when he sees it. There is normally no difficulty whatever about this—that is, when we employ our ordinary concept of an object and closely related concepts.[8] For instance, if I wish to identify Nassau Hall for you, I can tell you that it is a handsome large old brownstone building with an inappropriate cupola set on top of it, that it is located near the intersection of Nassau and Witherspoon Streets in

Princeton, New Jersey—and so on. If you shouldn't know where Princeton is, I may tell you that it is about half way between New York City and Philadelphia. If you do not know where those metropolises are either, I can locate them for you by giving (perhaps rough) distances and directions from the place where you now are. So given the commonsensical conception of physical things, which includes the conception of the single spatio-temporal framework in which they exist, we can easily identify objects and events for one another verbally.[9]

How is this kind of identification to be accomplished in Berkeley's system, however, using the conceptual resources that his system provides? Nassau Hall, according to Berkeley, is a collection of ideas of sense. (We may ignore God's ideas of Nassau Hall, since they are obviously not going to play any role here.) To identify Nassau ·Hall for you, then, I must identify that particular collection of ideas—and I must do it using just the concepts Berkeley's system permits one to use. It seems that I shall have to say something like this (or of this form): 'If you, or any other sighted creature, were in Princeton, New Jersey, and standing in such-and-such a place, facing in such-and-such a direction, when the conditions of visual observation are normal, then you (or he) would perceive the following kinds of visual ideas of sense: . These ideas of sense belong to that collection of ideas known as "Nassau Hall." ' But this merely creates new problems: e.g., if you don't know where Princeton, New Jersey, is, how could I identify that town for you, in terms of just ideas of sense and the other Berkeleyan concepts? Or how could I, with the same restrictions, specify the place at which the observer is supposed to stand, or the direction in which he is supposed to face? These things could easily be done if I were allowed to employ the ordinary concept of a physical object and other closely related concepts, but the tasks seem hopelessly complex if we are allowed to use only those in Berkeley's conceptual repertoire.

There have been philosophical arguments, from Kant right up to the present day, designed to show that we cannot possibly do without our ordinary conception of physical objects and of their spatio-temporal framework. These transcendental arguments are extremely complex and difficult, and there can be no question, here, of considering them. But whether or not the ordinary conception of a physical thing is absolutely necessary, this much seems evident even from our simple example: the ordinary concept of a physical object is extraordinarily useful, at the very least, and many of the everyday actions that we constantly want and need to perform are rendered exceedingly difficult, at least, in Berkeley's system.

There seems, then, to be a major defect in Berkeley's system. But if we look a bit further into his philosophy, we shall find that he has the means at his disposal to remedy the defect; we find, in fact—surprisingly—that he is able to introduce the ordinary concept of a physical object harmoniously into his system. To see how he can accomplish this, consider first what he has to say about the concept of *force* as it pertains to physical things—e.g., the force of gravity. We know that for Berkeley so-called physical things have no real force or power in them, no principle of *activity* (cf. p. 137). If we suppose that such terms as 'force' or 'gravity' stand for something real in the physical world, we are the victims of an illusion; what we take to be a reality can be nothing but a spectre—a mysterious or 'occult quality,' as Berkeley calls it in *De Motu*:

> *Force* likewise is attributed to bodies; and that word is used as if it meant a known quality, and one distinct from motion, figure, and every other sensible thing and also from every affection of the living thing. But examine the matter more carefully and you will agree that such force is nothing but an occult quality. (*De Motu* 5)

This does not mean, however, as Berkeley goes on to argue, that we cannot employ such terms as 'force' and 'gravity' in connection with so-called physical things: on the contrary, we can, and indeed should, do so, for those concepts are extremely useful. For example: if we imagine that every body in the universe exerts an attractive force on every other, according to a certain formula, we are thereby enabled to predict where the moon and earth, say, will be relative to one another, and to the sun, at any given time.[10] Again, if we imagine that there are forces in moving bodies, stretched springs, and so on, then, by employing the method of the 'parallelogram of forces,' we shall be able to compute what the result will be of two such bodies coming together in certain ways. These forces, to repeat, are not real attributes of things; they are extremely convenient fictions. We are to talk and think *as if* physical things exerted forces on one another, but, as philosophers, we are never to be fooled by this practice into thinking that they really do:

> *Force, gravity, attraction,* and terms of this sort are useful for reasonings and reckonings about motion and bodies in motion, but not for understanding the simple nature of motion itself or for indicating so many distinct qualities. . . . A similar account must be given of the composition and resolution of any direct forces into any oblique ones by means of the diagonal and sides of the parallelogram. They serve the purpose of mechanical science and reckoning; but to be of service to reckoning and mathematical demonstration is one thing, to set forth the nature of things is another. (*De Motu* 17, 18)

I want to suggest, now, that just as Berkeley, while denying that there are any real physical forces, can nevertheless legitimately find room for the concept of physical force in his system (as we have just seen), so can he accommodate in his system the commonsensical concept of a physical object, while still denying that there really are such objects. We have seen how useful our ordinary concept of an object is; why, then, shouldn't we talk and think as if there were such things, thus gaining all the advantages that concept has to offer, as long as we don't fall into the trap, when philosophizing, of thinking that they really exist? On this view, physical objects, understood in the commonsensical way, are convenient fictions, just as physical forces are. And, in fact, it would seem that the convenient fiction of a physical force cleary *presupposes* the convenient fiction of a commonsensical physical object.

The only reality answering to (mythical) physical forces are particular physical motions. But if we had at our disposal no more than the conception of such motions, it is exceedingly difficult to see how we could cope intellectually (and hence practically) with all the many different particular motions that we do, or might, run across in the enormously wide variety of circumstances that do, or might, occur; so it is extremely convenient—and perhaps even necessary—to pretend that there are physical forces at work in nature, and to learn a few general laws that specify how these forces operate. This enables us to predict, given such-and-such circumstances, that such-and-such motions are likely to occur.

An exactly parallel justification can be given for the employment of the ordinary concept of a physical object in Berkeley's system. The only relevant reality that there is in this area is the particular ideas of sense themselves. This is all we 'get' in sense experience. But how are we to cope with the huge and bewildering array of individual ideas of sense that we get in various circumstances? If we had at our disposal nothing more than the conception of an idea of sense, it is extremely difficult to see how we *could* cope with it—how we could learn anything more than a few crude generalizations, how we could come to master all the sophisticated techniques that everyone does master. To be able to do these things, it is *at least* extremely convenient—and perhaps it is even necessary—to pretend that there are physical objects in nature and to learn laws that specify how these 'objects' will appear to different kinds of perceivers in different kinds of circumstances. A 'physical object' is then thought of as an enduring, mind-independent something-or-other that appears so-and-so in such-and-such circumstances. In this way, the ordinary concept of a physical object allows us to group together vast numbers of actual and possible ideas of sense, and thus enables us to deal intellectually (and hence practically) with what would otherwise be largely a 'blooming, buzzing confusion' of ideas of sense.

On this view, physical objects, like physical forces, would be theoretical entities, conceived not realistically, but instrumentally. This sort of view of physical objects is labelled the 'New Phenomenalism' by Wilfrid Sellars and 'theoretical phenomenalism' by James Cornman.[11]

As far as I can tell, theoretical phenomenalism is a view that it is positively necessary for Berkeley to adopt, because in his system there seems to be absolutely no way for one to conceive of any particular collection or family of ideas of sense—i.e., to know *which* ideas of sense are to be gathered together into those various collections or families—other than by thinking of them as those ideas of sense one would have in perceiving such-and-such an object (conceived of in the ordinary commonsensical way) under such-and-such conditions (conceived of in the ordinary commonsensical way). In other words, his very conception of a *family* of ideas of sense *requires*, so it seems to me, theoretical phenomenalism. I cannot here enter into the complex question of just how sound the doctrine of theoretical phenomenalism is;[12] but it is a position that Berkeley really *must* take, and it is one, moreover, that he has the materials at hand to defend (as we see from his treatment of physical force in *De Motu*).

If we interpret Berkeley as a theoretical phenomenalist, we find that although, of course, his system still does not render our basic commonsensical beliefs about physical objects true, it nevertheless now brings them within striking distance of being true, so to speak. What I mean is this. If Berkeley's system is so interpreted as *not* to contain a theoretical phenomenalist's view of physical objects, then the fundamental commonsensical beliefs about physical objects that I mentioned earlier when describing what I called the common view of the world (p. 140f) are, in his system, not even false, but unintelligible, since his system, so construed, does not even allow the conception of a physical object that the common view of the world contains. But when he is interpreted as a theoretical phenomenalist, Berkeley becomes much more sympathetic to our commonsensical beliefs about physical objects. Those beliefs are not, as I said, rendered true, to be sure, but the error they contain is made thoroughly understandable, and almost respectable, even; it is simply the honest mistake of taking theoretical and therefore (for Berkeley) fictional entities to be real ones.

X

Berkeley's World View III: The Existence of Unperceived Objects

Although Berkeley believes that he must deny that we ever perceive so-called physical objects (e.g., trees and houses) and maintains that we perceive only our own ideas, he sometimes says things that imply that we do, after all, perceive things like trees and houses. Consider this passage from the *Principles*:

> Sensible objects may likewise be said to be without the mind, in another sense, namely when they exist in some other mind. Thus when I shut my eyes, the things I saw may still exist, but it must be in another mind. (*PHK* I 90; see also *PHK* I 3 and 48)

If 'the things I saw may . . . exist . . . in another mind,' then those things cannot be my own ideas of sense, for *my* ideas cannot exist in any other mind: so by 'the things I saw,' here, Berkeley must mean so-called physical objects. We should not charge Berkeley with contradicting himself, however, for we can interpret him to be implying only that we *mediately* perceive natural objects.

It is yet another non-conciliatory feature of Berkeley's world view, as he understands it, that all the things we immediately perceive, and hence all the things we really perceive, have only a fleeting existence. Since they are nothing but our own ideas, they cannot go on existing after we stop perceiving them. Must the same be said of the so-called physical objects that according to Berkeley we only *mediately* perceive?

In Berkeley's system, as we know, God causes all of our ideas of sense, and ordinary natural objects are nothing but collections, or families, of such ideas. This provides some kind of account of the nature and existence of those objects when they are actually being observed by a finite spirit. But what about all those indefinitely many times when they are not being so observed? Is Berkeley forced to hold

163

that trees and frogs pop into, and out of, existence as finite spirits begin to, and cease to, perceive them? The standard view of what Berkeley thinks about this has been that he believes that natural objects do not behave in any such bizarre way; rather, they exist continuously from the time of their creation to the time of their destruction, and they do so because God continuously perceives them, thus maintaining them in existence as ideas in His mind. Recently, however, Jonathan Bennett has disputed the standard view.[1] His position is summarized in the following passage:

> Berkeley does not regularly assume that objects exist when no human perceives them; he is not much interested in whether they do; and the continuity argument, which assumes that they do, is absent from the *Principles* and occurs in the *Dialogues* only in the two-sentence passage which I have quoted. That passage is right out of line with everything else Berkeley says about the continuity of objects, and should be dismissed as a momentary aberration.
> (Bennett (2), p. 171)

I propose to proceed as follows. First, I shall try to determine what Berkeley ought to say about God and the continuous existence of natural objects—that is, to determine what view best accords with Berkeley's fundamental principles. Then, I shall turn to the question of what Berkeley's view on these matters really is.

We can understand what Berkeley's attitude toward the continuity of sensible objects ought to be only if we keep firmly in mind exactly what his conception of such objects is. They are, as we know, collections, or families, of ideas of sense. But it is important to realize, now, that there are vastly more *possible* ideas of sense that would, if they were actual, belong to the family of such ideas that constitute what we call a single object, than there are *actual* ones. Suppose, for example, that you are alone in a field, looking at a fig tree. At any given time, you have merely one visual idea of sense of the tree. But at that very moment, we normally assume that there is also a back side to the tree, a very complicated insides, a root system, and so on—none of which is being perceived by anyone. Is Berkeley forced to say that these things don't exist at that moment? Certainly not. He can say that if, at that moment, you had been looking at the tree from the other side, you would have had such-and-such ideas of sense; if, at that moment, you had opened up the tree, you would have had such-and-such other ideas of sense—and so on. There are thus indefinitely many non-actual, possible, ideas of sense that give an extra degree of reality to any object. To say that there are possible ideas of sense is, of course, not to say that there are (actual) ideas of sense that belong to (or are perceived by) no finite mind; it is, rather, to say that God stands ready to cause those ideas of sense—to make them actual—in case any finite mind should be in a position to perceive (have) them. (Since minds are not really located in space, 'position' cannot be construed spatially here. A finite mind, M, is 'in a position to perceive [have] an idea of sense x' just in case M is in a certain state or has performed certain volitions, and in case one of God's rules of action is to cause in any mind that at time t is in such a state or has performed such volitions, an idea of type x soon after t.)

We can now see how Berkeley ought to understand the question of temporal continuity—the enduringness—of what we, in our bumbling way, call a single object, e.g., a fig tree. In particular, we can see that he should not be especially concerned about the reality of what we call an object during those times—and there will always be a huge number of such times—when no finite mind is perceiving 'it.' The reason he should not be concerned is that a so-called 'object' is nothing but a family of ideas of sense spread out over time; and just as a genuine family does not go out of existence when one of its members dies, thus leaving an unoccupied post in the family tree, so an 'object' does not go out of existence when there is an unoccupied position in its 'family tree'—i.e., when there happens not to exist any idea of sense belonging to that 'object.'

But the simple analogy with a family does not provide the whole story. For consider: the reason why a family does not cease to exist when one of its members dies is that there are other members of the family still in existence. A family exists only as long as at least one member of it is alive. But in the case of unobserved objects, there *are* no members of the family still 'alive.' So if the whole story about an object were that it is nothing but a family of ideas of sense, one would have to say that it ceases to exist every time that it is unobserved. But this is not the whole story, according to Berkeley; there is God to consider. It is not the case that there is just nothing in reality answering to an object at those times when it is unobserved: on the contrary, there is a readiness, indeed a positive intention, on God's part, to create whatever members of the family would have been required if various circumstances had existed. We may, therefore, call an object a *metaphysically grounded* family of ideas of sense. Such a family can survive the 'death' of all its members without going out of existence. This may be seen quite clearly if we consider what a genuine going out of existence—i.e., an annihilation—really amounts to. For example, suppose that a fig tree is blasted to smithereens by a bomb. After that catastrophe, no one, no matter what he does or where he goes, and no matter how hard he tries, can have an idea of sense that belongs to the family of such ideas that constitutes the tree. But that is not true of a fig tree, growing quietly in a field, to which nothing happens more drastic than that a lonely observer goes away, or blinks his eyes, leaving it for a time unobserved. Thanks be to God, innumerable ideas of sense of that tree continue to be available at any time, and no doubt many of them are eventually had by future observers. So no annihilation, no going out of existence, has occurred.

This way of accounting for the reality of the unobserved parts of observed objects and for the reality of unobserved objects can easily strike one as inadequate. One wants the object itself to be totally actual at all times and this would mean, for Berkeley, that there must at all times be actual ideas of sense belonging to the object. The temptation to think along these lines is entirely understandable—but also unjustifiable. Unjustifiable, that is, on Berkeley's conception of an object. When we demand something actual at all times, we are thinking of objects in a Lockean way—that is, as being entities that exist in their full reality (in three dimensions, with backs, insides, etc.) at every moment. An entity of that sort admittedly would not exist at any time during which there is nothing actual answering to it. But since that is not Berkeley's conception of an object, the same demand for continuous actuality cannot be made of him. Berkeley, by providing the aforementioned intention on God's part to cause ideas of sense, provides, as we have seen, enough reality to carry an object, as conceived of by him, across periods of not being observed.

To summarize: for Berkeley, what we ordinarily call a (single) physical object—e.g., a fig tree—is actually a huge metaphysically grounded family of ideas of sense. Some of these are actual ideas of sense, but most of them are non-actual, possible, ideas of sense. The series of *actual* ideas of sense that belong to the family that constitutes any given object is almost certain not to be temporally dense—that is, there will be moments at which none of them occurs. These are the moments when the object is unobserved. But Berkeley's system by no means entails that the object lapses into non-existence at such moments.

Still, the temptation to want something more, during periods of no observation, than God's readiness to provide ideas of sense is almost overwhelming. There is, moreover, an obvious move that looks as though it were open to Berkeley that would satisfy this felt need—namely, to say that God perceives all objects, and indeed all parts of all objects (even their insides), all the time. Ideas in God's mind would then yield existence to unobserved parts of observed objects and to all parts of unobserved objects: or we may say instead that God would be the perpetual observer of all parts of all things, thus maintaining them continuously in being.

Many readers of Berkeley think that he actually takes this step. In my opinion, however, it would be both pointless and impossible for Berkeley to try to make God into a kind of cosmic observer. It would be pointless, because what can ideas in God's mind do for the reality of unobserved objects that cannot be done by an intention on His part to cause suitable ideas of sense in the minds of finite observers, should the need have arisen? Ideas in God's mind are no more real, and provide no more reality, than such an intention on God's part provides. So nothing is to be gained by the proposed move.

But even if there were some advantage to be gained by the move, Berkeley in any case cannot make it. Whatever kind of act or process *perception* may be, it must at the very least be caused in part by something other than the perceiver. If this feature is missing, there may be hallucination, dreaming, fantasy, delusion, or whatever, but there will certainly not be the *perceiving* of anything. (Recall that for Berkeley ideas of sense are just those that are caused in us by God; he thus tacitly acknowledges that *human* perception, anyway, requires a cause external to the perceiver.) But nothing in Berkeley's system can fill the required causal role: 'no external being can affect [God]' (*3D* III (*W* II 241; A 203; T 186)). There could not be, in his world view, anything to act on God, for that would render God partially passive, whereas He must be 'an impassive, . . . purely active being' (*3D* II (*W* II 214; A 176; T 155)). So Berkeley's God cannot be a cosmic perceiver of anything.

It might be objected that although *human* perception requires a cause external to the perceiver, *divine* perception of things can be achieved by God's causing appropriate ideas of them in His own mind. But this proposal, too, makes God partially passive. It also suffers from being altogether *ad hoc*. God has ideas of all things, both actual and merely possible, in His understanding and He stands ready to cause ideas of sense of the actual things in finite minds; what conceivable motive could He have for wanting to cause perceptual ideas of actual things in His own mind?

This concludes my discussion of what I think Berkeley ought to say about God and the continuous existence of sensible objects. On my view, his system allows him to hold that the unobserved parts of observed objects, and all parts of unobserved objects, exist though not perceived by any finite mind; he has no reason to appeal to God's perception of sensible objects for this purpose, and there are anyway strong considerations preventing him from making any such appeal. It is time, now, to see what Berkeley himself actually says about these matters.

In the *Philosophical Commentaries*, we can see Berkeley wrestling with the problem of unobserved objects. It is fascinating, and instructive, to watch his dialectical labors. He begins with this view:

'Bodies etc do exist even w^n not perceiv'd they being powers in the active Being' (*PC* 52). At first glance, one might think that this is precisely the position that I have been saying Berkeley ought to adopt—but not so. If an object (e.g., a fig tree) is identified with God's powers when no finite spirit is observing it, then there is no avoiding the conclusion that the object is identical with those powers at *all* times; and then Berkeley would be forced to hold that our ideas of sense of the fig tree do not *constitute* the tree, but are mere *appearances* of the real fig tree (namely, the powers in God's mind), and he would thus be saddled with a view that is as fraught with skeptical consequences as the Lockean system is.

Berkeley soon shifts to a different account that makes no mention of God:

> The Trees are in the Park, that is, whether I will or no whether I imagine any thing about them or no, let me but go thither & open my Eyes by day & I shall not avoid seeing them. (*PC* 98; for another entry in the same vein, see *PC* 185a)

This is more promising: indeed, it could easily be elaborated into the very position I would have Berkeley adopt. But he takes a different line. He evidently supposes that what he has said implies that objects have a 'gappy' existence through time—i.e., that they do exist when they are being perceived, but do not exist when they are not being perceived—for when he next addresses himself to the problem, he writes:

> On account of my doctrine the identity of finite substances must consist in something else than continued existence, or relation to determin'd time and place of beginning to exist. the existence of our thoughts (wch being combin'd make all substances) being frequently interrupted, & they having divers beginnings, & endings. (*PC* 194)[2]

We can now, I think, detect an unfortunate assumption that Berkeley is making. He is assuming that the only way one can give God a rôle to play in the continuing existence of objects is by identifying objects with God's powers. I have suggested that there is another, far more satisfactory, way; but Berkeley evidently does not acknowledge that possibility. He rightly shrinks from holding that objects are divine powers, but then, seeing no other way for God to provide the continuity of objects, he leaves Him altogether out of the account and reasons that since objects are nothing but families of ideas of sense, and since these are in virtually every case gappy, the existence of objects is therefore gappy—they have 'divers beginnings, & endings.'

Notice, in *PC* 194, that there is no apparent panic in face of the gappiness in the history of objects; Berkeley just calmly contemplates it. Nevertheless, he must have felt some uneasiness about it—not surprisingly—for he soon reverts to the idea that objects are divine powers, although now he gives that view a new twist:

> Bodies etc do exist whether we think of 'em or no, they being taken in a twofold sense. Collections of thoughts & collections of powers to cause those thoughts. these later exist, tho perhaps a parte dei it may be one simple perfect power. (*PC* 282; see also *PC* 293)

This is not, however, a view that Berkeley can live with: it is nothing but a version of the hated Lockean dualism, with God's powers substituted for Lockean material objects.

His next effort is much better:

> Bodies taken for Powers do exist w^n not perceiv'd but this existence is not actual. w^n I say a power exists no more is meant than that if in ye light I open my eyes & look that way I shall see it i.e. ye body &c. (*PC* 293a)

As the final '&c' suggests, Berkeley does not want to restrict his explication of what it means to say that a power exists to just the first person nor to just vision: to say a power (of the kind here at issue) exists at a time *t* is to say that any suitable perceiver could perceive (see, hear, touch, etc.) the object at *t*. Although he does not explicitly say so, Berkeley is no doubt assuming that God is the metaphysical ground of the power he attributes here to bodies. With these qualifications, *PC* 293a comes as close as one could wish to the view that, in my opinion, Berkeley should adopt. (A similar view is implicit in *PC* 408.)

Later, however, Berkeley seems to lose faith in this view. He apparently becomes unwilling to accept the notion that when objects are not being perceived, there are no suitable ideas to constitute their existence; in the published works, anyway, he abandons the view of *PC* 293a and presents a different one. To be sure, traces of the *PC* 293a view remain. There is, for example, such a trace in this passage from the *Principles*:

> I think an intuitive knowledge may be obtained of this, by any one that shall attend to what is meant by the term *exist* when applied to sensible things. The table I write on, I say, exists, that is, I see and feel it; and if I were out of my study I should say it existed, meaning thereby that if I was in my study I might perceive it, or that some other spirit actually does perceive it. (*PHK* I 3)

169

If we correct the undue emphasis on the first person, what this passage says is that the existence of perceived objects consists in their being perceived, and the existence of unperceived objects consists in the fact that if, contrary to fact, there were suitable perceivers, they would perceive those objects.

There is another trace of the *PC* 293a view in the *Three Dialogues* where Berkeley attaches the following sense to the biblical account of the creation of the world:

> Philonous. Why, I imagine that if I had been present at the Creation, I should have seen things produced into being; that is, become perceptible, in the order prescribed by the sacred historian. (*3D* III (*W* II 251; A 214; T 199))

But these are mere remnants of an abandoned view; a new, and quite different, view replaces it in the published works.

The seeds of this final view are to be found in the *Philosophical Commentaries*. In the *Principles*, Berkeley merely hints at it, and it is not until the *Three Dialogues* that we find the final view clearly and confidently voiced. Let us trace these steps.

The beginnings are contained in these passages from the *Philosophical Commentaries*:

> You ask me whether the books are in the study now w^n no one is there to see them. I answer yes. you ask me are we not in the wrong for imagining things to exist w^n they are not actually perceiv'd by the senses. I answer no. the existence of our ideas consists in being perceiv'd, imagin'd thought on whenever they are imagin'd or thought on they do exist. Whenever they are mention'd or discours'd of they are imagin'd & thought on therefore you can at no time ask me whether they exist or no, but by reason of y^t very question they must necessarily exist. (*PC* 472)

> But say you then a Chimaera does exist. I answer it doth in one sense. i.e. it is imagin'd. but it must be well noted that existence is vulgarly restrain'd to actuall perception. & that I use the word Existence in a larger sense than ordinary. (*PC* 473)

Here, Berkeley copes with the problem of unperceived objects by a tactical maneuver: 'Just try to give me an example of an unperceived object that does not exist,' he dares his opponent, 'and you will refute yourself in the very attempt.' Berkeley does not employ this maneuver in his published writings to solve the problem of unperceived objects that is posed by his own system. (He uses it, rather, as we saw, in his attack against Locke.) But *PC* 472 and 473 nevertheless point the way to his final solution of that problem. What this final solution is may be seen—at last—if we consider this passage:

> The propertys of all things are in God i.e. there is in the Deity Understanding as well as Will. He is no Blind agent & in truth a blind Agent is a Contradiction. (*PC* 812)

The following is the view—what I claim to be Berkeley's final view—about the existence of unperceived objects that Berkeley will later construct from these materials found in *PC* 427, 473, and 812. God must be considered to have in His understanding ideas of all things, including ideas of all objects in the world. He certainly could not be thought to cause our ideas of sense without being guided by ideas of the relevant objects; for 'He is no Blind agent.' But if God has ideas of all the objects of the world in His understanding, then they may be said to exist in His mind—just as a chimaera exists in a person's mind when he thinks of one. This is not the usual, first-class kind of existence that belongs to things that are actually perceived, of course—a chimaera is not as real as the desk one can see before one's very eyes—but if, as Berkeley is determined to do, we 'use the word Existence in a larger sense than ordinary,' we may say that any object has existence just in virtue of the fact that God thinks of it (i.e., has ideas of it). Here, then, is a way for Berkeley to hold that unperceived objects continue to exist: they continue to exist in the mind of God, since He always has ideas of every object.

This is the view that I claim to be Berkeley's considered (or final) view about the existence of unperceived objects. I shall try to justify this claim by examining the relevant passages from the published works; but first I have to remark that I think the doctrine is by no means an attractive one. Anyone who wants to, or does, believe that objects continue to exist when no finite creature is observing them—and this includes at least all of mankind who are sane—should not be satisfied with the statement that they merely continue to exist in God's mind. It is, in the first place, little more than a bad joke to claim that a thing exists simply in virtue of the fact that someone has an idea of it in his understanding—i.e., is thinking of it. Imagine, for example, what your response might be to someone who asserted that there is a purple man with three heads, and who explained his remark by saying 'Yes, he exists in my daughter's mind, since she is thinking about such a man.' The truth is, of course, that to say a purple man with three heads exists in someone's mind is just another way of saying that there is no such creature. And why should this situation be any different when we shift from an idea in a finite understanding to an idea in an infinite one (God's)? The weakness of Berkeley's position can be seen, too, if we remember that

God must have ideas of all possible worlds in His mind, in addition to ideas of this actual world. The kind of existence that Berkeley accords to unperceived objects of this world, then, is precisely the kind that objects in merely possible, but non-actual, worlds have—e.g., the kind and amount that a purple man with three heads has. No one, I say, should be satisfied with so little.

The obvious way to remedy this defect in Berkeley's position, it might naturally be thought, would be to have God not merely *think* about unperceived objects, but actually *perceive* them. But this cure, I have argued, is not available; and we shall find, when we turn to the texts, that Berkeley wisely avoids taking that course. Rather than connecting the existence of unperceived objects to ideas in God's understanding, or to perceptual ideas in God's mind, Berkeley would do far better to tie their existence to God's *will*; this would be a move in the direction of the view I have suggested Berkeley ought to adopt. As a matter of fact, in the *Three Dialogues* Berkeley flirts briefly with the idea that there is an essential connection between the existence of unperceived objects and God's will, when he suggests that the creation of the world might have consisted in God's decreeing that objects 'should become perceptible to intelligent creatures' (*3D* III (*W* II 253; A 216; T 201)). But this is just a brief interlude, unhappily; the main thrust of Berkeley's remarks about the existence of unperceived objects, in the published works, lies in the direction of what I have been calling his final, or considered, view.

It might be thought that the final, or considered, view is open to the following objection: On the final view, God has in His understanding ideas of all objects. But His ideas must be of the objects as they really are. Since God's ideas must be totally different from ours, it looks as though we do not perceive objects as they really are.

The answer to this objection is that although God's ideas of objects are no doubt quite different from ours, and perhaps even in certain respects incomprehensible to us, there is still no reason why the final view must therefore lead to skepticism—for the view can maintain, altogether plausibly, that these ideas of objects in God's mind are ideas of how objects will appear to us, or how they will be perceived by us, in all possible circumstances. Or perhaps it would be better to put it this way: they are rules for the production of suitable ideas of sense in finite perceivers. These general rules in God's mind would constitute what Berkeley calls the *archetypes* of objects: 'And . . . so may you suppose an external archetype on my principles; *external*, I mean, to your own mind; though indeed it must be supposed to exist in that mind which comprehends all things' (*3D* III (*W* II 248; A 210f; T 195); see also Berkeley's second letter to Johnson (*W* II 292)).

Let us turn, now, to Berkeley's texts. I propose to go through the

Principles and then the *Three Dialogues*, picking out the most important passages that deal with the existence of unperceived objects. The first relevant passage is the one from *PHK* I 3 that was quoted and discussed above (p. 169f). It is a remnant of an earlier view that must still have had some appeal for Berkeley, but which is for the most part abandoned in the published writings. It will be instructive to consider together all the other relevant passages in the *Principles*; surprisingly, there are only three:

a. Some truths there are so near and obvious to the mind, that a man need only open his eyes to see them. Such I take this important one to be, to wit, that all the choir of heaven and furniture of the earth, in a word all those bodies which compose the mighty frame of the world, have not any subsistence without a mind, that their being is to be perceived or known; that consequently so long as they are not actually perceived by me, or do not exist in my mind or that of any other created spirit, they must either have no existence at all, or else subsist in the mind of some eternal spirit: it being perfectly unintelligible and involving all the absurdity of abstraction, to attribute to any single part of them an existence independent of a spirit. (*PHK* I 6)

b. [I]t will be objected that from the foregoing principles it follows, things are every moment annihilated and created anew. The objects of sense exist only when they are perceived: the trees therefore are in the garden, or the chairs in the parlour, no longer than while there is some body by to perceive them. Upon shutting my eyes all the furniture in the room is reduced to nothing, and barely upon opening them it is again created [*PHK* I 45]. . . . If we consider it, the objection proposed in *Sect.* 45 will not be found reasonably charged on the principles we have premised, so as in truth to make any objection at all against our notions. For though we hold indeed the objects of sense to be nothing else but ideas which cannot exist unperceived; yet we may not hence conclude they have no existence except only while they are perceived by us, since there may be some other spirit that perceives them, though we do not. Wherever bodies are said to have no existence without the mind, I would not be understood to mean this or that particular mind, but all minds whatsoever. It does not therefore follow from the foregoing principles, that bodies are annihilated and created every moment, or exist not at all during the intervals between our perception of them. (*PHK* I 48)

   c. Again, the things perceived by sense may be termed *external*, with regard to their origin, in that they are not generated from within, by the mind it self, but imprinted by a spirit distinct from that which perceives them. Sensible objects may likewise be said to be without the mind, in another sense, namely, when they exist in some other mind. Thus when I shut my eyes, the things I saw may still exist, but it must be in another mind. (*PHK* I 90)

An extraordinary feature of these statements is the studied refusal to make a firm commitment to the existence of unperceived objects. Objects not perceived by me or any other created spirit 'either have no existence at all, or else subsist in the mind of some eternal spirit' (passage a), 'It does not follow' from Berkeley's principles 'that bodies . . . exist not at all during the intervals between our perception of them' (passage b), 'When I shut my eyes, the things I saw may still exist . . .' (passage c). It is a stunning fact that Berkeley should display indecision in this definitive work on a matter of such importance. I want to suggest the following hypothesis to explain this fact: Berkeley, in the *Principles*, is between theories, as it were, and really does not know what to think about the status of unperceived objects. The view that I have called the *PC* 293a view must still have some hold on him, for we find a trace of it in the passage from *PHK* I 3 referred to at the beginning of this paragraph. But on this view, there are no actual ideas to constitute the reality of unperceived objects, and this feature doubtless leads Berkeley, by the time he writes the *Principles*, to regard the view with suspicion, at least, and in fact to think that it probably ought to be rejected. It seems perfectly clear, on the other hand, that in the *Principles* he has no other view to put in its place. The result is that Berkeley is unable to cope with the problem at all: he cannot decide whether or not unobserved objects, in his system, should be said to have any existence at all. The possibility of his final view, which offers a solution to the problem, has occurred to him, as we can tell from passage a; but he obviously has not even begun to adopt it as his considered position, for he mentions it nowhere else in the *Principles*, and even in passage a it is put forward merely as one side of a disjunction. In the *Principles*, then, Berkeley takes no definite stand on the question of whether unobserved objects exist or not, for he does not know what stand best to take.

If it is asked how Berkeley can publish a work when this issue has not been resolved in his own mind, the answer may very well be that although *we* consider the issue to be of great importance, and although Berkeley gives some thought to it in the *Philosophical*

Commentaries, nevertheless in the *Principles* he considers the matter to be of only secondary importance. He thinks, remember, that mere practical considerations account for the fact that our language contains the names of so-called physical objects (cf. *3D* III (*W* II 245; A 207; T 191) and *NTV* 49); and he implies that the existence of these names produces the confused belief that they signify some kind of entity. In the *Principles*, as I have already remarked, Berkeley is in a decidedly non-conciliatory mood, and so doubtless feels no need to speculate about the continuous existence of these alleged entities.

Let us turn, now, to the more conciliatory *Three Dialogues*. Here, Berkeley does finally come forward with an explicit theory about the existence of unobserved natural objects. It is not perfectly clear, however, precisely what theory he offers. There are only these two possibilities: first, that God preserves them in existence by continuously perceiving them, and second, that God preserves them in existence by thinking of them—i.e., by having ideas of them in His understanding. I shall call the first, the *Perception Theory*, and the second, the *Conception Theory*. The standard interpretation of Berkeley has him espousing the Perception Theory, whereas I think he embraces the Conception Theory.

It seems to me that there are three kinds of relevant passages in the *Three Dialogues*: (I) those that either explicitly state the Conception Theory or else are most plausibly read as asserting it, (II) those that are neutral as between the Conception Theory and the Perception Theory, and (III) those that seem to state the Perception Theory, but that can be read, without any, or any undue, forcing, in such a way as to be consistent with the Conception Theory. In view of the type-I passages, and in view of the fact that the Perception Theory, as I have argued, is not open to Berkeley, I think that we ought to read the type-III (and, of course, the type-II) passages in the way required by the Conception Theory.

Let us dispose quickly of the type-II passages. Here they are:

1. To me it is evident, for the reasons you allow of, that sensible things cannot exist otherwise than in a mind or spirit. Whence I conclude, not that they have no real existence, but that seeing they depend not on my thought, and have an existence distinct from being perceived by me, *there must be some other mind wherein they exist.* As sure therefore as the sensible world really exists, so sure is there an infinite omnipresent spirit who contains and supports it. (*3D* II (*W* II 212; A 174f; T 153))

2. Take here in brief my meaning. It is evident that the things I perceive are my own ideas, and that no idea can exist unless it

be in a mind. Nor is it less plain that these ideas or things by me perceived, either themselves or their archetypes, exist independently of my mind, since I know myself not to be their author, it being out of my power to determine at pleasure, what particular ideas I shall be affected with upon opening my eyes or ears. They must therefore exist in some other mind, whose will it is they should be exhibited to me. (*3D* II (*W* II 214f; A 177; T 156))

I take it as obvious that these passages are consistent with both the Perception Theory and the Conception Theory.

There are four type-I passages—i.e., passages that seem to require the Conception Theory:

3. Mark it well; I do not say, I see things by perceiving that which represents them in the intelligible substance of God. This I do not understand; but I say, the things by me perceived are known by the understanding, and produced by the will, of an infinite spirit. (*3D* II (*W* II 215; A 178; T 157))

4. Hylas. Supposing you were annihilated, cannot you conceive it possible, that things perceivable by sense may still exist?
   Philonous. I can; but then it must be in another mind. When I deny sensible things an existence out of the mind, I do not mean my mind in particular, but all minds. Now it is plain they have an existence exterior to my mind, since I find them by experience to be independent of it. There is therefore some other mind wherein they exist, during the intervals between the times of my perceiving them: as likewise they did before my birth, and would do after my supposed annihilation. And as the same is true, with regard to all other finite created spirits; it necessarily follows there is an *omnipresent eternal Mind*, which knows and comprehends all things, and exhibits them to our view in such a manner, and according to such rules as he himself hath ordained, and are by us termed the *Laws of Nature*. (*3D* III (*W* II 230f; A 193; T 175))

5. Hylas. But be your opinion never so true, yet surely you will not deny it is shocking, and contrary to the common sense of men. Ask the fellow, whether yonder tree has an existence out of his mind: what answer think you he would make?
   Philonous. The same that I should my self, to wit, that it doth exist out of his mind. But then to a Christian it cannot surely be shocking to say, the real tree existing without his mind is truly known and comprehended by (that is,

176

exists in) the infinite mind of God. (*3D* III (*W* II 234f; A 197; T 179f))

6. And . . . so may you suppose an external archetype on my principles; *external*, I mean, to your own mind; though indeed it must be supposed to exist in that mind which comprehends all things. (*3D* III (*W* II 248; A 210f; T 195))

Passage 3 provides very powerful support for the view that Berkeley accepts the Conception Theory. The others, I suggest, are most plausibly read as supporting that view; for it seems more plausible to think that God's *knowing* and *comprehending* objects involves His having ideas of them in His understanding than to think that it is a matter of His perceiving them.

Notice, before we proceed, that in passage 4, Berkeley attempts to *demonstrate* that God exists as the mind that maintains natural objects in existence when they are not being observed by finite spirits. Bennett calls this the continuity argument for God's existence (Bennett (2), pp. 169–72). I agree with him that the argument is vitiated by Berkeley's conflating these two quite distinct conceptions of an idea's *depending on* a mind: (a) an idea's *being caused by* a mind, and (b) an idea's *being had by* (and hence existing in) a mind. (See Bennett (2), pp. 166–9; the same conflation occurs in passages 1 and 2, above, as well.) My main concern here, however, is not with Berkeley's argument, nor with its validity or non-validity, but rather with the nature of its conclusion: that is, I am trying to determine just how, according to Berkeley, God maintains natural objects in existence when they are not being observed by finite spirits.

To continue: there are three passages of type-III— i.e., passages that seem to require the Perception Theory:

7. Philonous. Men commonly believe that all things are known or perceived by God, because they believe the being of a God, whereas I on the other side, immediately and necessarily conclude the being of a God, because all sensible things must be perceived by him.
Hylas. But so long as we all believe the same thing, what matter is it how we come by that belief?
Philonous. But neither do we agree in the same opinion. For philosophers, though they acknowledge all corporeal beings to be perceived by God, yet they attribute to them an absolute subsistence distinct from their being perceived by any mind whatever, which I do not. Besides, is there no difference between saying, *there is a God, therefore he perceives all things*: and saying, *sensible things do really exist: and if*

177

they really exist, they are necessarily perceived by an infinite mind: therefore there is an infinite mind, or God. This furnishes you with a direct and immediate demonstration, from a most evident principle, of the *being of a God.*
(*3D* II (*W* II 212; A 175; T 153f))

8. The question between the materialists and me is not, whether things have a real existence out of the mind of this or that person, but whether they have an absolute existence, distinct from being perceived by God, and exterior to all minds.
(*3D* III (*W* II 235; A 197; T 180))

9. every unthinking being is necessarily, and from the very nature of its existence, perceived by some mind; if not by any finite created mind, yet certainly by the infinite mind of God. (*3D* III (*W* II 236; A 198; T 181))

Let us consider each of these in turn. In the context of passage 7, there is a hint that Berkeley may be using the word 'perceive' loosely. In the passage immediately preceding passage 7, Hylas refers to the belief, held by all who believe in God, that God 'knows and comprehends all things.' As I remarked earlier, this expression suggests the view that God has ideas of things in His understanding, rather than the view that He perceives them. But at the beginning of passage 7, Philonous clearly takes himself to be simply repeating the belief just expressed by Hylas, when he says 'Men commonly believe that all things are known or perceived by God.' So it would not be implausible to read the 'perceived' as meaning *comprehended* or *understood*. We can even see why Berkeley should introduce the word 'perceived' at this particular juncture. In the later parts of passage 7, Berkeley has occasion to refer several times to the epistemic relationship between God and sensible objects. He does not want to have to use the cumbersome expression 'knows and comprehends' to designate this relationship each time; he prefers to use a *single* term. So when, at the beginning of passage 7, he says 'all things are known or perceived by God,' he introduces the word 'perceived' as a convenient term to be used in what follows to stand for God's awareness of objects. 'Perceive' thus means, in passage 7, no more than *have an idea of.* Read in this way, passage 7 is consistent with the Conception Theory. I do not, of course, say that it *has* to be read in this way, but only that it easily and plausibly can be so interpreted. And, since we have strong independent grounds for thinking that Berkeley accepts the Conception Theory rather than the Perception Theory, we have a right to read it in this way.

An exactly similar account can be given of passages 8 and 9. They, like passage 7, are immediately preceded by a passage in which Berkeley speaks of natural objects' being 'known and comprehended by (that is, *exist[ing] in*)' the mind of God. And, as in 7, I think we can reasonably read the 'perceive' in 8 and 9 as a convenient term that means no more than 'have an idea of.'

The most plausible conclusion to be drawn from our review of passages from the *Three Dialogues* is that Berkeley accepts the Conception Theory, not the Perception Theory.[3] This interpretation certainly accords with his last views on the subject, as the following words from *Siris* conclusively show:

> There is no sense nor sensory, nor anything like a sense or sensory, in God. Sense implies an impression from some other being, and denotes a dependence in the soul which hath it. Sense is a passion; and passions imply imperfection. God knoweth all things as pure mind or intellect; but nothing by sense, nor in nor through a sensory. (*Siris* 289)

The Conception Theory, although better than its rival, is still inadequate, since it gives no more reality to unobserved objects than any merely logically possible object has—for example, no more than a purple man with three heads has. The way to remedy this defect, within the limits of Berkeley's system, is not to augment the reality of unobserved objects by adding perceptual ideas of them in the divine mind (the Perception Theory), but rather to augment it with a dispositional state of God's will—namely, with God's being so disposed that if, contrary to fact, there were any appropriate observers, He would cause them to have suitable ideas of sense. By 'suitable ideas of sense' I mean ideas of sense that have the right sort of content, and that are 'more strong, lively, and distinct than [ideas] of the imagination' (*PHK* I 30) and that are coherent (*ibid.*). God *is* in such a state with respect to the toothbrush in my unoccupied bathroom, and *is not* in such a state, as far as I know, with respect to any purple man with three heads. This addition would be a great improvement on the Conception Theory, and the result would be a view that is, in essence, the same as the unhappily abandoned *PC* 293a view.

XI

Berkeley's View
of the Mind

We turn now to Berkeley's conception of the mind. His theories of its nature are inextricably bound up with his views on the meaningfulness of terms, as we shall see. I use the phrase 'views on the meaningfulness of terms' advisedly. The word 'views,' in the plural, indicates that Berkeley's beliefs on this subject changed over the years—and so, correspondingly, did his conception of the mind. I use the word 'meaningfulness,' which I dislike, rather than 'meaning,' because I want to avoid the suggestion that Berkeley at any time has a theory of what the meaning of a term is. He has views about such things as what it is for a word to 'be significant' or to have a meaning, and what it is to know or understand the meaning of a word; but wisely he nowhere attempts to specify what the meaning of a word actually is.

Berkeley's first doctrine about the meaningfulness of words is that every word stands for (signifies, or denotes) some ideas, and this relation to ideas renders words significant; their having a meaning just *is* their standing for some genuine ideas. (Let us call this the Idea Doctrine of the meaningfulness of terms—or, for short, the Idea Doctrine.) Thus, in his early notebooks he writes: 'All significant words stand for Ideas' (*PC* 378).

What the Idea Doctrine says, as I understand it, is that a meaningful *singular* term (e.g., a proper name) denotes a huge family of actual and possible ideas of sense—the family, namely, that on Berkeley's view actually constitutes the individual thing that the singular term is used to refer to—and that a meaningful *general* term denotes either a certain range of such families of ideas (as the general term 'chair,' for example, denotes all actual and possible chairs) or a range of individual ideas that instantiate a certain property (as the general term 'red,' for example, denotes all actual and possible ideas that embody redness). The Idea Doctrine also contains, implicitly, a thesis about what it is for a person to know the meaning of terms, and, in general, to use language meaningfully—that is, for a person to say something and to understand what he says, or to hear something and to understand what he hears. I am not sure that Berkeley, at this early stage, thinks that in order for a person to use language meaningfully, he must, every time he uses language, entertain one or more relevant ideas for each word that is used, but as he understands the Idea Doctrine, it certainly implies, anyway, that the person must at least *be able* to conjure up one or more relevant ideas for each word that is used. (I assume that it is clear what a *relevant* idea for each type of word would be: thus, for example, a relevant idea for a singular term would be a copy of one of the ideas of sense that constitute the denoted individual thing.)

No word to be used without an idea. (*PC* 422)

I affirm 'tis manifestly absurd. no excuse in ye world can be given why a man should use a word without an idea. Certainly we shall find that w^{t}ever word we make use of in matter of pure reasoning has or ought to have a compleat Idea annext to it. i.e.: its' meaning or the sense we take it in must be completely known. (*PC* 638)

Let us see, now, what consequences the Idea Doctrine has for Berkeley's conception of the mind. Descartes held that the mind is an unextended, immaterial, or spiritual substance entirely distinct from, though causally connected with, the body, a material substance. Locke, with misgivings, accepted essentially the same view. Given such views held by Berkeley's philosophical forbears, and remembering that he has eliminated material substance, we should be surprised if he were to deny that the mind is a special kind of substance. In his major works, notably in the *Principles* and in the *Three Dialogues*, as everyone knows, he does officially espouse the view that the mind is a simple immaterial, spiritual substance. We shall deal with this official doctrine later. But, first, we must notice that in the central part of the earlier *Philosophical Commentaries*, the Idea Doctrine leads Berkeley to vigorously deny that the mind is a mental substance. Let us see how this comes about.

On any mental substance view of the mind, it would seem, one must distinguish these two kinds of mental elements: on the one hand, such things as ideas, images, dreams, sensations, feelings, and so on, and, on the other hand, that which entertains, or is conscious of, the ideas, images, and the rest.[1] In the *Philosophical Commentaries*, Berkeley usually calls the first kind of elements 'perceptions,' but he also calls them 'ideas'; so I shall use both terms in what follows. To refer to the second element, I shall use part or all of the noncommittal, though awkward, expression 'the thing that has (or perceives) ideas (or perceptions).' In the main part of the *Commentaries*—I mean the part that runs up through the sections numbered in the middle 600s, roughly—we find Berkeley denying the existence of the thing that has, or perceives, ideas. The mind, on this early view, is nothing more than the perceptions that occur in its history: it is a bundle (to use Hume's phrase), or a congeries (to use Berkeley's) of perceptions:

The very existence of Ideas constitutes the soul. (*PC* 577)

Mind is a congeries of Perceptions. Take away Perceptions & you take away the Mind put the Perceptions & you put the mind. (*PC* 580)

This 'congeries of perceptions' view of the mind is a fairly direct consequence of the Idea Doctrine. According to Berkeley, we are not aware of the (alleged) thing that has, or perceives, ideas—we are aware only of the ideas themselves. The (alleged) thing that has, or perceives, ideas, then, is not itself an idea (nor, presumably, is it a family of ideas). This must seem obvious to Berkeley on other grounds as well; for he surely assumes that it is nonsense to speak of an idea perceiving another idea (see *3D* III (*W* II 233f; A 196; T 178f). Any term purporting to denote the (alleged) thing that has ideas, then, is meaningless, according to the Idea Doctrine. So the mind must consist of just 'its' perceptions alone:

Say you the Mind is not the Perceptions. but that thing wch perceives. I answer you are abus'd by the words that & thing these are vague empty words wthout a meaning. (*PC* 581; see also *PC* 579)

You would naturally suppose that this view of the mind has the consequence that one's mind does not exist when one has no ideas—that it simply goes out like a flame when there are no ideas to constitute its existence; and Berkeley even says at one point that 'in sleep & trances the mind exists not' (*PC* 651). But in fact, given his view of time, he should not say this, for according to that view, surprisingly, the mind never ceases to exist. However, I want to postpone our discussion of Berkeley's theory of time and its bearing on the mind's existence; see below, pp. 206–11.

For a while, Berkeley is content with the 'congeries of perceptions' view. He raises the question of the will, but for the moment sees nothing wrong with treating it as a congeries of individual volitions:

'The Will not distinct from Particular volitions' (*PC* 615). Like Hume, however, Berkeley does not remain satisfied for long with the bundle theory. His first worry about it makes a hesitant appearance in the following passage:

> Say you there must be a thinking substance. Somthing unknown wch perceives & supports & ties together the Ideas. Say I, make it appear there is any need of it & you shall have it for me. I care not to take away any thing I can see the least reason to think should exist. (*PC* 637)

Here Berkeley shows signs of becoming concerned about a certain fundamental unity that we experience in our mental lives. I may have several perceptions simultaneously: feeling an itch on my arm, hearing a sound outside, seeing a picture across the room, and perhaps others as well. These ideas do not exist, however, as a mere multiplicity, as just so many different experiences. No, one and the same thing seems to be having each of these experiences—namely, *I* myself (see *PC* 744). The same goes for perceptions that I have at different times. But it seems that a congeries of perceptions cannot provide its own unity; certainly no one of the ideas in the bundle can be thought to perceive all the rest! Berkeley later sees this inadequacy of his own early 'congeries of perceptions' view of the mind. Thus, in the *Three Dialogues*, he says 'I know that I, one and the same self, perceive both colours and sounds,' and he takes this to show that 'I my self am not my ideas,' but rather 'one individual principle, distinct from colour and sound; and, for the same reason, from all other sensible things and inert ideas' (*3D* (*W* II 233f; A 196; T 178f)).[2] Whether or not the unity of the mind demands that it be a substance, as Berkeley supposes in his later writings, he is surely right in thinking that the bundle theory, by itself, cannot account for this fundamental feature of our conscious lives.

I want now to digress briefly from the main line of argument to discuss a charge of inconsistency that might be raised against Berkeley when he talks about the unity of the mind. The charge is well put by S. C. Brown:

> He insists that our talk of *unity* in the case of extended things is no more than a convenience, that the unity ascribed is conferred by us upon mere collections of ideas: yet when he writes of spirits he is willing to grant them a real, and not merely a notional, unity.[3]

Berkeley says that number does not really exist in things themselves, but is entirely 'the creature of the mind' (*NTV* 109).[4] It is quite clear that by 'things,' he means so-called physical things. His fundamental point, I think, is that there is no intrinsic, or metaphysical, unity in the physical world, but only an imposed unity that derives from the concepts one happens to have. For example: if there exist in a given place a multitude of leaves, a trunk, some branches, twigs, and roots, all disposed in a certain familiar way and all functioning normally, then there is—necessarily—one tree in that place, for that is what we call a (single) tree. But the unity is not absolute, not inherent in the very nature of the things that constitute the multitude; it derives entirely from the fact that we happen to have the concept of a tree. We may say, to employ a terminology invoked by S. C. Brown, that between the multitude of tree parts and the tree there is a necessary many-one relation, but it is merely a semantically necessary many-one relation. When we consider the mind itself, however, the situation seems to be quite different. In any given mind, we have a multiplicity—namely, of ideas[5]—but in this case there is a necessary many-one relation to something (the mind whose ideas they are), a relation whose necessity cannot be totally accounted for in semantical terms alone. The ideas must all be had by (or perceived by) something—some *one* thing—namely, by the mind. There just are not, and cannot be, free-floating ideas that we simply happen to group together in certain ways and call 'minds'—ways that might be altogether different; because each of us knows, as I remarked earlier, that all of his ideas are had by one and the same 'thing,' namely, himself or his mind.

This argument is at least suggested by the things Berkeley says in his principal published works, and I think he really does subscribe to it, or something very like it. A full discussion of the important and complex issues involved is out of the question here; I shall have to content myself with the remark that the argument by itself certainly does not prove that the mind is an immaterial, unextended substance—and I'm sure Berkeley knows that it doesn't. It shows at most only that there is something-or-other, not an idea, that has a whole series of ideas; the nature of this 'thing' is left completely open. Let us return, now, to the main line of argument.

A related difficulty with the bundle theory of the mind that Berkeley does not explicitly mention in the *Philosophical Commentaries*, but which may nevertheless make him unhappy with it, is this: if, as the bundle theory seems to suggest, the perceptions that constitute a given mind just *happen* to be bundled together, then it ought to be possible for an individual perception to be detached from all other perceptions—that is, for it to be 'in,' or perceived by, no mind at all. Hume—sometimes, at least—considers such a possibility to be perfectly intelligible.[6] But Berkeley never wavers in his conviction that it is nonsense to speak of an unperceived idea. Thus, for example, in the *Three Dialogues* he says that 'a necessary relation to the mind is understood to be implied' by the term 'idea' (*3D* III (*W* II 235f; A 198; T 181); see also *PC* 377, and *PHK* I 4).

Another worry about the bundle theory bulks much larger in Berkeley's thought than the others: it concerns activity or power. Berkeley seems always to have been convinced that the will is active, and is indeed the only active thing that there is in the world: 'No active power but the will, therefore matter if it exists affects us not' (*PC* 131). There is, to be sure, a moment of doubt in the following remarkable entry:

> The simple idea call'd Power seems obscure or rather none at all. but onely the relation 'twixt cause & Effect. W^n I ask whether A can move B. if A be an intelligent thing. I mean no more than whether the volition of A that B move be attended with the motion of B, if A be senseless whether the impulse of A against B be follow'd by ye motion of B. (*PC* 461)

But this Humean doubt disappears at once, and Berkeley seems never again to waver in his conviction that the will is a, and in fact *the*, genuine active power in the world.

I suggested in Chapter VIII that there is considerable plausibility in this notion that the will is a real active force (cf. p. 133). But what we must notice now is that it creates problems both for Berkeley's bundle theory of the mind and for his Idea Doctrine. Let's consider the bundle theory first. The mind, Berkeley has said, is a congeries (bundle) of ideas. Volitions, however, as Berkeley apparently sees, are *not* ideas—that is, we are not directly aware of them, they are not direct objects of awareness. Although the point is not absolutely explicit in the *Philosophical Commentaries*, several passages strongly suggest that Berkeley wants to go along with the view that in standard cases of volition, one is directly aware of nothing more than (i) the idea of an action (or, more precisely, the idea of oneself performing a certain action), and (ii) a feeling of uneasiness that the action is not yet being performed. Neither one of these two ideas is the volition itself, nor is their combination:

> The act of the Will or volition is not uneasiness for that uneasiness may be without volition. (*PC* 611) Volition is distinct from the object or Idea for the same reason. (*PC* 612)
>
> Also from uneasiness & Idea together. (*PC* 613; see also *PC* 624)

(Berkeley adds that there can be volition even without any feeling of uneasiness: see *PC* 628, 630.) Berkeley does not doubt that an act of volition must be something real, in addition to the idea of the desired action and the feeling of uneasiness (if any) (cf. *PC* 598); but he sees that it cannot be an idea—i.e., an object of direct awareness. The will may be a congeries of volitions, but it certainly cannot be a congeries of ideas:

> The grand Cause of perplexity & darkness in treating of the Will, is that we Imagine it to be an object of thought (to speak wth the vulgar), we think we may perceive, contemplate & view it like any of our Ideas whereas in truth 'tis no idea. Nor is there any Idea of it. tis toto coelo different from the Understanding i.e. from all our Ideas. If you say the will or rather a Volition is something I answer there is an Homonymy in the world thing w^{n} apply'd to Ideas & volitions & understanding & will. all ideas are passive, volitions active. (*PC* 643)

Clearly, Berkeley's original view that the mind is a congeries of perceptions (i.e., ideas) must now be abandoned; for the will is at least an important part of the mind, and it is not a congeries of ideas. Berkeley could conceivably modify his original theory of the mind as follows: he could hold that the mind has two parts—a conscious part consisting of ideas, and an unconscious part consisting of volitions. But, in fact, he takes a more drastic course. Berkeley is impressed by the fact that ideas are inactive; he announces this doctrine, as we have just seen, in *PC* 643, and later in the published works.[7] At this stage of his evolving thought, Berkeley apparently wants to expel all inactivity from the mind, for he now abandons the 'congeries of perceptions' view and boldly identifies the mind with the will, and denies that ideas are any part of the mind: 'The Spirit the Active thing that wch is Soul & God is the Will alone. The Ideas are effects impotent things' (*PC* 712; see also *PC* 478a). (Notice that this new view entails that a person—i.e., his mind—is constantly performing acts of volition, as Berkeley clearly sees: 'While I exist or have any Idea I am eternally, constantly willing, my acquiescing in the present State is willing' (*PC* 791).)

The view that the mind is essentially active not only wrecks the 'congeries of perceptions' theory of the mind—it also forces Berkeley to scuttle his Idea Doctrine. As we have seen, Berkeley holds that we are not directly aware of any volitions. This leads him to maintain that we have no idea of a volition, because he supposes that an idea (i.e., an idea of reason, as contrasted with an idea of sense or an idea of introspection) must be a copy of (and indeed must resemble) something that we can be directly aware of or must anyway be reducible to copies of such things: 'To ask have we an idea of ye Will or volition is nonsense. an idea can resemble nothing but an idea' (*PC* 657; see also *PC* 663). To put the point in another way: since all

186

ideas are inactive, none of them can be a copy of—i.e., resemble—and hence be the idea of, a volition or the will: 'No Perception according to Locke is active. Therefore no perception (i.e., no Idea) can be the image of or like unto that wch is altogether active & not at all passive i.e. the Will' (*PC* 706).

If Berkeley were to hold on to the Idea Doctrine, he would have to say that it is nonsense to talk about volitions or the will—and this would mean, since the mind has now been identified with the will, that it is nonsense to talk about the mind. In that case, Berkeley would of course have to deny the existence of the mind, just as, earlier, he denied the existence of that (alleged) thing that has perceptions, when he espoused the 'congeries of perceptions' theory. But since Berkeley cannot possibly allow that the mind does not exist, he promptly, and rightly, abandons the Idea Doctrine:

> Some words there are wch do not stand for Ideas v.g. particles W<i>i</i>ll etc. (*PC* 661)

> Tis allow'd that Particles stand not for Ideas & yet they are not said to be empty useless sounds. The truth on't is they stand for the operations of the mind i.e. volitions. (*PC* 667)[8]

By his rejection of the engagingly simple Idea Doctrine, Berkeley creates a problem for himself that he will struggle with throughout the rest of his philosophical career; for if we have no idea of mental acts or of the mind itself, how is it that we are able to talk about them intelligibly? His later doctrine of notions is an attempt to cope with this problem.

I shall postpone further discussion of the developments in Berkeley's theory of the meaningfulness of terms, and continue, now, our account of his changing view of the mind. We have reached the point at which Berkeley identifies the mind with the will. But what does he take the nature of the will to be? (Let us assume, for the time being, that such questions are legitimate, despite the fact that we can have no idea of the will or of volitions.) Earlier, Berkeley had maintained that the will is a congeries of volitions (*PC* 615), but he is no longer satisfied with that view. I am not totally confident that I know what the reasons for this change are. Perhaps it just now seems obvious to Berkeley that there cannot be free-floating events that are genuinely active and that have real causal efficacy—and on the 'congeries of volitions' view of the will, individual volitions would have to be just such events. Whatever is genuinely active, he may suppose, must be a substantial *thing*, and in fact a substance. There is evidence that Berkeley is also newly impressed by what might be called the unity of volitional consciousness and by the apparent inability of a congeries view to account for it:

We see no variety or difference betwixt the Volitions, only between their effects. Tis One Will one Act distinguish'd by the effects. This will, this Act is the Spirit, operative, Principle, Soul etc. (*PC* 788)

So Berkeley abandons the view that the will (i.e., the mind) is a mere congeries of volitions in favor of the view that the will (i.e., the mind) is an immaterial or spiritual substance (cf. *PC* 829).

We should notice that here in the *Philosophical Commentaries* the proposition that the will, or mind, is a substance, is apparently put forward not as a known fact, but as an hypothesis. It is significant that in *PC* 788, he makes his point negatively: 'We see no variety or difference betwixt the Volitions.' He carefully does *not* claim that we are aware of some unifying element—the will itself—in all our volitions. Thus, he holds fast to his conviction that volitions, and the will, are not objects of direct awareness. And when he declares the will to be a substance, he steadfastly maintains its unknowability:

Substance of a Spirit is that it acts, causes, wills, operates, or if you please (to avoid the quibble y^t may be made on ye word it) to act, cause, will, operate its' substance is not knowable not being an Idea. (*PC* 829; see also *PC* 701)

(*Note*: In this passage, by the word 'substance,' we must understand *essence*. Berkeley is telling us what the essence of a spirit is, and asserting at the same time that we are not directly aware of, not 'acquainted with,' this essence. I take this latter claim to be that we are not directly aware of spirit, or will, itself.) I think we might well read Berkeley here as though he were saying something like this: Look here, whenever we *will* (i.e., perform a volition), we are being genuinely active. Furthermore, our volitions are not a mere series of discrete, disconnected items; there seems to be some kind of fundamental unity to them. I propose, as the best metaphysical explanation of these phenomena, the thesis that the will is an immaterial substance.

It is also quite possible that Berkeley regards the thesis that the will is a substance not merely as the *best* metaphysical explanation of the phenomena, but as the *only possible* explanation—in other words, that he looks upon the substantiality of the will as a 'demand of reason.'

As soon as Berkeley identifies the mind with the will, and then takes the will to be an unknowable spiritual substance, he begins to doubt the plausibility of excluding the understanding and the other so-called mental 'faculties' from the mind. To whatever degree it is clear that one and the same entity performs all of one's volitions, it is clear that the same entity that performs one's volitions also perceives one's ideas. (It is the same 'I' that wills this, imagines that, fears this other, and so on.) Berkeley's final view in the *Philosophical Commentaries*, then, is that the mind is an (unknowable) spiritual substance that both wills things and perceives all manner of ideas. Since the spiritual substance is unknowable, there can be no question of distinguishing different mental faculties (e.g., the will, the understanding, etc.) in its make-up; we must simply say that there is a spirit (i.e., an active entity) that wills things and perceives ideas:

> I must not Mention the Understanding as a faculty or part of the Mind, I must include Understanding & Will etc in the word Spirit by wch I mean all that is active. I must not say that the Understanding differs not from the particular Ideas, or the Will from particular Volitions. (*PC* 848; see also *PC* 854, 871)

Here, at the end of the *Philosophical Commentaries*, Berkeley finally arrives at the view that is to be his official doctrine in the published works: the mind is an unextended spiritual substance. I want now to investigate one important aspect of this doctrine— namely, the metaphysical relationship between the mind and the ideas it has (or perceives, to use Berkeley's terminology).

Berkeley devotes a lot of attention to the connection between ideas and such things as tables and chairs, but he is remarkably slapdash in his treatment of the connection between ideas and the mind that has them. I do not mean that he does not have strong opinions on the subject, for he does. But the opinions are only briefly and inadequately defended. And what is worse, they seem not to be consistent with one another.

Berkeley asserts each of the following propositions:

(J) The mind perceives ideas.

(K) The mind is wholly distinct from its ideas.

(L) The alleged distinction between (i) the perceiving of an idea and (ii) the idea perceived, is a bogus one; there is no such distinction.

I shall, first, give textual justification for my claim that Berkeley did in fact hold each of the theses (J), (K), and (L). I shall then show that (J), (K), and (L) together constitute an inconsistent triad of propositions. Then, since (K) and (L) are perhaps the most suspicious-looking of the three, I shall give Berkeley's reasons for asserting them. Next, I shall assess the merits of these reasons, and finally, indicate the most plausible moves Berkeley might make to extricate himself from inconsistency.

No one will dispute that Berkeley subscribes to (J). Here are some representative passages:

> Besides all that endless variety of ideas or objects of knowledge, there is likewise something which knows or perceives them, and exercises divers operations, as willing, imagining, remembering about them. This perceiving, active being is what I call *mind*, *spirit*, *soul* or *my self*. (*PHK* I 2)

> A spirit is one simple, undivided, active being: as it perceives ideas, it is called the *understanding*. (*PHK* I 27)

> I my self am not my ideas, but somewhat else, a thinking active principle that perceives, knows, wills, and operates about ideas. (*3D* III (*W* II 233; A 196; T 178))

That Berkeley holds (K) is almost as easy to verify. In addition to the passage just quoted in support of (J), one may also cite the following:

> tis most sure & certain that our Ideas are distinct from the Mind i.e. the Will, the Spirit. (*PC* 847)

> This perceiving, active being is what I call *mind*, *spirit*, *soul* or *my self*. By which words I do not denote any one of my ideas, but a thing entirely distinct from them, wherein they exist, or, which is the same thing, whereby they are perceived. (*PHK* I 2)

> *Thing* or *being* is the most general name of all, it comprehends under it two kinds entirely distinct and heterogeneous, and which have nothing common but the name, to wit, *spirits* and *ideas*. (*PHK* I 89)

> *Spirits* and *ideas* are things so wholly different, that when we say, *they exist*, *they are known*, or the like, these words must not be thought to signify any thing common to both natures. There is nothing alike or common in them. (*PHK* I 142)

> Ideas are things inactive, and perceived: and spirits a sort of beings altogether different from them. (*3D* III (*W* II 231; A 194; T 176))

Proposition (L) is one that Berkeley asserts most emphatically in the *Philosophical Commentaries*, where he writes:

> The Distinguishing betwixt an Idea and perception of the Idea has been one great cause of Imagining material substances. (*PC* 609)

> wherein I pray you does the perception of white differ from white. (*PC* 585)

It is not announced in such loud tones in the works meant for publication, but it does show up there, too:

> Light and colours, heat and cold, extension and figures, in a word the things we see and feel, what are they but so many sensations, notions, ideas or impressions on the sense; and is it possible to separate, even in thought, any of these from perception? For my part I might as easily divide a thing from it self.[9] (*PHK* I 5)

The distinction is denied again in the *Three Dialogues*. In the first dialogue, Philonous (Berkeley) picks up a remark made earlier by Hylas: 'To return then to your distinction between *sensation* and *object*; if I take you right, you distinguish in every perception two things, the one an action of the mind, the other not' (*3D* I (*W* II 195; A 159; T 135)). Philonous then proceeds to attack the distinction, on grounds that we shall be discussing in a moment. He thinks he shows the distinction to be illegitimate and near the end of his argument he says: 'Since therefore you are in the very perception of light and colours altogether passive, what is become of that action you were speaking of, as an ingredient in every sensation?' (*3D* I (*W* II 197; A 160; T 137)).

There can be no doubt, then, that Berkeley subscribes to all three propositions (J), (K), and (L). But it is not at all clear how (K), especially, is to be understood. This is due not only to the obscurity of the concepts of mind and of idea, but also to the obscurity of the concept of distinctness (or wholly-distinctness). The mind, according to Berkeley's official doctrine, is an unextended, immaterial, or spiritual substance. It is reasonably certain, I think, that whatever conception we have of such an entity must be based on an analogy with ordinary *physical* substances—with such things as the bodies of human beings, for example.[10] The passages I have quoted above in support of the claim that Berkeley avows (J) and (K)—and they are typical of his statements about minds and their ideas—strongly suggest that he is implicitly thinking of the relation between a mind and any one of its ideas as analogous to the relation between Bill's body and, say, a tree, when Bill kicks the tree. In this example, we may detect two kinds of distinctness, which I shall call strong distinctness and weak distinctness. Bill is (wholly) distinct from the tree in an obvious sense. I shall say that Bill is strongly distinct from the tree. If Bill kicks the tree, there may be some point in saying that Bill is distinct from his act of kicking the tree. Bill is not the same thing as his acts or his states, and so, in a *recherché* sense, he is distinct from them. But they, unlike the tree, qualify his being, to employ the terminology of another day. He is to some extent necessarily, even if only temporarily, different because of them. So he is not distinct from them in the strong way he is distinct from the tree: I shall say that Bill is weakly distinct from his acts and states.

We shall have to examine (K) much more critically later, but for the moment I shall assume that it must be understood as saying that the mind is distinct from its ideas in a way analogous to that in which Bill is distinct from the tree—in other words, that the mind is strongly distinct from its ideas. On this interpretation, an idea is not an element in the ontological make-up of the mind. To be sure, Berkeley says, as we have seen, that ideas exist in the mind, but he adds that he means by this only that ideas are perceived by the mind (PHK I 2)—and that is consistent with maintaining that ideas are no part of the metaphysical make-up of minds.

If it is, indeed, in this way that (K) is to be understood, then (J), (K), and (L) form an inconsistent trio of doctrines. One of the things the mind does is perceive ideas (proposition (J)); so the perceiving of an idea is either an act or a state of mind. Therefore the mind is not strongly, but only weakly, distinct from the perceiving of the idea. However, since the perceiving of an idea cannot be distinguished from the idea perceived (in virtue of (L)), the idea, like the perceiving, is only weakly distinct from the mind. And this contradicts (K), which says that an idea is strongly distinct from the mind.[11]

One or more of the three propositions clearly has to go. It would be possible to allow Berkeley to retain (K) and (L), thus forcing him to abandon (J). On this view, the perceiving of an idea and the idea perceived would be identified (in virtue of (L)), and the unified idea-perception would be kept wholly, or strongly, distinct from the mind, from mental substance (in virtue of (K)). This would mean, of course, that the mind is no longer the perceiver of ideas—i.e., the mind is no longer 'doing the perceiving'—and that proposition (J) is therefore rejected. Berkeley could hardly be expected to approve of this solution, since (J) seems to be central to his thinking. And it is, anyway, a profoundly unsatisfactory position to defend: for it makes the relationship between the mind and its ideas unintelligible. It is not enough to be told that the mind and its ideas are totally distinct: we want to know how they are related. For example, what is it that makes a certain idea an idea belonging to just this mind, rather than to some other? Berkeley cannot answer that this mind is the one that directly *causes* the idea; for according to him, all our ideas of sense are caused directly by God's mind, not by our own. And if we are forbidden to answer 'This mind is the one that *perceives* the idea,' we seem to have no answer whatever. And so we do not understand what the relationship between a mind and its ideas could possibly be on this view. I conclude, therefore, that proposition (J) cannot be rejected, and that either (K) or (L), or both, must be sacrificed.

We must cast suspicious looks at these two propositions, then. I shall begin with (L). In the passage in which Berkeley deals most explicitly with (L) (namely, in 3D I (*W* II 194-7; A 158-60; T 134-7)), we can discern two arguments against the alleged distinction referred to in that proposition. The first is that if you distinguish two elements in every perception of an idea—the perceiving of the idea and the idea perceived—the first element would have to be a (mental) act, since the phrase 'perceiving an idea' is simply short for the expression '*the act of* perceiving an idea.' But there is no such act, since we are entirely passive in perception: the only 'actions involved in seeing, for example, are such acts as opening one's eyes, turning oneself and one's eyes in the right direction, and so on. And none of these constitutes any part of perception itself—for *that* takes place only after these acts are performed, and when it does take place, we are totally passive, apprehending whatever patterns of light and color happen to impress themselves on our consciousness from outside.[12] Since there is no such thing as an act of perceiving an idea, the alleged distinction between that (non-existent) act and the idea perceived must be rejected.

This first argument for abandoning the distinction seems to be an incredibly weak one. Berkeley makes it quite clear that if something a person does is to be counted an *act*, it must be directly caused by one of that person's volitions. But this is far too strong a requirement to impose for the purpose at hand. The issue to be resolved is whether one can or cannot distinguish the perceiving of an idea from the idea perceived. Berkeley argues, in effect, that the distinction is allowable only if the former (i.e., the perceiving) is an act, that is, only if it is directly caused by a volition. Since perceiving is not so caused, the distinction is ruled out. But this requirement appears to rule out far too much. Imposing Berkeley's stricture, one could argue that if a wind blows you down and you fall on an ant, there can be no distinction between your falling on the ant and the ant fallen upon, since your falling on the ant, unpreceded as it was by a volition, was not an act. And this seems absurd.

Berkeley is anxious to deny the distinction between the perceiving of an idea and the idea perceived because he thinks that if you detach them from one another, then although the perceiving will, of course, be something occurring in the mind, the object of the perceiving—the idea perceived—will have to be located outside the mind in some 'unperceiving substance,' since all ideas are 'visibly inactive' and cannot be granted the status of mental entities. This brings us to Berkeley's second argument. He says that if we are to distinguish the perceiving of an idea from the idea perceived, we must do so for all kinds of ideas. But in the case of pain, it is absurd to suggest that the alleged object of the alleged act of perceiving might exist outside the mind in an unthinking substance. Berkeley is on stronger ground here, but still his argument is far from decisive; for it rests on the dubious assumption that if one grants the disputed distinction, then perceived ideas must be accorded extramental existence. Indeed, Berkeley's own argument could be turned around by a defender of the distinction: such a person could urge that since the distinction is obviously legitimate and since the object of the perceiving (the idea perceived) is at least sometimes not an extramental entity (as, for example, in the case of pains or dreams), it is just a mistake to assume that the distinction entails the extramental existence of the object that is perceived. Here we may begin to suspect that there might be something odd about proposition (L) and the distinction with which it deals—or at least that our understanding of the distinction may not be as perfect as we had supposed. We shall have to return to it later.

But let us, first, cast a jaundiced eye on proposition (K). Berkeley thinks he has proved conclusively that ordinary physical objects—things like tables and chairs—are nothing but families of ideas. This conclusion naturally makes him disposed to think of ideas as being strongly distinct from mind. Physical objects, after all, are normally conceived of as standing over against the mind, as being what the mind is not. It would be ludicrous to suggest that tables and chairs—or elements of them—might actually constitute parts of the mind. So ordinary common sense would urge. Berkeley, in so far as he is a conciliator, naturally wants to side with common sense; but as a philosopher, he must provide reasons for his agreement with common sense.

The ground Berkeley most often gives in support of (K) is that ideas are inactive and so must be strongly distinct from the mind, which is active. But this is a feeble excuse for accepting (K): as we saw, Berkeley takes pains to point out that perceiving an idea is not an act. Presumably, then, the perceiving of an idea is inactive, too, a mere passive process. And yet it is one of the things that goes on in the mind (see proposition (J)) and so is not strongly, but only weakly, distinct from the mind. So the mere fact that an idea is an inactive is not enough to make *it* strongly distinct from the mind, as (K) asserts.

I think it possible that Berkeley's own terminology may have beguiled him into a favorable attitude toward (K)—I mean his speaking of the mind as *perceiving* ideas. The model or picture embodied in this way of talking is that of ordinary sense perception: just as when a person sees a tree, the tree is something strongly distinct from the person (at least, unreflective common sense views the matter in this way), so when a mind perceives an idea, the idea must be something strongly distinct from the mind. But, of course, we have no reason whatever for thinking that this perceptual model for the mind's awareness of ideas is a suitable one, despite the fact that a great many good philosophers have employed it. On the contrary, it would not be difficult to think of reasons for viewing that model with great suspicion.

I want to hazard the guess that none of the foregoing considerations weighs as heavily with Berkeley in embracing (K) as this one: he thinks that the only alternative to (K) is the Cartesian view that an idea is a mode of consciousness or mind, and he regards that view as absurd. Descartes held that an idea is a mode of consciousness, a way for the mind to be conscious (and hence, for Descartes, to exist). Just as being spherical and blue are modes of extension, i.e., ways of being extended, so having an image of a blue sphere is a mode of consciousness, i.e., a way of being conscious. This conception denies that ideas are strongly distinct from the mind, and thus stands in stark opposition to proposition (K). As Descartes puts it: 'I allow only so much difference between the soul and its ideas as there is between a piece of wax and the various shapes it can assume.'[13] Berkeley does not attack this Cartesian view head-on, but it is quite clear from some of the things he says that he believes it to be absurd: for he thinks the view entails that when a person has an idea of sense or an image of, say, a blue sphere, that person's mind is then blue and spherical. Here are two passages in which this criticism is implicit:

> That there is no substance wherein ideas can exist beside spirit, is to me evident. And that the objects immediately perceived are ideas, is on all hands agreed. And that sensible qualities are objects immediately perceived, no one can deny. It is therefore evident there can be no *substratum* of those qualities but spirit, in which they exist, not by way of mode or property, but as a thing perceived in that which perceives it. (*3D* III (*W* II 237; A 199f; T 182F))

> [I]t may perhaps be objected, that if extension and figure exist only in the mind, it follows that the mind is extended and figured; since extension is a mode or attribute, which (to speak with the Schools) is predicated of the subject in which it exists. I answer, those qualities are in the mind only as they are perceived by it, that is, not by way of *mode* or *attribute*, but only by way of *idea*; and it no more follows, that the soul or mind is extended because extension exists in it alone, than it does that it is red or blue,

195

because those colours are on all hands acknowledged to exist in it, and no where else. (*PHK* I 49)

In these passages, Berkeley evidently assumes that if an idea is a mode of consciousness, the mind must actually have the properties that are contained (in whatever sense they are contained) in the idea. In the first of the two passages just quoted, Berkeley argues that the objects we immediately perceive are ideas, and (at least in sense perception) the objects we immediately perceive are sensible qualities. From this we are obviously meant to infer that sensible qualities *are* ideas. So when ideas are alleged to be modes of consciousness, sensible qualities are also necessarily accorded the same status. But if sensible qualities, such as blueness or sphericity, are modes of consciousness, then the mind must have those qualities—must be, for example, blue and spherical. Since this is an absurd consequence, the view that ideas are modes of consciousness must be rejected.[14]

Berkeley's attack on the Cartesian view of ideas looks terribly weak—and I think it really is. The Cartesian seems to have the following easy rejoinder: When I say the idea of a blue sphere is a mode of consciousness, I am not committed to holding that blueness and sphericity are modes of consciousness, but only that the *awareness* of blueness and sphericity is a mode of consciousness. And this does not in the least entail that the mind itself is blue and spherical.

This rejoinder seems eminently sensible, but I suspect that Berkeley may have thought he could not allow it. I think he may have thought that the rejoinder presupposes a distinction between the awareness of an idea (or, in his terminology, the perceiving of an idea) and the idea of which one is aware (the idea perceived). This distinction, as we know, is rejected in Berkeley's proposition (L). Since there is no such distinction, he may have reasoned, if the awareness of blue sphericity is a mode of consciousness, so also is the blue sphericity—for the two are identical. So the absurdity cannot be avoided: the rejoinder merely seemed to avoid it by appealing to a non-existent distinction.

But the Cartesian view cannot be so easily upset. The rejoinder I put into the mouth of its defender in the above paragraph was unfortunately worded, for it did suggest that the view rests on the distinction that Berkeley wishes to reject. This is ironic, because the whole point of the Cartesian view, when seen aright, is that it denies precisely this distinction. What the Cartesian view urges, to express it in Berkeleyan terms and to confine it to just one kind of idea of sense, is that the proper analysis for sentences of the form 'Mind M perceives an idea of an FG,' where F is a color term and G is a term designating a shape—for example:

(I) 'Mind M perceives an idea of a blue sphere'

is not

(IA) $(\exists x)\,(\exists y)$ (x is the mind M and x perceives y and y is an idea of a blue sphere)

but rather

(IB) $(\exists x)$ (x is the mind M and x perceives in a blue-spherical manner), or

  $(\exists x)$ (x is the mind M and x perceives blue-spherically).

The second conjuncts in (IB) are to be regarded as asserting that the mind M is in a not-further-to-be-analyzed state of consciousness. In particular, the analysis (IB) denies that the idea of a blue sphere is an object of awareness, separable from the awareness of it, as analysis (IA) suggests. Of course, a mind that is aware blue-spherically has those properties before itself as 'objects' of awareness, but these 'objects' are subjective sense-contents, essential aspects of the state of consciousness itself. According to (IB), the awareness of an idea is no more distinguishable from the idea than the turning of a somersault is distinguishable from the somersault turned, or than the swimming of the breaststroke is distinguishable from the breaststroke swum. Those who are tempted to analyze (I) along the lines of (IA), the Cartesian would maintain, are unconsciously assimilating (I) to such sentences as 'Bill kicks the tree' or 'Jane upsets the vase,' where there is an action (or at any rate a bodily movement) and a seemingly distinct object. But there is absolutely no need to do this; and it is, in fact, far better to assimilate (I) to such sentences as 'Jones turns a somersault' or 'Tarzan is swimming the breaststroke.' It is better because one thus avoids the positing of a class of objects—that is, ideas—that are metaphysically embarrassing. If only on grounds of parsimony, (IB) is preferable to (IA); both are committed to the existence of minds and both presuppose that minds can be in certain states (or perhaps (IA) presupposes rather that minds can perform actions), but (IB) requires nothing further, while (IA) requires the existence of another kind of object.

If someone should complain that while he understands the analysis (IA) well enough, he does not understand either version of (IB) at all, I would reply in the following way. Our conception of a spiritual substance, as I remarked earlier, must evidently be based on an analogy with material substance. A philosopher who wishes to defend the analysis (IA) is in effect urging that we use as our model, in construing sentences of the form (I), such sentences as 'Bill kicks the tree'; and a philosopher who defends analysis (IB) is urging that we use instead such sentences as 'Jones turns a somersault.' As far as I can see, on the score of intelligibility there is no *prima facie* warrant for preferring one model, or analogy, over the other. It may turn out, when the analogies are developed, that our intellectual hold on one is firmer than it is on the other—but there is no legitimate reason to prejudge the matter at the very outset.

Someone might object that on the Cartesian view, the perceiving of an idea is a *state* of consciousness, not an *act* of consciousness; and yet I have maintained that on that view, sentences of the form (I) should be assimilated to such sentences as 'Jones turns a somersault' and 'Tarzan is swimming the breaststroke,' both of which clearly attribute *actions* (or perhaps in the case of swimming, it is rather an *activity*) to an agent. This is not a formidable objection, however. The essence of the Cartesian view[15] is not that the mind's perceiving an idea is necessarily a *state*, as opposed to an *action*, of the mind; it is that the words 'an idea' in the expression 'the mind perceives an idea' do not designate an object distinct from the perceiving. It does not matter here whether the perceiving is an act, a state, a process, or something else; rather, the words 'an idea' designate a way the mind perceives—whether perceiving is an act, a state, a process, or whatever it is. If we think an idea *must* be an object distinct from the perceiving of it, then we are being misled by a model suggested to us by the form of words we use. To rid ourselves of the model, we need only stop thinking of perceiving ideas as being at all analogous to kicking trees and upsetting vases, and start thinking of it instead as being analogous to dancing jigs and swimming breaststrokes. The words 'a jig' in the expression 'dancing a jig' do not designate an object distinct from the dancing of it, whether the dancing is an act, a state, a process, or whatever it is;[16] rather, the words 'a jig' designate a way of dancing, whether the dancing is an act, a state, a process, or whatever it is. (If the objector insists on holding out for an analogue from the class of what are undoubtedly *states*, as opposed to acts or activities, then the Cartesian could reply that although suitable examples may be hard to come by in the real world, it is easy to find them in the realm of fantasy. Thus, imagine that we spoke not of sitting in a lotus position, but rather—as we easily might—of sitting a lotus.)

Notice how plausible the Cartesian view is in the case of sensations: for example, it certainly makes sense to deny that a pain is one thing and the feeling or awareness of it, another. There is just the feeling of pain. So accepting the Cartesian view for the whole range of ideas is tantamount to assimilating our awareness of all ideas to our awareness of sensations.

(IA) represents what we may call, adapting the terminology of modern sense-datum theories, an *act-object* analysis[17] of the perceiving of ideas of sense, while (IB) represents an *adverbial* analysis of such perceiving. Looking back to our original triad of Berkeleyan propositions, we see now that (IA) finds expression in proposition (K), and (IB) finds expression in (L). It is just this fact that accounts for the inconsistency in that triad of propositions: Berkeley shifts from an act-object analysis of perceiving ideas in (K) to an adverbial one in (L). This shift sets up an unresolved conflict that runs all through Berkeley's philosophy. I do not mean that a philosopher could not consistently accept an adverbial analysis for the perceiving of some ideas (e.g., pains) and an act-object analysis for the perceiving of other ideas (e.g., ideas received in sense perception). But there is no indication that Berkeley thinks our perceivings of ideas may be of two different sorts, and every indication that he thinks all ideas enjoy the same metaphysical status. His shifting back and forth between the adverbial and the act-object points of view is not governed by any explicit or implicit rules that I can discover; so I can only judge that he means to have just *one* view about our awareness of ideas. Since he does not, I say he falls into inconsistency.

I have been examining Berkeley's reasons for embracing propositions (K) and (L), and have found them wanting. If my criticisms of these reasons have been well taken, and if they are, as I believe, his *only* reasons, then Berkeley has provided no good ground for accepting either of those propositions. But there may well *be* such grounds—especially so if one wishes to defend the general metaphysical position that Berkeley does. So there may be good reasons why Berkeley *should* clasp either (K) or (L) to his bosom, despite the fact that he himself does not put them forward nor, presumably, realize what they are. And I think that, in fact, there are good reasons of this sort. I shall now try to show which of the two propositions Berkeley had better accept, and why—that is, which of the two leads to fewer and less embarrassing difficulties, and/or is consistent with more that is essential in his metaphysical system. To do this, I shall take a critical look at the distinction denied in (L); doing that will also, necessarily, be taking a critical look at proposition (K), for as we now realize, (K) affirms, at least, the very distinction that (L) denies.

I shall assume that Berkeley, in so far as he subscribes to proposition (L), is advocating an adverbial analysis of the perceiving of ideas. I shall also assume that in so far as he subscribes to proposition (K) he is advocating an act-object analysis. There may be more than the act-object analysis in (K), but it surely includes at least that. Rather than discuss (K) and (L) directly, then, I shall examine the act-object and adverbial analyses of the perceiving of ideas. I want to ask what someone who accepts the act-object analysis believes, or is committed to, that someone who accepts the adverbial analysis denies, or at least is not committed to.

Here is one answer to this question that looks promising: a defender of the act-object analysis maintains that although a given idea I_1 may, in fact, be the object of an act (or state) of perceiving, P_1, occurring at time t_1, the same idea I_1 could exist also as the object of a different act (or state) of perceiving, P_2, occurring at a different time t_2. The words 'the same idea I_1' in this answer cannot be construed as meaning *generically* the same idea I_1, because then, apart from the superficial matter of his expressing it in his own different terminology, a defender of the adverbial analysis would presumably agree with the proposition. He would agree, for example, that a mind can perceive blue-spherically at t_1 and blue-spherically at t_2; and doing this would be perceiving the generically same idea at two different times. In order to have any chance of marking a real difference between the act-object and the adverbial analyses, then, our answer must be interpreted so that 'the same idea I_1' means *numerically* the same idea. Now we *seem*, at least, to have something that an act-object analyst would say 'Yes' to, and that an adverbial analyst would say 'No' to. But this seeming is, as yet, deceptive. For there are two plausible choices still open to the act-object analyst. He can say either (a) ideas exist only when they are perceived, or (b) ideas exist when they are perceived and also when they are not perceived.

Let us explore the first possibility, (a). This proposition may be intended either as a necessary truth or as a contingent one. If the act-object analyst construes it in the first way, as a necessary truth, then, as far as I can tell, he is adopting a view that is indistinguishable from the adverbial analysis. For what is the difference between saying, as the adverbial analyst does, that sense-contents exist, of necessity, only when a mind is aware in a certain mode, and saying, as the act-object analyst does if he accepts (a) as a necessary truth, that ideas exist, of necessity, only when a mind perceives them? This is a mere seeming-difference; the act-object analyst's 'object' is nothing but the adverbial analyst's sense-contents with a different label.[18]

The only hope for an act-object analyst to keep his analysis really distinct from the adverbial analysis is for him to deny that (a) is a necessary truth. But then he owes us an explanation of why an idea, although it could well exist when not being perceived, never in fact does so, of why ideas pop into, and out of, existence as minds start, and stop, perceiving them. If he were to give such an explanation, the act-object analyst would then have endowed ideas with an extremely thin, barely perceptible, margin of objecthood over the subjective sense-contents of his adverbial analyst opponent; but it is unlikely that the offered explanation would be anything but wildly implausible and unconvincing—which explains, I suppose, why no act-object analyst (as far as I know) has ever tried to formulate one. So if an act-object analyst is going to deny that (a) is a necessary truth—as he must if his analysis is to differ from the adverbial analysis—then he would be well advised not to hold on to (a) as a contingent truth but rather to reject it altogether and to accept (b) instead. For (b) accords ideas exactly the same metaphysical status that (a) does, when (a) is understood as a contingent proposition, but is simpler and more plausible.

If I am right, then, the difference between the adverbial analysis and the act-object analysis amounts to this: on the adverbial analysis, it is a necessary truth that no ideas can exist unperceived, while on the best version of the act-object analysis, ideas can and do exist unperceived. Before drawing what are doubtless the obvious conclusions from all this, I should like to point out that Berkeley agrees with me that any philosopher who denies proposition (L) (which embodies the adverbial analysis of the perception of ideas) and, thus, accepts what I have been calling the act-object analysis, is committed to the existence of unperceived ideas: 'Twas the opinion that Ideas could exist unperceiv'd or before perception that made Men think perception was somewhat different from the Idea perceived' (PC 656).

I cannot undertake here a full discussion of the relative merits of the adverbial and act-object analyses of the perception of ideas; I want only to extricate Berkeley, as painlessly as possible, from what I take to be a serious inconsistency. It should now be fairly clear how this can be done. Proposition (K) embodies the act-object analysis which entails, if I am right, that ideas can exist when unperceived; proposition (L) embodies the adverbial analysis which entails that it is necessarily false that ideas exist when unperceived. Obviously, then, the simplest and best way to preserve the largest bulk of Berkeley's central philosophical doctrines is to have him abandon proposition (K). And he would lose nothing of importance by doing this; for the characteristics he is anxious to attribute to ideas—passivity above all else—he could simply attribute to the 'sense-contents' of the adverbial analysis. Indeed, it seems easier to understand why such sense-contents should be inactive than why ideas, conceived as objects, should be so.

There is at least one famous Berkeley scholar, namely, A. A. Luce, who would violently object to my suggestion. He does not think that Berkeley is guilty of any inconsistency: ignoring, or at any rate attaching no importance to, the passages I have cited above in support of proposition (L), Luce maintains that Berkeley simply holds propositions (J) and (K). On this view, ideas—or rather, just ideas of *sense*—are objects that are sharply to be distinguished (i.e., are strongly distinct) from anything mental:

> Such ideas are not mental. . . . The Berkeleian idea of sense is *from* and *in* the mind of God, and *for* and (sometimes) *in* the mind of man, but it is not mental. It is not a constituent of mind, divine or human. It is the non-mental *other* of mind.[19]

This interpretation has Berkeley accepting the act-object analysis of ideas of sense, and spurning the adverbial analysis that I have urged on him.

But this conception of ideas is disastrous for Berkeley. Let us see why. If ideas are the kind of objects that Luce suggests, then if what I have said about the act-object analysis is correct, Berkeley must hold that it is logically possible for ideas[20] to exist unperceived. He would then have the further option of saying that

(i) ideas do in fact exist unperceived, or
(ii) ideas in fact exist only when perceived.

Berkeley would, of course, have to reject option (i) out of hand; its acceptance would radically change the entire character of his metaphysical position, making it virtually indistinguishable from a form of materialism.

Option (ii) is even worse; for if he accepts (ii), Berkeley must give us some account, some explanation, of *why* these objects (i.e., ideas) happen to exist only when they are perceived by some mind or other—and it seems extremely unlikely that any plausible account of this kind could possibly be formulated. Certainly Berkeley makes no attempt to provide one. And incidentally, Luce must agree with me that some such account is really required on his reading of Berkeley, for he argues that Berkeley's ideas (of sense) are public objects, accessible to any number of different observers[21]—and surely anyone would have to admit that if such objects exist only when they are perceived, this is an extraordinary fact that cries out for some explanation.

I conclude that Luce's 'act-object' interpretation of Berkeley saddles our philosopher with a hopeless position. My suggestion, then, is that we allow Berkeley to abandon proposition (K), with its act-object analysis of the perceiving of ideas, and have him adopt instead the adverbial analysis implicit in proposition (L). This move has the great advantage of allowing him to retain the necessary non-existence of unperceived ideas as part of his system. Furthermore, everything else of importance that Berkeley wishes to maintain can be accommodated within the adverbial analysis. On this analysis, Berkeley can even insist, as he is wont to do, that the mind is (wholly) distinct from its ideas—not, of course, strongly distinct, but weakly so. The very words of proposition (K) may thus be preserved, as long as we understand by 'distinct,' *weakly distinct*. There can be little doubt that when Berkeley talks in the (K)-vein, he implicitly thinks of the mind as being strongly distinct from its ideas. On this point, I am in complete agreement with Luce. But if we understand weak distinctness where Berkeley intends strong distinctness, we can free him from the charge of inconsistency.

Having dealt, now, with the question of how minds, viewed as mental substances, are related to their ideas in Berkeley's philosophy, I turn to an even more fundamental problem that faces his theory of the mind—that of specifying what the nature, or essence, of the mind is. Berkeley must of course have a position on this matter, for minds, after all, are in his system the basic kind of thing that exists, so he owes us some account of what these basic things *are*. It is not enough to say that they are immaterial, unextended substances, because this tells us only what they are *not*, and we need to know what they *are*. Nor will it do to say merely that they are spiritual or mental substances; for once we are told that a mind is a (unique kind of) substance, it follows much too easily that it must be a mental or spiritual substance. We still want to know what the nature of that kind of substance is.

Berkeley realizes full well that it is incumbent upon him to have an opinion about what the essence of the mind is, and he in fact discharges this obligation. When he abandons his early view that the mind is a congeries of perceptions and takes up the view that it is a substance, he first identifies the mind, remember, with the will. The mind, then, is a willing, that is to say, an active, substance, and so its essence, as Berkeley tells us, is 'to act, cause, will, operate' (*PC* 829). Several questions about this doctrine immediately arise—one might, for example, ask, with Berkeley's American correspondent Samuel Johnson, 'Can actions be the *esse* of anything?' (*W* II 277)—but since the view is a transitional one, it will be more profitable to deal with the relevant issues in connection with Berkeley's final view (or anyway, with his final *official* view). That view is that the mind is a simple immaterial substance that both performs volitions (i.e., wills) and perceives ideas: 'A spirit is one simple, undivided, active being: as it perceives ideas, it is called the *understanding*, and as it produces or otherwise operates about them, it is called the *will*.' (*PHK* I 27). In *PHK* I 139, the soul is declared to be a substance that 'perceives ideas, and wills, and reasons about them'; but reasoning, or thinking, may be regarded as a complex process that can be reduced to perceiving ideas and willing, and no doubt is so regarded by Berkeley, for he sometimes refers to thinking as *operating about ideas* (see *3D* III (*W* II 233; A 196; T 178)). So the essence of the mind, on this view, presumably, is to perceive ideas and to will. And this is what Berkeley maintains. Thus, he says that the existence of spirit—which I take to mean the *essence* of spirit—consists 'in perceiving ideas and thinking' (*PHK* I 139); since thinking reduces to perceiving ideas and willing, Berkeley's contention is that the essence of spirit is perceiving ideas and willing. This is precisely the purport, too, of the following entry in the *Philosophical Commentaries* with its later emendation:

Existence is percipi or percipere ʌ   . . . (*PC* 429)
ʌ or velle i.e. agere   (*PC* 429a)

The existence—that is, the essence—of spirit, Berkeley is saying here, consists in its perceiving ideas or willing (i.e., acting). (Notice that this means that the mind is not altogether active, for perceiving ideas, in Berkeley's view, is a passive state of the mind. See *PC* 301, *3D* I (*W* II 196f; A 159f; T 136f), and Berkeley's last letter to Johnson, where he says 'That the soul of man is passive as well as active, I make no doubt' (*W* II 293).)

How satisfied ought we to be with Berkeley's thesis that the essence of the mind—of the human mind, at any rate—is to perceive ideas and to will? Well, here are two complaints that one is tempted immediately to make:

1 'Berkeley is telling us what the mind can *do* (namely, that it can perform volitions) and what kind of passive state it can be in (namely, that it can perceive ideas), whereas we need to be told what the mind *is*.'

2 'There are times when the mind is neither willing anything nor perceiving ideas—e.g., during sleep or when the person is in a coma—so its essence cannot be what Berkeley says it is.'

If we were to ignore the point of the second objection, and assume instead that the mind *is* always either willing or perceiving (or both), then the first complaint would not, I think, be a fair objection to Berkeley's theory of the mind's essence; for then the theory *would* be telling us what the mind is—namely, that it is essentially a thing that wills and perceives. The idea behind the objection might, however, be that if two things are essential to a kind of substance, then any substance of that kind must at every moment of its existence have *both* things. Thus, for example, if material things existed, and if their essential properties were extension and impenetrability, then any material thing would have to be both extended and impenetrable throughout its history. 'But surely,' the objector would then go on, 'the mind can either simply perceive an idea (without willing anything) or simply will something (without perceiving any idea); so Berkeley's view cannot be that the essence of the mind is to perceive ideas and to perform volitions. The most he can say is that the essence of the mind is to perceive ideas *or* to perform volitions—and he even does say this in *PC* 429 and 429a. But that is a very strange view: for how can a thing lose one part of its essence at some times and lose another part at other times? That is not an intelligible doctrine.'

Berkeley would, I think, deny a premiss of this objection; for there are passages in the early notebooks which indicate that he thinks that there can be no such thing as willing without the perception of ideas, and no such thing as the perceiving of ideas without volition. Thus he says: 'While I exist or have any Idea I am eternally, constantly willing, my acquiescing in the present State is willing' (*PC* 791). So the perceiving of an idea entails volition. But volition also entails the perceiving of an idea, as we have seen (cf. p. 185); for to will something involves having the idea of some as yet unperformed action. His real view, then, is that the essence of the mind is to perceive ideas *and* to perform volitions—and *PC* 429 and 429a should be regarded as mistaken in suggesting that the mind's essence is to perceive *or* to will.[22]

But if Berkeley thus escapes the first objection, he is nevertheless still in deep trouble; for his escape presupposes that the mind is constantly perceiving ideas and willing, and this seems clearly not to be the case. (The thesis that the mind's essence is to perceive ideas *or* to perform volitions would offer no help on this front, for it would require that the mind be constantly either perceiving or willing, and this, too, seems clearly to be false.) In other words, even if Berkeley escapes the first of the two complaints against his theory, the second will apparently still refute him. Let us turn, then, directly to the second objection.

The objection seems, at least, to make a perfectly valid point when it says that there are times when the mind is neither performing a volition nor perceiving ideas. If so, then it cannot be the essence of the mind to perceive ideas and to will, because a thing must have its essential features at every moment of its existence. Berkeley might take the line of conceding that there are, for any mind, times of non-willing and non-perceiving, but then boldly claim that what this fact shows is that the mind does not exist continuously throughout its career—it exists when, and only when, it is willing and perceiving, and lapses into non-existence at other times. This would be a desperate measure on behalf of Berkeley's thesis about the essence of the mind, however; it would, in fact, be an abandonment of the view that the mind is a substance, and a reversion to the bundle theory.

205

Whatever a substance may be, it must at least endure continuously throughout its history; so a mind that kept popping into, and out of, existence would be no substance, but a mere bundle of volitions and perceptions.

A more promising course for Berkeley would be to deny that there are any times when the mind is not willing something and perceiving ideas, and to maintain that whenever it is not consciously willing and perceiving, the mind is unconsciously doing those things. But this option is closed for Berkeley since, as we know, he finds the suggestion that there might be unconscious mental states or processes unintelligible (see, for example, *NTV* 19). The mind, for him, is a transparent medium; everything in it is necessarily illuminated by consciousness.

Perhaps the best way, ideally, for Berkeley to respond to the present objection would be to abandon his thesis about the essence of the soul, and to offer some other attributes as its essence—attributes that it has continuously, as long as it exists. Not surprisingly, Berkeley makes no move in this direction; it is actually very doubtful that there are any known attributes that would satisfy the requirements. Could he hold, then, that the mind has some unknown, and indeed unknowable, essential attribute(s)? And does he not, in fact, adopt precisely this position when he claims, as he sometimes does, that the essence of the mind is unknowable? The answer to the second of these questions, anyway, is 'No.' When Berkeley says that the essence of the mind is unknowable (as he does, for example, in *PC* 829), he means that we are not directly aware of (not 'acquainted with') the mind itself. But to claim that the mind is unknowable in this sense is not at all the same thing as saying that we do not, and cannot, know what the essential attributes of the mind are; thus in the very passage (i.e., *PC* 829) where Berkeley says that the essence of the mind is unknowable, he tells us what its essence is! It is perfectly consistent to maintain that one cannot be directly aware of (i.e., one cannot know by acquaintance) one's own mind itself, or the essence of one's own mind, but at the same time to insist that one knows in some other way that the essence of one's mind is to perform volitions and to perceive ideas.

The move that Berkeley actually does make to meet the second objection is remarkable both for its ingenuity and for its implausibility: he boldly denies the apparently obvious truth that there are times when the mind is not willing something and perceiving ideas—and he does it without having recourse to unconscious willings and perceivings. He adopts instead a view of time according to which there simply is no lapse of time between any two non-simultaneous conscious episodes of a mind. There just is no time between any of the conscious episodes of a mind. Therefore, the mind is always willing and perceiving, and Berkeley's thesis that the mind's essence is to will and to perceive thus survives the second objection. The theory of time that so dramatically saves the day is the incredibly simple one that time is nothing more nor less than the succession of conscious willings and perceivings that occur in each mind—or, to put it in the inaccurate, but more convenient, way that Berkeley himself regularly does, the view is that time is the succession of ideas that occur in each mind:

> Time therefore being nothing, abstracted from the succession of ideas in our minds, it follows that the duration of any finite spirit must be estimated by the number of ideas or actions succeeding each other in that same spirit or mind. Hence it is a plain consequence that the soul always thinks. (*PHK* I 98)

> A succession of ideas I take to *constitute* Time, and not to be only the sensible measure thereof, as Mr. Locke and others think. (Berkeley's second letter to Johnson (*W* II 293))

It is important to realize that this view of time does *not* entail that the mind goes out of existence between its non-simultaneous willings and perceivings; on the contrary, it entails that the mind exists continuously as long as it wills and perceives. Since there is literally no time between any of its non-simultaneous willings and perceivings, it would make no sense to say that the mind sinks into non-existence *during* the time that elapses between its non-simultaneous willings and perceivings. (There is no time for a mind to non-exist in, as it were.) Berkeley does not always keep this point firmly in his mind in the *Philosophical Commentaries*. He gets it right when he says: 'No broken Intervals of Death or Annihilation. Those Intervals are nothing. Each Person's time being measured to him by his own Ideas' (*PC* 590). But then he goes wrong a little later: 'Certainly the mind always & constantly thinks & we know this too In Sleep & trances the mind exists not there is no time no succession of Ideas' (*PC* 651). This is incoherent; for if there is no time when there is no succession of ideas, then in sleep and trances there is no time at which, or during which, the mind fails to exist—and so Berkeley should not say that 'in sleep & trances the mind exists not.'

Notice that it is just possible to have a 'succession of ideas' view of time according to which there would be one common time that serves as an objective measure for everyone: the succession of ideas in God's mind might be held to constitute the one common time series. Whatever the merits of this divine view of time might be, Berkeley explicitly spurns it on the grounds that there is no succession of ideas, and indeed no succession of any kind, in God's mind. (See Berkeley's second letter to Johnson (*W* II 293).) The divine view of time, or any other theory that posits a single objective time, would of course wreck Berkeley's attempt to save his thesis that the essence of mind is to will and to perceive; for if such theories were correct, then there *would* be times when the mind is not willing and perceiving, just as the second objection to Berkeley's doctrine asserts.

Berkeley's own view of time is what we might call a solipsistic one: there is no common time for everyone, but a separate, unique time for each mind. There are no temporal relationships among the different time series: for example, it cannot be the case that you perceive an idea at the same time that I do, or that you perceive an idea before, or after, I do—because there is no common time in which alone such relationships could exist. There are just the various different time series—one for each mind—running along independently, with no temporal relationships among them. It would, in fact, be embarrassing for Berkeley's view of the mind as a substance if there were temporal relationships among the different time series, because then for each person there would be periods *in other people's time* during which he did not exist, and that would seem to impugn the substantiality of his soul. (Berkeley tells Johnson that one error in thinking about time is 'supposing that the Time in one mind is to be measured by the succession of ideas in another' (*W* II 293).)

How did Berkeley arrive at his solipsistic view of time? I suggest that he might have reasoned as follows. Suppose a person tries to form an idea of time—i.e., to think of time. One cannot think of just time itself, abstracted from everything that happens in it (*PHK* I 97); he can think only of some concrete temporal sequence of events—for example, the sequence of getting up in the morning, then washing, then dressing, then taking the dogs for their usual walk, and so on. To think of this sequence of events, on Berkeley's view, is to think of a sequence of ideas—of the ideas, namely, that one might have while participating in, or observing, those events. But the idea of time passing, or of the time in which these events occur, is not any one of the ideas in the thought-of sequence, nor is it any mere set of them; it can only be the succeeding of one idea after the other, that is, the succession of ideas. The result so far, however, is only that time is the succession of ideas *in some mind or other*: how could Berkeley have reached the stronger conclusion that time, for each person, is the succession of ideas *in his own mind*? I think he must have reasoned that those thought-of ideas are, after all, thought of by the person who is trying to think of time, and that therefore they are ideas in his own mind. For each person, then, time is inconceivable apart from, and can only *be*, a succession of ideas in his own mind.

I would blush to attribute this argument to Berkeley, except that (a) I can think of no other path that could lead him to the solipsistic view of time, and (b) the argument is of the same form as one in which Berkeley has great faith—namely, his so-called desert island argument. In the desert island argument, recall, Berkeley argues that since a person cannot think of a desert island without having an idea of it in his own mind, the desert island must simply *be* an idea in his own mind (cf. p. 112). The weaknesses of the desert island argument, discussed in Chapter VII, therefore ruin the above argument for the solipsistic view of time as well. Berkeley may have another defense of it, but I cannot think what it might be.

I must conclude that Berkeley has no adequate defense to offer for his solipsistic view of time. Does it, nevertheless, have any merits? Well, the view does seem to save Berkeley's doctrine that the mind is a substance whose essence is willing and perceiving, but that is surely its only virtue; for otherwise, it is a total disaster. I think the view is in fact incomprehensible. It states that there is no single time series, but a host of separate individual times; one for each mind. There is your time, my time, Bunny's time, and so on. But can we understand the expressions 'your time,' 'my time,' 'Bunny's time,' when they are specifically *not* meant to be referring to such things as Pacific Coast Time or London Time, but rather to just *time* (in general)? I do not think we can. When you and I are living in the same time zone, what could be meant by speaking of 'your Tuesday,' 'my Tuesday,' and so on?[23] Your Tuesday *is* my Tuesday—and indeed, quite generally, as Rudy Vallee used wisely to point out, your time is my time. It is Bunny's time, too. The point is this: the conception of a real world is the conception of one in which (real) events are ordered temporally in a common way, the same for all people.[24] It is perhaps not essential that there be a *single* time series; things might begin to behave in strange ways that would lead us to suppose that there are several different time series—but if the events in these different series are to be *real*, or *objective*, events, then it is essential that they be ordered in a single way within their series; that is, the temporal orderings must be the same for everyone. Temporal ordering, as Kant taught us, just *is* one of the fundamental ways in which happenings that we consider to be real are ordered; and it is essential to our conception of time that the temporal ordering(s) of events belong among their objective features. We distinguish between the real temporal order of events and the way they merely seem to be ordered to this or that individual person, just as we distinguish between the real shape or weight of a stone and the shape or weight it merely appears to have to this or that person. So when Berkeley removes the feature of objectivity from time, and speaks of 'each person's time' (*PC* 590), we literally cannot understand what he is saying. There is, I suppose, such a thing as the succession of ideas in people's minds, but if they are real ideas in real minds, we can think of the successions only as occurring *in* time; so we cannot make sense of the suggestion that the successions might *be* time. Even Berkeley himself cannot live with that view of time; thus, he very often says things that are irreconcilable with it. For example, in the *Three Dialogues*, Philonous at one point asks: 'And is it not possible ideas should succeed one another twice as fast in your mind, as they do in mine, or in that of some spirit of another kind' (*3D* I (*W* II 190; A 154; T 130)). If this is indeed possible, it is so only in case there is a common time in which both series of ideas (i.e., of idea-perceivings) occur, because in order for ideas in one mind to succeed each other *twice as fast* as they do in a second mind, twice as many ideas must occur in the first mind as occur in the second mind *during the same period of time*—and nothing can count as 'the same period of time' if each mind has its own time.[25]

Berkeley is, of course, well aware that in our everyday speech, we constantly say things whose very sense seems to require that there be one common objective time. Thus, to take a humble example, I may say that I have made a dentist's appointment for next Thursday at 3:30 p.m. This means, evidently, that my dentist and I have agreed to meet in his office at a certain time next week—that is, that we have committed ourselves to being in his office next week at *the same time*. What sense can be made of this perfectly ordinary kind of agreement if there is not, for both the dentist and me, a common time? Berkeley would hold that here, once again, we are being misled by our language: we are supposing that the expression 'the same time' must pick out a point in a single objective time series. According to Berkeley, however, we ought to consider 'the true use and end of words, which as often terminate in the will as in the understanding, being employed rather to excite, influence, and direct action, than to produce clear and distinct ideas' (Berkeley's second letter to Johnson (*W* II 293)).

What Berkeley means here may be interpreted, rather freely, as follows: We ought not to construe the expression 'next Thursday at 3:30 p.m.' as a denoting expression, picking out a point in a single objective time series. There is no such series. We should, rather, notice what sort of use the expression actually has in our lives. For instance: when I say to my dentist 'I shall be in your office at 3:30 p.m. next Thursday,' the purpose of my remark is not to enlighten him—i.e., not to influence his understanding—but to guide both his actions and mine toward a useful end—i.e., to fix my will and to influence his. Once we see in this way how temporal expressions (such as 'next Thursday at 3:30 p.m.') really work in our linguistic practice, we shall rid ourselves of the preconception that temporal expressions *must* do just the one job of *naming*, or *denoting*, something. Then we shall be free of the notion that time is some kind of objective flowing current in which events occur.

This intriguing Wittgensteinian move on Berkeley's part unfortunately will not achieve his main purpose, which is to impugn the view that time is an objective ordering of events, the same for everyone. This becomes evident when we notice that in giving any account of what the 'true use and end' of temporal expression is, one cannot avoid the unwanted presupposition that time is an objective ordering of events. Consider again the example of next week's dentist appointment: the point of the remark to the dentist 'I shall be in your office at 3:30 p.m. next Thursday' was said to be 'to guide.both his actions and mine toward a useful end.' But in any attempt to specify what that useful end is, the idea of an objective time will necessarily intrude itself. Expressed in terms appropriate to Berkeley's own system, for example, the immediate 'useful end' will be that the dentist and I shall have harmonizing perceptions—he will have perceptions of me coming into his office and I shall have perceptions of him in his office. But the rub, of course, is that these perceptions must occur *at the same time*—and, in particular, next Thursday at 3:30 p.m.! If we follow Berkeley's advice to consider 'the true use and end of words,' we may rid ourselves of the idea that time is some kind of vast empty container or a huge flowing current; that would be a useful result, for as Berkeley says, in attempting to work out such ideas, one becomes 'lost and embrangled in inextricable difficulties' (*PHK* I 98). But there is just no avoiding the conception of time as some sort of objective ordering of events. And it is true *a fortiori* that paying attention to 'the true use and end of words' will lend no support whatever to Berkeley's contention that 'a succession of ideas . . . *constitute*[*s*] Time.'[26]

I conclude that Berkeley's solipsistic view of time collapses. His doctrine that the mind is a substance whose essence is willing and perceiving collapses with it; and so if he wishes to continue maintaining that the mind is a substance, he is still faced with the problem of specifying what the nature of that substance is.

It might be thought that there is a way of coping with this dire situation (namely, by holding that each of us has a direct awareness of his own mind) and that Berkeley actually takes this course in the *Principles* and *Three Dialogues*, thus reversing his earlier position in the *Philosophical Commentaries*. It is certainly not unreasonable to think that there might be some form of self-consciousness that would provide us with information about the nature of mind—but I shall not pursue that matter. I want to concentrate instead on the question of whether Berkeley really does think that we have a kind of direct intuitive awareness of our own minds. The standard line is that he does;[27] but S. C. Brown has argued recently against the usual interpretation.[28] I shall try to show that in the passages that are supposed to support the standard line, Berkeley does not, in fact, assert that we have a direct awareness of our own minds; what he says, rather, is that we have a 'direct knowledge' of what sort of things our minds are. So it is the truth of certain propositions that he claims we have 'direct knowledge' of; and he is not, in these passages, maintaining that we have 'direct knowledge' (i.e., direct awareness) of an entity, i.e., our own mind. (What 'direct knowledge' of a proposition's truth is will have to be explained, of course.)

There is an apparent development in Berkeley's thought on this general subject from the first edition of the *Principles*, through the first edition of the *Three Dialogues*, to the 1734 editions of both works. In the first edition of the *Principles*, he is firm in his conviction that there is, and can be, no idea of soul or spirit, on the grounds that all ideas are 'passive and inert' and so 'cannot represent unto us, by way of image or likeness, that which acts' (*PHK* I 27; see also *PHK* I 135–42). There is no explicit assertion, in this edition of the work, that we have any kind of direct, intuitive awareness of our own minds. (It might be argued that the following passage presupposes that we do have such an awareness:

> Moreover, as we conceive the ideas that are in the minds of other spirits by means of our own, which we suppose to be resemblances of them: so we know other spirits by means of our own soul, which in that sense is the image or idea of them, it having a like respect to other spirits, that blueness or heat by me perceived hath to those ideas perceived by another. (*PHK* I 140)

But as I urge below, in discussing a similar passage from the *Three Dialogues*, there is no need to interpret this passage as presupposing any direct awareness of one's own mind.) Berkeley does insist that we know what the meaning of such terms as 'soul,' 'spirit,' and 'mental substance' is: 'by the word *spirit* we mean only that which thinks, wills, and perceives; this, and this alone, constitutes the signification of that term' (*PHK* I 138).

We find, here, a natural and almost inevitable extension of the early Idea Doctrine of the meaningfulness of terms. The Idea Doctrine itself, as a general thesis about the meaningfulness of all terms, is clearly still being rejected by Berkeley, since he holds that the terms 'spirit,' 'soul,' and so on, have meaning though they denote no ideas whatever. The Idea Doctrine has now been widened, apparently, so that a term has meaning if it denotes an idea, or group of ideas, *or any other actually existing thing of whose existence we have knowledge.* Since minds really exist, and we know that they do, the terms that denote them have meaning:

> But it will be objected, that if there is no idea signified by the terms *soul*, *spirit*, and *substance*, they are wholly insignificant, or have no meaning in them. I answer, those words do mean or signify a real thing, which is neither an idea nor like an idea, but that which perceives ideas, and wills, and reasons about them. (*PHK* I 139)

But although this liberalization of the Idea Doctrine is perfectly plausible, there are still large gaps in Berkeley's general position at this point that need to be filled in; for there is no account yet of how we know that minds exist, and hence no account of how we can have any conception of a mind at all. (There is, perhaps, the germ of an answer to these questions in the contention that we know what terms such as 'mind' and 'spirit' mean; but this germ comes to fruition only later.)

In the first edition of the *Three Dialogues*, Berkeley repeats the points made earlier—namely, that there is no idea of spirit (*3D* III (*W* II 231; A 193; T 176)), and that we know what is meant by the terms 'I' and 'myself,' and hence, I presume, what is meant by 'spirit' or 'soul' (*ibid.*). But he *seems*, now, to make the additional claim that we have some sort of direct awareness of our own minds. The crucial passage is a long speech by Philonous in the third dialogue (*W* II 231-2; A 193-4; T 176-7). It should be noted at the outset that Berkeley is not, in this passage, directly confronting the question of what conception we can have of our own minds; the issue, rather, is the possibility of our having a conception of God or a conception of matter. One suspects that Berkeley might not be as careful in stating his position about our conception of our own minds here as he would be if he were addressing himself directly to that question; in any case, it would surely be hazardous to rely *heavily* on such a passage. But now that we have given due weight to these exegetical qualms, let us turn to Philonous' remarks.

There is no doubt whatever that his speech can plausibly be interpreted as maintaining that we have a direct awareness of our own minds. He says, for instance:

(1) Farther, I know what I mean by the terms *I* and *myself*; and I
    know this immediately, or intuitively, though I do not
    perceive it as I perceive a triangle, a colour, or a sound. (*3D* III
    (*W* II 231; A 193f; T 176))

The referent of the 'this' that he claims to know 'immediately, or intuitively' is not absolutely clear: to be sure, one natural interpretation would be to regard 'this' as short for 'what I mean by the terms "I" and "myself," ' but it would be equally natural, apparently, to take the referent of 'this' to be the same as that of the 'it' in 'I do not perceive *it* as I perceive a triangle'—and the referent of 'it' here is clearly his own mind. On this second reading, therefore, Berkeley would be claiming in (1) that he knows his own mind immediately or intuitively, that is, he has a direct awareness of it. One might wonder why, if I have a direct awareness of my own mind, I do *not* 'perceive it as I perceive a triangle, a colour, or a sound'—i.e., as I perceive an idea; but Berkeley provides the key to a solution of this difficulty a little later in the same speech of Philonous:

(2) For you neither perceive matter objectively, as you do an inactive being or idea, nor know it, as you do your self by a reflex act. (*W* II 232; A 194; T 176f)

The suggestion is that you cannot simply direct an inward gaze at your own mind as if it were just another ordinary object of awareness (cf. *PC* 643); no, you can become aware of it only by first being aware of something else—one or more ideas, presumably. When you are perceiving an idea, you can at the same time become aware, 'by a reflex act,' of your mind's state of perceiving that idea—and to be aware of a state of your mind *is* to be aware of your mind, just as to perceive the shape and color of a table *is* to perceive that table. So passage (2) itself seems clearly to require that Berkeley be read as holding that each of us has a direct awareness of his own mind.

Further corroboration of this reading can be found in the fact that Philonous goes on to say that his own soul furnishes him with 'an image, or likeness of God':

(3) For all the notion I have of God, is obtained by reflecting on my own soul heightening its powers, and removing its imperfections. (*W* II 231f; A 194; T 176)

It is not implausible, I think, to assume that one's own mind could not provide one with a model for God's mind unless one had some sort of direct awareness of it; so if Berkeley is making that assumption, (3) supports the present interpretation of Philonous' speech. The case seems to be irrefutably closed with Philonous' subsequent remark that:

(4) My own mind and my own ideas I have an immediate knowledge of. (*W* II 232; A 194; T 176)

(Let us call the doctrine that the mind has, or can have, a direct awareness of itself, the *Direct Awareness* doctrine, for short; and let us call the foregoing interpretation of Philonous' speech—i.e., of Berkeley's position—the *Direct Awareness* interpretation.)

Philonous' speech can be read in quite a different way, however—and plausibly, too. Thus, consider passage (4). In the sentences that follow it in Philonous' speech, he talks about his knowledge of the existence of other (finite) spirits and ideas, and his knowledge of the existence of God's mind and ideas. Therefore, it is apparent that in (4), what Philonous is claiming to have an immediate knowledge of is: the existence of his own mind and its ideas. He is saying, to put it in another way, that he has an immediate knowledge of the fact that his mind and its ideas exist, or an immediate knowledge of the truth of the proposition that his mind and its ideas exist. On this interpretation, (4) is simply a recapitulation of the assertion, made earlier in Philonous' speech, that 'I do nevertheless know, that I who am a spirit or thinking substance, exist as certainly, as I know my ideas exist' (*W* II 231; A 193; T 176). This is compatible with the claim that he has a direct awareness of his own mind, of course, but it is also compatible with the contention that he does not.

But what is it to have immediate knowledge of a fact, or of the truth of a proposition? We have the answer to this question in what Philonous goes on to say, right after (4). It is clear, in those remarks, that he thinks his knowledge of the existence of other minds and ideas is obtained only by processes of discursive reasoning—e.g., inference—and that this fact renders such knowledge mediate or indirect. By contrast, then, direct or immediate knowledge of the truth of a proposition is knowledge that is obtainable without recourse to inference or any other kind of discursive reasoning. Propositions that are knowable in this way must be obviously, or self-evidently, true. The claim being made in (4), on this interpretation, then, is that the existence of one's mind and its ideas are self-evident truths. Berkeley clearly believes that they are, moreover. It is indisputable that he takes the existence of one's own ideas to be an obvious truth; he would dismiss as absurd the suggestion that one has to *infer* that they exist. But he also regards it as a self-evident truth that one's own mind exists, in that he deems it obvious that ideas can exist only in a mind that perceives them (cf. *PHK* I 3, 6; and *3D* III (*W* II 235f; A 198; T 181)). One might argue that there is an inference involved here: from the fact that my ideas exist, I infer, albeit with certainty, that my mind exists; but Berkeley might plausibly contend, in response, that the knowledge that an idea exists as *mine* already contains the knowledge that it is perceived by *my mind*, and hence that my mind exists. Perhaps this is why he says: 'Cogito ergo sum, Tautology, no mental Proposition. answering thereto' (*PC* 738).

So (4), at least, not only can plausibly be read, but must be read, as maintaining, not that one has an immediate awareness of one's own mind and its ideas, but that one has an immediate—i.e., an intuitive, as opposed to a discursively reasoned—knowledge that one's own mind and its ideas exist. (Let us call the doctrine that the existence of one's own mind and its ideas is a self-evident truth, the *Self-evident Existence* doctrine, for short; and let us call the interpretation of Philonous' speech that attributes this doctrine to Berkeley, the *Self-evident Existence* interpretation.) But what, now, about passages (1), (2), and (3)? Well, (1) can be comfortably accommodated by the Self-evident Existence interpretation. According to this interpretation, Philonous would be saying in the first part of (1) that he knows *what sort of a thing* it is that he is referring to when he uses the terms 'I' and 'myself'; this reading is rendered highly plausible by the fact that Philonous goes on, in the sentence that immediately follows (1), to tell us what sort of a thing it is: 'The mind, spirit or soul, is that indivisible unextended thing, which thinks, acts, and perceives' (*W* II 231; A 194; T 176). In the second half of (1), Philonous would not, on the present Self-evident Existence interpretation, be claiming to have a direct awareness of his own mind, but claiming, rather, to know 'immediately, or intuitively' what sort of thing his mind is—namely, the sort of thing he describes in the very next sentence, just quoted. In other words, he is contending that it is a self-evident truth that the mind is an 'indivisible unextended thing, which thinks, acts, and perceives.' (Clearly, some account is needed to explain this alleged self-evidence—an account, furthermore, that does not require that a person have direct awareness of his own mind. Berkeley provides the bare bones of such an account; I shall describe it later when we come to the 1734 editions of the *Principles* and *Three Dialogues*.) In the very last clause of (1), Philonous would be asserting, as on the earlier Direct Awareness account, that he does not perceive his own mind as he perceives a triangle, a color, or a sound. I find this reading of (1) wholly convincing. It certainly makes the context of (1) thoroughly coherent: in the sentence that immediately precedes (1), Philonous lays claim to the knowledge *that* his mind exists: 'I do nevertheless know, that I who am a spirit or thinking substance, exist as certainly, as I know my ideas exist' (*W* II 231; A 193; T 176). Then, in (1), he lays claim to the knowledge of *what* his mind is—what sort of a thing it is; and in the sentence that follows (1), he tells us what sort of a thing it is. The Direct Awareness interpretation does not ring nearly as true, on this score.

The Self-evident Existence interpretation has no real difficulty coping with (3): for there is no need to embrace the assumption that only if a person has direct awareness of his own mind, can it provide him with a model of God's mind. It is sufficient for such a purpose that the person know what sort of entity his mind is; and this knowledge, as we shall see, need not require that the person have direct awareness of his own mind.

Passage (2), finally, can easily be handled by the Self-evident Existence interpretation. The 'reflex act' need not be an act of intro-

216

spective awareness, as on the Direct Awareness rendition; it may be a purely intellectual act in which the mind thinks about itself—about its own nature, or its own existence, or both.

It seems to me that, everything considered, though the Direct Awareness interpretation of Philonous' speech is quite plausible, the Self-evident Existence interpretation is preferable. If I am right in this, and if there are no relevant passages that I have overlooked, then we may conclude that Berkeley, in the first editions of the *Principles* and *Three Dialogues*, does not claim that we can, or do, have direct awareness of our own minds.

Let us turn, finally, to the 1734 editions of the *Principles* and the *Three Dialogues*. Berkeley persists in his denial that we can have any idea of mind, but he claims, now, that we have some *notion* of it. This claim represents no new doctrine, or no new evasion, as is sometimes thought, because to have a notion of something, as Berkeley explains, is just to know the meaning of some term that signifies, or denotes, it—and he has maintained right along that we know what terms such as 'mind' and 'spirit' mean: 'Though it must be owned at the same time, that we have some notion of soul, spirit, and the operations of the mind, such as willing, loving, hating, in as much as we know or understand the meaning of those words' (*PHK* I 27; see also *PHK* I 140, 142). I suggested earlier that knowing what the term 'mind' means, or knowing what the meaning of the term 'mind' is (I treat these two locutions as equivalent, as I think Berkeley himself does), is knowing what sort of thing the mind is. Berkeley seems, at least, to suggest now that we have this knowledge because we have a direct awareness of our own minds:

(5) We comprehend our own existence by inward feeling or reflexion, and that of other spirits by reason. We may be said to have some knowledge or notion of our own minds, of spirits and active beings, whereof in a strict sense we have not ideas. (*PHK* I 89)

(6) I say lastly, that I have a notion of spirit, though I have not, strictly speaking, an idea of it. I do not perceive it as an idea or by means of an idea, but know it by reflexion. (*3D* III (*W* II 233; A 195; T 178))

I shall take up these passages separately, and in reverse order. Everything hinges, in (6), on what the word 'reflection' means. As Brown points out,[29] Berkeley uses the term 'reflection' and its cognates in two quite different ways. In the first of its two senses, reflection is 'non-cognitive' introspection; it is a direct awareness of mental 'things' such as feelings, emotions, and sensations. It seems to be viewed as a kind of internal sense analogous to the usual external senses:

217

For what is there on our part, or what do we perceive amongst all the ideas, sensations, notions, which are imprinted on our minds, either by sense or reflexion, from whence may be inferred the existence of an inert, thoughtless, unperceived occasion? (*PHK* I 74)

But whoever shall attend to his ideas, whether of sense or reflexion, will not perceive in them any power or activity. (*PHK* I 25)

Notice that as far as these passages go, we are aware, in reflection, of nothing but 'ideas, sensations, notions';[30] if Berkeley thinks that it is somehow in the nature of reflection to have only such things as these for its objects (as he thinks it is in the nature of an external sense to have nothing but ideas of sense for its objects), then it is extremely unlikely that he would express the unadorned and unexplained opinion, here in the 1734 editions of his major works, that in reflection we are also directly aware of our own minds.

But before we can reject this first sense of 'reflection' as the correct meaning of the term in (6), we must consider the famous opening sentence of the *Principles*, Part I:

It is evident to any one who takes a survey of the objects of human knowledge, that they are either ideas actually imprinted on the senses, or else such as are perceived by attending to the passions and operations of the mind, or lastly ideas formed by help of memory and imagination, either compounding, dividing, or barely representing those originally perceived in the aforesaid ways. (*PHK* I 1)

Although the word 'reflection' is not used, it is obvious that the second and third of the three items in his 'survey of the objects of human knowledge' are objects presented to us in reflection (in our first sense of the term). It is not clear whether the 'such' in the description of the second item in the survey means 'such *ideas*' or whether it means 'such *objects of knowledge*.'[31] If it means 'such *ideas*,' then, as before, the objects given to us in reflection are apparently limited to ideas. But if, as seems overwhelmingly likely, it means 'such *objects of knowledge*,' then the passage can plausibly be viewed as extending the range of objects given to us in reflection. This may be seen as follows. On this reading, Berkeley seems plainly to be saying that in reflection we are directly aware of 'the passions and operations of the mind'; but one can plausibly argue, as I urged earlier, that to be (directly) aware of a passion, which is probably best viewed as a *state* of the mind, or to be (directly) aware of an operation, or action, of the mind, is to be (directly) aware of the mind itself. But whatever the merits may be of such an argument, it is clear from the very next section of the *Principles* that Berkeley does not endorse it, for he says there:

> But besides all that endless variety of ideas or objects of knowledge, there is likewise something which knows or perceives them, and exercises divers operations, as willing, imagining, remembering about them. This perceiving, active being is what I call *mind, spirit, soul* or *my self*. (*PHK* I 2)

With these words, Berkeley specifically excludes the mind from his 'survey of the objects of human knowledge.' It is abundantly clear that by 'objects of human knowledge,' here, he means objects of direct awareness. So Berkeley is rejecting the view that in reflection, in particular, we are directly aware of our own minds.

I conclude that in the pre-1734 editions of the *Principles* and the *Three Dialogues*, Berkeley denies that reflection, in the first sense of the term, affords us a direct awareness of the mind. But if so, then it is extremely unlikely that in the 1734 editions he adopts the view that reflection *does* afford such an awareness. The point is not that such a change of heart would be impossible or even unusual; the point is rather that Berkeley gives no indication whatever that he now regards reflection (in the first sense) as having an extraordinary new object. That would be a radical change of view and would call for special comment or emphasis; but there is nothing of the kind. On the contrary, the sentences in the 1734 editions that speak of reflection—e.g., (6)—are positively subdued, and give the distinct impression that Berkeley is using the term in full accordance with the views expressed elsewhere in those works. If there were no other sense of 'reflection' in the *Principles* and the *Three Dialogues*, we might be forced to hold that Berkeley quietly—i.e., without proper warning—introduces a dramatic new doctrine in the 1734 editions; but there is another sense of the term.

In the second sense of 'reflection' to be found in Berkeley, it is also a kind of introspection, but it is more 'cognitive' than the first kind and involves more activity. It is a process of inspecting one's ideas, and of actively performing various sorts of experiments with them, to see what one can and cannot conceive of:

> Some truths there are so near and obvious to the mind, that a man need only open his eyes to see them. Such I take this important one to be, to wit, that . . . all those bodies which compose the mighty frame of the world, have not any subsistence without a mind, that their being is to be perceived or known; . . . To be convinced of which, the reader need only reflect and try to separate in his own thoughts the being of a sensible thing from its being perceived.

219

From what has been said, it follows, there is not any other substance than *spirit*, or that which perceives. (*PHK* I 6, 7)

But I desire any one to reflect and try, whether he can by any abstraction of thought, conceive the extension and motion of a body, without all other sensible qualities. For my part, I see evidently that it is not in my power to frame an idea of a body extended and moved, but I must withal give it some colour or other sensible quality which is acknowledged to exist only in the mind. (*PHK* I 10)

For to what purpose is it to dilate on that which may be demonstrated with the utmost evidence in a line or two, to anyone that is capable of the least reflexion? It is but looking into your own thoughts, and so trying whether you can conceive it possible for a sound, or figure, or motion, or colour, to exist without the mind, or unperceived. (*PHK* I 22)

(See also *PHK* I 27; it is clear that Berkeley is talking about reflection in this second sense in *PHK* I 24, too, even though the word is not used.) With the doctrine of reflection expressed in these passages, Berkeley joins the rationalists in holding that by the use of reason alone, one can arrive at substantial truths about reality. If, by reflection, one cannot conceive of an x without a y (or of an x without x's being y-ed, or of an x without x's y-ing, and so on), then it is nonsense to talk about the existence of an x without a y (or of an x without x's being y-ed, or of an x without x's y-ing, and so on)—and therefore, necessarily, there are no x's existing without y's (no x's existing without being y-ed, no x's existing without y-ing, and so on). As we shall see, Berkeley's rationalism is explicitly restricted in the following way: he denies that if one cannot conceive of an x, then one can conclude that there are no x's. (See *3D* III (*W* II 232; A 195; T 177), and below, p. 222.) Even this restricted form of rationalism is an extremely hazardous doctrine at best, since one's inability to conceive of some state of affairs may simply reveal a limitation of one's knowledge, imagination, ingenuity, or whatever, rather than revealing a deep truth about the way reality must be. But that Berkeley espouses this doctrine is undeniable.

I want to suggest, as the most plausible hypothesis, that when Berkeley says, in (6), that he knows his mind by reflection, he means reflection not in the first, but in the second, sense. He is claiming to know, by reflection, what sort of a thing the mind must be. As I reconstruct his reasoning, it goes something like this: You cannot conceive of an idea existing by itself—i.e., independently of being perceived by something. So wherever there is an idea, there is, necessarily, something that perceives it. This something is called the mind. You cannot conceive that an idea is perceived by another idea; so the mind must be something quite different from any idea. You find further that, simply by willing it, you can bring certain ideas before your mind, and move parts of your body. You cannot conceive that this sort of thing should happen without a cause, that is, without some principle of activity. So the mind must be a genuinely active entity, as well as a perceiver of ideas. (And so on, for other features of the mind—e.g., its simplicity.)

As I interpret (6), then, Berkeley is not claiming to have a direct awareness of his own mind, but claiming rather that simply by consulting his own thoughts, he can 'see' there what sort of a thing his mind must be. If Berkeley assumes, as he very well might, that reflection in his second sense yields self-evident truths, and that all self-evident truths are knowable 'immediately or intuitively' (i.e., without inference), then this interpretation of (6) agrees perfectly with passage (1), as we construed it—for (1) asserts in part, we decided, that we know 'immediately, or intuitively' what sort of thing our minds are. A notable virtue of this reading of (6) is that it yields a wholly natural account of what Berkeley means by a *notion*. To have a notion of spirit, he has told us, is to know or understand the meaning of the term 'spirit' (*PHK* I 27, 140)—i.e., to know what is meant by that term (*PHK* I 142). To know what is meant by the term 'spirit' is to know what the term 'signifies,' what it denotes—and to know this is to know what sort of thing the denotatum is. It is reflection in his second sense that provides us with precisely this knowledge. Reflection, thus, provides us with a notion of spirit.

The doctrine of reflection, in which Berkeley's philosophy takes a decidedly rationalist turn, is an attempt to solve the problem of how, without being able to have an idea (or image) of spirit, we can have any conception of it at all. We can have a conception of it because its existence is a demand of reason, and reason tells us at the same time what sort of thing it must be. In the first edition of the *Three Dialogues*, Berkeley had taken the same sort of line about our conception of God: 'And though I perceive Him not by sense, yet I have a notion of Him, or know Him by reflexion and reasoning' (*3D* III (*W* II 232; A 194; T 179)). The existence and nature of God are demands of reason: in the case of God, our conception is formed by the intuitive apprehension of self-evident truths ('reflection') and by processes of discursive argumentation ('reasoning'), while in the case of finite spirits, our conception requires only reflection, not discursive reasoning as well. (I think that as a matter of fact there is more inference involved in obtaining knowledge of our own mind, on Berkeley's account, than he acknowledges; but we may let that pass.)

We may express Berkeley's view of our conception of spirit by saying

221

that our notion of it is a *relative notion*.[32] To have a 'direct and positive notion' of something, evidently, one must be directly aware of it, but we can have a (merely) relative notion of a thing, *x*, that we do not have a direct awareness of, in case the existence of something that we *do* have direct awareness of demands the existence of *x*. Berkeley had already admitted the possibility of such (merely) relative notions in the first edition of the *Three Dialogues*:

> That from a cause, effect, operation, sign, or other circumstance, there may reasonably be inferred the existence of a thing not immediately perceived, and that it were absurd for any man to argue against the existence of that thing, from his having no direct and positive notion of it, I freely own. But where there is nothing of all this; where neither reason nor revelation induce us to believe the existence of a thing; where we have not even a relative notion of it; where an abstraction is made from perceiving and being perceived, from spirit and idea: lastly, where there is not so much as the most inadequate or faint idea pretended to: I will not indeed thence conclude against the reality of any notion or existence of any thing: but my inference shall be, that you mean nothing at all. (*3D* II (*W* II 223; A 186; T 166))

As I interpret (6) and the other passages in the 1734 editions of the *Principles* and *Three Dialogues* in which Berkeley speaks about notions and reflection, with respect to mind or spirit, he is contending that from reflection, in his second sense, we have a (merely) relative notion of spirit.

Turning, now, to passage (5), we can see that despite initial appearances, it poses no threat whatever to the present interpretation of Berkeley. He is not discussing our knowledge of the nature of our minds here, but our knowledge of its existence. Such knowledge, he is telling us, depends on 'inward feeling or reflexion'—that is, on an introspective awareness of our passions, sensations, states of perceiving ideas, and so on. From the existence of these, we know with certainty that we exist, as Descartes had long ago pointed out. So although 'reflection' is indeed being used in its first sense in (5), Berkeley is not claiming that we have direct awareness of our own minds.

Assuming, now, that our interpretation of Berkeley is correct, what conclusions are to be drawn about the essence of the mind? It is a demand of reason that the mind exist and that it be an entity of a certain sort—it must be an unextended thing, wholly different in kind from ideas, one that perceives ideas and performs volitions. Although this characterization tells us a lot about the mind, it does not tell us what its essence is, as I have argued. So Berkeley's view ought to be that the essence of the mind is unknown and unknowable. He should restrict himself, as he usually does, to the statement that the mind is an unextended substance that perceives ideas and wills. He should not go on to say that this is the essence of spirit, as he does when he says that the existence of soul or spirit consists 'in perceiving ideas and thinking' (*PHK* I 139). (See also the passage in the 1734 edition of the *Three Dialogues* where he characterizes the mind in the now familiar way, and then goes on to say 'I am not in like manner conscious either of the existence or essence of matter' (*3D* III (*W* II 234; A 196; T 179)) which suggests that the foregoing characterization of the mind had stated what its essence is.) And there is no need for his desperate effort to defend his thesis about the essence of the mind against the obvious objection—the objection, namely, that the mind does not constantly perceive ideas or perform volitions—an effort that embroils him in a grotesque theory of time. No doubt it is the spectre of skepticism that moves Berkeley to go further than he is entitled to; but if we know as much about the mind as he makes out that we do, skepticism about its very essence is not so frightening. It is, for him, in any case, unavoidable.

I want, now, to discuss what I regard as a fascinating possibility; I want to ask what doctrine of the mind would result if Berkeley were to apply his new instrumentalist view of language to such terms as 'mental substance.' His official position, we have seen, is that the existence of the mind, viewed as an unextended substance that perceives ideas and performs volitions, is a demand of reason. What this really means, as far as I can see, is that the existence of such an entity is the only possible hypothesis that can explain certain phenomena that we encounter in our so-called 'mental life'; so we *must* posit the existence of a mental substance. This is somewhat stronger than, but nevertheless close in spirit to, the view that we ought to posit the existence of a mental substance, not because it is the only possible hypothesis, but because it is the best hypothesis to explain the observed data. If Berkeley were to adopt this weaker, and surely more plausible, position, it would be reasonable for him also to hold that the term 'mental substance,' and various closely related terms, such as 'spiritual substance' and 'unextended entity', have perfectly respectable uses in our language, and *therefore* have meaning. To do this would be to apply his instrumentalism, or pragmatist, view of language to terms such as 'mental substance,' and I want to explore this possible move on Berkeley's part.

It is not difficult to see what uses Berkeley might attribute to the term 'mental substance.' He would certainly maintain that it has moral uses. To call the mind a mental, or spiritual, substance—and, more specifically, to call it a simple mental substance—would tend to foster the belief that it is immortal (see *PHK* I 141, and the sermon 'On Eternal

Life' (*W* VII 108)), and this belief has the most beneficial moral results: 'And indeed there is no such antidote to vice, no such guard of virtue, no such comfort in affliction as a right belief and thorough persuasion of a future state' ('On Eternal Life' (*W* VII 106)). (See also the Preface to the first two editions of the *Three Dialogues* (*W* II 167; A 132; T 106).) Berkeley would also, of course, maintain that the term 'mental substance' has intellectual uses, since it figures prominently in what he regards as the correct explanation of both the unity of consciousness and the activity that we find in ourselves.

After agreeing with this much—and there is no reason why Berkeley should not agree with it—there are two possibilities open to him. He can say, first, that the term 'mental substance' has *only* these sorts of pragmatic meaning, and that it does not also denote a real entity; or he can say, second, that the term also denotes a real entity. In either case, 'mental substance' would be a theoretical term, but it would receive an instrumentalist interpretation on the first option, and a realist interpretation on the second.

On the instrumentalist account, mental substance would be a convenient fiction, just as he holds physical force to be; it is useful to talk as if there were mental substances, but actually the mind is nothing but a congeries of perceptions and volitions. This would be Berkeley's secret doctrine of the mind, the same in essence as the one he espoused in the earlier part of the *Philosophical Commentaries*. He would then have a phenomenalistic view of the mind, and a phenomenalistic view of so-called physical objects: the result would be a neutral monism of the type expounded by William James—a world of pure experience.

Professor Colin Turbayne, if I understand him correctly, thinks that something very like what I have called his secret doctrine of the mind is the view that Berkeley actually accepts.[33] But I do not think that this can be true. In the first place, we would have to charge Berkeley with intellectual dishonesty if he privately believed that the mind is in reality nothing but a congeries of perceptions and volitions, and yet publicly declared it to be an unextended, active substance.[34] In the case of the term 'force' when applied to so-called physical things, Berkeley makes it perfectly clear that although it is useful to speak as if there were physical forces, in fact there are, and can be, no such things. By contrast, he gives no indication in the published works that the term 'substance,' applied to the mind, is merely useful and that it does not denote a real entity. On the contrary, he explicitly asserts that it does denote a real entity:

> But it will be objected, that if there is no idea signified by the terms *soul, spirit*, and *substance*, they are wholly insignificant, or have no meaning in them. I answer, those words do mean or signify a real thing, which is neither an idea nor like an idea, but

that which perceives ideas, and wills, and reasons about them. What I am my self, that which I denote by the term I, is the same with what is meant by *soul* or *spiritual substance*. (*PHK* I 139)

It is quite impossible to believe that Berkeley is capable of misleading his audience in this flagrant way about something that lies at the very center of his metaphysical system. (To be sure, Berkeley has a pragmatic view of truth, as we shall see in Chapter XII; but it is pretty well confined to moral or practical truths, and he would certainly not in any case extend it to the area of metaphysics.)

Another serious objection to the 'secret doctrine of the mind' thesis is that the most important use of the term 'substance,' when applied to the mind, is its use in explaining certain mental phenomena—notably, the unity of our consciousness and our activity in volition; but for Berkeley, there would not be the right kind of explanation of these phenomena unless there really *were* mental substances, i.e., unless such things literally existed.[35] It might be suggested that the secret doctrine does not merely embrace the term 'mental substance,' but reaches also to such terms as 'unity' and 'activity'; mental unity and mental activity, it could be argued, are convenient fictions, just as mental substance is. But this would make the plot thicken beyond our ability to comprehend it; for if we cannot take Berkeley to be speaking literally when he says that the mind is 'entirely distinct' from its ideas (*PHK* I 2), that he knows he is 'a thinking active principle' (*3D* III (*W* II 233; A 196; T 178)), that he knows he is 'one individual principle' (*ibid.* (*W* II 234; A 196; T 179)), and so on, then we would lose our grip on what he takes the literal truth to be. Convenient fictions must rest on a solid foundation of literal truth; thus, for example, it is only because we think we know what Berkeley takes the literal truth about so-called physical objects to be, that we can understand what he means when he says that physical forces are a convenient fiction. The solid basis of literal truth that allows us, so we thought, to understand what Berkeley could mean if he believed mental substances to be a convenient fiction, is that there is genuine unity and activity in the mental realm; but if this supposed solid basis is itself a fiction, then we have lost our intellectual moorings. How are we to know where the literal truth lies that our understanding of these new fictions requires?

Moreover, Berkeley would find himself in deep trouble if his talk about the activity of the mind were not literally true. If he were to think that the mind is not really active, then since he presents no other candidates for genuine active agency (on the contrary, he asserts that 'we cannot possibly conceive of any active power but the Will' (*PC* 155)[36]), he would have to think that nothing in reality is genuinely active. But then his distinction between true or metaphysical causality (which requires activity) and scientific or commonsensical causality (which does not) would collapse; there would be only one kind of causality, and it would be of the Humean, constant conjunction, variety. In that case, however, Berkeley's proof of God's existence could not even get off the ground; the only causal explanation of our ideas of sense would have to be wholly 'naturalistic' (involving reference to light rays, retinas, and so on—that is, in Berkeley's system, to other ideas of sense), and there would be no reason to bring God into the picture.

The 'secret doctrine of the mind' interpretation of Berkeley, it seems to me, is confronted with the following unsavory options:

1 It can hold that Berkeley simply goes wrong in thinking he needs God in his system; for the reasons just given, God is entirely eliminable.

2 It can hold that Berkeley's talk of God is not to be construed as laying claim to literal truth; God, too, is a convenient fiction.

3 It can hold that God is needed in Berkeley's system, and not simply as a convenient fiction, but as a genuine immaterial substance (in the literal sense).

I take it that options (1) and (2) are sufficiently implausible to make any comment on them unnecessary: if one had to go to those lengths to defend the 'secret doctrine of the mind' interpretation of Berkeley, then that fact alone would be enough to refute the interpretation. But the third option is hardly better: if it has to be conceded that God is a genuine spiritual substance, then Berkeley would have no motive for denying that we are.

I conclude that there is no secret doctrine of the mind to be found in Berkeley, and that he takes 'mental substance' to be a theoretical term which he construes realistically—that is, he thinks the term denotes a real entity.[37] This does not involve Berkeley in the simple-minded kind of inconsistency that Hylas, and many others, charge him with:

> We have therefore no idea of any spirit. You admit nevertheless that there is spiritual substance, although you have no idea of it; while you deny there can be such a thing as material substance, because you have no notion or idea of it. Is this fair dealing? To act consistently, you must either admit matter or reject spirit.
> (3D III (W II 232; A 194f; T 177))

Berkeley's reply to this accusation is perfectly correct, given his own principles: first, the alleged conception of material substance is incoherent, while the conception of spiritual substance is not, and second, even if the conception of material substance were coherent, there is no reason to posit its existence, while there is good reason to posit the existence of spiritual substance. So the two cases are altogether different. My interpretation of Berkeley does have him positing the existence of an entity that he takes to be beyond the reach of any sort of direct awareness; but that is not a philosophically scandalous thing to do.

XII

Passive Obedience

It is surprising that Berkeley does not devote more of his energies to moral philosophy, and, in particular, that there is no systematic work on fundamental moral issues from his hand. Surprising, because it was perhaps the overriding concern of his life to promote the welfare of mankind, so that one might expect him to have carefully thought-out views on such questions as what the well-being of man is and what sort of life a person should strive to lead. Of course he has views about these matters, but it cannot be said that he anywhere provides, or tries to provide, adequate backing for them. It is true that Part II of his *Principles of Human Knowledge* was to deal with moral theory and that he actually completed some of the work; but the manuscript was lost and Berkeley could not bring himself to rewrite it.[1] His most sustained treatment of a moral issue—and it is also an issue in political philosophy—is contained in the tract *Passive Obedience* (first published in 1712), and I want, in this chapter, to examine what he says there.

Berkeley's aim is to demonstrate that every citizen of a country has an absolute or unconditional duty of passive obedience to the supreme civil power in that state. (For variety, I shall often use the noun 'sovereign' in place of the expression 'supreme civil power.') He does not, of course, mean to be arguing that citizens have a *legal* duty to passively obey the supreme civil power; that they do is an obvious, and perhaps even a necessary, truth. He is arguing, rather, that they have a moral and, as it turns out, even a religious, duty—or anyway a duty as God's creatures—to passively obey the sovereign.

What does the expression 'passive obedience' mean? What contrast is implied by the term 'passive' here? Is the kind of obedience intended by Berkeley supposed to be contrasted with *active* obedience? But what is active obedience? One bit of evidence as to what Berkeley might mean is that he uses the term 'non-resistance' as an alternative to 'passive obedience': 'I shall endeavour to prove that there is an absolute unlimited non-resistance or passive obedience due to the supreme civil power, wherever placed in any nation' (PO 2). But this does not help us very much until we know what kind of actions Berkeley would call 'resistance' to the supreme power. So let us see just how far, on his view, an obligation to obey the supreme civil power goes. Does he take the extreme position that we ought to obey any and all of its commands, no matter what they may require us to do?

The answer to this question is clearly 'No,' and his reason is relatively straightforward. Berkeley distinguishes between positive and negative precepts of morality. The former enjoin us to do something—e.g., 'Honor your parents,' 'Keep your promises,' while the latter require that we refrain from doing certain kinds of acts—e.g., 'Do not tell lies,' 'Do not commit adultery.' He holds further that although our obligation to obey any given *positive* precept of morality is limited, since there may well be occasions when it has to be violated, our obligation to obey the *negative* precepts is absolute and unconditioned; it is never permissible to violate a negative precept of morality. (I shall consider his defense of this view in a moment.) It follows at once that it cannot be our duty to obey any and all commands of the sovereign, no matter what they may be; for it is quite possible that he might enact a law, or issue a direct command, that would require us to perform an action that is prohibited by a negative moral precept, and in that case it would be our moral duty *not* to obey the sovereign's law or command.

Before proceeding, let us examine Berkeley's distinction between positive and negative precepts of morality, and his thesis that although we may, on appropriate occasions, violate a positive precept, we may never violate a negative precept. In defense of this thesis, Berkeley argues as follows (PO 26). Any moral precept, whether positive or negative, is binding on a moral agent and must be obeyed unless obeying it is, for some reason, impossible, or unless obeying it is ruled out by some higher moral consideration. But positive and negative precepts are importantly different here. On any given occasion, it is always possible that two or more positive moral precepts will require that a person do two or more different and incompatible actions. On such occasions, the agent must decide where his strongest duty lies, and violate the weaker precepts. So our obligation to obey positive moral precepts is not unconditional, since there may be occasions on which it would be wrong to obey them. (Berkeley fails to consider here the possibility that there might be one supreme positive moral precept that may never, under any circumstances, be overridden; but I shall not pursue this point.) With negative moral precepts, by contrast, we do not encounter such complications; they tell us to refrain from doing certain positive actions, and it is always easy for a person to obey all of them at once simply by abstaining from any positive action. Thus, our duty to obey them is unconditional; there are no circumstances in which it is permissible to violate them.

So runs Berkeley's argument. But the distinction between positive and negative moral precepts is not nearly strong enough to bear the weight that he places on it; the distinction, in fact, seems to be more verbal than real. For example: 'Keep your promises' looks like a positive injunction, but how does it differ, except verbally, from the negative injunction 'Do not break your promises'? Again: 'Do not steal' is presumably negative, but is equivalent to the positive 'Let other people keep their possessions' or 'Honor the right of others to hold on to their possessions.'

The corresponding distinction between doing some (positive) action and 'abstaining from all manner of positive actions whatsoever' (*PO* 26)—i.e., doing nothing—is correspondingly unreal. Am I doing some (positive) action if I sit quietly in a chair or am I doing nothing? It all depends on the circumstances. In most cases, it could plausibly be called 'doing nothing,' for all this means is that this mode of behavior fails to satisfy the descriptions of any action that happens to be relevant to some present interests or purposes; but if I know that there is a freight train bearing down on me, to sit quietly in a chair is to commit suicide, which is presumably to do some (positive) action.

So there is no mode of behavior that counts, in all circumstances, as 'doing nothing.' So 'doing nothing' is not an absolute state (of non-action) in this strong sense. But, of course, Berkeley does not need so much; all he requires is that *given any situation*, there will always be some mode of behavior that counts as 'doing nothing.' Even this weaker requirement cannot, however, be fulfilled; there just is no guarantee that, for any situation, there will always be a mode of behavior that qualifies as 'doing nothing.' Hence, there is no guarantee that I can always avoid violating all allegedly negative moral precepts. On the contrary, there are describable cases where I cannot avoid doing this. Here is one simple example: I promise a friend that I will tell his wife a falsehood about his actions on a particular night, thus helping him to avoid an argument with her. When the time comes to keep my promise, I cannot possibly avoid violating either the negative precept 'Do not tell falsehoods' or the negative precept 'Do not break your promises.' The most plausible candidate here for 'doing nothing' would, I suppose, be keeping silent: but to keep silent would be to break my promise.

Since Berkeley's principle of the absolute inviolability of negative moral precepts—let us call it the AINMP principle for short—presupposes that the distinction between doing a (positive) action and doing nothing is an absolute or, as we might say, a metaphysical, one, when in fact, as we have seen, it is no such thing, I conclude that he offers no adequate support for the principle.[2] I want to argue now that the principle is in any case patently false. It implies that if, by breaking a negative moral injunction, I could save the human race from destruction, it would be morally wrong to do so! And Berkeley actually believes that it would be wrong! Here are his extraordinary words:

> We are now come to the second point, which was to shew that
> the prohibitions of vice, or negative precepts of morality, are
> to be taken in a most absolute, necessary, and immutable
> sense; insomuch that the attainment of the greatest good, or
> deliverance from the greatest evil, that can befall any man or
> number of men in this life may not justify the least violation
> of them. (PO 26)

This is utterly incredible. It could conceivably be true, though I very much doubt it, that there are certain extremely weighty negative moral precepts that should not be violated even if doing so would mean saving the human race from destruction; but whether that is true or not, there are certainly any number of negative moral injunctions that only a moral maniac would refuse to infringe where doing so would mean, say, the saving of a life or the saving of many lives. Surely it is easy to imagine circumstances in which it would be permissible to tell a lie, or deceive a friend, or steal something, or commit adultery, if such an act would save a life or save many lives. I can only appeal to one's moral intuition here, but the verdict of my intuition, anyway, is strong and clear.

I submit, against Berkeley, that there is no essential connection between the 'negativity' of a moral precept and its being exceptionless or inviolable, nor between the 'positiveness' of a moral precept and its allowing exceptions. Most negative moral precepts—such as 'Do not tell falsehoods,' 'Do not break your promises,' even 'Do not kill'—permit occasional exceptions, just as most, and perhaps all, positive moral precepts do. What gives the illusion that negative precepts are inviolable, perhaps, is the existence of certain terms that have inviolability built into them, as it were. I have in mind such terms as 'murder.' It is true that the negative moral precept 'Do not murder' or 'One ought not to murder' is absolute or unconditional; but its unconditionality is due not to its negativity, but rather to the special feature of the term 'murder.' Murder is the taking of another person's life where such an act is morally wrong; so if I am locked in mortal combat with a man who has actively tried to kill me, then if I kill him, it is not murder, but killing in self-defense, whereas if he kills me, it is murder most foul. The precept 'One ought not to murder,' therefore, is exceptionless because vacuous; it says that one is morally at fault for taking another person's life in cases where such killing is morally wrong (cf. *PO* 32).

I conclude that the reasoning which leads Berkeley to claim that our obligation to obey the supreme civil power is limited or subject to exceptions, is faulty, since it turns on the false AINMP principle. Nevertheless, what he claims is clearly right: for there surely *are* circumstances in which it would be morally wrong to obey the supreme civil power. If the sovereign issues a law, or a direct command, that requires certain citizens to do something highly immoral—e.g., to assassinate a foreign head of state because he is a communist, or to break into a doctor's office to get incriminating evidence against a political enemy—then those citizens have the duty to refuse to obey, just as Berkeley says. Berkeley, of course, is committed to something stronger than this. He is committed, that is, not merely to the view that in case the supreme civil power commands citizens to infringe certain *very weighty* negative moral precepts, they are entitled, and even obliged, to disobey; he is committed further, by his AINMP principle, to the very much stronger thesis that whenever the supreme power commands citizens to infringe *any negative moral precept whatever*, they are entitled, and even obliged, to disobey. (Berkeley might even concede further that if the sovereign commands a citizen to infringe a very important *positive* moral precept, the citizen may rightfully refuse to obey.)

But what, then, is the absolute or unconditional duty of passive obedience that Berkeley claims all citizens owe to the supreme civil power? It is the duty to obey all commands of the sovereign that are not in conflict with one's moral conscience, and to refrain from using any force, or any violence, against the supreme power, either by way of attempting to overthrow it or by way of resisting the punishment it metes out when one disobeys its commands. So even when a citizen is perfectly justified, morally, in disobeying the sovereign, he must submit patiently to the punishment such disobedience calls down upon him. Berkeley sums all this up by saying that citizens have an unconditional duty to obey the injunction 'Thou shalt not resist the supreme power' (*PO* 15). (It seems to me that the term 'passive obedience' is an extremely misleading one for Berkeley to have used as a name for his doctrine, since in fact he defends a citizen's right to non-violent civil *disobedience*.)

Now that we know what Berkeley's doctrine of passive obedience is—or, better, what his doctrine of non-resistance is—we must turn to the question of how he attempts to justify it. His strategy, briefly, is to show that the injunction 'Thou shalt not resist the supreme civil power' is a negative moral precept and thus, like all the others, absolute or unconditional. The proof proceeds as follows.

Berkeley assumes that it can be demonstrated, and that anyway the audience of his *Passive Obedience* will grant, that God exists, that He 'alone is maker and preserver of all things' (*PO* 6), and that human beings are immortal spirits capable of experiencing pleasure and pain after their so-called bodily deaths. Berkeley takes it as self-evident that God alone is capable of making 'us for ever happy, or for ever miserable' (*PO* 6). It follows that we ought, as a matter of prudence, to obey God's will. In addition, it is our moral duty to obey God's laws. Berkeley offers only the skimpiest argument for this latter claim. The world and everything in it, including us human beings, are created by God, and it must just seem obvious to Berkeley that creatures ought, morally, to obey their creator. This does not seem at all obvious to me, but I shall not press the point.

Before proceeding with the argument, I want to digress very briefly to say something—or rather raise a question—about Berkeley's views on human motivation. He is much concerned to show that we humans have a very strong motive of self-interest to obey God's laws—that is, to do what He wants us to do; and his conception of God, and of our relationship to God, makes easy work of this attempt.[3] Does Berkeley think that self-interest provides the *only* motive we have for obeying God's will, or does he think that our knowledge that obeying God's will is our moral duty *also* provides us with a motive? I am not sure what the answer to this question is. Berkeley certainly holds that self-interest (or self-love, as it was usually called in Berkeley's day) is the dominant human motive. In *Passive Obedience*, he says that self-love is 'a principle of all others the most universal, and the most deeply engraven in our hearts' (*PO* 5). In a version of another sermon he writes, 'Every one knows the prevailing principle in human nature is self-love' (*W* VII 48; see also *W* VII 90). Berkeley also asserts, in a remarkable entry in the *Philosophical Commentaries*, that self-interest is the only rational motive: 'I'd never blame a Man for acting upon Interest. he's a fool that acts on any other Principle. the not understanding these things has been of ill consequence in Morality' (*PC* 542). All of these passages imply that there *are* other motives for human actions, without saying what they actually are. It is clear from the following passage that he regards emotions and desires as motives for some acts:

Tenderness and benevolence of temper are often motives to the best and greatest actions; but we must not make them the sole rule of our actions: they are passions rooted in our nature, and, like all other passions, must be restrained and kept under, otherwise they may possibly betray us into as great enormities as any other unbridled lust. (*PO* 13)

I do not know of any place where Berkeley specifically acknowledges the existence of a purely moral motive: it is quite probable, however, that he simply takes it for granted that people—right-minded people—are sometimes motivated to do a certain action because, and only because, they think that the action is the morally right thing to do.

To continue, now, with Berkeley's argument: he has reached the conclusion, so far, that we ought to obey God's will. God's will is expressed in certain general laws, commonly called laws of nature. These laws are of two kinds (*PO* 33). Everything that happens in the universe happens in accordance with natural laws (e.g., laws of physics), which in Berkeley's philosophy, as we have seen, are indeed expressions of God's will. These we may call *descriptive* laws of nature; and they have nothing directly to do with human morality. The second kind of laws we may call *prescriptive* laws of nature; these laws prescribe the ways in which God wants us, of our own free wills, to act. They are commands that God issues to us, and it is our moral duty to obey them. The moral law just consists of God's commands (or commandments) to His creatures that have free will—i.e., to us humans and to any other free spirits that there might be.

Notice that Berkeley takes it for granted that the set of God's commands to creatures with free will is identical with the set of moral laws or precepts. Thus, he never considers the possibility that there may be some moral laws that lie outside the scope of God's will. It might be thought—wrongly—that the reason behind Berkeley's position here is this: since moral laws tell us how we ought to act, God, in His infinite wisdom and in His infinite love for us, would not fail to command us to act in *all* of the ways we ought to, since He wants us to be perfectly virtuous. But this won't do as an account of Berkeley's thought, because it suggests that moral laws are independent of God's will, in the sense that they would be binding on us whether or not God commanded that we obey them. But Berkeley clearly holds that the laws of morality are in no way independent of God's will; they just *are* edicts that He commands us to obey: 'all the particular laws of nature or morality are to be looked upon, as so many decrees of the divine will' (Sermon X (*W* VII 130)). Hence moral laws have no authority from any source other than God: as Berkeley puts it, they 'derive their obligation . . . immediately from the Author of nature himself' (*PO* 12; see also *PO* 31).

At this point, a problem arises: how can we tell what decrees God has issued to us humans—that is, how can we determine what the laws of morality are, in so far as they apply to us human beings? Berkeley could refer us to the Holy Scripture here, but he specifically abjures any such move, since his purpose is to establish the doctrine of passive obedience by purely rational argument (*PO* 2). What we must do, then, Berkeley says, is to figure out, from our knowledge of God's nature, what ends He would want to achieve in issuing His moral commandments to us; whatever kinds of human action would serve those ends, it is reasonable to suppose, must be prescribed in God's commandments to us.

What ends *does* God want to achieve in issuing His moral edicts to us? Obviously He wants to achieve some good; and not some good for Himself, because He has every perfection, but rather some good for His creatures. Since human actions evidently have no consequences for whatever non-human rational creatures there may be, Berkeley concludes that God must intend to accomplish just the good of His human creatures (*PO* 7). (This is a parochial view that I find morally objectionable and indeed pernicious. I agree with Berkeley when he says that the laws of human morality are not concerned with the good of non-human rational creatures—e.g., angels—but I can see no warrant for his eliminating the good of non-human non-rational, but sentient, creatures—e.g., gorillas, horses, and dogs—from the scope of human morality. Why should God not want us to act in ways that would, for example, reduce the amount of pain and increase the amount of pleasure in the lives of dogs? Why should God care that little about the welfare of dogs, when He created them, and gave them the ability to feel pain and experience pleasure? Perhaps Berkeley would reply that God does want us to act in ways that will produce more pleasure and less pain for dogs and other sentient creatures, but that these desirable modes of action lie outside the scope of morality. But it is precisely this restricted view of morality that I object to: it seems obvious to me that it is morally wrong to cause needless pain to a dog, just as it is morally wrong to cause needless pain to a person. Berkeley could agree with this only if he could show that causing needless pain to dogs somehow works against the good for man—but it seem perfectly clear to me that causing needless pain to dogs is morally wrong *whether or not* such action works against the good for man.)

On Berkeley's view, then, God wants us, and indeed commands us, to act in ways that will further the good for man. Since God loves all human beings equally—where this means all men now living as well as past and future generations of men—we must act in ways that further the good of all mankind (see *PO* 7; Sermon X (*W* VII 130)). A possible objection to this that Berkeley considers a: Surely God loves virtuous people more than He loves sinners, and therefore He must want the virtuous to fare better than the wicked. It seems, then, that our moral charge ought to be to act in ways that will further the good of the virtuous more than they will further the good of the wicked.

Berkeley replies that virtuous people are just those who obey God's commandments, and wicked people are those who don't. This means that before there is even the logical possibility of virtue or wickedness, God's commandments must *already* be formulated; it would be logically impossible, therefore, that God's commandments should be designed or formulated in such a way as to distinguish between the virtuous and the wicked. That distinction can be made only *after* His commandments have been formulated:

> as nothing in a natural state can entitle one man more than
> another to the favour of God, except only moral goodness; which,
> consisting in a conformity to the laws of God, doth presuppose the
> being of such laws, and law ever supposing an end, to which it
> guides our actions; it follows that, antecedent to the end proposed
> by God, no distinction can be conceived between men; that end
> therefore itself, or general design of Providence, is not determined
> or limited by any respect of persons. (*PO* 7)

But this is a bad argument. There is nothing to prevent a private club, for example, from having a set of regulations designed to work for the advantage of those who obey them and for the disadvantage of those who do not. This could be done in a variety of ways. One way is to fix the clubhouse in suitable ways: for instance, there could be a regulation stating that club members are to show their identification cards to the doorman before entering the clubhouse. To punish those who choose to disobey this rule, the club could install a trap door just inside the main entrance, operated by the doorman, and sending transgressors down a shoot and into a pit of hungry crocodiles. Another way is simply to issue a second-order regulation stating that violators of its rules will be thrown out of the club. Berkeley would have to say that there cannot conceivably be any such thing as a violator of the rules until the rules have already been formulated; but this is simply not true. No doubt there must be some rules on the books, or anyway contemplated, before there can be conceptual space for a violator of the rules; but as we have seen, there is nothing to prevent a set of rules from being designed to favor the rule-obeyers over the rule-violators.

If God really does love virtuous people more than He loves sinners, then, there is no conceptual difficulty preventing Him from designing His commandments so as to take account of this preference; He could simply arrange things so that sinners do not fare as well as the virtuous do—and, indeed, this is precisely what He has done, because murderers and thieves do not generally fare as well in this life as the morally upright do, and even if they should escape punishment here on earth, the fires of hell are nevertheless waiting for them. Alternatively, He could issue such second-order commandments as 'Shun ye all those who break My laws.' So Berkeley's argument fails. Where does he go wrong? I would diagnose his mistake as follows. Let us assume that there are certain individuals who are wicked (e.g., Hitler) and certain classes of wicked individuals (e.g., capitalists). Berkeley is right that it is logically impossible that God should *first* pick out as wicked these individuals and classes of them (e.g., Hitler and capitalists) and only *then* formulate His commandments so as to discriminate against them. My guess is that Berkeley goes astray by assuming that since God, in formulating His commandments, cannot take account of the wicked in *this* way, He cannot take account of them in any way at all, and must therefore formulate His commandments so that they tend to benefit all men, wicked and virtuous alike. This assumption is wrong, for as we have seen, there is a perfectly coherent way in which God, in formulating His commandments, can take account of the wicked and discriminate against them if He wishes.

To continue the main line of Berkeley's thought, however, let us assume that he has shown that God wants us to act in ways that will produce the maximum good for all mankind. This gives us some help in answering our current problem—the problem, namely, of how we can determine what the laws of morality are; but we still need to know more. We need to know what form God's commandments take. According to Berkeley, there are only two possible choices open to God (*PO* 8):

1 He can issue just one sweeping injunction, telling us always to act in ways that seem to us most likely to lead to the maximum good for man.

2 He can issue several determinate injunctions, commanding us to perform certain acts (e.g., to honor our debts) and to refrain from certain acts (e.g., to refrain from stealing). These determinate rules would be such that if everyone were to obey them, the public good would almost certainly be increased, though occasionally, through some misfortune, obedience to them might well do a lot of harm.

A minor point about the second option. In the characterization of this option, it does not seem to be necessary, or even desirable, to require that *everyone* should observe the determinate rules. Given the imperfection of human nature, it would be unreasonable of God to expect that everyone would always observe His commandments; if He were to choose the second option, He would be well advised, then, to assume that the best He can hope for is that people will *for the most part* obey His commandments, and to issue commandments that, given the truth of that assumption, have the best chance of increasing human welfare. (Berkeley could not agree with this point because it presupposes that there is the conceptual possibility of a violator of God's commandments before they are formulated, and we have seen that he explicitly denies this presupposition.)

Berkeley believes that there are several strong objections to the first of the options, but he confines himself to just two connected shortcomings (*PO* 9f). First, it would be so difficult as to be virtually impossible for a person to calculate the good and bad effects of each action open to him at every turn; and even if he could do this, the process would take far too much time to be of any practical use. Second, on this option, there would be no ascertainable standards by which to judge whether people are acting morally or sinfully, since different people would calculate the good and bad effects of any action differently, so that, for example, although an agent may deem it his duty to do a certain act, others may think that to do it would be a terrible sin. Berkeley thinks that this would entail 'the most horrible confusion of vice and virtue, sin and duty, that can possibly be imagined' (*PO* 10).

A full discussion of these objections would take us too far afield; I shall simply say, dogmatically, about the second that I doubt very much that the moral scene would be nearly so chaotic as Berkeley fears that it would. The first objection seems much stronger; it is, by now, a familiar objection to act utilitarianism. Act utilitarianism is the doctrine, to put it roughly, that the rightness (or wrongness) of an individual act is its potentiality for causing an increase (or a decrease) in the general sum of human happiness. Difficulties of the kind raised by Berkeley have led some philosophers who were sympathetic with utilitarianism to abandon act utilitarianism in favor of rule utilitarianism; this is the view—again, to put it briefly but much too crudely—that the rightness (or wrongness) of an individual act is its being in accord with (or not in accord with) a set of moral rules, when the rules are such that their general observance would have the effect of enhancing human welfare. The difference between the two versions of utilitarianism, then, is this: on act utilitarianism, one would appeal directly to the tendency to increase human happiness in order to justify any individual action, whereas on rule utilitarianism, one would appeal rather to a set of moral rules in order to justify an individual action, and would appeal to the tendency to increase human happiness only to justify the rules themselves.

Berkeley considers the objections to the first of God's two possible options to be crippling, and concludes that God must therefore choose the second; Berkeley thus makes the very move, just described, that those philosophers make who abandon act utilitarianism to embrace rule utilitarianism. Is Berkeley a rule utilitarian, then? Almost, but not quite. Berkeley and a rule utilitarian would agree in all their moral judgments, and they would even give the same reasons to support them. The difference comes in what they say about the source of the authority of the moral rules. The rule utilitarian says that such-and-such moral rules are the right ones because, and only because, their general observance leads to more human happiness than would the general observance of any other set of rules. It is our duty to obey them whether God exists or not; for their status of being the rules we ought to follow just *is* their status of being the rules whose general observance leads to more human happiness than would the general observance of any other set of such rules. For Berkeley, on the other hand, it is their being God's commands to us that makes them the set of rules we ought to obey; our obligation to obey them stems not, then, from the fact that their general observance leads to more human happiness, but directly from the fact that God has willed them: 'nothing is a law merely because it conduceth to the public good, but because it is decreed by the will of God, which alone can give the sanction of a law of nature to any precept' (*PO* 31). To be sure, given God's nature, it is certain that His moral commandments will be identical with the moral rules that a rule utilitarian would accept; but Berkeley would say that if, *per impossibile*, God should have issued different moral laws from the ones He in fact did issue, then it would have been our duty to obey those other laws. A rule utilitarian, by contrast, would say that if God should have issued a different set of moral rules, He would have made a ghastly mistake: He would have issued the *wrong* set of laws, and we would have no obligation to obey them.[4]

Berkeley has now found, he thinks, a way of determining what God's commandments are, that is, what the laws of morality are:

Hence, upon an equal comprehensive survey of the general nature,
the passions, interests, and mutual respects of mankind,
whatsoever practical proposition doth to right reason evidently
appear to have a necessary connexion with the universal well-being
included in it is to be looked upon as enjoined by the will of God.
(*PO* 11)

This calls for comment. Despite what Berkeley implies in this passage, one cannot, it would seem, consider a single 'practical proposition,' by itself, and determine whether its universal acceptance will promote the well-being of all mankind; for the good and bad effects of any single rule will be influenced in part by the other moral rules that are generally observed along with it. Thus, the precept 'Do not commit adultery' would have certain kinds of good and bad effects if it were permissible to have three hundred wives, or to have a spouse, or several spouses, of the same sex, and quite different effects if, as in our society, it is permitted to have only one spouse, and of the opposite sex. Again, the effects of that precept in a society where telling falsehoods is allowed would no doubt be different from what they would be in a society such as ours where telling falsehoods is not allowed. So as Berkeley himself later realizes, what he wants to say is that moral laws are characterized by the fact that the universal observance of the *whole set* of them leads to the well-being of mankind: 'The law of Nature is a system of such rules or precepts as that, if they be all of them, at all times, in all places, and by all men observed, they will necessarily promote the well-being of mankind, so far as it is attainable by human actions' (*PO* 15).

Now, however, Berkeley is faced with a problem. In this passage, he offers a criterion that applies to a set of propositions; it suggests a way of telling whether a whole set of purported moral rules or precepts is the set of valid moral rules or precepts. But his concern in *Passive Obedience* is to show that a *single* precept (namely, 'Thou shalt not resist the supreme civil power') is a genuine moral law, and in fact an inviolable moral law. He needs a criterion that will determine whether or not a single practical rule is a genuine moral law—and how can such a criterion be derived from a criterion that tells us only whether a whole set of practical propositions is the set of genuine moral rules? This is a complication for Berkeley, but not in itself an insuperable difficulty, I think. He can say that when one is testing a single rule, P, one must imagine that it is embedded in a certain plausible set of other rules, and then try to determine whether P would or would not make a positive contribution to the well-being of a group of people who accepted the whole set of rules. Such a trial will probably have to be run again, for it is likely that some of the 'plausible set of other rules' will turn out not to be acceptable when they are similarly tested; but I see no reason in principle why this procedure should not eventually yield a single set of rules that satisfies Berkeley's criterion. Here, then, is what I propose as Berkeley's *main criterion* of a (single) moral law: a rule P is a law of morality if, and only if, P is a member of a set of rules S which is such that the universal observance of S promotes the well-being of mankind, so far as it is attainable by human actions, and the universal observances of *P* makes a positive contribution to this well-being of mankind.

What is the well-being of mankind, for Berkeley? He says very little about this, but he does offer some remarks about the good for man. He identifies the good for man with happiness, and happiness, in turn, with pleasure (*PO* 5). At one point early in his career, he makes the surprising claim that 'Sensual Pleasure is the Summum Bonum. This the Great Principle of Morality. This once rightly understood all the Doctrines even the Severest of the Gospels may clearly be Demonstrated' (*PC* 769). His considered view, however, is that there are pleasures associated with our sensual nature, others with the imagination, and still others with the rational part of our soul, and that these last are the highest and best pleasures.⁵ So the well-being of mankind is their having a maximum amount of happiness—i.e., a maximum amount of the highest kinds of pleasures that they are capable of experiencing.

This conception of the well-being of mankind shows us how Berkeley's criterion for the set of true moral rules is to be construed: it should be understood as saying that the true moral laws are that system of rules or precepts *S* which, when all of them are universally observed, produces more human happiness than would be produced by the universal acceptance of any other such system of rules or precepts. To determine whether a single rule *P* satisfies Berkeley's main criterion for a law of morality, then, one must establish that the universal observance of *P*, along with the other members of *S*, produces more human happiness than would the universal observance of any alternative to *P*.

Berkeley thinks he has now discovered an *easy* way to determine what the genuine moral laws are (*PO* 15), but this is far from true in most cases. It is no doubt fairly obvious that we are better off (i.e., happier) if there are moral prohibitions against our stealing from one another and against our killing one another casually, than if there were no such prohibitions; but is it so clear that we are better off with, than without, moral prohibitions against, say, adultery or homosexuality? To find out by using the procedure of Berkeley's main criterion, we should have to carry out the most complex calculations imaginable. These calculations would require a vast amount of knowledge—about human psychology, sociology, physics, politics, and every other branch of human learning; and we should need to use this knowledge to make hypothetical predictions about huge numbers of people over great stretches of time. And there are, of course, innumerable familiar problems about measuring and comparing pleasures. So it is clear that the task of determining what most of the moral laws are, on Berkeley's account, is not nearly so easy as he makes it out to be; on the contrary, it is staggeringly difficult.

The criterion that Berkeley has now set forth—what I have called his *main criterion* for a law of morality—is not, in fact, sufficient to pick out the laws of morality, as he himself well realizes; it specifies at most a necessary condition for a moral law, but not also a sufficient one. Thus, there are very many systems of rules which, if generally followed, will produce more good for mankind than would be produced by the general observance of any other such system, but which would not be called rules of morality—e.g., rules of etiquette, rules of wise investment of capital, rules of good house construction, rules of good farming, and innumerable others. Berkeley, recognizing the need for further restrictions, lists three:

(a) Rules of morality deal only with matters of great importance. (*PO* 17)
(b) Rules of morality deal only with universal matters—that is, with things of concern not just to special groups of people, but to all people everywhere. (*PO* 18)
(c) Rules of morality deal only with matters that are in many cases too difficult to be left to the judgment of individuals. (*PO* 19)

The question of what the essential features of moral laws are is a vexing one that has perhaps not even yet been satisfactorily answered, but it seems clear enough anyway that Berkeley has not given a fully adequate account. Once again, I cannot discuss this question with the thoroughness it deserves; I shall simply remark that the four conditions together seem to be too generous, allowing some clearly non-moral rules to be counted as moral rules (e.g., rules to be followed for good health, the rules of good farming).

Now that Berkeley has, as he thinks, a set of criteria allowing him to identify the genuine laws of morality, he moves to the task of showing that the precept 'Thou shalt not resist the supreme civil power'—let us call this the *non-resistance precept*—is an inviolable moral law. He tries to do this in two different ways. In the first, he shows that the non-resistance precept satisfies his four criteria for being a law of morality (*PO* 16–19), and therefore is such a law. He then presents the principle of the absolute inviolability of negative moral precepts—the AINMP principle—and draws the conclusion that the non-resistance precept, being a negative rule, is inviolable. This first way is a dead end, because, as I have already urged, the AINMP principle is false.

The second way, which I shall now describe, is much more

interesting. Berkeley argues, as before, that his non-resistance precept satisfies criteria (a), (b), and (c) for being a moral law, and then attempts to show that the precept, when regarded as inviolable, is superior to its alternatives, in that a system of rules that includes it leads to more good for mankind than an otherwise similar system of rules that does not include it. That is, he attempts to show that his non-resistance precept (when regarded as inviolable) satisfies his main criterion for being a moral law. Since the precept, so regarded, satisfies all four criteria, it is a valid moral law.

The argument occurs in section 20 of *Passive Obedience*. Berkeley says that there must be *some* rule to guide people when it comes to the question of resistance to the supreme civil power: there must be a rule stating whether or not it is ever permissible to resist the supreme power, and if it is ever allowed, what conditions justify the resistance. Chaos would result if no restrictions at all were laid down, so that citizens could resist the supreme power whenever they wanted to or thought they could get away with it. But the required rule must either be Berkeley's non-resistance precept (regarded as inviolable) or a rule stating that one should not resist the supreme power except in cases where greater public good can be achieved by resisting than by not resisting. (Let us call this second precept the *utilitarian alternative*.) Now comes the crucial phase of the argument. Berkeley next claims that since people have wildly different views about what the public good is, to adopt the utilitarian alternative would be tantamount to having no rule at all. It has already been agreed that to have no rule at all in this area would be disastrous, and so Berkeley's non-resistance precept (regarded as inviolable) must be acknowledged as binding on us.

This argument fails. Berkeley goes wrong when he says that the variety of views different people have about what constitutes the public good means that adopting the utilitarian alternative is tantamount to adopting no rule at all. Everything depends on *why* there is such a variety of views. Berkeley might be right if the variety were due to the fact that there is no objectivity at all concerning what the public good is—that is, if there were no such thing as one view on the subject being better or worse than any other. But Berkeley cannot, and does not, of course, explain the variety of views in that way; for he is deeply committed to the objectivity of judgments about what the public good, or the good for man, is. (For example, his main criterion for a moral law presupposes the objectivity of such judgments.) He must say that the variety is due to the extreme difficulty of determining just what the public good requires in any given situation—and he is no doubt right about this. But if so, then the fact that there are a variety of views about what the public good requires does not mean, as Berkeley thinks it does, that opting for the utilitarian alternative is as good (or bad, rather) as having no rule at all, and that it would permit all sorts of resistance to the supreme civil power; it means, rather, that a citizen must be extremely cautious, very sure of his ground, before he takes it upon himself to indulge in such resistance in the name of the public good. The disadvantage of adopting the utilitarian alternative—and this is the feature of it that distresses Berkeley—is that well-meaning people would surely sometimes appeal to it to justify some drastic resistance to the sovereign when, contrary to their opinion, the public good would be seriously diminished by their rebellion. But to concede that such unfortunate incidents would occasionally happen if people accepted the utilitarian alternative is very far from saying that the acceptance of that precept is tantamount to having no precept at all. Most people most of the time regard the overthrow of their government as a kind of disaster, and indeed will scrupulously avoid resisting the sovereign. They will support a rebellion only in the most extreme situations, when they are positively driven to it by insufferable tyranny; so if they adopted the utilitarian alternative, there is good reason to suppose that they would invoke it to justify rebellion only rarely, in the direst of circumstances. It is by no means clear that the best interests of mankind would not be served by their adopting the utilitarian alternative, rather than Berkeley's non-resistance precept, when this latter is regarded as inviolable.

One thing is certain: there are describable situations in which a system of rules that includes the utilitarian alternative would serve mankind better than a similar system that includes Berkeley's non-resistance precept (regarded as inviolable). One such situation is the kind that existed in Hitler's Germany. Berkeley's precept (regarded as inviolable) would disallow any attempt on the part of citizens to overthrow a Hitler, despite the fact that he might be systematically exterminating millions of innocent people, whereas the utilitarian alternative would sanction such attempts, provided, of course, that they did not involve even greater harm to mankind. It would, thus, give honest citizens a clear motive for attempting to overthrow a wicked tyrant. If Berkeley is right about the method one must use to determine what the moral laws are, then this one kind of case does not prove that the utilitarian alternative is morally preferable to Berkeley's non-resistance precept.[6] To determine whether it is or not by Berkeley's method would be a tremendously complex affair, as I have already argued. One would have to reckon the effects of adopting each precept in a huge variety of possible situations, calculate the probability of these situations actually occurring, and so on—a staggering job. I have no idea whether, in the end, Berkeley's non-resistance precept (regarded as inviolable) or the utilitarian alternative would emerge as the true moral principle by this procedure; but it is certain that Berkeley has not even come close to proving that his precept (regarded as inviolable) is superior to the utilitarian alternative. And he is most certainly mistaken in his claim that espousal of the utilitarian alternative is tantamount to having no rule at all.

I think that the example of Hitler's Germany is more damaging to Berkeley's position than I have so far indicated. I have just argued that mankind would benefit, in horrible situations such as that of Hitler's Germany, if people accepted the utilitarian alternative rather than the non-resistance precept (regarded as inviolable); and I conceded that this fact, by itself, does not prove that the utilitarian alternative is a better moral principle than the non-resistance precept (regarded as inviolable). When I said that in those circumstances mankind would benefit from an acceptance of the utilitarian alternative, I meant that its acceptance would give honest citizens a motive for overthrowing a wicked Hitler-like tyrant at the head of their government; I was assuming, of course, that the downfall of such a tyrant would be a gain for mankind. But I think something much stronger can be said about rebelling against a Hitler-like tyrant; not only would mankind benefit from his downfall, but citizens of his country have a moral right, and perhaps even a moral duty (though that is a hard judgment needing a great deal of defense), to rebel against him. I claim, in fact, that we know, with complete certainty, that any attempt by the citizenry to overthrow a Hitler-like government, within certain bounds (e.g., the attempt must not involve the destruction of half the human race), would be not only a morally right action, but an act of supreme moral heroism. I take it as perfectly obvious that if one's government is slaughtering millions of innocent people, then it is one's moral right, and perhaps even one's duty, to seek the overthrow of that government by lawful means, or, in case lawful means are out of the question, by unlawful means. If this intuition of mine is correct, then it follows at once that Berkeley's non-resistance precept is not a valid moral precept—that is, not when conceived of as Berkeley does, namely, as an inviolable moral precept. Berkeley holds that it is never morally permissible to rebel against the supreme civil power; but if my intuition about the kind of situation that existed in Hitler's Germany is right, then Berkeley is mistaken in this.

In section 52 of *Passive Obedience*, Berkeley says something that might seem to give him an answer to my objection: he says that the non-resistance precept (regarded as inviolable) is clearly not meant to oblige us citizens 'to submit the disposal of our lives and fortunes to the discretion . . . of madmen.' This means that his non-resistance precept ought to be reworded to take account of this fact. The proper formulation of it might, for example, be something like this: 'Thou shalt not resist the supreme civil power when this power is either a sane person or a body dominated by sane persons.' Hitler was clearly mad, it might be argued, and so as Berkeley now construes the non-resistance precept, it allows citizens in Hitler's Germany to attempt to overthrow their demented leader. I do not think that this defense will work, however. It is not clear to me whether Berkeley means that we have no duty of passive obedience at all to a sovereign who is mad, or whether he means that our duty of passive obedience to a mad sovereign lapses only when he threatens our lives or fortunes. Either way, Berkeley is skating on thin ice. Why, we may ask, should our obligation not to resist a mad sovereign be any weaker than our obligation not to resist a sane one? The only plausible answer, as far as I can see, is that more harm would be inflicted on the populace by not resisting a mad supreme civil power than would be suffered by rebelling against it. But then Berkeley is implicitly admitting an exception to the non-resistance precept, from considerations of the public welfare—i.e., he is implicitly espousing what I have called the utilitarian alternative—and this he cannot permit himself to do. There is also another weakness of Berkeley's alleged answer to my objection: Hitler happened to be mad, let us grant—but it is easy enough to imagine a non-actual example, where a sovereign commits Hitler-like atrocities but is not mad. (It could be claimed that any tyrant who commits atrocities that are sufficiently grave to morally justify a rebellion against him must be mad, but I do not know how such a claim might be defended.)

I have argued that Berkeley does not establish that his non-resistance precept, as he conceives of it—i.e., as inviolable—is a valid moral law. I have argued, further, that if my moral intuition about the kind of situation that existed in Hitler's Germany is right, Berkeley's precept, as so conceived, cannot be a valid moral law. The strongest position he can plausibly take, I think, is that the non-resistance precept is a law of morality, but not an inviolable one. But that thesis is just the hated utilitarian alternative, and Berkeley would, of course, not want to defend it.

I want, now, to raise some metaethical questions, that is, some questions about ethical propositions, in Berkeley's philosophy. He holds that there are no ideas of the virtues and vices (*PC* 669)—and let us agree, for the sake of argument, that this does indeed follow from his imagist conception of ideas. He would also consider himself committed to the position that there are no ideas answering to such terms as 'ought,' 'right,' 'duty,' 'obligation,' and so on. Some special account will have to be given, then, of what ethical propositions are. We know that Berkeley specifically rejects the view that there must be an idea corresponding to every term that has a meaning; some terms, he says, have meaning in virtue of having a use (or uses). It is eminently plausible, moreover, to view ethical terms as having precisely this kind of pragmatic meaning. Berkeley certainly so views them, at any rate. For example, in the first draft of his introduction to the *Principles of Human Knowledge*, he remarks that when the Apostle says to us that God has prepared wondrous good things for those who love Him, his purpose is not to raise ideas of those good things in our minds—there are no such ideas—but simply 'to beget in us a chearfulness and zeal and perseverance in well doing' (*W* II 138). But this raises certain questions. If utterances containing ethical terms have only pragmatic meaning, in what sense, if any, can they be said to have a truth value (i.e., to be either true or false)? Are there, in other words, on this view, any ethical *propositions*? And what can it be to *prove* a moral pronouncement? In *Passive Obedience*, in particular, are we to suppose that Berkeley is trying to prove that it is our inviolable duty not to resist the sovereign, or is he rather merely trying to persuade us to act in that way; that is, is he seeking to influence our understanding or to influence our will?

It will be instructive, in answering these questions, to examine Berkeley's earliest reflections on the subject. In the *Philosophical Commentaries*, he is concerned about the demonstrability of ethical principles. Consider the following passage:

> We have no Ideas of vertues & vices, no Ideas of Moral Actions wherefore it may be Question'd whether we are capable of arriving at Demonstration about them, the morality consisting in the Volition chiefly. (*PC* 669)

Here Berkeley raises what appear to be the very doubts that motivated our questions just now; but although he raises them, he does not share them. He himself, in the *Philosophical Commentaries*, is confident that, despite the lack of ideas answering to the crucial moral terms, demonstration in morality is possible. In fact, instead of the words '*despite* the lack of ideas answering to the crucial moral terms,' I could almost have put '*because* of the lack of ideas . . .'; for Berkeley thinks it is those who assert the existence of moral ideas who have difficulties with demonstration in moral philosophy—and here he no doubt has Locke in mind: 'The opinion that men had Ideas of Moral actions has render'd the Demonstrating Ethiques very difficult to them' (*PC* 683). The difficulties do not stem from the fact that the alleged ideas have to do specifically with morality; on Berkeley's view, whatever the subject matter may be, there can be no demonstration with ideas, no demonstration with what he calls 'mental propositions' (see, e.g., *PC* 731, 809). All demonstration is purely verbal (*PC* 734, 804).

We have already seen, in the chapter on abstract ideas, why the early Berkeley must hold that all demonstration is verbal: it is because he thinks, at the time of the *Philosophical Commentaries* and even as late as the unpublished first draft of the introduction to the *Principles of Human Knowledge*, that there are no general ideas. (He rejects general ideas, remember, because he assumes that a general idea would have to be an abstract idea, and there cannot be any such ideas.) The lack of general ideas means the lack of general mental propositions—and indeed of virtually all mental propositions (though Berkeley himself does not acknowledge this latter fact (see *PC* 809))—and so there cannot be any proofs carried out with mental propositions, since any proof (or at least any non-trivial proof) seeks to establish a proposition with some degree of generality, and this requires that among the premises there must also be propositions with some degree of generality. There are general *words*, however, and general verbal propositions, and so demonstration must be accomplished with words. (In point of fact, Berkeley states his own view misleadingly when he says, as he does in *PC* 804, that 'Demonstration can be only verbal.' He thinks that there can be demonstration in geometry, and that geometrical proofs require the use of a figure or diagram (*W* II 132). These diagrams are signs standing for all objects of a certain sort—all triangles or all straight lines, for example; they are therefore general signs.[7] General words, too, are general signs—so Berkeley's early thesis may best be expressed as the view that demonstration can be accomplished only by verbal and non-verbal signs. The reason that Berkeley does not put it this way is simply that he uses the term 'word' to cover all sorts of signs (see *PC* 750).[8])

We find, in the *Philosophical Commentaries*, confident statements that demonstration is possible in morality; the method consists of formulating definitions of certain terms (e.g., 'God') and then finding the moral principles that are contained, implicitly or explicitly, in them: 'To demonstrate Morality it seems one need only make a Dictionary of Words & see which included which. at least. This is the greatest part & bulk of the Work' (*PC* 690). Berkeley cannot mean that we should simply invent arbitrary verbal definitions, and then draw their moral consequences; he means that we should work out, in whatever ways we can—e.g., by philosophical reflection—correct or adequate definitions. We might, for instance, try to discover what God's nature is, and express it in a definition of

'God.' Berkeley thinks that if we do this correctly, and have true definitions also of 'worship' and 'ought,' we can easily demonstrate that God ought to be worshipped (*PC* 705).

There is another relevant passage in the *Philosophical Comment-uries* that warrants a brief discussion: 'Morality may be Demonstrated as mixt Mathematics' (*PC* 755). As an example of 'mixt mathematics,' Berkeley gives geometry (*PC* 770). The idea, I take it, is this: in geometry, as in all mathematics, there is demonstration—and it is verbal demonstration (in the broad sense of 'verbal' just indicated). But geometry also applies to, and indeed is *about*, real points and their spatial disposition—i.e., it states truths about what we call extension or space. It is the fact that geometry has real extension for its subject matter that makes it '*mixt* mathematics'; the contrast here is with such branches of mathematics as arithmetic and algebra. Arithmetic, for Berkeley, is 'pure, i.e., entirely nominal' (*PC* 770). Part of what he means by this is that proof in arithmetic is entirely 'verbal'—it is a matter of manipulating arithmetical signs in accordance with certain formal rules. But he also means more: he means that although arithmetical propositions are useful in dealing with objects in the real world, they are in no sense about real units, real pairs of things, real trios of things, and so on—that is, they do not have real units, pairs, trios, etc. for their subject matter—for the simple reason that there are no real units, real pairs, real trios, and so on. Numbers, Berkeley argues, have no objective reality, since the very same chunk of reality can be considered to be one, two, or any number of things, depending on how the mind thinks of it (cf. *PC* 104, 110, 325; *NTV* 109; *PHK* I 12, 13; *Siris* 288, 357). (Berkeley's argument for the purely subjective, or 'mental,' character of number is faulty, as commentators have shown;[9] I shall not stop to consider their criticisms.)

Just as the propositions of geometry are truths about (what is called) real extension, so the propositions of morality are truths about real human actions. Neither geometry nor morality is empirical, however, in the sense of containing empirical generalizations about extension or about how human beings actually behave. Their propositions, rather, are what might be called normative or ideal truths; they set up standards for reality. For example, geometry does not tell us whether there are any perfect plane triangles in reality or not, but it tells us what features any such triangle that there may be must have. Similarly, the science of morality does not tell us whether anyone has ever behaved as duty requires, but it tells us how people must behave if they ever do behave as duty requires (see *PO* 53).

Given that the early Berkeley holds that all demonstration is purely verbal, one might reasonably expect him to think very highly of verbal reasoning, and to take a dim view of reasoning in ideas. But just the opposite is true. He regards verbal reasoning as being of a rather inferior sort. To be sure, he acknowledges the usefulness, in practice, of its results—as in the case, for example, of mathematics (*PC* 853)[10]—and even concedes that it can lead to a kind of knowledge and truth (*PC* 676, 750, 830). But it is not reasoning of the highest or most important kind. In arithmetic or algebra, for example, we do not gain any knowledge of reality—we gain no 'speculative knowledge,' as Berkeley puts it (*PC* 768; see also *PHK* I 120). And the demonstrations in morality only draw out the truths that are already contained in our definitions. The really important kind of reasoning in moral theory is the kind that would lead to correct definitions of the relevant terms (see *PC* 162, 163). And what kind of reasoning is that? Reasoning purely in ideas, presumably. In the first draft of the introduction to the *Principles of Human Knowledge*, Berkeley tells us that in his speculations, he will attempt to spurn words as far as possible and confine his 'thoughts and enquirys to the scene of [his] own particular ideas' (*W* II 142). So Berkeley must think that reasoning in ideas is the proper way to carry on the real work in philosophy, including moral philosophy.[11] (I have argued that thinking in ideas—in mental propositions—is impossible without general ideas, but Berkeley, of course, disagrees.)

By now it might seem that Berkeley is saddled with a problem. He holds, remember, that there are no ideas of the virtues and vices, and no ideas, presumably, answering to such terms as 'right,' 'ought,' 'duty,' and so on. But if the thinking required to forge a moral theory is to be carried out in ideas, and if the aim is to formulate correct definitions of the relevant moral terms, then those definitions must presumably be mental definitions—definitions consisting of ideas—and this is impossible if, as Berkeley thinks, there are no ideas of the virtues and vices, and of the other moral terms. There is, however, a flaw in this objection, and Berkeley is not in trouble. As we know, he insists that there are other uses of language beside that of raising ideas in the minds of one's audience, and that words can have these uses even if they stand for no ideas at all. It is open to him to say, therefore, that words such as 'ought' and 'duty' can have verbal definitions, and that these definitions are evaluated not by seeing whether the words in them express the right ideas (for some of the words in them will not express any idea at all) but rather by determining whether the definitions show accurately how people actually do, or perhaps should, use the relevant terms. And there is no incoherency involved in saying that the best way for one to arrive at such verbal definitions, and to evaluate them, is to do one's thinking in ideas, rather than in words.

This line of defense, I say, is open to the early Berkeley, though he does not himself offer it. In any case, judging from what he does in *Passive Obedience*, by the time he writes that work he has arrived at a new conception of what demonstration in morality is. Definitions no longer occupy center stage, and moral principles are not derived from them. Instead, a moral principle (in this case, the principle that a citizen has the inviolable duty of not resisting the supreme civil power) is directly demonstrated, by showing that it is useful—i.e., by showing that if it is generally accepted, it leads to the well-being of all mankind. Given that moral terms signify no ideas and that their meaning lies in their use, it is not at all implausible to hold, as Berkeley evidently does, that to show that general sentences containing moral terms are beneficial to mankind *is* to demonstrate the truth of those sentences. He holds the same kind of view about certain principles in physics—e.g., those which employ the term 'force'; there can be no idea of physical force, but certain sentences containing the term 'force' are useful, and can therefore presumably be called 'true.' This is not the usual kind of truth; we might call it pragmatic truth. (We know from the *Philosophical Commentaries* that Berkeley is sympathetic to the view that there are different kinds of truth: 'Truth. three sorts thereof Natural, Mathematical & Moral' (*PC* 676).) The thesis that the best—and we might as well say, the *true*—moral principles are those that benefit mankind most, is one that Berkeley holds for the rest of his career. Thus, we find him saying in the late work *Alciphron*:

> But is not the general good of mankind to be regarded as a rule or measure of moral truths, of all such truths as direct or influence the moral actions of men? . . . Since, therefore, we are so far agreed, should it not seem to follow from the premises that the belief of a God, of a future state, and of moral duties are the only wise, right, and genuine principles of human conduct, in case they have a necessary connection with the well-being of mankind? (*Alciphron* I 16)

(These passages are contained in a section of *Alciphron* where Berkeley is explicitly countering the claim that 'convenience is one thing, and truth is another' (*W* III 60).)

It may not be quite right to say that Berkeley altogether abandons his early view that demonstration in morality is verbal, for he could still hold that demonstrations of that kind are possible. But he certainly demotes them, at least. His final position is that the most cogent and direct way of demonstrating a moral principle is to show that its general acceptance improves man's lot. Berkeley has support for this position from two quarters. The first comes from his metaphysical and theological views about God and His will. God issues His moral commandments with the aim of promoting the welfare of all mankind. It follows that in order to prove that a principle is a valid—or true—moral principle, one has to show that its general observance improves man's lot.[12] The second comes from Berkeley's views about language. Moral terms stand for no ideas, but they have a use and hence have meaning. General sentences that contain them in an essential way—i.e., purported moral principles— are (pragmatically) true in case they are useful, that is, in case their general acceptance by people leads to an improvement in their lot.[13] Thus do Berkeley's new pragmatic conception of language and his fundamental beliefs about God unite to form a beautifully coherent doctrine of proof in morality.[14]

I asked earlier whether Berkeley, in *Passive Obedience*, is trying to influence our understanding or trying to influence our will. The answer, I think, is 'both'; he is trying to influence our will, and hence our lives, for the better, by influencing our understanding. Berkeley passionately believes that the search for understanding and the search for happiness or the good life cannot be divorced, as if they were two entirely independent ventures. In *Alciphron* I 16, for example, he argues that a genuine philosopher—i.e., a seeker after truth—will try to establish principles that promote the general well-being of mankind: 'He who promotes the general well-being of mankind, by the proper necessary means, is truly wise, and acts upon wise grounds.' And later in *Alciphron*, he says: 'The true end of speech, reason, science, faith, assent, in all its different degrees, is not merely, or principally, or always, the imparting or acquiring of ideas, but rather something of an active operative nature, tending to a conceived good' (*Alciphron* VII 14). Berkeley's opposition to the 'free-thinkers' of his time stems from his conviction that their doctrines are false: but this opposition amounts to positive loathing because he thinks their views are also pernicious—though their falsity and their perniciousness are, again, not two altogether independent features of their doctrines:

> But to see men without either wit or argument pretend to run down divine and human laws, and treat their fellow-subjects with contempt for professing a belief of those points on which the present as well as future interest of mankind depends, is not to be endured. For my own part, I shall omit no endeavours to render their persons as despicable, and their practices as odious, in the eye of the world, as they deserve. (Essay on Immortality, originally published in *The Guardian* (*W* VII 224))

At the heart of all Berkeley's work—as a minister of the church, as an advocate of tar-water, as the proposer of a college in America, as a political economist (in *The Querist*), but above all, as a philosopher—there lies the purest desire to promote the welfare of all human beings. Those who knew him best certainly considered him to be a paradigm of virtue, and some of them were moved to words of high praise. Pope, for instance, wrote:

Ev'n in a bishop I can spy desert,
Secker is decent, Rundel has a heart;
Manners with candour are to Benson giv'n,
To Berkeley ev'ry virtue under heav'n.[15]

Richard Steele, in a letter published in his paper *The Guardian*, had this to say:

I cannot but look upon myself with great contempt and mortification, when I reflect that I have thrown away more hours than you have lived, though you so much excel me in everything for which I would live. Till I knew you, I thought it the privilege of angels only to be very knowing and very innocent.[16]

His wife Anne, writing to their son some time after Berkeley's death, paid glowing tribute to his character:

You never heard him give his tongue the liberty of speaking evil. Never did he reveal the fault or secret of a friend. . . . Humility, tenderness, patience, generosity, charity to men's souls and bodies, was the sole end of all his projects, and the business of his life.[17]

Virtue, as experience attests, is no safeguard against contumely and hatred in others; quite the contrary. Berkeley, so lavishly praised by his friends, was lavishly abused by the numerous critics of his works.[18] In all of his theoretical and practical endeavors, Berkeley was daring, imaginative often courageous, even; and his projects were by no means the flimsy affairs that some of his critics charged. Derision was never a warranted response to them. But it is not difficult to understand why ridicule and anger were nevertheless directed at our philosopher. From the purest of motives, he sought to reform and educate his fellow men. To have such an aim in life, one must think that humanity is in a bad way and that one knows what the remedies are for its various ills. Neither of these thoughts endears the reformer to those he is only trying to help; but the explanation of the hostility that Berkeley's work met goes further than that.

There is no doubt that the young Berkeley was (perhaps attractively) brash, as he well knew:

I am young, I am an upstart, I am a pretender, I am vain, very well. I shall Endeavour patiently to bear up under the most lessening, vilifying appellations the pride & rage of man can devise. But one thing, I know, I am not guilty of. I do not pin my faith of the sleeve of any great man. I act not out of prejudice & prepossession. I do not adhere to any opinion because it is an old one, a receiv'd one, a fashionable one, or one that I have spent much time in the study and cultivation of. (PC 465)

He never lost this fervent independence of spirit and the self-assurance that alone makes it possible. In the course of his career, he spoke out against virtually all the recognized authorities of the day—not just in philosophy, but in science, mathematics, medicine, and economics as well.

And Berkeley really did, I think, have a low opinion of the general spiritual condition of most people: he saw them as the victims of error and selfishness. And so he naturally had no great respect for the deliverances of ordinary common sense, although he paid lip-service to it. There is a profound difference of philosophical orientation between a person who considers the dictates of common sense to be, on the whole, a body of firm knowledge about how things in the world, generally speaking, are, and one who views them with deep suspicion and who is thus ready to dismiss as vulgar error any commonsensical belief, no matter how basic, that conflicts with his principles. In his heart of hearts, Berkeley was a thinker of the second kind, while most of his readers, naturally, have always belonged to the first.

Berkeley's unyielding confidence that his principles were true and his arguments sound, even though they led to rude violations of common sense shows him to be a man of the highest kind of intellectual integrity and even courage; but to most of his readers, of course, this same trait can look very like intellectual arrogance—and they are bound to view it that way, since they feel badly threatened when their deepest convictions about the world are attacked. So while Berkeley's metaphysical system never fails to impress and excite, it is also profoundly disturbing to most people. There are few indeed who can embrace it as their own.

Notes

I Biographical Sketch

1 All of my biographical facts are taken from Luce.
2 Though Luce thinks it is virtually certain that Berkeley had already met Swift in Dublin (Luce, p. 65).
3 Whitehall, Berkeley's house in Middletown, is maintained as a museum by the Society of Colonial Dames of Rhode Island. One can also visit the handsome Trinity Church in Newport where Berkeley often preached.
4 Davis and Hersh, p. 81.
5 See Berkeley's first letter to Thomas Prior (*W* V 175).

II The Visual Perception of Distance

1 I have added the '(A)' and '(B)' as a means of convenient reference. See also *3D* I (*W* II 202; A 165f; T 143) and *Alciphron* IV 8.
2 Cf. *PC* 215.
3 I take it that the 'of itself' in (A) means simply *itself*; Berkeley is claiming that distance itself cannot be immediately seen.
4 Dretske, ch. II.
5 This kind of seeing is what Dretske calls secondary epistemic seeing (cf. Dretske, p. 153).
6 I am painfully aware that my account of these two distinctions is drawn in the broadest—i.e., crudest—strokes. Innumerable refinements and qualifications would have to be made to tell the full story of direct versus indirect perception; and of course I do not even try to present a formal analysis of any of the four types of perception. The full story could not possibly be attempted here; but I hope the sketch offered in the text will do for our purposes. For more on the subject, the reader may profitably consult Dretske, and Cornman (3).
7 Similarly, Dretske's primary epistemic seeing positively *includes*

non-epistemic seeing (cf. Dretske, p. 79).

8 I shall not use the subscripts 'w/o.inter.' or 'w/o.inf.,' for the difference between the two kinds of immediate perception is irrelevant here. I shall in fact regularly drop these subscripts, and the subscripts 'w.inter.' and 'w.inf.' to the term 'mediate (or indirect) perception,' when the differences they mark are irrelevant.

9 Here, and throughout this investigation, I assume that there is a perfect correlation between immediate seeing and full-blooded looking, and a perfect correlation between mediate seeing and anemic looking. This is an assumption that Berkeley would certainly make; but I think it is actually false. Consider the visual perception of distance, for example: suppose a perceiver (consciously) infers that an object O is at such-and-such a distance; I think it is quite possible that this might make O look to the perceiver, in the full-blooded sense, to be that far away from him.

10 One of the 'other things' is the fact of compensatory movements: as one moves about, or moves parts of his body (e.g., his head or trunk), the compensatory movements (e.g., of his eyes) that he has to make in order to keep a given object, O, visually fixated will vary with the distance of O. I shall not discuss this aspect of distance perception.

11 See Klein, p. 524.

12 I shall use 'event' here to mean event or state.

13 The diagram ignores a problem that Berkeley himself also ignores— namely, how the two different patterns of retinal stimulation (due to retinal disparity) normally produce just *one* visual presentation. I shall not discuss this problem.

14 See Klein, pp. 522–37, and esp. 524f.

15 Berkeley, we remember, criticizes his opponents for thinking that we judge the distance to a seen object by consciously noting such things as the angle that our two optic axes make when they meet at the object and then consciously inferring what the distance to the object must be; but if the process were not thought of in that way—i.e., if it were not understood according to the view represented in Figure 3, but rather in accordance with the view represented in Figure 4—the disagreement between Berkeley and his opponents would vanish.

16 See Taylor.

III Visible Objects; the Visual Perception of Magnitude

1 Henceforth I shall usually drop the qualifying term 'immediately' in such phrases as 'immediately see' and 'immediately perceive'; except where otherwise indicated, words such as 'see' and 'perceive' are to be understood as though the qualifying term were present, however.

2 'Although we think we govern our words . . . certain it is that words, as a Tartar's bow, do shoot back upon the understanding of the wisest, and mightily entangle and pervert the judgment' (Bacon, *The*

Advancement of Learning, quoted in Hacking, p. 5).

3 'A *picture* held us captive' (Wittgenstein, Pt I, § 115), I have discussed Wittgenstein's treatment of pictures in Pitcher (1), pp. 201-11.

4 See note 5, below.

5 Again, let us not think of the visual appearance of *x* as an image (or resemblance) of *x*. I say this because I mean now to be talking within the framework of Berkeley's system, and in that system, according to (F), the visible objects are 'not so much as the ideas or resemblances of things placed at a distance.'

6 In *NTV* 35, Berkeley admits that faintness is a distance clue; but for some reason or other, in his explicit treatment of distance clues, he fails to include faintness among them.

7 See *NTV* 77, however.

8 Berkeley himself raises an objection to this part of his account when he asks, in the *Philosophical Commentaries*, 'why a mist encreases not the Apparent magnitude of an object in proportion to the faintness?' (*PC* 244). By the time he writes the *Essay*, however, he thinks that the facts are quite different: 'in misty weather it is a common observation that the appearance of the horizontal moon is far larger than usual, which greatly conspires with and strengthens our opinion' (*NTV* 71).

9 Section 73 of the *Essay* seems itself to have peculiar optical properties, for it has altogether escaped the notice of at least two commentators: see Armstrong (1), p. 41, and Klein, p. 515.

10 Another possibility, not considered by Berkeley, is that the effect of the abnormal surrounding conditions will be to produce no judgment of tangible size at all, but sheer confusion.

11 As I do here, I shall usually 'speak with the vulgar,' saying things that seem to presuppose that we actually *see* tangible objects. The reader can easily translate these expressions into their proper Berkeleyan form if he wishes.

12 It is not, however, a *completely* idle accompaniment. Kaufman and Rock found in their experiments that 'eye elevation would appear to exert a slight effect' (p. 123). But they add: 'it cannot really account for the moon illusion.'

13 Cf. Berkeley's criticism of what I have called the true account of the moon illusion, which in his own day was propounded by 'the celebrated Dr. Wallis' (*NTV* 76f).

IV Retinal Images; the Heterogeneity of Tangible and Visible Objects

1 See Armstrong (1), p. 9, 51f; Turbayne (1); Furlong (1); Thrane.

2 Here, and (except where otherwise noted) hereafter, by '(1),' I mean the second version of (1), in which the retinal image is a picture on the visible retina.

3 Berkeley concedes that they do resemble each other in one respect; for

the visible square has four equal parts corresponding to the four equal sides of the tangible square and also four equal parts corresponding to its four equal angles. He insists, however, that the correlated parts do not resemble each other. Even this single point of resemblance is non-essential, on Berkeley's view: it merely makes the visible square 'fitter' than certain other visible objects to be correlated with, and hence to be a sign of, the tangible square (cf. *NTV* 142, 143). Actually I think Berkeley here concedes more than he should. What the elements of a thing are, and hence what their number is, are questions whose answers depend entirely on how we 'analyze' the things into parts (see Wittgenstein, Pt I, §§ 47, 48). So Berkeley's view ought to be that any visible object is as fit as any other to correspond to a tangible square. But I shall not insist further on this point.

4 This, of course, is hardly a universal feature of the relationship between written words and their spoken counterparts, however.

5 For example, see *NTV* 43, 55, 59, 61, 127, 149.

6 In *NTV* 158, Berkeley says, 'What we strictly see are not solids, nor yet plains variously coloured: they are only diversity of colours.' But it is clear from the preceding section (157) that the 'plains' here spoken of are *tangible* plains.

7 See, for example, von Senden.

8 See von Senden.

9 I offer one such explanation in Pitcher (2); see esp. pp. 212-16.

10 Cf. Thomson.

V   Abstract Ideas

1 These characteristics constitute what Locke, anyway, would call the nominal essence of dogs, not what he would call their real essence. (See Locke, Bk III, ch. 3, §§ 12-17.)

2 Clearly, my account of the doctrine of abstract ideas is only the roughest sketch; it has dealt, moreover, with only one kind of general term—namely, those that designate a natural kind (in my main example, dogs). But this incomplete picture still brings out the points that are relevant for our limited purposes. (I should perhaps add that Locke's own discussion of the names of substances and other natural kinds presupposes that there is *another* use of these terms, quite different from the one I have dealt with and not easily reconcilable with it, in which they refer not to abstract ideas or to nominal essences, but rather to real essences or to real kinds. See John Troyer's fine article 'Locke on the Names of Substances.')

3 Locke, Bk III, ch. 3, § 13.

4 For a similar defense of Locke, see Aaron, pp. 195-7. See also Bennett (2), pp. 37-9.

5 I doubt, however, that Locke really has any definite or precise view on this point. Some of the things he says certainly suggest that abstract

ideas must be sketchy images (and Bennett, among others, takes this to be Locke's true view [cf. Bennett (2), pp. 21–2]), but other passages in Locke suggest that abstract ideas are not images at all (see Aaron, pp. 195–203).

6 In the paragraph that contains this statement, the present argument is explicitly formulated.

7 Hume, Bk I, Pt II, § 6.

8 Here, and in what immediately follows, I use the term 'idea' in one ordinary sense—namely, so that 'idea of x' stands for what one has in his mind when he is (merely) thinking about x and not perceiving it. Berkeley, as we shall see, uses 'idea' in a much broader sense.

9 See, for example, *PHK* Intro. 10; and a passage from the first draft of the Introduction to the *Principles* (*W* II 129).

10 See Bennett (2), pp. 39–43.

11 See Bennett (2), p. 21f. But for some doubts on this point, see the caveat I entered, above, on p. 67.

12 For convenience, I omit '(or writer)' after 'speaker,' and '(or reader)' after 'hearer.'

13 Berkeley seems to think that he shows, somewhere in the Introduction, that 'names do not always stand for ideas,' because he says in its penultimate section: 'And he that knows names do not always stand for ideas, will spare himself the labour of looking for ideas, where there are none to be had' (*PHK* Intro. 24). I assume he thinks that the argument of section 20 shows that 'names do not always stand for ideas.' But it doesn't. What Berkeley demonstrates in section 20 is only that a word oftentimes raises passions in the mind of the hearer without causing the occurrence of any intervening idea—and this is quite consistent with the word's nevertheless standing for an idea, as Berkeley himself would have to agree, given his rebuttal of (β) in the preceding section of the Introduction. (See also *PHK* Intro. 19.)

14 See Mill, Bk I, ch. ii, § 5.

15 Warnock, p. 77f. See also p. 85.

16 In the first draft of the Introduction, too, Berkeley vows that in his inquiries he will abjure words, so far as he is able, in favor of his own 'particular ideas' (*W* II 142). But since he there thinks that generality can be achieved only in words, not in ideas, such a vow is empty.

17 For one cogent criticism of the theory, see Geach, § 6–11.

18 See Bennett (2), pp. 47–52.

VI The Objects of Immediate Perception: Ideas of Sense

1 Berkeley himself uses the term 'idea of sense'—e.g., in *PHK* I 30. He also uses a variety of other phrases to refer to them—e.g., 'ideas imprinted on the sense(s)' (*PHK* I 1, 3, 33, 90) and 'ideas actually

perceived by sense' (*PHK* I 29).

2 Hereafter, I shall drop the qualification '(consciously),' but it should be understood.

3 The remark is put in the mouth of Hylas, who is Berkeley's opponent in the *Dialogues*: but in this case, Berkeley certainly agrees with Hylas.

4 In at least two important respects, the *Three Dialogues* marks an advance over the *Principles*: (1) In it, Berkeley presents a much-needed defense of (I), where none is offered in the *Principles*. (2) Berkeley there faces up to the issue of the existence of objects that are not perceived by any finite minds, whereas in the *Principles* the whole issue is simply ignored, as we shall see. I, therefore, disagree with the usual assessment of these two works, in which the *Principles* is 'the complete, final, and authoritative statement of the immaterialist theory' and the *Three Dialogues* is 'a sequel saying the same thing in a more vivid, popular, and picturesque way' (Luce, p. 47). (See also p. 52, where Luce remarks of the *Three Dialogues* that 'nothing of any importance is added, unless the discussion of the Creation and of identity in the third dialogue are to be so regarded.').

5 Given the usual concepts of a property and of an idea, perceptual properties cannot literally *be* ideas of sense; so the claim should rather be that perceptual properties are *instantiated by* just ideas of sense, or that ideas of sense, and only ideas of sense, are *characterized by* perceptual properties. For the sake of convenience, however, I shall follow Berkeley's (strictly incorrect) way of talking here.

6 The attackers include Austin, Sellars, and Wittgenstein.

7 In order not to beg any relevant questions, we must here think of visual appearances neutrally; that is, we must not suppose that they are physical entities, or that they are mental entities, or that they have any other particular metaphysical status.

8 But why does Berkeley use the argument from the relativity of perception to support (III) in the *Three Dialogues*? Nancy Newman, in her unpublished doctoral dissertation ' "To Perceive is to Have a Sensation": a Study of the Philosophy of Perception of the Seventeenth and Eighteenth Centuries' (Princeton University, 1975) argues persuasively that (a) there are stylistic signs in the text showing that Berkeley does not himself accept the argument, (b) he thinks his Lockean opponents regard the argument as a sound one *as far as secondary qualities are concerned*—i.e., they think it proves that secondary qualities are ideas of sense, and (c) Berkeley, in the *Three Dialogues* really means simply to show that the argument works as well for primary qualities as it does for secondary qualities, so that there is no warrant here for assigning different ontological statuses to the two sorts of qualities.

9 Cf. Pitcher (2), pp. 28-42.

10 The last three paragraphs are taken, with minor alterations, from

Pitcher (2), pp. 46–8. (Reprinted by permission of the Princeton University Press.) I discuss the argument from the causation of perception more fully in that book, pp. 43–59.

VII The Attack against Lockean Matter

1 And he means, of course, not only that you can conceive of some object, *x*, that, as it happens, is not at the moment being perceived by anyone, but that you can conceive of an object, *x*, and conceive of it as not being perceived by anyone.
2 Cf. Armstrong (2), p. 10; Tipton, p. 161; Williams, p. 117.
3 Cf. *PC* 473.
4 Tipton (p. 174) points out that there is at least one other passage in which Berkeley makes the same mistake of confusing an idea and what it is an idea of—namely, in *PHK* I 36, where he says, 'the sun that I see by day is the real sun, and that which I imagine by night is the idea of the former.' This is wrong, for what I imagine by night is not the *idea* of the real sun, but *the real sun*.
5 In this paragraph, I borrow points made by Bernard Williams.
6 There are, of course, situations in which the remark would make perfectly good sense; but we are not now considering those situations.
7 (There is not even a single *term* of which it is true to say that it *could not* (without changing or extending its meaning) be used to refer to unobservables. "Red," for example, was so used by Newton when he postulated that red light consists of *red corpuscles*.

In short: if an "observation term" is a term which *can*, in principle, only be used to refer to observable things, then *there are no observation terms*' (Putnam, p. 243).
8 Amazingly, Locke concedes the point:
It is evident the mind knows not things immediately, but only by the intervention of the *ideas* it has of them. *Our knowledge*, therefore, is *real* only so far as there is a conformity between our *ideas* and the reality of things. But what shall be here the criterion? How shall the mind, when it perceives nothing but its own *ideas*, know that they agree with things themselves?
(Locke, Bk IV, ch. 4, § 3)

How can I know the picture of anything is like that thing, when I never see that which it represents? (Locke, *Examination of Malebranche's Opinion*, § 51)
9 See Bennett (2), ch. 4. Bennett himself, however, would deny that his discussion could show that we have good reason to think that unobservable material objects resemble ideas of sense in certain respects, for on his view about ideas of sense, it cannot be literally true that they have those properties (such as shape, color, size, and so on) that we attribute to physical things (Bennett (2), ch. 2, § 5).
10 See Curley, esp. pp. 450–4.

11 It should be remarked that Berkeley himself violates the principle stated in *PC* 51. In writing *PC* 51, Berkeley is thinking only of the contrast between ideas and Lockean material objects, and is thus forgetting altogether about the contrast between ideas and *minds*. Minds, too, are not ideas, and although, as Berkeley concedes, we cannot perceive them and hence (if the principle of *PC* 51 is correct) cannot compare them with ideas, nevertheless Berkeley definitely wants to say, and does say, that minds are unlike ideas. (See, e.g., *3D* III (*W* II 231; A 194; T 176).)

12 I ought rather to say '*apparently* embraced by Locke,' or 'embraced by Locke *according to the usual interpretation of what he says*'; for M. R. Ayers, in his article 'The Ideas of Power and Substance in Locke's Philosophy,' argues persuasively that Locke does not mean by 'substratum' what Berkeley and most others take him to mean.

13 Locke acknowledges the possibility that matter might think (Bk IV, ch. 3, § 6), but in the end, his view is that mind is most probably a separate, immaterial substance. We shall discuss Berkeley's conception of the mind later.

14 Locke himself acknowledges Berkeley's point—see his *Examination of Malebranche*, §§ 1–16—but this does not lead him to abandon what I have been calling the Lockean hypothesis.

VIII Berkeley's World View I: Ideas of Sense

1 In one remarkable passage in his early notebooks, however—i.e., *PC* 461—Berkeley expresses some doubts about the idea of power and hints at a Humean regularity view of causation.

2 Hume makes precisely the same point when he says, 'We never have any impression, that contains any power or efficacy' (Hume, Bk I, Pt III, § 14 (p. 161 of the Selby-Bigge edition)).

3 See Berkeley's first letter to Johnson (*W* II 282).

4 I ignore the dubious phenomenon of ESP. Even if there is such a thing, it is by no means obvious that it can occur without some kind of purely physical medium.

5 Grice, p. 142.

6 Malebranche taught that we see all things in God (*Treatise Concerning the Search after Truth*, Bk III, ch. 6).

7 Berkeley is understandably most impressed by the complicated but orderly way in which our *visual* ideas, especially, signify other ideas of sense; visual ideas, he holds, constitute a natural language in which God speaks to us (see *NTV* 147, 152; *TVV* 38–40; *PHK* I 44; *Alciphron* IV 7–12). (In the 1734 edition of the *Principles*, Berkeley for some reason changes two passages (that is, *PHK* I 66 and 108) that refer to a divine *language*, so that they refer instead to a system of *signs* instituted by God.)

IX Berkeley's World View II: Berkeley and Common Sense

1 I shall also use these terms in some closely related ways. For example, I shall say that a philosophical doctrine or proposition that accords with the commonsense view of the world is conciliatory, and one that does not, non-conciliatory.

2 In general, the *Principles* is not nearly as conciliatory as the *Three Dialogues* nor the early notebooks, where Berkeley wrote: 'I side in all things with the Mob' (*PC* 405; see also *PC* 368, 406, 408, 740, 747, 748, and 751).

3 Some philosophers would deny that there are *two* senses of 'same' and 'different' in connection with ideas; they think that ideas (along with sensations, moods, and many other things) cannot intelligibly be spoken of as numerically the same or numerically different. David Braybrooke, for example, in his useful article 'Berkeley on the Numerical Identity of Ideas' says: '[T]he ideas that different people have . . . are neither numerically identical nor numerically different. There is no procedure for telling apart cases of exact duplication and cases of numerical identity; and therefore there is no point in the distinction' (p. 634). I do not want to enter into this dispute here, but shall simply state dogmatically that I agree with Berkeley, against Braybrooke and the others, that there really are two senses of 'same' and 'different' with respect to ideas.

4 *Part* of a single cause, rather; for God's will is also part of the cause.

5 Actually, it would probably have to be a set of several tactual ideas of sense in this case.

6 This is obviously only the roughest sketch: a proper characterization of the principle would have to fill in numerous details.

7 'Ideas of sense in the O-family' are the ideas of sense that belong to the family of ideas that constitute O.

8 By 'closely related concepts' I mean such concepts as those of a city or town, the intersection of two streets, and so on—that is, concepts of things that have a more or less definite location in space and time.

9 See Strawson, ch. 1.

10 See *PHK* I 104, 105. Berkeley warns, however, that gravity may not be, and even appears not to be, an absolutely universal phenomenon (*PHK* I 106; see also *Siris* 235).

11 Sellars, ch. 3; Cornman (4).

12 Sellars attacks the view, while Cornman defends it against Sellars's attack.

X Berkeley's World View III: The Existence of Unperceived Objects

1 Originally, in Bennett (1) and then, more fully, in Bennett (2), ch. 7.

2 I am assuming that the 'finite substances' spoken of here are so-called material objects (e.g., tables and fig trees); but it is a real possibility

that Berkeley is talking rather about finite *minds*.

3 After I had written this chapter, George H. Thomas's article appeared, 'Berkeley's God Does Not Perceive,' *Journal of the History of Philosophy*, 14, 1976, 163-8. I was happy to see that he, too, thinks that Berkeley would reject what I have called the Perception Theory.

XI Berkeley's View of the Mind

1 We can ignore for now the question of whether (a) the ideas, images, and the others, are to be thought of as kinds of objects, while the other element is thought of as performing just the one act of being conscious of these objects, or whether, instead, (b) the first element should really be construed as the act or state of having ideas, the act or state of having images, and so on, while the second element is thought of as being the entity that performs these acts or is in those states. For a discussion of this issue, see below, pp. 189–203.

2 See also *Siris* 347 and 358, where the unity of the mind is made much of.

3 Brown, p. 65. Brown seeks to partially defend Berkeley against this charge. In his extremely interesting article, Brown defends the view, which I cannot share, that it is Berkeley's anti-abstractionism that provides the main support for his view that the self is a simple substance.

4 See also *PC* 104, 110, 325; *PHK* I 12, 13; *Siris* 288, 357.

5 Strictly speaking, a multiplicity of perceivings and willings; but the 'idea' terminology is more convenient.

6 See Hume, Bk I, Pt IV, § ii (p. 207f of the Selby-Bigge edition).

7 See, for example, *PHK* I 25, and our earlier discussion on p. 132.

8 This view of particles is taken directly from Locke, I would imagine. Particles are connectives joining parts of sentences to form a whole sentence or joining whole sentences to form a still longer sentence; and according to Locke, they 'are not truly by themselves the names of any *ideas*,' but are rather '*marks of some action or intimation of the mind*' (Locke, Bk III, ch. 7). Philosophers have continued to wrestle with the problem of how such 'logical' words as 'if then,' 'or,' and 'not' are best to be understood, right up to the present day. The view that they signify some mental act or state has been quite popular until fairly recently: thus Russell, for example, in *Human Knowledge: its Scope and Limits* (Simon & Schuster, New York, 1948) holds that 'the word "or" expresses my hesitation, not something objective' (p. 126).

9 This passage may be construed, however, as asserting that the existence of an idea consists in its being perceived, and hence as not necessarily asserting (L).

10 Berkeley has a related point in mind when he writes: 'Speech metaphorical more than we can imagine insensible things & their

modes circumstances &c being exprest for ye most part by words borrow'd from things sensible. the reason's plain. Hence Manyfold Mistakes' (*PC* 176).

11 S. A. Grave, to the best of my knowledge, first noticed this inconsistency in Berkeley (see Grave (2)).

12 Berkeley discusses only sense perception in this passage, and hence only one limited class of ideas; but it would not be difficult to construct parallel arguments for other kinds of ideas—e.g., images.

13 Descartes, Letter No. 347, in *Descartes: Philosophical Writings*, tr. E. Anscombe and P. T. Geach (Thomas Nelson, London, 1954), p. 288.

14 Locke rejects the Cartesian view on similar grounds: see his *Examination of Malebranche*, § 39.

15 I mean the view I am in the process of defending: I do not pretend that it corresponds in all respects with Descartes' actual view.

16 It is easy enough, by the way, to think of cases of jig-dancing, somersault-turning, and breaststroke-swimming that are not *actions*, at any rate. For example, suppose that Jones, while standing, is suddenly rendered unconscious and that in falling, he turns a perfect somersault. Similarly, imagine a floating, but comatose Tarzan studded with electrodes that are able to inflict muscle-activating impulses; when Jane operates the impulse-generator, Tarzan swims a jerky, but passable, breaststroke.

17 Perhaps 'passive state-object analysis' would be preferable to 'act-object analysis' from Berkeley's point of view, but I shall nevertheless use the latter in what follows.

18 This is not quite right: to put the point precisely, I should say that there is no difference if the act-object analyst claims that (a) is necessarily true *and, in addition, holds that no idea-residues exist when the corresponding ideas are not being perceived.* For the act-object analyst can maintain that the relationship between a mind and any one of its ideas is analogous to that between a husband and a wife: the two are strongly distinct, and yet there is a logical connection between them, since there can be no wife without a husband. But when a woman's husband dies, she does not need to cease existing: she may continue to exist, not of course as a wife, but as a woman, or, as we may put it, as a wife-residue. Similarly, the act-object analyst can hold that it is a necessary truth that ideas *as such* exist only when perceived, but maintain that they exist as idea-residues when they are not being perceived. (Cf. the early Russell on sense-data and sensibilia.) If the act-object analyst takes this line, there certainly is an important difference between his view and that of the adverbial analyst. Therefore, to be precise, I must add the second requirement specified (and italicized) in the first sentence of this note. In the text, I ignore this option that is open to the act-object analyst, because for our present purposes, (b), above, represents essentially the

same option.

19 A. A. Luce, 'The Berkeleian Idea of Sense,' *Proceedings of the Aristotelian Society*, supplementary vol. 27, 1953, p. 3.

20 In what follows, by 'ideas' I shall mean ideas *of sense*.

21 See Luce, *op. cit.*, pp. 17–18.

22 Even if Berkeley were to hold that the mind can simply perceive an idea (without willing anything) or simply will something (without perceiving any idea), I am not sure he would be in trouble; for I must confess that I can see no incoherency in the view that there is a kind of thing whose essence is to have either property P or property Q (or perhaps both at once). But there is little point in pursuing the matter, because even if I am right in this, Berkeley does not stay out of trouble for long, as we shall see.

23 Such expressions do make sense, of course, if they are simply short for something like 'your (my) regular schedule on Tuesday,' as in 'Your Tuesday is really rough.'

24 Within, that is, a given objective frame of reference. I shall henceforth ignore this qualification.

25 See G. Dawes Hicks, p. 173.

26 For a balanced and perceptive discussion of Berkeley's view of time, see Tipton, pp. 277–89.

27 See, for example, Tipton, p. 269f; Cornman (1), p. 172f.

28 My own discussion is heavily indebted to Brown's.

29 S. C. Brown, p. 66.

30 Here, Berkeley is apparently using the term 'notion' in a non-technical sense to denote ideas of the imagination or of the understanding.

31 See Furlong (2).

32 Cf. Brown, p. 71.

33 See Turbayne (2).

34 S. A. Grave makes this point in Grave (1).

35 See Cornman (2), esp. p. 83.

36 See also *PHK* I 28, 89; *3D* II (*W* II 217; A 180; T 159), *3D* III (*W* II 239; A 201f; T 185); *De Motu* 40; *Siris* 154, 247, 290.

37 This is the line taken by Cornman in his articles Cornman (1) and (2). He, however, seems to think that Berkeley holds that we have a direct awareness of our own minds, while I think he does not.

XII *Passive Obedience*

1 See Berkeley's letter to Johnson dated Nov. 25, 1729 (*W* II 282).

2 There are two short subsidiary arguments in its defense in section 27 of *Passive Obedience*, but I shall not consider them because (a) they are very weak, and (b) they presuppose various Berkeleyan doctrines that we have not yet discussed.

3 See Sermon X, entitled 'On the Will of God' (*W* VII 129–38, esp. p. 135).

4 Unless, of course, the utilitarian happened, improbably, to believe in the existence of a vengeful and powerful God who visits the most horrible punishments on those who disobey His commandments.

5 See Berkeley's essay 'Public Schools and Universities' (*W* VII 203); *Alciphron* II 13–18; and *PO* 5.

6 Indeed, even if a society that finds itself in a situation like that of Hitler's Germany accepted Berkeley's non-resistance precept, some of its members might still of course try to overthrow their wicked leader, motivated perhaps by compassion for the slaughtered millions, or by a lust for power (see *PO* 44). But if they accepted Berkeley's precept, and if they agreed with Berkeley that it is an inviolable moral principle, then they would have to think that their rebelling is an immoral action, and that thought would surely diminish their zeal, at least.

7 See *The Analyst*, § 50, question 6.

8 Berkeley, at this stage of his career, apparently does not see that if the drawn diagram of a square, for instance, can be a general sign, then so can the determinate image—the idea—of a square. That is to say: he does not see that ideas, as he conceives of them, can be general. At this early time, he apparently supposes, wrongly, that the generality of an idea would have to be an intrinsic feature of it, rather than a matter of how it is used by the person whose idea it is. He later corrects this misconception: see *PHK* Intro. 15.

9 Bennett (2), p. 112f; Brook, p. 149f.

10 In *PC* 768, Berkeley calls arithmetic and algebra 'entirely useless but for Practise in Societys of Men,' but I think he must be speaking there of the more esoteric branches of those disciplines that do not, as he evidently supposes, have practical applications.

11 Berkeley does not make this point explicitly in the *Philosophical Commentaries*, but it seems to me to be implicit in *PC* 736. The following entry seems at first glance to speak against the spurning of words: 'Tis not to be imagin'd w^t a marvellous emptiness & scarcity of Ideas that man shall descry who will lay aside all use of Words in his Meditations' (*PC* 600). But the passage is ironical; Berkeley means that if one abjures words, one will not suffer the hallucination of all sorts of non-existent ideas engendered by language. The passage, in fact, is found, almost verbatim, in the first draft of the introduction to the *Principles* (*W* II 142) where Berkeley is in the process of listing the advantages of abandoning words in favor of ideas in philosophical work.

12 This is a simplified and not quite accurate account, given here just to make the present point shorter and therefore, I hope, clearer.

13 Again, for expository reasons, I indulge in some oversimplification and inaccuracy.

14 The two strands are not independent. Here is one example of how one influences the other. Suppose, invoking Berkeley's pragmatic

conception of language, we have determined that certain candidates for the role of true moral principles have won, in virtue of being the most useful to mankind, *leaving God out of account*: then we can see that these same winning principles have an enormous additional amount of utility when we consider God's purposes, for we know— invoking, now, Berkeley's views about God—that God wants people to obey these winning principles, and that He will reward those who do and punish those who do not.

15 Epilogue to the *Satires*, Dial., ii. i. 70; quoted in Luce, p. 60.

16 The letter (quoted in Luce, p. 63) is addressed to the unnamed writer of two essays in earlier editions of *The Guardian*; the author of the essays was almost certainly Berkeley.

17 Quoted in Luce, pp. 181–2.

18 For an account of the scornful attacks that greeted his metaphysical views, see Bracken.

Works (other than Berkeley's) Referred to in the Text

Aaron, R. I., *John Locke* (3rd ed.), Clarendon Press, Oxford, 1971.

Armstrong, D. M. (1), *Berkeley's Theory of Vision: a Critical Examination of Bishop Berkeley's* 'Essay towards a New Theory of Vision,' Melbourne University Press, 1960.

Armstrong, D. M. (2), Introduction to *Berkeley's Philosophical Writings*, Collier-Macmillan, New York and London, 1965.

Austin, J. L. *Sense and Sensibilia*, Oxford University Press, London, 1962.

Ayers, M. R., 'The Ideas of Power and Substance in Locke's Philosophy,' *Philosophical Quarterly*, 25, 1975, 1–27.

Bennett, J. (1), 'Berkeley and God,' *Philosophy*, 40, 1965, 207–21.

Bennett, J. (2), *Locke, Berkeley, Hume: Central Themes*, Clarendon Press, Oxford, 1971.

Bracken, H. M., *The Early Reception of Berkeley's Immaterialism* (rev. ed.), Martinus Nijhoff, The Hague, 1965.

Braybrooke, D., 'Berkeley on the Numerical Identity of Ideas,' *Philosophical Review*, 64, 1955, 631–6.

Brook, R. J., *Berkeley's Philosophy of Science*, Martinus Nijhoff, The Hague, 1973.

Brown, S. C., 'Berkeley on the Unity of the Self,' in *Reason and Reality: Royal Institute of Philosophy Lectures, Volume 5, 1970–1*, Macmillan and St Martin's Press, London, 1972, 64–87.

Cornman, J. W. (1), 'Theoretical Terms, Berkeleian Notions, and Minds,' in *A Treatise Concerning the Principles of Human Knowledge / George Berkeley, with Critical Essays*, ed., C. M. Turbayne, Bobbs-Merrill, Indianapolis and New York, 1970, 161–81.

Cornman, J. W. (2), 'A Reconstruction of Berkeley: Minds and Physical Objects as Theoretical Entities,' *Ratio*, 13, 1971, 76–87.

Cornman, J. W. (3), 'On Direct Perception,' *Review of Metaphysics*, 26, 1972, 38–56.

Cornman, J. W. (4), 'Theoretical Phenomenalism,' *Nous*, 7, 1973, 120–38.

Curley, E. M., 'Locke, Boyle, and the Distinction between Primary and

Secondary Qualities,' *Philosophical Review*, 81, 1972, 438–64.

Davis, M. and Hersh, R., 'Nonstandard Analysis,' *Scientific American*, vol. 226, no. 6 (June 1972), 78–86.

Dretske, F. I., *Seeing and Knowing*, Routledge & Kegan Paul, London, 1969.

Furlong, E. J. (1), 'Berkeley and the "Knot about Inverted Images,"' *Australasian Journal of Philosophy*, 41, 1963, 306–16.

Furlong, E. J. (2), 'An Ambiguity in Berkeley's *Principles*,' *Philosophical Quarterly*, 14, 1964, 334–44.

Geach, P., *Mental Acts*, Humanities Press, New York, 1957.

Grave, S. A. (1), 'A Note on Berkeley's Conception of the Mind,' *Philosophy and Phenomenological Research*, 22, 1961–2, 574–6.

Grave, S. A. (2), 'The Mind and its Ideas: some Problems in the Interpretation of Berkeley,' *Australasian Journal of Philosophy*, 42, 1964, 199–210.

Grice, H. P., 'The Causal Theory of Perception,' *Proceedings of the Aristotelian Society*, suppl. vol. 35, 1961, 121–52.

Hacking, I., *Why Does Language Matter to Philosophy?*, Cambridge University Press, 1975.

Henze, D. F., 'Berkeley on Sensations and Qualities,' *Theoria*, 31, 1965, 174–80.

Hicks, G. D., *Berkeley*, Russell & Russell, New York, 1932.

Hume, D., *A Treatise of Human Nature*, ed. L. A. Selby-Bigge, Clarendon Press, Oxford, 1888.

Kaufman, L. and Rock, I., 'The Moon Illusion,' *Scientific American*, vol. 207, no. 1 (July 1962), 120–30.

Klein, D. B., *A History of Scientific Psychology: its Origins and Philosophical Backgrounds*, Routledge & Kegan Paul, London, 1970.

Locke, J., *An Essay concerning Human Understanding*, ed. P. H. Nidditch, Clarendon Press, Oxford, 1975.

Luce, A. A., *The Life of George Berkeley, Bishop of Cloyne*, Thomas Nelson, Edinburgh, 1949.

Mill, J. S., *A System of Logic, Ratiocinative and Inductive*, Parker, London, 1843.

Pitcher, G. (1), *The Philosophy of Wittgenstein*, Prentice-Hall, Englewood Cliffs, N.J., 1964.

Pitcher, G. (2), *A Theory of Perception*, Princeton University Press, 1971.

Putnam, H., 'What Theories are Not,' in E. Nagel *et al.*, eds, *Logic, Methodology and Philosophy of Science*, Stanford University Press, 1962, 240–51.

Sellars, W., *Science, Perception and Reality*, Routledge & Kegan Paul, London, 1963.

Strawson, P. F., *Individuals*, Methuen, London, 1959.

Taylor, J. G., *The Behavioral Basis of Perception*, Yale University Press, New Haven and London, 1962.

Thomson, J. J., 'Molyneux's Problem,' *Journal of Philosophy*, 71, 1974, 637–50.

Thrane, G., 'Berkeley's "Proper Object of Vision,"' *Journal of the History of Ideas*, forthcoming.

Tipton, I. C., *Berkeley: the Philosophy of Immaterialism*, Methuen, London, 1974.

Troyer, J., 'Locke on the Names of Substances,' *Locke Newsletter*, no. 6, 1975, 27–39.

Turbayne, C. M. (1), 'Berkeley and Molyneux on Retinal Images,' *Journal of the History of Ideas*, 16, 1955, 339–55.

Turbayne, C. M. (2), 'Berkeley's Two Concepts of Mind,' *Philosophy and Phenomenological Research*, 20, 1959–60, 85–92.

von Senden, M., *Space and Sight*, Methuen, London, 1960.

Warnock, G. J., *Berkeley*, Penguin Books, Melbourne, Harmondsworth and Baltimore, 1953.

Williams, B. A. O., 'Imagination and the Self,' *Proceedings of the British Academy*, 52, 1966, 105–24.

Wittgenstein, L., *Philosophical Investigations*, Blackwell, Oxford, 1953.

Additional Selected Bibliography

Collections of Berkeley's Works

Armstrong, D. M. (ed.), *Berkeley's Philosophical Works*, Collier-Macmillan, New York and London, 1965.

Ayers, M. R. (ed.), *George Berkeley: Philosophical Works, including the Works on Vision*, Dent, London; Rowman and Littlefield, Totowa, N.J., 1975.

Calkins, M. W. (ed.), *Berkeley: Essay, Principles, Dialogues*, with selections from other writings, Scribner, New York and Chicago, 1929.

Fraser, A. C. (ed.), *The Works of George Berkeley* (4 vols), Clarendon Press, Oxford, 1901.

Luce, A. A. and Jessop T. E. (eds), *The Works of George Berkeley, Bishop of Cloyne* (9 vols), Thomas Nelson, London and Edinburgh, 1948–57.

Turbayne, C. M. (ed.), *George Berkeley: Principles, Dialogues, and Philosophical Correspondence*, Library of Liberal Arts Book no. 208, Bobbs-Merrill, Indianapolis, New York, and Kansas City, 1965.

Warnock, G. J. (ed.), *Berkeley: The Principles of Human Knowledge, Three Dialogues between Hylas and Philonous*, Collins Fontana, London, 1962.

Collections of Articles on Berkeley

Engle, G. W. and Taylor, G. (eds), *Berkeley's Principles of Human Knowledge: Critical Studies*, Wadsworth, Belmont, Calif., 1968.

Martin, C. B. and Armstrong, D. M. (eds), *Locke and Berkeley: a Collection of Critical Essays*, Doubleday, New York, 1968.

Pepper, S. C., Aschenbrenner, K., and Mates, B. (eds), *George Berkeley: Lectures Delivered before the Philosophical Union of the University of California*, University of California Press, Berkeley and Los Angeles, 1957.

Steinkraus, W. E. (ed.), *New Studies in Berkeley's Philosophy*, Holt,

ADDITIONAL SELECTED BIBLIOGRAPHY

Rinehart & Winston, New York and Chicago, 1966.

Turbayne, C. M. (ed.), *A Treatise concerning the Principles of Human Knowledge/George Berkeley, with Critical Essays*, Bobbs-Merrill, Indianapolis and New York, 1970.

Books on Berkeley

Ardley, G., *Berkeley's Renovation of Philosophy*, Martinus Nijhoff, The Hague, 1968.

Bracken, H. M., *Berkeley*, Macmillan, London and Basingstoke, 1974.

Luce, A. A., *Berkeley and Malebranche*, Clarendon Press, Oxford, 1934.

Luce, A. A., *Berkeley's Immaterialism*, Thomas Nelson, Edinburgh, 1946.

Luce, A. A., *The Dialectic of Immaterialism*, Hodder & Stoughton, London, 1963.

Olscamp, P. J., *The Moral Philosophy of George Berkeley*, Martinus Nijhoff, The Hague, 1970.

Park, D., *Complementary Notions: a Critical Study of Berkeley's Theory of Concepts*, Martinus Nijhoff, The Hague, 1972.

Ritchie, A. D., *George Berkeley: a Reappraisal*, Manchester University Press, Barnes & Noble, New York, 1967.

Stack, G. J., *Berkeley's Analysis of Perception*, Mouton, The Hague and Paris, 1970.

Wild, J., *George Berkeley*, Harvard University Press, Cambridge, Mass., 1936.

Wisdom, J. O., *The Unconscious Origins of Berkeley's Philosophy*, Hogarth Press, and the Institute of Psycho-Analysis, London, 1953.

Articles

Acton, H. B., 'George Berkeley,' in P. Edwards, ed., *Encyclopaedia of Philosophy*, vol. 1, Macmillan, Free Press, New York; Collier-Macmillan, London, 1967, 295–304.

Allaire, E. B., 'Berkeley's Idealism,' *Theoria*, 29, 1963, 229–44.

Ayers, M. R., 'Substance, Reality, and the Great, Dead Philosophers,' *American Philosophical Quarterly*, 7, 1970, 38–49.

Craig, E. J., 'Berkeley's Attack on Abstract Ideas,' *Philosophical Review*, 77, 1968, 425–37.

Cummins, P. D., 'Berkeley's Ideas of Sense,' *Nous*, 9, 1975, 55–72.

Davis, J. W., 'Berkeley and Phenomenalism,' *Dialogue*, 1, 1962, 67–80.

Day, J. P. de C., 'George Berkeley, 1685–1753,' *Review of Metaphysics*, 6, 1953, 83–113, 265–86, 447–69, 583–96.

Doney, W., 'Two Questions about Berkeley,' *Philosophical Review*, 61, 1952, 383–91.

Flew, A., 'Critical Notice of Jonathan Bennett's *Locke, Berkeley, Hume: Central Themes*,' *Canadian Journal of Philosophy*, 3, 1974, 691–701.

Flew, A., 'Was Berkeley a Precursor of Wittgenstein?,' in W. B. Todd, ed., *Hume and the Enlightenment: Essays Presented to Ernest*

273

Campbell Mossner, Edinburgh University Press; University of Texas Humanities Research Center, Austin, 1974, 153–63.

Gallois, A., 'Berkeley's Master Argument,' *Philosophical Review*, 83, 1974, 55–69.

Margolis, J., 'Esse est Percipi Once Again,' *Dialogue*, 5, 1967, 516–24.

Murphy, J. G., 'Berkeley and the Metaphor of Mental Substance,' *Ratio*, 7, 1965, 170–9.

Odegard, D., 'Berkeley and the Perception of Ideas,' *Canadian Journal of Philosophy*, 1, 1971, 155–71.

Prior, A. N. 'Berkeley in Logical Form,' *Theoria*, 21, 1955, 117–22.

Shaffer, J., 'Minds, Bodies, and Theoretical Entities,' *Ratio*, 14, 1972, 83–6.

Thomas, G. H., 'The Implications of Berkeley's Earliest Philosophy concerning Things,' *Journal of the History of Philosophy*, 10, 1972, 425–30.

Thomson, J. F., 'Berkeley,' in D. J. O'Connor, ed., *A Critical History of Western Philosophy*, Free Press, New York; Collier-Macmillan, London, 1964, 236–52.

Vesey, G. N. A. (1), 'Berkeley and the Man Born Blind,' *Proceedings of the Aristotelian Society*, 61, 1960–1, 189–206.

Vesey, G. N. A. (2), 'Berkeley and Sensations of Heat,' *Philosophical Review*, 69, 1960, 201–10.

Watson, R. A., 'Berkeley in a Cartesian Context,' *Revue internationale de philosophie*, 17, 1963, 381–94.

White, A. R. (1), 'The Ambiguity of Berkeley's "Without the Mind,"' *Hermathena*, 83, 1954, 55–65.

White, A. R. (2), 'A Linguistic Approach to Berkeley's Philosophy,' *Philosophy and Phenomenological Research*, 16, 1955–6, 172–87.

Note: There is a superb bibliography of Berkeley for the years 1933–62, by C. M. Turbayne and R. Ware, in *Journal of Philosophy*, 60, 1963, 93–112. It is continued for the years 1963–74 by C. M. Turbayne and R. Appelbaum in *Journal of the History of Philosophy*, 15, 1977, 83–95.

Index

Aaron, R. I., 258
Addison, J., 1
AINMP principle, 231f, 242
Anscombe, E., 264
Archetypes, 149f, 171f
Armstrong, D. M., 257, 261
Austin, J. L., 260
Ayers, M. R., 262

Bacon, F., 29, 256
Bennett, J., 119, 164, 177, 258, 259, 261, 263, 267
Bermuda project, 2
Blind, man born, 55–7
Bracken, H. M., 267
Braybrooke, D., 263
Brook, R. J., 267
Brown, S. C., 183f, 212, 217, 264, 266

Causality; 40f, 124, 137f; between mind and body, 122–4, 134f; as involving activity, 132f, 225f
Chimaera, existence of, 170
Color, 26, 30, 48, 53–5, 104–6
Common sense, 59–61, 140–62 (passim), 254
Conceivability, 53–5, 57f, 68, 110–24 (passim)
Conception Theory (vs. Perception Theory), 175–9
Conciliator defined, 141
Cornman, J., 162, 255f, 263, 266
Creation of the world, 170, 172
Crusoe, R., 113f
Curley, E. M., 119, 261

Data, primal perceptual, 144
Davis, M., 255
Demonstration: only verbal, 248–50; in geometry, 75f, 84f, 249; in morality, 248–52
Descartes, 108, 181, 195–8, 222, 264, 265
Desert Island argument, 111–15
Direct Awareness doctrine stated, 214
Distance: clues (or cues), 6f, 12f, 17–20, 257; idea of, 13f; illusion, 20–2
Dreams, 23f, 181
Dretske, F., 9, 255f

Essence, 63f, 110

Forces: parallelogram of, 160f; physical, 160f, 251
Furlong, E. J., 257, 266

Geach, P., 259, 264
Geometry, 75f, 84f, 249
God: archetypes in the mind of, 149f, 171f; as cause of ideas of sense, 92, 130, 133–7, 138f, 192; as moral law giver, 234f, 239, 252, 266; as perceiver of natural objects, 166f, 179; as preserver of unperceived objects, 163–79 (passim); as responsible for laws of nature, 53, 134, 138f; not a blind agent, 171; notion of, 214, 221; proofs for the existence of, 91f, 133–5, 176f, 226
Grave, S. A., 264, 266
Gremlin, 10f, 150

Grice, H. P., 136, 262

Hacking, I., 256
Heat, perception of, 100–3
Henze, D., 101
Hersh, R., 255
Hicks, G. D., 266
Hume, D., 68, 123f, 128, 132, 182, 184f, 258, 262, 264

Idea Doctrine (of the meaningfulness of terms), 180f, 186f, 212f
Ideas: abstract, 49f, 54, 62–90; as inactive, 132, 186, 194; association of, 13; existence of, 93f, 184f; general, 82–7, 89f; perception of the same (by different people), 146–9
Ideas of sense: act-object analysis of, 199–203, 265; adverbial analysis of, 199–203; criteria of, 127–30
Illusion, 97, 104–6; distance, 20–2; moon, 37–41, 257
Images, 67, 70–4, 77, 81–5, 89f
Incorrigibility, 86f, 97–100
Information, effective, 16f
Introspection, method of, 40f, 72f, 102f

James, W., 224
Johnson, S., 203, 204, 207, 208, 210, 262, 266

Kant, I., 128, 159
Kaufman, L., 38, 41, 257
Klein, D. B., 256, 257

Language: connection between words and things, 63–5, 74, 80–90; misleading features of, 28f, 73f, 86f, 267; uses of, 78–80, 88, 160f, 223f, 250, 259
Likeness principle ('An idea can be like nothing but an idea'), 115–20
Locke, J., 13, 55, 65–7, 69, 70, 72, 75, 76f, 80, 82, 91f, 95, 96, 108f, 110–24 (passim), 125–31, 134f, 142, 157, 181, 207, 247, 258, 261, 262, 264
Looks: anemic sense, 8, 9, 256; full-blooded sense, 8, 9, 16, 20, 23, 256
Luce, A. A., 201–3, 255, 260, 265, 267

Malebranche, N., 1, 262
Meaning (meaningfulness), 88f, 180f, 186f, 212f

Melampus, 82, 86f
Microscopes, 61, 143f
Mill, J. S., 80, 259
Mind: as active, 132f, 185f, 225f; as a transparent medium, 21f, 72, 131; bundle theory of, 182–6, 224; essence of, 203–5, 222f, 265; existence in, 25f, 28–33, 60f, 62, 93, 111; place-picture of, 29–33; no idea of, 213, 226; relationship to ideas, 182–6, 189–203; secret doctrine of, 223–6; unity of, 183f, 187f, 203, 225
Minimum visibilia, 29, 34f
Molyneux, W., 5, 44, 55
Moon illusion, 37–41
Moral terms, no ideas of, 246f

Neutral monism, 224
Newman, N., 260
Newport, Rhode Island, 2
Newton, I., 261
Notion, 71, 187, 221; relative, 120f, 222

Objects, natural (or so-called 'physical'): concept of, 158–62; existence of, when unperceived, 163–79; nature of, 92, 137, 143f, 156f, 164–6; perception of, 144–6, 150–3; real properties of, 153–8
Objects: tangible, 28f, 31, 35f, 42f, 46–61, 62, 152f; visible, 34f, 42f, 46–61, 143f

Pain, 54; the pleasure/pain argument, 100–4
Particles, logical, 187, 264
Perception: argument from the causation of, 106–8; argument from the relativity of, 104–6; immediate (or direct), 6, 9–13, 16, 25, 27, 54, 95–9, 107f, 120, 256, identified with sense perception, 144f, without interference, 9–12, 95, 150, 152, without intermediary, 9–12, 95, 150, 152; inference in, 7, 9–13, 16, 98, 144f; mediate (or indirect), 6f, 9–13, 16, 18f, 28, 256, with inference, 9–12, with intermediary, 9–12; not an activity, 191, 193; suggestion in, 6f, 9f, 13f, 18f, 20–2, 37, 94, 144–6; tactual, 7, 13f
Perception Theory (vs. Conception Theory), 175–9, 263

Phenomenalism, theoretical, 162
Pope, A., 1, 253
Principle non-P/C, stated, 154
Principle PC, stated, 155; weaker PC principle, stated, 157
Prior, T., 255
Properties, basic visual, 96f, 99, 116f
Psycho-physical correlations, 12, 17–20, 22, 39, 41, 42
Putnam, H., 261

Qualities, primary, 115f

Reflection, two senses of, 217–20
Retinal images, inversion of, 42, 44–8
Rock, I., 38, 41, 257
Russell, B., 264, 265

Seeing, non-epistemic, 9, 256
Self-evident Existence doctrine, stated, 215f
Self-interest (self-love), 233f
Sellars, W., 162, 260, 263
Sense perception: Berkeley's view of, 95, 144–6; identified with immediate (or direct) perception, 144f
Signification, 80f, 89
Signs, 58f, 138
Simplicity, 102–4
Size clues, 36–9
Snowman example, 153–5
Steele, R., 1, 253
Strawson, P. F., 263
Substance, mental, 91, 92f, 181f, 188f, 223f; essence of, 203–5, 222f; knowability of, 182, 188f, 211–22, 227
Substance, physical, 91, 110–24 (passim), 226
Substratum, 121f
Suggestion, 10, 13f, 18f, 20–2, 37, 94, 144–6
Swift, J., 1, 255

Tar-water, 3
Taylor, J. G., 256
Thomas, G. H., 263
Thomson, J. J., 258
Thrane, G., 257
Time, Berkeley's view of, 182, 206–11
Tipton, I. C., 261, 266
Trinity College, Dublin, 1f
Troyer, J., 258
Turbayne, C. M., 224, 257, 266

Utilitarian alternative, 243–6
Utilitarianism, act vs. rule, 238f

Volition, 132f, 185f; no idea of, 133, 186f
von Senden, M., 258

Wallis, Dr, 257
Warnock, G. J., 82, 259
Will, 182f, 185–9, 225f; no idea of, 186f
Williams, B. A. O., 261
Wittgenstein, L., 29, 30, 79, 102f, 211, 256, 258, 260

A NOTE ABOUT THE TYPE

The text of this book has been film set in a type face named Bembo. The roman is a copy of a letter cut for the celebrated Venetian printer Aldus Manutius by Francesco Griffo, and first used in Cardinal Bembo's *De Aetna* of 1495— hence the name of the revival. Griffo's type is now generally recognized, thanks to the researches of Mr. Stanley Morison, to be the first of the old face group of types. The companion italic is an adaption of the chancery script type designed by the Roman calligrapher and printer Lodovico degli Arrighi, called Vincentino, and used by him during the 1520's.

Composed by ComCom, a division of The Haddon Craftsmen, Inc.,
Allentown, Pennsylvania. Printed and bound by
R. R. Donnelly & Sons, Harrisonburg, Virginia.
Typography and binding design by Virginia Tan.